Contents

SUCCESS IN

PRINCIPLES OF ACCOUNTING

3RD EDITION

GEOFFREY WHITEHEAD, B.Sc. (ECON)

JOHN MURRAY

to Joan

Success Studybooks

Advertising and Promotion
Book-keeping and Accounts
Business Calculations
Chemistry
Commerce
Commerce: West African Edition
Communication
Economics
Electronics
European History 1815–1941
Information Processing
Insurance
Law
Managing People
Marketing
Politics
Principles of Accounting
Principles of Accounting: Answer Book
Psychology
Sociology
Statistics
Twentieth Century World Affairs
World History since 1945

First published 1974
by John Murray (Publishers) Ltd
50 Albemarle Street
London W1S 4BD

Second edition 1987
Third edition 2001

Layouts and illustrations by Wearset
Typeset in 9/11 pt Times by Wearset, Boldon, Tyne and Wear
Printed and bound in Great Britain by Biddles Ltd., www.biddles.co.uk

A catalogue entry for this title is available from the British Library

ISBN 0 7195 7212 6

Foreword to Third Edition

A knowledge of the principles of accounting is essential to anyone who has to take part in keeping accurate records of the financial affairs of a business. Today computerized accounting systems are widely used, and never has it been so vital for anyone contemplating a business career to understand the methods of book-keeping and accounting that lie behind the computer's activities. Whether the transactions of a business are recorded and processed by computer or are handwritten in books of original entry, the basic thinking is the same. No one can hope to understand either the programming of a computer or the straightforward day-to-day entries in a ledger without a thorough grounding in the accounting systems common to both.

Success in Principles of Accounting provides a clear and detailed introduction to the basic concepts and practices of book-keeping and accounting for students working towards a whole range of examinations. Many students enrol on high-level courses without the early grounding they require. Such students will find that *Success in Principles of Accounting* explains everything they need to know to make their main course meaningful. The book is particularly directed at international courses for students preparing for the GCE Ordinary level/School Certificate examination (7110), but will be of great help to those embarking straight away on the A Level Accounting Course (5120).

In this new edition we have changed the currency symbols from £ sterling to dollars ($) and euros (€). These changes reflect the reduced use of the £ symbol around the world, but students are urged to use their own national currency symbols if they differ from $ or €.

This third edition includes 'Revise and Test' material at the end of each chapter, which ensures a sound grasp of the basic material covered and facilitates recall as tests or examinations approach.

The book is divided into units of study, each with a wide variety of exercises. To get the maximum benefit from the book students are advised to work through the exercises, then check them against the detailed answers given in the companion text *Success in Principles of Accounting: Answer Book*. This approach is particularly important for anyone preparing for an examination. It helps to reinforce understanding of the topic being studied and it also shows students the high standard of presentation required in examinations.

Acknowledgements

In preparing this revised edition, I have received help from various firms and institutions. I am particularly indebted to the following:

Safeguard Systems (Europe) Ltd, for permission to reproduce their three-in-one systems;
George Vyner Ltd, for permission to reproduce a page from a simple Receipts and Payments Book;
Formecon Services Ltd, Gateway, Crewe, for permission to reproduce a bill of exchange.

I should also like to express my appreciation for the help from Carolyn Burch and the publishers, with thanks for their continued support of this book.

G.W.

UNIT 1

Accounting to the Trial Balance

1.1 A Definition of Accounting

Accounting is the art of controlling a business by keeping accurate book-keeping records, measuring and interpreting the financial results of the business by using the information in these records, and communicating the results to management and other interested parties.

Every business proprietor must have an understanding of accounting, for it is a major factor in the success of all firms. It is perhaps most important to very large companies, for only by the most careful control can these enormous enterprises keep prosperous and successful. Not only their own prosperity, but the prosperity of shareholders, managers, staff, and even the nation itself, depend upon maintaining efficiency and competitiveness in the free-enterprise world.

1.2 Why Start a Business?

The purpose of business is to make a profit, and we may define profit as the *reward for enterprise and risk*. So one of the chief aims of accounting is to reveal whether or not a business is being conducted profitably.

At one time profits were calculated only once in a lifetime—when the owner of the firm died. There was little need to calculate them more often. If the business was not profitable it soon became obvious for all to see: the premises would not be repaired or redecorated and the owner's family would be shabbily dressed. Rumour and gossip would spread news of their difficulties far and wide. By contrast, the prosperous merchant displayed his prosperity: the beautiful homes of early merchants are still to be seen in nearly every European city.

Today, profit must be calculated at least once a year, for the State requires its share. This contribution to the State is called *taxation*. Individuals pay *income tax* and companies pay *corporation tax*. After taxation has been paid, the shareholders of companies have to be rewarded for investing their money by paying them a *dividend* made up from the remainder of the profits. The directors of the company may keep some of the profits back, however, as *reserves* to strengthen the business in the coming year. But an annual calculation of profits is unlikely to keep an efficient check on the business. More frequent calculations of the profits are necessary, and many companies today actually know how much profit they have made on every day's activities. Such feats of calculation are, of course, only made possible by the use of computers.

1.3 Book-keeping—the Basis of Accounting

The true purpose of accounting is to maintain proper control of the finances of a business. Accounting must be based on careful and efficient *double-entry book-keeping*. This is a system of accounting entries devised by the early merchants of Lombardy in northern Italy, who gave their name to Lombard Street, the banking centre of the City of London. These early accountants used a book with pages divided down the middle, called the *ledger*. This is still the most important book of account. The name 'ledger' is of Dutch origin, and means 'the book on the ledge'. In early counting houses the book lay open on a ledge under the window, and double entries were made immediately after customers had called at the shop. A page from the ledger looks like this:

							L1
Dr.							*Cr.*
Date	Details	Folio	Amount $	Date	Details	Folio	Amount $

You should note the following points:

(i) Every page in the ledger is called an *account*. Since the pages are always used on both sides, an account is really a leaf in the ledger and it is given the name *folio*, from the Latin *folium*, a leaf.

(ii) Every account is therefore given a *folio number*. On the ledger page above the number is L1 (Ledger 1), written in the top right-hand corner where it can easily be seen as the pages are turned.

(iii) There is a line at the top of every ledger page for the name, address and telephone number of the person whose transactions with the business are being recorded, thus:

T. Smith, 9 High Road, Summerville, Barsetshire BS0 0AB (042-29 13477)

Some accounts are not *personal accounts* but refer to other matters of importance, like assets of the business or losses incurred by the business. Such an account might be headed 'Typewriters Account' or 'Light and Heat Account'.

(iv) The page is clearly divided down the middle, and the two halves of the page are identical, each having columns for the date, the details of the transaction, the folio number and the amount of money involved.

(v) The left- and right-hand sides of the page are called respectively the *debit side* (headed *Dr.*) and the *credit side* (headed *Cr.*). The debit side is always used when the person or thing named at the top receives goods or services or money and thus becomes a *debtor* of the firm. The credit side is used when the person or thing gives goods or services or money to the firm and thus becomes a *creditor*.

Note: We shall see later (Unit 2.2) that today many accounts are not kept in this traditional form, but are kept in what is called 'running-balance style'.

1.4 Double-entry Book-keeping

Whenever a piece of business is arranged, there are always two parties involved: one is the 'giver' and one the 'receiver'. Every piece of business activity is called a *transaction* and millions of them occur every day. If you buy a bar of chocolate from a confectioner, that is a transaction. If the Port of London Authority orders a container crane from a manufacturer, that is another transaction. The first involves the payment of a few pence to the confectioner—it was a *cash transaction*. The other involves perhaps a quarter of a million pounds sterling, and is almost certainly not a cash transaction. Such transactions, where there is a time-lag between the contract for the goods and the payment of the money, are called *credit transactions*. In both types of transaction a giver and receiver take part. This dual nature of transactions—there are two sides to every bargain made—gives rise to the system of double-entry book-keeping.

Under this system, every transaction must be recorded in two accounts. One account will be debited because it receives value; the other will be credited because it has given value. The rule for double entries is therefore as follows:

Always debit the account that has received goods or services or money.
Always credit the account that has given goods or services or money.

Let us now consider the double entries required in a few simple transactions. We will imagine that Arthur Upson has just set up in business in a small way, with capital of $200.00.

(a) Double Entry No. 1

On 1 January 20.. Arthur Upson contributes the sum of $200.00 as capital for the new business, placing it in a bank account with one of the big banks, say Lloyds TSB.

A very important principle at once arises. In accounting *we always treat the business as quite a different person from the proprietor, or owner, of the business*. The proprietor, when he/she makes this capital available, becomes a creditor of the business *for he/she has given it $200.00*. The Bank Account is debited with $200.00, *for it has received $200.00*. We therefore have a double entry, thus:

Bank Account L1

Dr.					*Cr.*
20..		$			
1 Jan.	Capital	200.00			

Capital Account (A. Upson) L2

Dr.					*Cr.*
			20..		$
			1 Jan.	Bank Account	200.00

(b) Double Entries Nos 2 and 3

Upson now pays out $50.00 to a supplier for cloth required in his workshop, and $25.00 each for two second-hand sewing machines.

This requires two further double entries, shown below:

Bank Account L1

		$			$
20..			20..		
1 Jan.	Capital	200.00	1 Jan.	Purchases (cloth)	50.00
			1 Jan.	Machinery	50.00

Capital Account L2

					$
			20..		
			1 Jan.	Bank Account	200.00

Purchases Account L3

		$			
20..					
1 Jan.	Bank Account	50.00			

Machinery Account L4

		$			
20..					
1 Jan.	Bank Account	50.00			

Notes:

(i) Whenever we buy goods for resale, or raw materials to be made up into goods for resale, we call these *purchases* and enter them in the Purchases Account. This is a very important point; later, we shall use the purchases figure as part of the process for finding profit.

(ii) In contrast to (i) above, the purchase of machines is not the purchase of goods to be resold, but is the purchase of an *asset*—something to be kept in the business for regular use by the business.

(iii) In each of these double entries the Bank Account was credited because it gave money out for the purchase of these items, i.e., *we credit the account that gives value.*

(iv) The Purchases Account was debited with $50.00 of cloth, and the Machinery Account was debited with $50.00 of machinery, because they received these items, i.e., *we debit the account that receives value.*

You have now seen the basic idea of double entry. There is nothing difficult about it, but of course there are a great many accounts and only with regular practice will you develop a real understanding of all possible entries. Before we go on to consolidate this knowledge, however, one or two further pieces of vocabulary are necessary. First, the three classes of accounts.

1.5 The Three Classes of Accounts

These are:

- *personal accounts*, which are the records of our transactions with other firms and individuals, our customers and suppliers;
- *nominal accounts*, which are records kept of losses and profits of the business (for example, Rent and Rates Account or Commission Received Account); and finally
- *real accounts*, which are the records we keep of the real things the business owns (i.e. the assets of the business); examples are Land and Buildings Account, Plant and Machinery Account and Cash Account.

Let us consider these in detail.

(a) Personal Accounts

There are many people with whom the business deals. Some are suppliers who make available raw materials and goods for resale, or the assets we need to make the business operate. Others are customers to whom we supply goods or services. All these people are either creditors or debtors. The creditors have given us goods or services, and the debtors have received goods or services from us. Thus we have personal accounts:

Debtors
(who have received value)

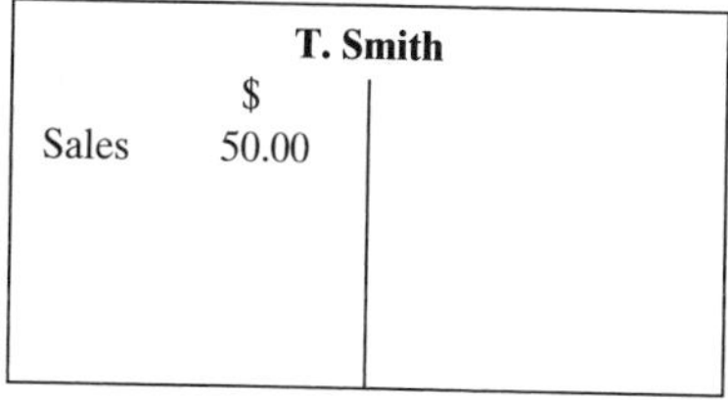

T. Smith

	$		
Sales	50.00		

Creditors
(who have given value)

R. Jones

			$
		Purchases	75.00

There are two personal accounts which are rather special. One of them is the Capital Account, already mentioned. This is the personal account of the proprietor. In a limited company there are many contributors of capital, called *shareholders*. They too have a personal account called, for example, the Ordinary Share Capital Account, or a similar title. Here all the capital is lumped together in one personal account, but the individual shareholder's share of this is recorded in a special shareholders' register.

Capital Account (A. Upson)

			$
		Bank	200.00

Ordinary Share Capital Account

			$
		Bank	1 000 000.00

The other special account is the Value Added Tax (VAT) Account. This is a particular type of taxation account. It is really the personal account of HM Customs and Excise Department, and it shows what is the business's position with regard to that department's VAT office. Most businesses owe the department tax moneys, and consequently HM Customs is their creditor. Some businesses may be in the opposite position—the department owes them refunds of tax; HM Customs is therefore their debtor. (This is explained more fully in Unit 1.6.)

(b) Nominal Accounts

The word 'nominal' means 'existing in name only'. This implies that there is nothing really there, so that you might say nominal accounts are the opposite of real accounts. Suppose we decide to mail all our customers with a leaflet about a new product. The cost of this mailing, at the cheapest postage today, might be $600.00. We send the office junior round to the post office to buy stamps for this value. What will the double entry be? Here it is:

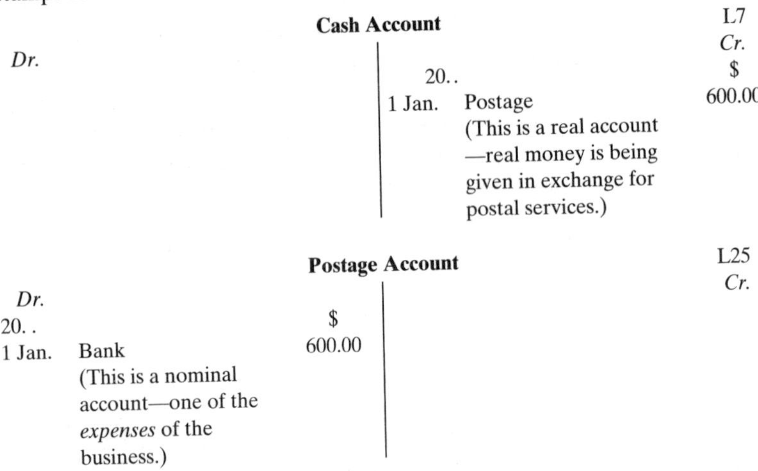

Cash Account L7

Dr.					*Cr.*
					$
			20. .		
			1 Jan.	Postage (This is a real account —real money is being given in exchange for postal services.)	600.00

Postage Account L25

Dr.					*Cr.*
		$			
20. .					
1 Jan.	Bank (This is a nominal account—one of the *expenses* of the business.)	600.00			

The Cash Account gave value, so it is credited with $600.00. The money was used to buy postage stamps so it is debited to Postage Account, which has received value. In fact where are the stamps? Stuck on the letters now going through the post to our customers. Clearly the $600.00 on the Postage Account does not represent anything real at all; it is only a nominal entry—an entry in name only. It is recorded here for convenience so that at the end of the year, when we come to work out our profits, we shall remember to deduct from the profits this expenditure of $600.00.

By contrast, suppose we arrange the sale of a piece of property for a customer, and earn commission of $200.00. This will probably be received as a cheque and be paid into the Bank Account. The double entry for it will be in Commission Received Account:

Bank Account L1

Dr.					*Cr.*
20..		$			
1 Jan.	Commission Received (The cheque paid into the Bank Account will give us control of real money.)	200.00			

Commission Received Account L27

Dr.					*Cr.*
			20..		$
			1 Jan.	Bank (This nominal account is one of the *profits* of the business.)	200.00

It is clear that this nominal account is quite the opposite of the Postage Account, for it shows a profit, not a loss. The actual money is in the Bank Account, but this nominal record will remind us at the end of the financial year to include this $200.00 as part of the firm's profits.

(c) Real Accounts

When we pay money for postage, the real stamps are stuck on envelopes and are lost to the business as soon as we post the letters in the letter box. On the other hand, if we purchase such things as computers, plant and machinery or furniture and fittings they are not lost to the business, but are permanent assets available for use over a period of years. These assets are recorded in the third class of accounts—real accounts. Suppose we want to record the purchase of a motor vehicle by cheque for $12 850.00:

Bank Account L1

Dr.					*Cr.*
			20..		$
			1 Jan.	Motor vehicle	12 850.00

Motor Vehicles Account L23

Dr.					*Cr.*
20..		$			
1 Jan.	Bank	12 850.00			

Notice that both the Bank Account and the Motor Vehicles Account are real accounts. The balance at the bank (not shown here) is one of the assets of the business, just like the motor vehicle we have purchased.

1.6 The VAT Account

This, as we have said, is a rather special account. The Value Added Tax system is discussed in detail later (see Unit 9.4(e)), but here we need to look at the procedure by which the tax is collected in the United Kingdom. The VAT system spreads taxation over the vast majority of the nation, so that the Government can raise the money it needs from every family in the land. What it does is charge tax on every supply of goods and services. If we buy a car or a bicycle, tax is added to the purchase price. If we call in a decorator to redecorate our homes, he must add tax to the bill for his services. So a business must charge tax every time it supplies goods or services to its customers, and it will also pay tax on everything it buys from other businesses. The tax it collects on its sales of goods and services is called *output tax* and must be paid over to the Customs and Excise Department at regular intervals. The tax it pays on the goods and services that it buys from other firms is called its *input tax*, and can be reclaimed from the Customs and Excise. At the time of writing, food, children's clothing and some other items are not taxed (zero-rated goods) so that traders who sell only such goods do not collect any output tax, and so only have to reclaim their input tax from the Department.

Now consider the ledger entries necessary for the following transactions, in which the VAT rate has been taken arbitrarily as 10 per cent. (In fact, of course, VAT rates vary from time to time at the discretion of the Government.)

1. Mr Smith sells goods value $800 to A. Parsons, adding on VAT at 10 per cent (i.e. $80). The total charge is therefore $880.
2. Mr Smith buys furniture from Shopfitters Ltd for $700, and finds that VAT has been added to the bill (i.e. $70), making $770 in all.

Let us look at these transactions as though we were Mr Smith's accountant. A. Parsons has to pay the total charge, making him a debtor for $880, but only $800 of this will be a credit entry in Mr Smith's Sales Account—the other $80 will be a credit in his VAT Account as he owes the Customs and Excise Department this amount of output tax.

Similarly Mr Smith still has to pay Shopfitters Ltd the full value of the bill of $770, so they are a creditor for that amount. Only $700 of this will be a debit to Furniture Account, however, because Mr Smith has only received furniture to the value of $700. The other $70 is input tax which has been paid to Shopfitters Ltd. Mr Smith is entitled to reclaim this $70 from the Customs and Excise Department, so it is debited to VAT Account.

Notice that in each case we still have a perfect double entry, even though three accounts are involved. As far as the sales were concerned the entry in the debtor's account (A. Parsons Account) is a debit entry of $880; this exactly balances the $800 in Mr Smith's Sales Account and the $80 in his VAT Account, which are both credit entries. The same is true of Smith's purchase of furniture: the debit entries in Furniture Account and VAT Account exactly balance the credit entry in Shopfitters Ltd's Account.

The entries therefore look like this:

A. Parsons Account L1

	$		$
Sales	880		

Sales Account L2

	$		$
		A. Parsons	800

VAT Account L3

	$		$
Shopfitters Ltd	70	A. Parsons	80

Shopfitters Ltd Account L4

	$		$
		Purchases	770

Furniture Account L5

	$		$
Shopfitters Ltd	700		

We can see from the VAT Account that we actually owe the Customs and Excise only $10—the difference between the output tax we collected ($80) and the input tax we paid ($70). Later (see Unit 1.9(a)) we shall learn how to balance off an account and show the difference (in this case of $10) on whichever side it should appear (in this case, on the credit side).

1.7 Entering Items in the Three Classes of Accounts

Table 1.1 The commonest accounts

Dr.	*Cr.*
Personal accounts:	
T. Smith Account and all other trade debtors	J. Brown Account and all other trade creditors and expense creditors
The proprietor's Drawings Account (see Unit 4.3)	The proprietor's Capital Account (see Unit 1.5(a))
VAT Account (whenever we pay input tax to a supplier)	Loan Accounts, Mortgage Accounts and any other admissions of debts like VAT due
	Reserves (see Unit 27.2(e)), unappropriated profits
Nominal accounts:	
Rent Paid Account	Rent Received Account
Wages Account	Commission Received Account and all other profits of the business
Salaries Account	Sales Account
Light and Heat Account	Purchases Returns Account
Telephone Expenses Account	
Motor Vehicle Expenses Account and all other losses of the business	
Purchases Account	
Sales Returns Account	
Stock Account (at start)	
Real accounts:	
Cash Account	There are no real accounts with credit balances
Bank Account	
Motor Vehicles Account	
Furniture and Fittings Account	
Land and Buildings Account and all other asset accounts	

Table 1.1 shows the commonest accounts in each of the three classes. Of course every account will have entries on both the debit and credit sides, because every account will eventually be cleared off the books in some way or other, and the only way to 'clear' an account is to have an entry on the other side of it. Thus the motor vehicle purchased in Unit 1.5(c) will be cleared from the books by a series of depreciation entries over a number of years, and eventually it will be traded in as a second-hand car to some garage in part-exchange for a new one. The listing in Table 1.1 is only intended to show the side of the account (debit or credit) which will usually have a balance.

Clearly we must have rules for making the entries in this very large collection of accounts. Learning accounting is rather like learning to drive: you have to face a very complex pattern of new ideas. You cannot expect to learn everything at once. The very best thing to grasp firmly at first is the idea of debit and credit, the two sides of the ledger page. Let us look at this in pictorial form again (Fig. 1.1).

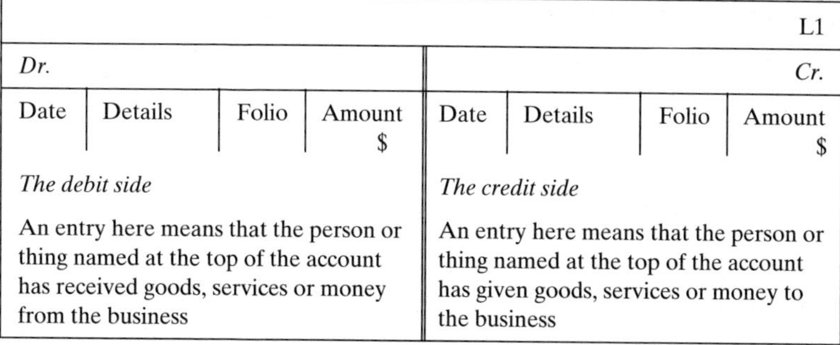

							L1
Dr.							*Cr.*
Date	Details	Folio	Amount $	Date	Details	Folio	Amount $
The debit side An entry here means that the person or thing named at the top of the account has received goods, services or money from the business				*The credit side* An entry here means that the person or thing named at the top of the account has given goods, services or money to the business			

Fig. 1.1 The meaning of debit and credit entries

Printed ledger paper often carries the abbreviations *Dr.* and *Cr.* at the tops of the pages. These are not essential, and in this book they have been included as a reminder only in the early pages, and then omitted. The simple rule:

Debit the receiver—credit the giver.

This is just a shortened statement of the rule first given in Unit 1.4:

Always debit the account that has received goods, services or money.
Always credit the account that has given goods, services or money.

Here are some detailed aspects of this rule for the three classes of accounts.

(a) Personal Accounts

Debit the person who receives value (goods, services or money). He/she will thus become a *debtor* of the business.

Credit the person who gives value (goods, services or money). He/she will thus become a *creditor* of the business.

(b) Nominal Accounts

Debit the loss accounts, which have received 'in name only' the benefits from money expended. Examples are Postage Account and Motor Vehicle Expenses Account.

Credit the profit accounts, which have given 'in name only' benefits to the business. Examples are Commission Received Account and Fees Received Account.

(c) Real Accounts

Debit the asset account (Motor Vehicles Account, for instance) when the stock of the assets is increased. The asset has received an increased share of the resources of the business because money has been expended on a further supply.

Credit the asset account when the stock of the asset is reduced either by fair wear and tear or disposal of a worn-out or obsolete asset. The asset has given up some of its value in the service of the business.

1.8 An Exercise in Double-entry Book-keeping

We are now ready to make a set of entries following double-entry rules. Let us, as an example, make the appropriate entries in a set of accounts for a series of transactions. Remember that every transaction will appear in two accounts, and that if VAT (at 10 per cent) is concerned the double entry will be spread across three accounts.

(a) On 1 January 20.., T. Smith starts business with capital of $2 000.00 which he puts in the bank.
(b) On the same day he buys goods for resale $220.00 by cheque. This includes VAT of $20.00.
(c) He also pays by cheque for the hire of a market stall, lighting and so on, for one month, $25.00.
(d) He buys an account book for $5.50 by cheque. Of this, VAT is $0.50.
(e) On 2 January he buys a second-hand machine for $440.00, of which $40.00 is VAT.
(f) Sales for the week by 6 January total $385.00, which he banks. Of this $35.00 is VAT.

Notes on the six transactions:

(a) This is the contribution of capital by the proprietor. Bank Account has received $2 000.00; Capital Account (T. Smith) has given value. Debit Bank Account, credit Capital Account.
(b) All goods purchased for resale are recorded in Purchases Account. Bank Account has given $220.00. Debit Purchases Account $200.00 and debit VAT Account with $20.00. Credit Bank Account with $220.00.
(c) This payment of $25.00 is one of the expenses, or losses, of the business. Bank Account has given $25.00. The debit entry will be made in an expense account. We can give such accounts any name we like, but as rent of a business place is a regular item which will recur every month, we will call the expense account Rent of Stall Account. Debit Rent of Stall Account, credit Bank Account. (Note that VAT is not payable on rent.)
(d) An account book is a necessary office expense. It will not recur very often but we will enter it in Stationery Account. Bank Account has given $5.50. Debit Stationery Account and VAT Account, credit Bank Account.
(e) This is the purchase of an asset of the business. Debit Machinery Account with $400.00 (always debit the asset account when you purchase an asset) and debit VAT Account with $40.00. Credit Bank Account.
(f) When he cashes up his takings at the end of the week T. Smith sees that what he has sold has realized $385.00. No doubt he still has some goods in stock, so that it has been a profitable week. The Bank Account is debited because it has received $385.00, and we shall credit the Sales Account with $350.00 and the VAT account with $35.00. The Sales Account is always credited with the sales figure; it is the opposite of the Purchases Account mentioned in (b).

Looked at in ledger form, we have:

Bank Account L1

	$		$
Capital	2 000.00	Purchases	220.00
Sales	385.00	Rent	25.00
		Stationery	5.50
		Machinery	440.00

Capital Account (T. Smith) L2

			$
		Bank	2 000.00

Purchases Account L3

	$		
Bank	200.00		

Rent of Stall Account L4

	$		
Bank	25.00		

Stationery Account L5

	$		
Bank	5.00		

Machinery Account L6

	$		
Bank	400.00		

Sales Account L7

			$
		Bank	350.00

VAT Account L8

	$		$
Bank	20.00	Bank	35.00
Bank	0.50		
Bank	40.00		

1.9 The Trial Balance

This first Unit is called 'Accounting to the Trial Balance'. It is a most important section of accounting, and many people spend their entire business lives carrying out book-keeping transactions which only go as far as the Trial Balance level. If you examine the 'situations vacant' columns of a newspaper, you are likely to find an advertisement for a book-keeper who can keep records 'to the Trial Balance'. You may then ask 'Do you really mean I have now learned enough book-keeping to go out and get a job?' Well, not quite, but by the end of this Unit you will have learnt the *principles* underlying work to the Trial Balance level. You will then need only a little more knowledge, chiefly connected with books of original entry, and you will certainly be ready for useful, if perhaps routine, employment.

What is a *Trial Balance*? It is an attempt to check the accuracy of the book-keeping by striking a balance of the books. Since a debit entry is never made without a corresponding credit entry, a list of all the items entered on the debit side should balance, or agree, with a list of items on the credit side. This is called *striking a balance*, and it should reveal any mistake of double entry. It would, however, be rather boring to extract all the entries we have just made and draw up two lists of debit and credit entries. Instead we take the opportunity of clearing up one or two little difficulties that exist on the accounts, and we draw up a Trial Balance *which consists only of the balances on the accounts.*

(a) Balancing-off an Account

Look again at the accounts in Unit 1.8, and consider which accounts are difficult to understand. Most of them are perfectly clear, because each has only one item on the account. But the first account, the Bank Account, is very muddled at present, for it has six entries on it. We cannot tell at a glance how much money is in the account; we need a pencil and paper to work out the balance. Let us look at this account again, and balance it off so that it is clear.

Bank Account L1

	$		$
Capital	2000.00	Purchases	220.00
Sales	385.00	Rent	25.00
		Stationery	5.50
		Machinery	440.00

If we add up the two sides of this account we find:

debit side (money received by the Bank Account)	= $2385.00
credit side (money given out by the Bank Account)	= $ 690.50
Difference	= $1694.50

We now add the difference to the credit side—the smaller side—and that balances off the account level at $2385.00. We then bring the balancing figure down to the debit side to show the true balance on the account. The account now looks like this:

Bank Account L1

	$		$
Capital	2000.00	Purchases	220.00
Sales	385.00	Rent	25.00
		Stationery	5.50
		Machinery	440.00
		Balance	1694.50
	$2385.00		$2385.00
	$		
Balance	1694.50		

Notes:

(i) The balancing figure is called *the balance on the account.*
(ii) This balance is first entered on the side which is smaller in value, but is brought down on the proper side of the account to show the true position, which is that we have $1694.50 in the bank.
(iii) These two balancing entries are a 'double entry'.
(iv) To make the account neat we use a currency sign—a $, € or whatever is appropriate—against the total, and rule lines above and below the sum.
(v) Since we balance the sides at the same level, we must leave some empty lines on the shorter side. There is a rule in accounting which says: *never leave empty lines*. Fill them in with ruled lines in red so that no one can enter sums of money by mistake on the lines. Some people fill in the lines where wording is written (that is, under the word 'sales'), instead.
(vi) Notice that no line is drawn under a balance that has been brought down.

(b) More About Balancing Accounts

Some students think that it is necessary to balance off every account. This is not so. It is only necessary to balance off an account if there are items on both sides of the account, so that the balancing off makes the account simpler to understand. Consider an account with only one item recorded:

Machinery Account L6

	$		
Bank	400.00		

Suppose we now balance off this account:

Machinery Account L6

	$		$
Bank	400.00	Balance	400.00
	$400.00		$400.00
	$		
Balance	400.00		

The balancing off has not simplified the picture at all; the picture was perfectly clear anyway. Machinery worth $400.00 is recorded on the books as an asset of the business.

Even in the following example it is not necessary to balance off the account:

R. Brown Account L21

20..		$	
4 Jan.	Sales	242.75	
11 Jan.	Sales	36.50	
19 Jan.	Sales	16.18	

A much simpler process is to add it up and pencil in the total figure to one side. Only accounts that have items on *both* sides of the page need to be balanced off before preparing a Trial Balance.

We are now ready to prepare the Trial Balance from the accounts in our example: it is shown below.

Trial Balance of T. Smith's ledger as at 6 January 20..

		Dr.	*Cr.*
		$	$
Bank Account	L1	1694.50	
Capital Account	L2		2000.00
Purchases Account	L3	200.00	
Rent of Stall Account	L4	25.00	
Stationery Account	L5	5.00	
Machinery Account	L6	400.00	
Sales Account	L7		350.00
VAT Account	L8	25.50	
		$2350.00	$2350.00

Notes:

(i) The book-keeping would appear to have been well done because the debits and credits agree, so it seems that a proper double entry has been done in each case.

(ii) A currency sign is used to make the total stand out.

(iii) All the accounts with a debit balance are listed in the debit column.

(iv) All the accounts with a credit balance are listed in the credit column.

(v) The heading should always show the date on which the Trial Balance was extracted.

You should now work through several exercises in double-entry book-keeping to the Trial Balance. Remember to use your own currency symbol instead of dollars ($) if you wish, as explained in the Foreword.

1.10 Exercises Set 1. Accounting to the Trial Balance

1. David Thomas begins to trade in machinery on 1 March 20.. with a capital of $10 000.00, which he banks. Record this opening capital and then the following transactions. Balance off the accounts where necessary and extract a Trial Balance as at 7 March 20... VAT is levied at 10 per cent.

2 March	Buys second-hand machine for $500.00 plus VAT $50.00, which he intends to resell. Buys spare parts for repair work for $100.00 plus VAT $10.00. Pays for both by cheque.
3 March	Buys second-hand machine $1 450.00 plus VAT $145.00, for resale; pays by cheque. Draws $50.00 cash from bank (enter in Cash Account).
4 March	Resells first machine for $720.00 plus VAT $72.00 to A. Debtor, who will pay on 31 March.
5 March	Sells second machine for cash $1 750.00 plus VAT $175.00.
6 March	Banks $1 900.00 from cash received on previous day.

2. On 1 May 20.. R. Brown goes into business as a scrap metal dealer with capital of $1 000, which he banks. He rents a yard that day for $100.00 per month, paying by cheque for the first month.

2 May	Purchases scrap boiler and spare piping, $55.00 by cheque.
3 May	Withdraws cash from bank $100.00 (record the cash in Cash Account). Purchases two cars for scrap, paying $40.00 for one and $25.00 for the other, in cash.
4 May	Purchases scrap aluminium $75.00 by cheque from US Army depot.
5 May	Sells scrap copper $180.00 plus VAT $18.00. Sells scrap aluminium $110.00 plus VAT $11.00. Payment received for both by cheque.

Record these items in R. Brown's ledger; balance off those accounts that need to be balanced and extract a Trial Balance as at 5 May 20...

3. Nick Whiteside begins business as a market trader on 20 March 20.. as a dealer in electronic equipment and related goods, with a capital of $1 200.00 in cash. Record this capital and enter the following items in his ledger accounts.

20 March	Buys radio sets for cash, $285.00 plus VAT $28.50. These are for resale.
21 March	Cash sales for the day $346.00 plus VAT $34.60. Buys hi-fi equipment for resale $385.00 plus VAT $38.50, paying in cash.
22 March	Pays for hire of stall (Rent Account) $30.00. Pays deposit on electricity bill (Light and Heat Account) $25.00. Purchases batteries, $68.00 plus VAT $6.80, for resale. All these in cash.
23 March	Sales for the day $386.00 plus VAT $38.60 cash.
24 March	Banks $400.00 for safe keeping. Purchases hi-fi equipment for resale for $116.00 plus VAT $11.60 cash.
25 March	Sales for the day $295.00 plus VAT $29.50 cash.
26 March	Balance off the accounts where necessary and prepare a Trial Balance.

4. On 1 April 20.. M. Logan begins business as a decorator with a capital of $400.00 in cash. He purchases second-hand ladders, trestles and other equipment for $135.00 (no VAT), also materials for use in the business (Purchases Account) for $123.00 plus VAT $12.30. Enter these items in his ledger and then the following:

2 April	Receives payment for redecorations in cash $45.00 plus VAT $4.50 (Fees Received Account). Sells materials $14.50 plus VAT $1.45 for cash.
3 April	Purchases wallpaper, $26.40 plus VAT $2.64 cash.
4 April	Receives payment for redecorations, $154.00 plus VAT $15.40, by cheque (Bank Account opened). Sells materials, $11.20 plus $1.12 VAT. Payment is by cheque.
5 April	Received for shop alterations $135.00 plus VAT $13.50 cash.
6 April	Pays for hire of power spray (Equipment Hired Account) $13.00 plus VAT $1.30, in cash. Sale of materials $24.40 plus VAT $2.44, cash.
7 April	Received for redecoration work $86.00 plus VAT $8.60, by cheque. Buys ledger and other stationery, $14.40 plus VAT $1.44 in cash.

Balance off the accounts where necessary and extract a Trial Balance as at 7 April 20...

5. D. Lobley sets up in business as a master locksmith with a capital of $2000.00, which he banks on 1 July 20... He then pays by cheque for two copy-cut machines for $385.00 plus VAT $38.50, tools for $165.00 plus VAT $16.50 and a supply of blank keys and other goods for resale, $480.00 plus VAT $48.00. Enter these items and then record the following transactions in his ledger:

2 July	Draws cash from bank, $100.00. Pays signwriter for supplying sign and painting name on door (General Expenses Account) $33.00 plus VAT $3.30 cash.
3 July	Cash sales of cut keys $24.00 plus VAT $2.40.
4 July	Receives for repairs of antique casket (Fees Received Account), $42.00 plus VAT $4.20 by cheque.
5 July	Cash sales of cut keys $58.00 plus VAT $5.80. Sale of metal cash boxes $72.00 plus VAT $7.20, cash.
6 July	Pays rent by cheque $40.00. Sales of storage chests and other items, $54.00 plus VAT $5.40, cash.

Balance off those accounts that require it, and extract a Trial Balance.

6. Ros Sparrow is a market gardener who sets up in business on 1 April 20... She has capital in cash of $500.00 and also brings in as part of her capital the following items: land and buildings $27 500.00; tools and equipment $840.00; a delivery van $585.00. Enter these items, and then the following transactions:

5 April	Purchases artificial fertilizer in cash $28.50 and seeds $1.50 (VAT $3.00), for resale. Purchases bedding plants $54.00 plus VAT $5.40, paying cash.
13 April	Purchases garden fork $12.40 plus VAT $1.24, cash.
21 April	Sells seedling lettuces for $76.00 plus VAT $7.60, cash.
28 April	Sells seedling cabbages, etc, for $83.00 plus VAT $8.30.
30 April	Pays wages for casual worker, $48.00.

Extract a Trial Balance as at 30 April 20...

7. Complete these sentences:

a) Accounting is .... (see Unit 1.1).

b) The purpose of business in a free enterprise society is .... (see Unit 1.2).

8. Complete the sentences below by inserting the correct word from the list in italics.

a) The government's share in the rewards of enterprise is called ....

b) A person running a business of his own pays a tax called .... tax.

c) A company pays a tax called ....

d) The basis of accounting is a very careful record of transactions called .... book-keeping.

e) The chief book of account is called the ....

f) A .... is a person who owes our firm money.

g) A person or firm to whom we owe money is said to be our ....

h) A number written in the top corner of a ledger page is called a .... number.

i) The three classes of ledger accounts are called .... accounts, ... accounts and .... accounts.

j) Every business deal of any sort in which goods or services are supplied, or money is paid, is called a ....

Word list: *transaction, taxation, double-entry, corporation tax, income, personal, creditor, nominal, debtor, real, ledger, folio.*

1.11 Revise and Test 1. Basic Ideas of Accounting

Each chapter in this book ends with a Revise and Test exercise. The idea of these exercises is that you take a sheet of paper and cover up the page. Then reveal one question at a time, and try to answer it. Slide the cover sheet down to find the correct answer, and the next question. You can test yourself as often as you like until you are quite sure of all the answers.

Answers	*Questions*
—	**1.** What is accounting?
1. It is the art of controlling a business by keeping accurate book-keeping records, either in basic books of account, or in computerized records. These records enable the accountant to calculate the profit (or loss) being made, and to detect weaknesses before they become serious.	**2.** What is the purpose of business activity?
2. To make a profit by supplying the goods and services required by the world.	**3.** What is profit?
3. It is a reward for the enterprise shown by the proprietors of a business, and for the risks they took in starting and maintaining the activity.	**4.** Why do we draw our book-keeping to a close once a year and work out our profit?
4. Because the state requires the government's share of our prosperity in the form of taxation levied on the profits made each year.	**5.** What is the basis of accounting?
5. The routine book-keeping records which start at 'Dawn on Day 1' and continue every day until the business ceases to trade.	**6.** What do we call these endless events to be recorded?
6. Transactions. To buy a factory for $100000 is a transaction. To buy a penny stamp is another transaction. Both are important.	**7.** What is a cash transaction?

7. A transaction where the goods and the money both move at the same time. The customer gets the goods (or services) and the shopkeeper (or the service provider) gets the money.	**8.** What is a credit transaction?
8. One where the goods move first and the money moves later.	**9.** What is the main book of account?
9. The Ledger—so called because in the old counting-houses it lay on a ledge under the window.	**10.** What do we call each leaf in the ledger?
10. An Account. Each person we deal with has a double-sided page (a leaf). Each leaf has a folio number, from the Latin *folium*—a leaf.	**11.** What are the three types of account?
11. Personal, nominal and real.	**12.** What sort of accounts are personal?
12. The accounts of our debtors and our creditors. Debtors owe us money, and creditors are people to whom we owe money.	**13.** What sort of accounts are real?
13. Accounts where we record assets of the business, Land and Buildings Account, Furniture and Fittings Account, etc.	**14.** Which accounts are nominal?
14. Accounts which are only records 'in name only', the actual money has been spent (or earned), e.g. Rent Account, Wages Account, etc. or Discount Received Account, Rent Received Account, etc.	**15.** What is the rule for making entries in accounts?
15. Debit the account that receives goods, services or money. Credit the account that gives goods, services or money.	**16.** Go over the page again until you are sure of all the answers.

UNIT 2

A More Detailed Look at the Ledger

2.1 Book-keeping to the Trial Balance

We have already learned seven important points:

(a) Accounting records are kept by a system of *double-entry book-keeping.*
(b) The chief book of account is the *ledger.*
(c) Every leaf in the ledger is called an *account.*
(d) The left-hand side of an account is called the *debit side* and is used whenever the person or thing named at the top of the account *receives* goods, services or money from the firm whose records are being kept in the ledger.
(e) The right-hand side of an account is called the *credit side* and is used whenever the person or thing named at the top of the account *gives* goods, services or money to the firm whose records are being kept in the ledger.
(f) There are three classes of account: *personal accounts, nominal accounts* and *real accounts.*
(g) At the end of any accounting period a *Trial Balance* may be struck. The various balances are listed in two columns, debit and credit, and the accuracy of the double entry checked by seeing that the two columns agree.

The whole of book-keeping to the Trial Balance is illustrated diagrammatically in Fig. 2.1. We must now go on to look more closely at these accounts and have some practice in making entries in typical accounts.

2.2 Traditional Accounts and Computerized Accounts

The accounts already shown in Unit 1 may be described as *traditional accounts*, that is, they have debit and credit sides to the account, and are balanced off at the end of the month, ready for the Trial Balance. This type of account has been improved upon by the introduction of computers, which add up and subtract automatically. While it would be a terrible labour for a human book-keeper to balance off an account every time he or she made an entry in it, a computer can do it with no trouble at all. Where a computer can perform the calculations electronically, the accounts might as well be balanced off to a new balancing figure every time an entry is made. This has brought about a change in the style of accounting. Where a business has a computerized system, accounts are laid out as shown in Fig. 2.2. These are called *continuous-balance* or *running-balance accounts*. Read the notes carefully to be sure you follow the revised layout of the debit and credit sides. As a student without access to a computer, however, you would waste a good deal of time working out all the arithmetic involved in accounts of this kind, so we must return to traditional accounts for our study of the ledger.

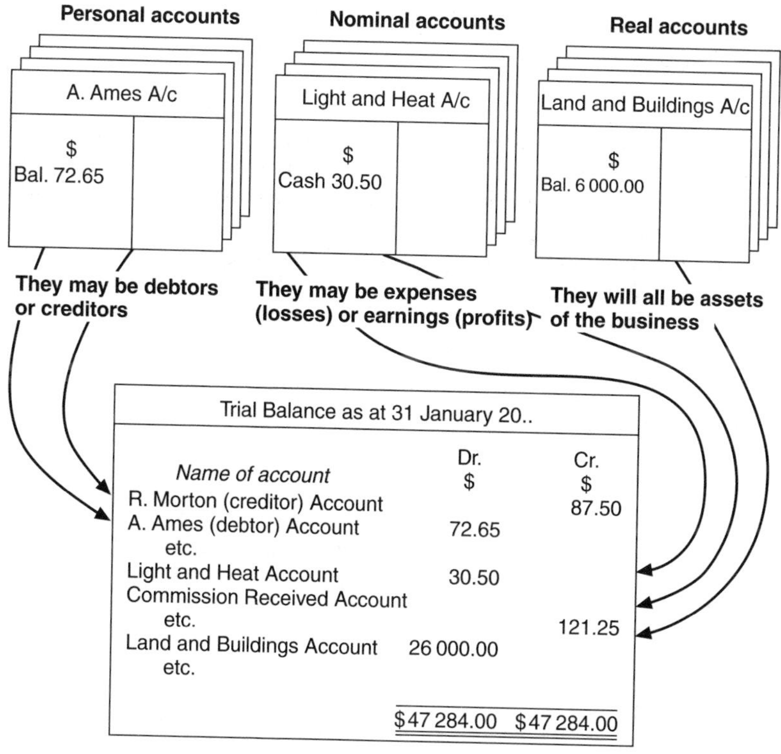

Fig. 2.1 Book-keeping to the Trial Balance

```
Account of John Murray (Publishers) in the books of J.M. Arden

John Murray (Publishers) Ltd.
50 Albemarle St, London W1S 4BD                    VAT = 10%
```

Date	Type	Ref. No.	Goods	VAT	Cash	Disc.	Total	O/S Amt	Balance
14-12-20.0	INV	3	195.00	19.50	0.00	0.00	214.50	0.00	214.50
4- 1 -20.1	CASH	204	0.00	0.00	214.50	0.00	-214.50	214.50	0.00
11- 1 -20.1	INV	36	20.00	2.00	0.00	0.00	22.00	0.00	22.00
16- 1 -20.1	INV	76	115.95	11.60	0.00	0.00	127.55	22.00	149.55
26- 1 -20.1	C/N	231	-16.50	-1.65	0.00	0.00	-18.15	149.55	131.40
29- 1 -20.1	INV	89	221.40	22.14	0.00	0.00	243.54	131.40	374.94
31- 1 -20.1	INV	103	79.50	7.95	0.00	0.00	87.45	374.94	462.39

```
Transaction types                              Outstanding Balances
                                               Curr. Month    Prev. Month
INV = Invoice
C/N = Credit Note CASH = Cash Receipt          $462.39        $0.00
```

Fig. 2.2 A continuous-balance computerized account

Note the following:

(a) The page is no longer divided down the middle but instead the debit and credit columns are side by side. Each is in two parts: the debit column records goods and VAT separately, and the credit column records cash and discount.

(b) When the customer (John Murray (Publishers) Ltd) is supplied with goods—as on 14 December, for example—the account is debited.

(c) Since this is the account of a customer, in other words of a debtor, these debit entries are added to the running balance, which shows what John Murray's firm owes to J. M. Arden's at any given time.

(d) When Murray's pays cash to Arden's—as on 4 January, for example—the account is credited. This payment reduces the amount owed on the running balance.

(e) On 26 January Murray returned goods to J. M. Arden (Portway) Ltd, who issued a credit note (coded C/N). The returns have not been added into the credit column but have been deducted from the debit column, which has exactly the same effect. This enables the computer to keep track of both sales and VAT.

(f) The column heading O/S AMT stands for 'outstanding amount'. This entry shows the final balance of the previous line, and is used by the computer to calculate the new balance.

(g) The lines at the foot of the account showing the outstanding balances for the current month and the previous month enable the credit controller to check whether debtors are paying promptly each month for their supplies.

2.3 Cash Transactions and Credit Transactions

(a) Cash Transactions

In these transactions the goods supplied are paid for immediately, as with most purchases in shops. Clearly a person who pays in this way cannot become a debtor of the business, and the proprietor of the business cannot suffer any bad debts. There is no need to record the transaction at all, so that book-keeping time is saved. As the money is struck up on the cash register, it is usually printed on the till roll, which gives at the end of the day a total 'daily cash takings' or 'daily cash sales' figure. This figure will be recorded in the Sales Account to enable profits to be calculated later on. Many small businesses prefer to keep all transactions in cash and many large firms, like supermarkets, deal similarly in cash only, while at 'cash-and-carry' warehouses retailers may purchase goods in bulk for spot cash, carrying them away in their own vans. Naturally they are able to buy very cheaply, getting good cash discounts (price reductions) on purchases, because they are not asking the wholesaler for the usual services he/she supplies, i.e. transport and credit.

(b) Credit Transactions

The word 'credit' sometimes confuses students, for it is commonly used in several different senses, some of which appear to conflict with others. Consider the following explanations of the word 'credit'.

(i) Credit is the name given to the right-hand side of the ledger page, on which entries are made when a person, or thing, has given goods, services or money to the business.

(ii) Credit is also the name given to a transaction for which payment is not made immediately, but is postponed to some future time. The usual period of credit in business is one month. The person receiving goods or services pays for them at the end of the month, when a *statement of account* is sent out requesting payment for all those transactions that have occurred in the last thirty days. This kind of trading is said to be on *monthly credit terms*.

(iii) Long-term credit—often called 'hire purchase credit' or 'extended credit'—requires payment to be made over a longer period of time, often up to three years. Hire purchase credit terms are sometimes controlled by Government orders, since they can be used to control the economy.

What is confusing about the term 'credit' is that the person concerned becomes a 'debtor'. Some students find this muddling, but it is not really difficult. The point is that someone who holds out the credit as an inducement to other traders to do business intends to become one of their 'creditors'. When inviting firms to do business with you on 'monthly credit terms' you are offering to become a creditor until the end of the month. They will become your debtors, and you will incur some risk of bad debts. The proprietor of a small business, fearful of bad debts, often exhibits a notice reading 'Please do not ask for credit as a refusal may offend'. He/she prefers to deal in cash only.

2.4 Credit Control

The people to whom we sell goods, or to whom we give services of some sort, become debtors of the business—perhaps for large sums of money—and must eventually pay for the goods or services received. Obviously, it would be unwise to make credit available to anyone who asks for it regardless of his or her ability to pay. This is the purpose of *credit sanctioning*.

Every business appoints one member of staff (usually the supervisor of the Debtors Ledger) to act as *credit controller*. This person tries to ensure that no account is opened with a new customer unless the following things have been done:

(i) A banker's reference or trade reference (from a supplier the debtor already deals with) has been taken up on the debtor to discover whether he or she is a reliable customer with funds available to honour any bills we send. If such a reference is not available it is possible to consult a specialist *credit reference agency*.

(ii) A credit limit has been set beyond which the customer may not go without the sanction of the credit controller. It is not unknown for a customer to place one or two small orders, paying promptly, and then send in a very large order for which it is beyond his or her capacity to pay.

(iii) A date has been set each month by which the accounts should have been settled. Orders received when the account is in arrears are held up while a letter is sent requesting payment before the new order can be fulfilled.

These measures of credit control may save us serious bad debts, and are essential for all businesses.

2.5 Debtors' Personal Accounts

Debtors may be invoiced for goods and services. They also occasionally return goods which are unsatisfactory for some reason, or they may be made an allowance for some overcharge or as compensation for some dissatisfaction they feel about the service provided. It follows that any debtor's account may have the following entries:

(a) Debit Entries in a Debtor's Account

(i) The opening balance This will almost always be a debit balance at the start of the month, since the debtor is in debt (debit).

(ii) Invoice entries Invoices are made out whenever goods or services are supplied (see Unit 9.4) showing how much the debtor must pay for the goods or services he/she has received.

(iii) Debit note entries These are very much like invoices; they are generally used to correct some undercharge on an invoice, or to charge the debtor with items such as carriage or packing expenses.

(b) Credit Entries in a Debtor's Account

(i) Credit note entries Credit notes are made out when goods are returned, or when allowances are made after some complaint (see Unit 9.10).

(ii) Cash or cheques When these are received by the firm, the debtor is credited as he/she has paid some or all of the debt.

(iii) Discount entries These may be cash or settlement discounts given for prompt payment (see Unit 10.2(a)). They reduce the debtor's debt.

(iv) The closing balance This will be carried down to the debit side as the outstanding debt at the end of the month.

A debtor's account might look like this:

M. Rostov, 15 High Road, Saltsea, Sussex — DL18

Dr.							*Cr.*
20..			$	20..			$
1 Apr.	Balance	B/d	145.50	7 Apr.	Bank		138.22
2 Apr.	Sales		36.80	7 Apr.	Discount Allowed		7.28
3 Apr.	Sales		12.50	12 Apr.	Sales Returns		8.40
3 Apr.	Carriage Outwards		1.50	30 Apr.	Balance	c/d	383.80
8 Apr.	Sales		45.50				
11 Apr.	Sales		149.00				
17 Apr.	Sales		65.00				
29 Apr.	Sales		80.50				
29 Apr.	Insurance		1.40				
		$	537.70			$	537.70
20..			$				
1 May	Balance	B/d	383.80				

Note:

(i) The year is written at the top of the date column. To save constant alteration only the figures 20.. have been shown here. You should read this as if it were the current year.

(ii) The words used in the details column are sometimes a source of some difficulty. The rule is: *always use the name of the account where the double entry will be found.* Thus on 2 April the double entry would be on the Sales Account, since Rostov has been sold goods to the value of $36.80. On 7 April the payment was by cheque, which will have been entered in the Bank Account, and the discount allowed to Rostov for prompt payment will have been entered in the Discount Allowed Account.

(iii) Only three *folio numbers* have been entered here. They are B/d, c/d, and B/d. These refer to 'Brought down' and 'carried down', and are used whenever an account is balanced off. (Traditionally a capital letter was always used for 'Brought down', but not for 'carried down'.) An explanation of folio numbers is given in Unit 3.5; here you should note that this account, which is a debtor's account, is in the *Debtors Ledger*, and has a folio number DL18.

(iv) The balancing off of the account is carried out on the same line so that the two sides are level, and a currency symbol is inserted to emphasize that a 'balance' has been struck at this point. The unused lines on the shorter side are struck through, in red ink, to prevent later entries being made in the spare lines. (You should always insert these lines when balancing off an account; but in this book they would serve no purpose and have been omitted except in the early Units, where they serve as a reminder.)

(v) An account with a balance on it must have the balance brought down before it can be called complete. *It would be quite wrong to leave the account levelled off*—in this case at a total of $537.70. This would give the impression that the account was clear, when in fact Rostov still owes us the sum of $383.80.

(vi) As the balance is brought down the date is changed to 1 May (i.e. the first day of the next month) to show clearly what the debtor owes at this date.

Do the following exercises without worrying about the double entry for each transaction you are entering. Of course in real business you would never make an entry in one account without making an equal and opposite entry in some other account, but here we are just concerned about practising the keeping of a single account. Remember the rules for entries in a debtor's account:

Debit the debtor's account when he/she receives goods, services or money from your business.

Credit the debtor's account when he/she gives back goods, or deserves an allowance off his/her debt because of some dis-service you have done to him/her, or when he/she gives money in payment.

2.6 Exercises Set 2. Debtors' Personal Accounts

1. C. Hadland is a debtor of ours, whose account has the folio number DL17. On 1 January 20.. he has a debit balance of $402.97. Then these transactions take place:

2 January	Hadland pays us the amount owed on 1 January, by cheque, less discount of $20.15.
3 January	Hadland orders goods which he collects by private messenger, value $47.50.
14 January	He orders more goods, value $72.50. We charge him carriage $4.25.
16 January	Hadland orders goods, value $285.00, and agrees to pay $100.00 on account. His cheque for this amount is brought by his van driver when he collects the goods.
27 January	Hadland returns packing cases, value $4.50.

Open Hadland's account with the balance shown, and enter these transactions into it. Balance off the account on 31 January and bring down the balance.

2. George Wakeman is a debtor of ours for the sum of $5.25 on 1 May 20... His account number is DL32. During May the following transactions take place:

2 May	Wakeman pays the balance owing by cheque, less discount of $0.13.
5 May	Wakeman orders goods valued at $27.55.
7 May	He orders further goods for $62.50 and is charged for insurance $1.50.
18 May	Wakeman returns goods sold to him on 5 May. Their value is $8.50.
29 May	Wakeman orders goods for $12.25.
31 May	We balance off the account and bring down the balance.

Enter these transactions into Mr Wakeman's account.

3. M. Watts is a debtor of ours for the sum of $720.50 on 1 July 20... His account number is DL194. During July the following transactions take place. Enter them into Watts's account after you have opened it with the balance shown above. Close the account on 31 July and bring down the balance.

3 July	Watts pays the balance owing on 1 July by cheque, less a discount of $2\frac{1}{2}$ per cent = $18.01.
4 July	Watts is sold goods valued at $41.25.
5 July	Watts returns goods, damaged in transit, worth $7.77.
15 July	Watts purchases more goods value $142.50. He is charged carriage $1.25 and insurance $0.75.
29 July	Watts agrees to sell us a surplus machine, valued at $650.00, the sum to be set against his account.
30 July	Watts is sold goods valued at $380.50.

Explain what is unusual about this balance in the debtor's account on 31 July.

4. a) Here is a ledger account in the books of Peter Lee. Copy it out on a piece of ledger paper, balance it off on 31 March and bring down the balance. Then answer the questions below.

R. T. Crafty, 14 High Street, Rowford, Essex							DL31
20..			$	20..			$
1 Mar.	Balance	B/d	405.75	3 Mar.	Bank		395.61
11 Mar.	Sales		274.50	3 Mar.	Discount		10.14
19 Mar.	Sales		100.00	27 Mar.	Returns		12.50
20 Mar.	Carriage		5.50	28 Mar.	Motor Vans		150.00

b) On 1 March, was Crafty a debtor or a creditor?
c) What happened on 27 March, according to this account?
d) What happened on 28 March, according to this account?
e) On 31 March, was Crafty a debtor or a creditor?

5. a) Here is Margaret Fisher's account in William Sandon's books. Copy it out and complete it for the month of May 20... Then answer the questions below.

M. Fisher, 87 Peartree Way, Newtown, Herts							DL72
20..			$	20..			$
1 May	Balance	B/d	15.25	2 May	Bank		14.49
14 May	Sales		10.50	2 May	Discount		0.76
29 May	Sales		12.25	30 May	Sewing Machines		68.50
29 May	Carriage		0.55				

b) On 1 May, was Margaret Fisher a debtor or a creditor?
c) What happened on 2 May?
d) What happened on 30 May?
e) What is unusual about the balance on 31 May?

2.7 Creditors' Personal Accounts

When we buy from a supplier, the supplier becomes a creditor of the business. The personal account of a creditor operates along exactly the same lines as the personal account of a debtor, but the items appear on the opposite side. Instead of receiving goods from our business (a debit entry) the creditor is giving goods to our business, so we must *credit the giver*. A creditor's account might look like this:

Dr.	R. Michaelson, 17 Low Road, Upper Hilton, Staffs						CL27 *Cr.*
20..			$	20..			$
2 Jan.	Purchases Returns		9.55	1 Jan.	Balance	B/d	490.55
30 Jan.	Bank		481.00	17 Jan.	Purchases		235.60
31 Jan.	Purchases Returns		5.50	17 Jan.	Purchases		71.90
31 Jan.	Balance	c/d	500.36	19 Jan.	Interest due		4.81
				28 Jan.	Purchases		64.50
				28 Jan.	Purchases		125.30
				29 Jan.	Carriage		3.75
		$	996.41			$	996.41
				20..			$
				1 Feb.	Balance	B/d	500.36

Notice the item 'interest due' on 19 January. Michaelson has charged us 1 per cent interest on the balance still owing from 1 January. It appears we should have paid more promptly.

You should now practise the keeping of creditors' accounts by making the entries for the exercises below. Remember the rules for entries in a creditor's account:

> *Credit the creditor whenever he/she gives goods, services or money to the business.*
>
> *Debit the creditor when he/she receives payment from your firm or receives back goods you have returned to him/her, or makes you an allowance because you are dissatisfied.*

2.8 Exercises Set 3. Creditors' Personal Accounts

1. R. Bolton is a supplier of ours, to whom we owe a balance of $40.75 on 1 August 20... Open his ledger account CL21 and then enter the following transactions for the month:

2 August	We pay the outstanding balance by cheque, less $2.04 discount.
13 August	Bolton supplies goods valued at $85.00.
17 August	He supplies more goods valued at $16.50.
18 August	We return goods to Bolton $5.75.
19 August	He makes us an allowance on goods that need repolishing because of damage in transit $8.40.
27 August	He supplies goods value $132.50 and also charges insurance on transit $1.50.
31 August	Account balanced off and brought down.

2. R. Lucas is in business as a manufacturer and the following are his transactions with T. Robertson for the month of January 20..:

1 January	Balance due to Robertson $500.00.
10 January	Buys from Robertson 30 tonnes scrap at $95.00 per tonne = $2 850.00.
12 January	Pays Robertson, by cheque, the balance due to him, on 1 January, less 5 per cent settlement discount.
14 January	Buys from Robertson 4 tonnes scrap zinc at $97.00 per tonne = $388.00.
16 January	Returns to Robertson 5 tonnes scrap purchased on 10 January.
16 January	Pays carriage on above return, $12.50 chargeable to Robertson.
27 January	Sells to Robertson a bulldozer at agreed valuation $880.00.
29 January	Buys from Robertson aluminium scrap sheeting valued at $42.00.

You are required to open Robertson's account in Lucas's books CL47; balance off the account and bring down the balance.

3. A. Miller is in business in the household durable goods trade and is supplied by Universal Warehouses Ltd. On 1 January 20.. the supplier is owed $729.54 by Miller. Open the supplier's account in Miller's book CL94, and make the following additional entries:

2 January	Miller pays the full amount owing by cheque.
4 January	Goods supplied to Miller $248.50.
11 January	Goods supplied to Miller $320.75. Miller returns empties, etc., $4.55.
18 January	Goods supplied to Miller $452.65. Miller returns discoloured goods $16.75 and empties $4.05.
19 January	Miller buys for use in the shops a cash register (Furniture and Fittings Account) valued at $215.50.
25 January	Goods supplied $184.55. Returned empties $15.25.
31 January	Account balanced off and brought down.

4. Here is the ledger account of R. Jones as it appears in the books of Lee Bros. Copy out the account and balance it off at the end of the month.

R. Jones							CL55
20..			$	20..			$
2 Jan.	Purchases Returns		7.70	1 Jan.	Balance	B/d	234.70
3 Jan.	Bank		221.32	14 Jan.	Purchases		48.60
3 Jan.	Discount		5.68	15 Jan.	Carriage		4.40
23 Jan.	Purchases Returns		4.12	17 Jan.	Purchases		133.10
30 Jan.	Motor Lorry (Exchange)		150.00	18 Jan.	Insurance and Carriage		7.12

Now answer these questions:

a) What does each line mean? Deal with them in date order.

b) Who owes the balance to whom?

5. Here is a ledger account in the books of M. Bright. Copy out the account on a piece of ledger paper; balance it off on 28 February 20.. and bring down the balance. Then answer the questions below.

P. B. Rowe, 27 Hill Road, Canewdon, Essex							CL39
20..			$	20..			$
2 Feb.	Bank		702.39	1 Feb.	Balance	B/d	720.40
2 Feb.	Discount		18.01	11 Feb.	Purchases		425.50
14 Feb.	Returns		25.50	19 Feb.	Purchases		285.50
18 Feb.	Motor Vehicles		1 650.00	20 Feb.	Carriage		12.50

a) On 1 February, was Mr Rowe a debtor or a creditor?

b) What happened on 14 February, according to this account?

c) What happened on 18 February, according to this account?

d) On 28 February, was Mr Rowe a debtor or a creditor?

2.9 Exercises Set 4. Running-balance Ledger Accounts

In this set of exercises you are asked to keep the ledger accounts in running-balance form, as in Fig. 2.2 (see page 24). Rule columns on a sheet of exercise paper for Date, Details, Debit, Credit and Balance. After each entry you must work out the running balance.

1. R. Molyneaux is a supplier of ours, to whom we owe a balance of $168.50 on 1 August 20... Open his ledger account CL29 and then enter the following transactions for the month:

7 August	We pay the outstanding balance by cheque, less $4.21 discount.
12 August	Molyneaux supplies goods valued at $94.60.
15 August	He supplies more goods valued at $54.80.
18 August	We return goods to Molyneaux $12.84.
19 August	He makes us an allowance on goods that need repairing because of damage in transit $25.00.
27 August	He supplies goods value $188.50 and also charges insurance on goods in transit $4.50.

2. M. Cosgrove is a debtor of ours, whose account has the folio number DL47. On 1 January 20.. he has a debit balance of $581.94. Then these transactions take place:

2 January	Cosgrove pays us the amount owed on 1 January, by cheque, less discount of $29.10.
3 January	Cosgrove orders goods, which he collects by dispatch rider, of value $84.60.
16 January	He orders more goods, value $197.28. We charge him carriage $8.50.
19 January	He orders goods value $326.84, and agrees to pay $200.00 on account. His cheque for this amount is brought by his van driver when he collects the goods.
28 January	Cosgrove returns package cases, value $17.25.

3. Here is the ledger account of Pauline Murray in our books. It is in running-balance style but the balances have not been calculated on the various entries. Copy out the account, calculate the running balances, and then answer the questions (a) to (e) below.

P. Murray				L15
Date	*Details*	*Debit*	*Credit*	*Balance*
20..		$	$	$
1 Mar.	Balance		284.74	284.74
11 Mar.	Purchases		328.24	
17 Mar.	Purchases		162.62	
20 Mar.	Purchases Returns	24.60		
23 Mar.	Bank	277.62		
23 Mar.	Discount	7.12		
29 Mar.	Purchases		94.24	
31 Mar.	Motor Vehicles	350.00		

a) On 1 March, was Miss Murray a debtor or a creditor?
b) What happened on 20 March?
c) What happened on 23 March?
d) What happened on 31 March?
e) On 31 March, was Miss Murray a debtor or a creditor?

2.10 Revise and Test 2. More about the Ledger

Cover the page with a sheet of paper, then read one question at a time.

Answers	*Questions*
—	**1.** Normally an account is divided down the middle. What do we call the two sides?
1. The debit side and the credit side.	**2.** Suppose we make an entry on the debit side of Tom Smith's account. What does it mean?
2. It means he has received goods, services or money from us. Consequently he is our debtor. He owes us money.	**3.** Suppose we make an entry on the credit side of Mary Jones' account, what does it mean?
3. It means she has given goods, services or money to us. Consequently she is our creditor, and we owe her money.	**4.** Suppose we keep our accounts on a computer. How will this change the records?
4. The account will really be in running-balance style, and the computer can tell us instantly what 'the balance' is on any account.	**5.** Name four real accounts.
5. Land and Buildings Account; Motor Vehicle Account; Furniture and Fittings Account; Cash Account.	**6.** What can we call all real accounts?
6. Asset Accounts. Assets are the real things a business owns.	**7.** Why do all real accounts have debit balances?
7. Because the item named at the top of the page (say, Motor Vehicles Account) has received that amount of the wealth of the proprietor(s) to buy the asset named.	**8.** What is a nominal account?

8. One where the money is there in name only (*nomen* = name—Latin). The actual money has gone elsewhere, and all we have is a record of it.	**9.** All nominal accounts must be either . . . Finish the sentence!
9. They are either losses or profits.	**10.** Name three losses of the business.
10. Rent, wages, telephone expenses.	**11.** All losses are entered on the debit side of the account. Why?
11. Because the item (say, telephone expenses) has received the amount entered on the account. The payment was probably made by cheque, so the money has gone to the telephone company.	**12.** Name three profits of the business.
12. Rent Received Account (if we have a tenant); Discount Received Account (if we pay promptly) and Commission Received Account (if we earn commission).	**13.** All profits are entered on the credit side of the account. Why?
13. Because the item named at the top of the account has given value to the business (say Rent Received).	**14.** But what about the actual money?
14. It is either in the Cash Box (Cash Account) or we may have paid it into the bank (Bank Account).	**15.** Say it again—what is the basic rule of book-keeping and accountancy?
15. Debit the account that receives goods, services or money. Credit the account that gives goods, services or money.	**16.** Go over the page again if necessary.

UNIT 3

More Advanced Accounting to the Trial Balance

3.1 Business Documents

If a transaction is a cash transaction (for instance, when a child buys an ice-cream from a van), no accounting records are kept, and no documents pass between the two parties. But where a transaction is a credit transaction an accounting record must be kept at least until payment is received, and generally much longer. The law says that a legal action on a simple bargain may be brought at any time within six years of the bargain being struck (Limitations Act 1980). Therefore if the transaction is a credit transaction, requiring records to be kept of the bargain, these records should be preserved for at least six years.

The usual documentary record of a bargain is an *invoice*, but of course there are more formal agreements which are drawn up by lawyers—deeds and leases are examples. Other documents are *credit notes*, for returns, *cheques* and *credit transfer slips* for payments, *receipts* for acknowledging payments, and so on. Not all documents lead to book-keeping records—for instance, an *order* is an offer to buy, but it does not become a bargain between the parties until it is accepted by the supplier, who prepares an invoice. The documents that lead to book-keeping records are called *original documents* and lead to entries in *books of original entry*. These books are discussed later (see Units 9 to 13).

3.2 Documents Leading to Book-keeping Entries

The documents that lead to book-keeping entries are discussed in full in Units 9.4, 9.10 and 10.5. Here we will look at them briefly in turn.

(a) Invoices

These are made out by the supplier (seller) of goods and given to the receiver (buyer) as evidence of the bargain struck.

They are prepared with the names and addresses of both parties to the transaction and include a description of the goods and their value. Then the ledger entries are as shown in Figs 3.1 and 3.2. Here we are keeping the books of A. Retailer.

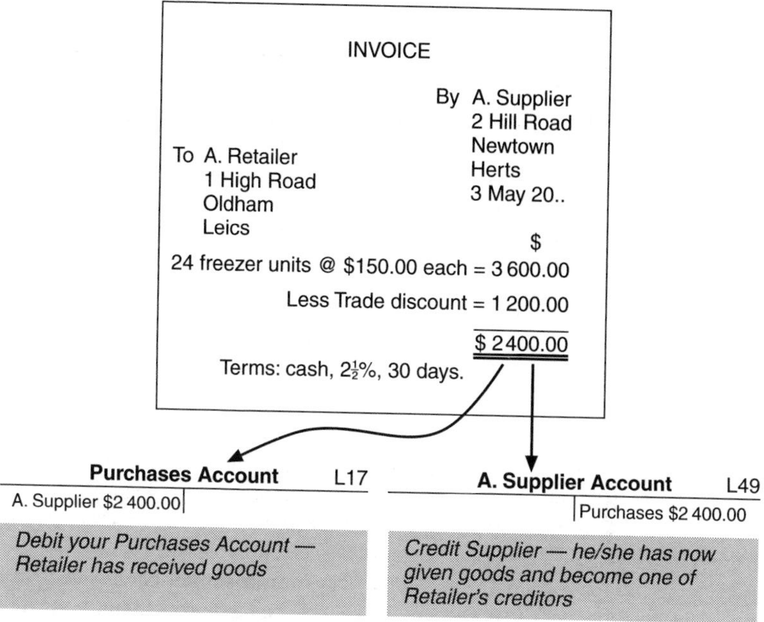
INVOICE

By A. Supplier
2 Hill Road
Newtown
Herts
3 May 20..

To A. Retailer
1 High Road
Oldham
Leics

	$
24 freezer units @ $150.00 each =	3 600.00
Less Trade discount =	1 200.00
	$ 2400.00

Terms: cash, 2½%, 30 days.

Fig. 3.1 Double entries for purchases invoices for goods received

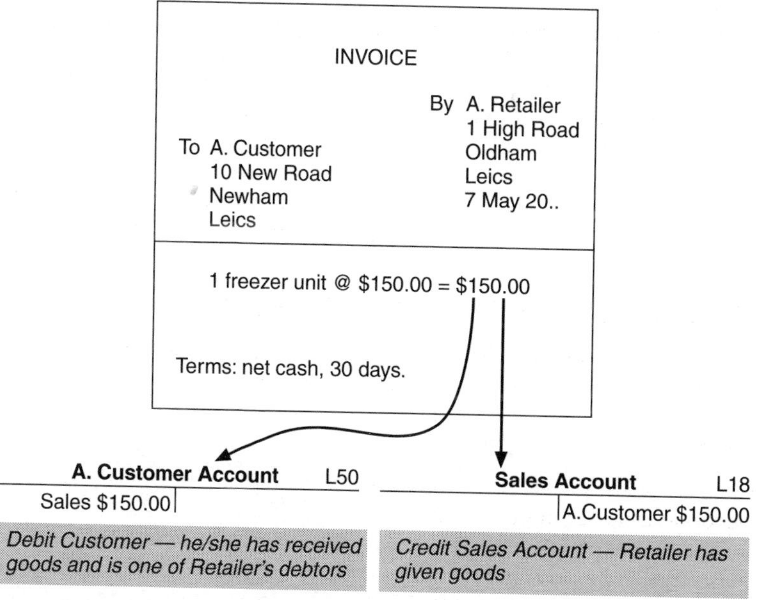
INVOICE

By A. Retailer
1 High Road
Oldham
Leics
7 May 20..

To A. Customer
10 New Road
Newham
Leics

1 freezer unit @ $150.00 = $150.00

Terms: net cash, 30 days.

Fig. 3.2 Double entries for sales invoices for goods dispatched

(b) Credit Notes

These are always printed in red and are made out (again) by the seller of goods when customers send back goods that are unsatisfactory. They may also be used to give an allowance where goods are not actually returned but are for some reason not worth the full invoice price—for example, where they were slightly damaged in transit. The ledger entries are as shown in Figs 3.3 and 3.4.

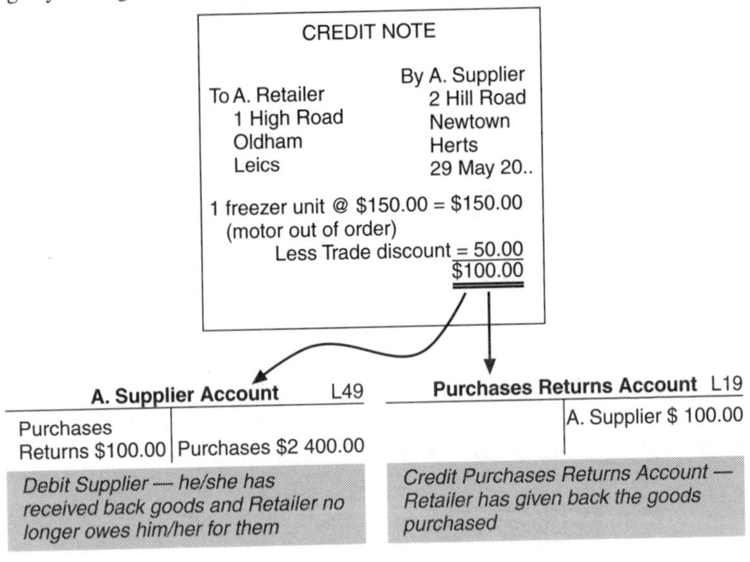

Fig. 3.3 Double entries for returns outwards

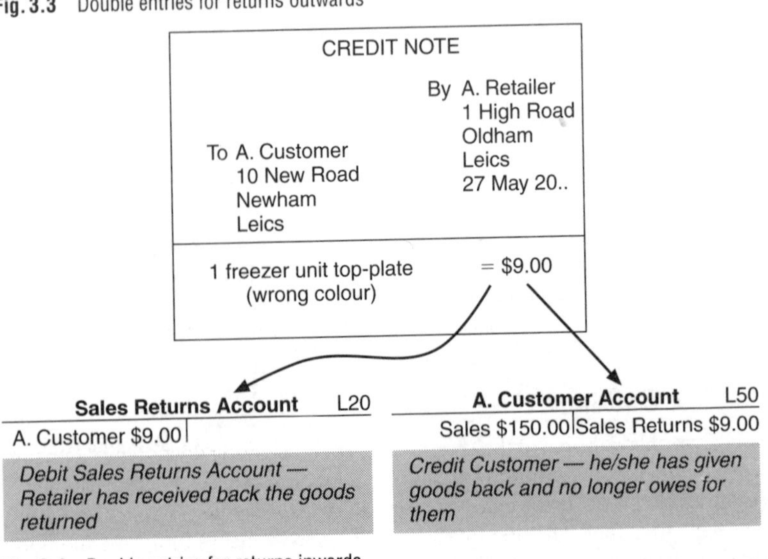

Fig. 3.4 Double entries for returns inwards

(c) Cheques, Bank Giro Credits and Postal Orders

These are used to settle indebtedness between businesses. They lead to entries in the Bank Account as shown in Figs 3.5 and 3.6.

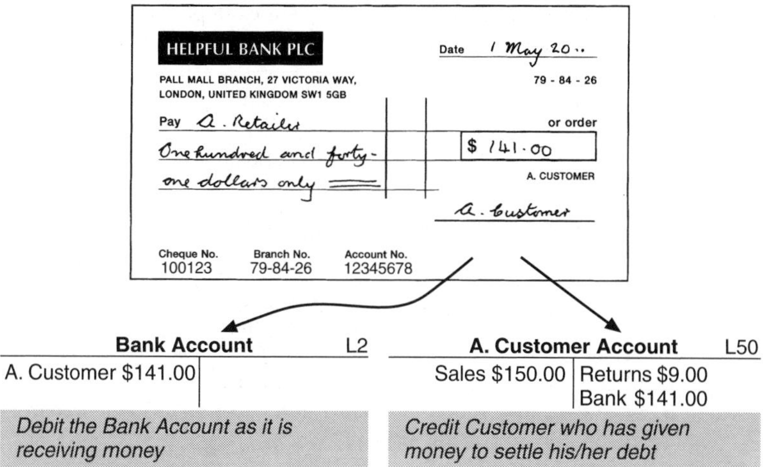

Fig. 3.5 Double entries for a cheque received

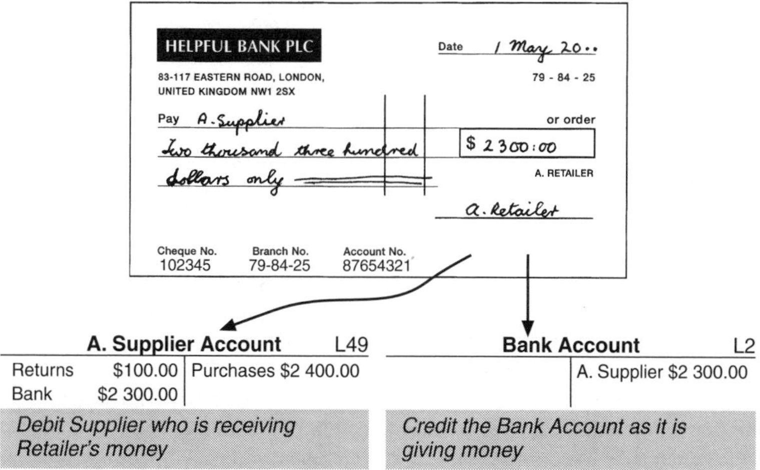

Fig. 3.6 Double entries for a cheque paid

Having looked at some of the most important accounting documents, a further word on the use of accounting paper is helpful here. There are many rulings of paper used, but the three chief ones are *ledger paper*, *journal paper* and *three-column cash paper*. The first two are all that need concern us for the moment; three-column cash paper is discussed in Unit 10.2.

3.3 Using Ledger Paper for Accounting Exercises

As we said earlier, in a ledger in a business office each leaf of the book—that is both sides of a sheet of paper—are reserved for the transactions with the one person, or thing, named at the top. We must never put Tom Smith's transactions on Peter Brown's page. But this is not practical when students are doing exercises involving, perhaps, twenty accounts with only one or two entries on each. It would waste too much ledger paper. The usual solution is to put about six accounts on a page, but pretend that they are separate accounts and give them separate folio numbers.

3.4 Journal Paper in Accounting

'Journal' comes from the French word *jour*, which means 'day', and journal paper is often called 'day book' paper. The Journal, or Day Book, is a very important book which we shall meet later (see Unit 9.2), but the ruling is shown here because it is very useful for Trial Balances. The two columns on the right-hand side are used for the debit and credit balances. The columns can be ruled across at the end of the Trial Balance and neat totals can be prepared, as shown in the model exercise on page 44.

Day	Month	Details	Folio	*Dr.*	*Cr.*

3.5 Folio Numbers

All book-keeping papers have special columns for folio numbers. These are used as cross-references for page numbers. In the ledger of the model exercise that follows, the folio numbers have been inserted as cross-references. On every line of this example there appears the folio number of the ledger account where the other half of the double entry will be found. In your own exercises from now on you should put in the folio numbers. You should also use these numbers throughout the model exercise and check the accuracy of the cross-references given.

The exercises in this Unit are a little longer than those in Unit 1. They use the new knowledge you will have acquired in this Unit by referring to documents such as invoices, credit notes and cheques, and they introduce a wider variety of expenses of the business. In every case, however, simple double-entry book-keeping is all that is required. *If you need to revise, you should do so at this point* so that you gain more confidence. The model exercise shown below will help you in your revision of double entry. (*Note:* from this point in the book onwards, we shall no longer separate the two sides of an account with a vertical line. You may of course continue to do so in your own work if you find it helpful.)

3.6 Model Exercise to the Trial Balance

Celia Peabody sets up in business on 1 January 20.. as a retail grocer, with the following assets: land and buildings $33 850.00; equipment $3 720.00; stock $2 350.00; cash at bank $650.00 and cash in hand $35.00. VAT input tax has been paid on equipment and stock to give $607.00 on the VAT Account. Open up the necessary accounts, including the Capital Account, and then enter the following items:

4 January	Cash sales $432.50 plus VAT $43.25. Sales on credit to R. Johnston $42.50 plus VAT $4.25. Pays rate demand by cheque, $112.50.
11 January	Buys shop shelving and equipment from Dexter Ltd by cheque, $127.00 plus VAT $12.70. Pays signwriter (General Expenses Account) $24.35 plus VAT $2.44, by cheque. Buys goods for resale from Ivor Brown Ltd on credit, $234.50 plus VAT $23.45.
15 January	Cash sales $378.50 plus VAT $37.85. Pays travelling expenses in cash, $23.25. Pays for repairs to premises in cash, $64.20 plus VAT $6.42. Returns goods to Ivor Brown Ltd, $15.50 plus VAT $1.55.
24 January	Cash sales $442.60 plus VAT $44.26. Purchases goods for resale from Mohican Bros Ltd, $405.25 plus VAT $40.52, on credit.
31 January	Pays Ivor Brown's outstanding account by cheque. Cash sales $937.50 plus VAT $93.75. Banks $1 600.00 from cash till.

Notes:

The double entries would be as shown below, and in the accounts that follow.

1 January — For the opening situation, all the assets brought in, except the VAT balance, are real items and must be debited in their real accounts. The VAT is a debit in the personal account of the Customs and Excise Department. The Capital Account will be credited with the total value contributed to the business. We therefore have:

Debit	Land and Buildings	$33 850.00
	Equipment	$3 720.00
	Stock	$2 350.00
	Cash at bank	$650.00
	Cash in hand	$35.00
	VAT	$607.00
Credit	Capital Account	$41 212.00

4 January — Debit Cash Account $475.75; credit Sales Account $432.50 and VAT Account $43.25.
Debit R. Johnston Account $46.75; credit Sales Account $42.50 and VAT Account $4.25.
Debit Rates Account $112.50; credit Bank Account $112.50.

11 January — Debit Equipment Account $127.00 and VAT Account $12.70; credit Bank Account $139.70.
Debit General Expenses Account $24.35 and VAT Account $2.44; credit Bank Account $26.79.
Debit Purchases Account $234.50 and VAT Account $23.45; credit Ivor Brown Ltd Account $257.95.

15 January	Debit Cash Account $416.35; credit Sales Account $378.50 and VAT Account $37.85.
	Debit Travelling Expenses Account $23.25; credit Cash Account $23.25.
	Debit Repairs Account $64.20 and VAT Account $6.42; credit Cash Account $70.62.
	Debit Ivor Brown Ltd $17.05; credit Purchases Returns Account $15.50 and VAT Account $1.55.
24 January	Debit Cash Account $486.86; credit Sales Account $442.60 and VAT Account $44.26.
	Debit Purchases Account $405.25 and VAT Account $40.52; credit Mohican Bros Ltd $445.77.
31 January	Debit Ivor Brown Ltd $240.90; credit Bank Account $240.90.
	Debit Cash Account $1 031.25; credit Sales Account $937.50 and VAT Account $93.75.
	Debit Bank Account $1 600.00; credit Cash Account $1 600.00.

Land and Buildings Account L1

20..	F	$
1 Jan. Capital	L7	33 850.00

Equipment Account L2

20..	F	$
1 Jan. Capital	L7	3 720.00
11 Jan. Bank	L4	127.00

Stock Account L3

20..	F	$
1 Jan. Capital	L7	2 350.00

Bank Account L4

20..	F	$	20..	F	$
1 Jan. Capital	L7	650.00	4 Jan. Rates	L10	112.50
31 Jan. Cash	L5	1 600.00	11 Jan. Equipment	L2	139.70
			11 Jan. General Expenses	L11	26.79
			31 Jan. Ivor Brown	L12	240.90
			31 Jan. Balance	c/d	1 730.11
		$2 250.00			$2 250.00
20..		$			
1 Feb. Balance	B/d	1 730.11			

Cash Account L5

20..	F	$	20..	F	$
1 Jan. Capital	L7	35.00	15 Jan. Travelling Expenses	L14	23.25
4 Jan. Sales	L6 & 8	475.75	15 Jan. Repairs	L15	70.62
15 Jan. Sales	L6 & 8	416.35	31 Jan. Bank	L4	1 600.00
24 Jan. Sales	L6 & 8	486.86	31 Jan. Balance	c/d	751.34
31 Jan. Sales	L6 & 8	1 031.25			
		$2 445.21			$2 445.21
1 Feb. Balance	B/d	751.34			

VAT Account L6

20..	F	$	20..	F	$
1 Jan. Capital	L7	607.00	4 Jan. Cash	L5	43.25
11 Jan. Bank	L4	12.70	4 Jan. R. Johnston	L9	4.25
11 Jan. Bank	L4	2.44	15 Jan. Cash	L5	37.85
11 Jan. Ivor Brown	L12	23.45	15 Jan. Ivor Brown	L12	1.55
15 Jan. Cash	L5	6.42	24 Jan. Cash	L5	44.26
24 Jan. Mohican Bros	L17	40.52	31 Jan. Cash	L5	93.75
			31 Jan. Balance	c/d	467.62
		$692.53			$692.53
20..		$			
1 Feb. Balance	B/d	467.62			

Capital Account L7

			20..	F	$
			1 Jan. Sundry assets	L1–6	41 212.00

Sales Account L8

			20..	F	$
			4 Jan. Cash	L5	432.50
			4 Jan. R. Johnston	L9	42.50
			15 Jan. Cash	L5	378.50
			24 Jan. Cash	L5	442.60
			31 Jan. Cash	L5	937.50

R. Johnston Account L9

20..	F	$
4 Jan. Sales	L6 & 8	46.75

Rates Account L10

20..	F	$
4 Jan. Bank	L4	112.50

General Expenses Account L11

20..	F	$
11 Jan. Bank	L4	24.35

Ivor Brown Ltd Account L12

20..	F	$	20..	F	$
15 Jan. Purchases Returns	L6 & 16	17.05	11 Jan. Purchases	L13	257.95
31 Jan. Bank	L4	240.90			
		$257.95			$257.95

Purchases Account L13

20..	F	$			
11 Jan. Ivor Brown	L12	234.50			
24 Jan. Mohican Bros	L17	405.25			

Travelling Expenses Account L14

20..	F	$			
15 Jan. Cash	L5	23.25			

Repairs Account L15

20..	F	$			
15 Jan. Cash	L5	64.20			

Purchases Returns Account L16

			20..	F	$
			15 Jan. Ivor Brown	L12	15.50

Mohican Bros Ltd Account L17

			20..	F	$
			24 Jan. Purchases	L6 & 13	445.77

Trial Balance as at 31 January 20..

	F	*Dr.* $	*Cr.* $
Land and Buildings	L1	33 850.00	
Equipment Account	L2	3 847.00	
Stock Account	L3	2 350.00	
Bank Account	L4	1 730.11	
Cash Account	L5	751.34	
VAT Account (refund due)	L6	467.62	
Capital Account	L7		41 212.00
Sales Account	L8		2 233.60
R. Johnston Account	L9	46.75	
Rates Account	L10	112.50	
General Expenses Account	L11	24.35	
Purchases Account	L13	639.75	
Travelling Expenses Account	L14	23.25	
Repairs Account	L15	64.20	
Purchases Returns Account	L16		15.50
Mohican Bros Ltd	L17		445.77
		$43 906.87	$43 906.87

3.7 Exercises Set 5. More Practice in Book-keeping to the Trial Balance

(*Note:* In the first four of these exercises VAT has been disregarded. Not all countries have Value Added Tax, and the difficulties it presents are therefore not encountered everywhere. Questions 5 and 6 do involve VAT.)

1. On 1 June 20.. Sarah Saxby, who has experience in the clothing industry, sets up in business with capital of $39 300.00, made up of land and buildings $32 000.00, furniture and fittings $3 300.00 and the rest in cash, which she banks except for $250.00. Open up the necessary accounts to record these matters and then enter the following further transactions:

1 June	Buys goods for resale on credit from R. Marsh, value $1 280.00.
2 June	Pays rates $115.50 electric light deposit $35.00, and telephone connection fee $63.50, all by cheque.
3 June	Buys materials for use in making up goods for resale, $35.00 cash.
4 June	Cash sales $265.00. Credit sales to R. Lebon $68.50.
5 June	Pays for postage $12.25, cottons and threads (Purchases Account) $27.50, and buys goods for resale, $115.00, all in cash.
6 June	Sends invoice to R. Johns for goods sold to him on credit, $227.50. Receives invoice from M. Walker for goods supplied by him on credit, for resale, $342.00.

Balance off the accounts and extract a Trial Balance as at 6 June.

2. On 1 July 20.. G. Parker sets up in business as a stationer with capital of $4 800.00, consisting of furniture and fittings $1 000.00, stock $2 000.00, cash at bank $1 000.00 and the rest in cash. Open the necessary accounts and then enter the following transactions:

1 July	Pays rent $30.00 in cash, purchases goods for resale on credit from H. Roach $285.50, and pays for hire of till and scales in cash, $27.50.
2 July	Cash sales $218.55, credit sales to Rose and Frank Ltd, $137.50.
3 July	Postage $4.50 cash, travelling expenses $23.65 cash, and cash sales $242.65. Agrees to employ assistant for $75.00 per week; gives him a $25.00 advance on salary in cash.
5 July	Receives invoice from T. Law for goods supplied by him on credit, $120.00. Banked $900.00 from cash in till.
6 July	Cash sales $384.75. Cash purchases of goods for resale $23.75. Purchases on credit from T. Yates goods valued at $75.50.

Balance off the accounts and extract a Trial Balance.

3. On 1 April 20.. Chris Lawrence sets up in business with capital of $34 500.00, made up of land and buildings $25 000.000, furniture and fittings $4 200.00, and the rest in cash which he banks, except for $125.00. Open the necessary accounts to record these matters and then enter the following further transactions:

1 April	Buys goods for resale on credit from R. Sims, value $56.50.
2 April	Pays rates $95.00, electric light deposit $45.50, and telephone connection fee $33.50, all by cheque.
3 April	Buys materials for use in making up goods for resale, by cheque $425.00.
4 April	Cash sales $348.00. Credit sales to R. Morton $215.00.
5 April	Pays for postage $5.50 cash, travelling expenses $14.20 cash, and buys goods for resale, $275.00, on credit from R. Large.
6 April	Sends invoice to R. J. Moss for goods sold to him on credit $250.00. Receives invoice from M. Rowe for goods supplied by him for resale $45.00. Banks $300.00 from till.

Balance off the accounts and extract a Trial Balance as at 6 April.

4. On 1 July 20.. Karen Rowcliffe sets up in business as a stationer with capital of $3 850.00, consisting of furniture and fittings $1 200.00, equipment $435.00, stock $1 350.00, and the rest in cash. Open the necessary accounts and then enter the following transactions:

1 July	Banks $500.00 for safe keeping. Pays rent $125.00 by cheque, purchases goods for resale on credit from H. Rogerson $442.00, and pays for hire of till and scales, $42.00, cheque.
2 July	Cash sales $218.55, credit sales to Roach and Lane Ltd, $48.50.
3 July	Postage $8.50 cash, travelling expenses $13.25 cash and cash sales $214.75. Agrees to employ assistant for $75.00 per week; gives him $37.50 cash advance on salary.
5 July	Receives invoice from R. Lyons for goods supplied on credit, $150.00. Banks $600.00 from till.
6 July	Cash sales $327.25. Cash purchases of goods for resale $45.30. Purchases on credit from M. Loman goods valued at $147.50.

Balance off the accounts and extract a Trial Balance.

5. On 1 November 20.. R. Turf sets up in business as a landscape gardener with a capital made up of tools and equipment $2 320.00, stock of materials $472.00 and cash $1 550.00, of which $1 500.00 is banked. The VAT Account is clear at this date. Open up the accounts necessary to record these matters and then record also the following transactions:

6 November	Purchases materials for use in draining land, $442.00 plus VAT $44.20, by cheque. R. Coombes agrees to settle his account on 30 November for work done, $350.00 plus VAT $35.00. Recorded him as a debtor, and credited Fees Received Account.
13 November	Purchases materials $30.00 plus VAT $3.00 by cheque. Sale of rock for decorative work, $125.50 plus VAT $12.55 cash. Pays wages to casual worker, $26.00 cash.

20 November	Purchases materials, $184.00 plus VAT $18.40 by cheque. Receives cash for work done (Fees Received Account) $280.00 plus VAT $28.00. Banks $350.00.
27 November	Wages to casual worker, $20.00 cash. Pays for materials, $235.00 plus VAT $23.50 by cheque, and for transport $24.50 cash.
30 November	Balances off accounts and prepares a Trial Balance.

6. R. Tilehurst is a smith and wrought-iron specialist who sets up in business on 1 June 20.. making decorative ironwork. He has capital consisting of premises $26 550.00, stock $820.00, equipment $2 200.00, a bank balance of $1 270.00, $80.00 in cash and there is a debit balance on VAT Account of $18.50. Record these items, then enter the following transactions:

2 June	Pays telephone connection fee in cash, $43.50 plus VAT $4.35.
3 June	Pays for small fittings in cash, $12.25 plus VAT $1.22. Receives invoice from Imperial Iron Co for metal, $250.00 plus VAT $25.00, on credit until 30 June. Sells iron gates for cash, $122.35 plus VAT $12.24.
4 June	Pays wages of part-time assistant, $20.00 cash. Pays for charcoal and solder $23.00 plus VAT $2.30, cash. Sends invoice to Ocean Hotel Ltd, $337.50 plus VAT $33.75, for goods supplied.
10 June	Cash sales $218.50 plus VAT $21.85. Purchases raw materials at auction, $37.50 plus $3.75, for use in making up goods for resale, by cheque. Pays carrier $25.50 and casual helper $22.00, both in cash.
17 June	Cash sales $336.00 plus VAT $33.60. Invoices Alhambra Garden Works for goods supplied, $86.50 plus VAT $8.65. Pays carriage $14.50 in cash.
23 June	Receives invoice from Imperial Iron Co Ltd for goods supplied by them on credit, $186.50 plus VAT $18.65.
30 June	Pays wages to part-time assistant $24.50 by cheque. Pays for fuel oil, $27.20 plus VAT $2.72 cash, and for small items for use in making up goods for resale $41.50 plus VAT $4.15 cash. Balances off accounts and draws up a Trial Balance.

3.8 Revise and Test 3. Accounting to the Trial Balance

Cover the page with a sheet of paper; then read one question at a time.

Answers	*Questions*
—	**1.** What is a Trial Balance?
1. It is a check on the basic entries made in a set of books, to see whether their double entries have been done correctly.	**2.** When is it drawn up?
2. Usually once a month—not longer as it would be hard to find the mistake if we leave too many weeks to pass by.	**3.** How does the Trial Balance show us a mistake has been made?
3. The two sides of the Trial Balance must come to the same figure if proper double entries have been made for every transaction. If the Trial Balance does not agree we must look for an error in our double entries.	**4.** Just what is a double entry?
4. Whenever any transaction takes place one account receives value and the other gives value. Every debit entry must be balanced by a credit entry of the same amount. If this has been done the Trial Balance will balance.	**5.** I buy a motor vehicle for the business and pay for it in cash. What is the double entry?
5. Motor Vehicles Account receives value. Debit it. Cash Account gives value. Credit it.	**6.** I buy furniture for the office and pay by cheque. What is the double entry?
6. Debit Furniture and Fittings Account. Credit Bank Account which has given the money.	**7.** I pay wages to all the staff in cash.
7. Debit Wages Account (the workers have received the money, but we record it in this nominal account). Credit Cash Account which has given the money in the wage packets.	**8.** I buy goods for re-sale, $2 864.00 from Produce Supplies Ltd, who will be paid in 30 days' time.

8. Debit Purchases Account (in business 'purchases' is the correct term for goods purchased for re-sale). Credit Produce Supplies Ltd who are now a creditor for $2 864.00.	**9.** I sell goods to Peter Parker for $450.00. He will pay later. What is the double entry?
9. Debit Peter Parker. He is now a debtor. Credit Sales Account. (Sales is the correct term for goods which are sold in the normal line of business with a view to making a profit.)	**10.** John Bates, a friend gives me $25.00 cash for helping him sell his car by a notice in my shop window.
10. Debit Cash Account which receives the money. Credit Commission Received Account (a profit of the business).	**11.** How does a computer do a Trial Balance, to check the accuracy of the entries?
11. It doesn't really. The software designer builds into the software a validation program which checks every entry for correctness. If it isn't a valid double entry the computer rejects it. You have to get the double entry right and put it in again.	**12.** Go over the page again until you are sure about your double entries.

UNIT 4

Accounting to Final Accounts Level. 1. The Trial Balance

4.1 Accounting to Final Accounts Level

In Unit 1 we saw that the first level of maturity in accounting is to reach the Trial Balance level of work, where the student can enter transactions in the ledger, balance off the accounts at the end of a month and prepare a Trial Balance of the ledger, getting the two sides to agree.

The second level of work in accounting is called 'Final Accounts level', because here you move on past the Trial Balance to prepare two Final Accounts: the *Trading Account* and the *Profit and Loss Account*. The first of these is used to discover what is known as the *gross profit* or overall profit. The second is used to prepare the *net profit* or clear profit of the business. This net profit of course belongs to the owner, or owners, of the business, and depending on the nature of the business it will be handed over to the *sole proprietor*, or shared among the *partners or shareholders*, as a reward for the enterprise they have shown.

Final Accounts work is therefore concerned with *discovering the profits of an enterprise, and paying them over to the person or persons entitled to enjoy them.*

The starting point for the preparation of these Final Accounts is the Trial Balance. We must now analyse a typical Trial Balance very carefully to make quite sure we understand its contents exactly.

4.2 Analysing the Trial Balance

Figure 4.1 shows a typical Trial Balance, prepared on 31 December 20.., after D. Webster has been in business for one month. Note that a Trial Balance is always made out 'as at a certain date'. This is because it is only really valid at that moment in time—the close of business on a given date. The next morning things will start to change and the Trial Balance would have to be altered too.

Also in Fig. 4.1 is a set of notes, arranged in two columns. Study these notes carefully. You will notice that a summary of the notes reveals that the debit and credit columns contain the following types of item:

Dr.	*Cr.*
3 Trading Account items	2 Trading Account items
Loss items	Profit items
Assets	Liabilities
A special asset	A special liability
(drawings of the proprietor)	(capital of the proprietor)

To make the picture complete, we should point out that outside the Trial Balance, not yet recorded on the books of the business, is the closing stock which, like the opening stock shown, is a Trading Account item.

It is very important to realize where all these balances belong. The outstanding balance of an asset account, for example, will always be a debit balance and will appear in the debit column of the Trial Balance. If a Trial Balance had an asset account with a credit balance it would clearly be wrong, for assets never appear in the credit column. The liabilities, which are the opposite of assets, appear in that column. Similarly the losses are all debit items, and the profits of the business all credit items.

Note that VAT Account, which can finish up with either a debit or a credit balance, does not need to appear separately. The Customs and Excise Department is either a debtor (a debit balance) and owes us money, or a creditor (we owe them money). VAT Account therefore appears as part of either Sundry Debtors or Sundry Creditors. In our example, D. Webster is not registered for VAT, and this account does not appear.

Trial Balance of D. Webster's books as at 31 December 20..

Accounts	*Dr.* $	*Cr.* $	*Notes (Dr.)*	*Notes (Cr.)*
Purchases	6400.00		Trading A/c	
Sales		11865.50		Trading A/c
Purchases Returns		460.00		Trading A/c
Sales Returns	65.50		Trading A/c	
Stock (as at 1 Dec. 20..)	1200.00		Trading A/c	
Warehouse Wages	600.00		Loss	
Warehouse Expenses	256.00		Loss	
Light and Heat	128.50		Loss	
Repairs	65.50		Loss	
Rent (branch shop)	150.00		Loss	
Discount Allowed	242.50		Loss	
Discount Received		132.50		Profit
Commission Received		112.00		Profit
Land and Buildings	28750.00		Asset	
Furniture and Fittings	4250.00		Asset	
Motor Vehicles	6500.00		Asset	
Sundry Debtors	650.50		Asset	
Sundry Creditors		2430.50		Liabilities
Plant and Machinery	2880.00		Asset	
Cash	164.75		Asset	
Bank	2047.25		Asset	
Drawings (D. Webster)	620.00		Special asset	
Mortgage on Premises		22000.00		Liability
Loan (Finance Co.)		1000.00		Liability
Capital (D. Webster)		17000.00		Special liability
Carriage In	30.00		Loss	
	$55000.50	$55000.50		

The closing stock was found to be worth $1300.00.

Fig. 4.1 A Trial Balance (with notes)

4.3 The Drawings Account—a Special Type of Asset

As we saw in Unit 1.5 the Capital Account is a liability, because the business owes back to the proprietor the amount contributed as capital. Normally he/she will not be repaid unless the business closes down or, for example, on retirement. The proprietor needs to live, however, and pay his/her personal bills. Proprietors cannot draw wages, for they are not employees, even if they work in the business full time. They are entitled to the profits of the enterprise when they are discovered at the end of the financial year but in the meantime what are they to live on? The answer is on *drawings*; that is, the withdrawal of such sums of money as are necessary. The drawings are said to be 'in expectation of profits made'. Cash may be drawn from the cash box (debit Drawings Account and credit Cash Account) or by cheque from the bank (debit Drawings Account and credit Bank Account). The proprietor may even draw goods (called *drawings in kind*), taking home goods bought for re-sale, but now taken for personal use. This is treated as a sale to the proprietor (debit Drawings Account and credit Sales Account).

Whatever the type of drawings, the proprietor becomes a debtor of the business for the amount until the end of the trading year. At the end of the year, if the business has been profitable, he/she will be entitled to the profits made, less the sums already drawn. If the business has made a loss, the proprietor will be in debt to the business for the amount drawn which will have to be set against the capital originally contributed. He/she has been 'living off his/her capital', which consequently reduces by the amount both of the Drawings Account and of the losses.

4.4 The Trading Account Items

There are five items in the Trial Balance (and a sixth item outside it, the closing stock) which are described as Trading Account items. These are the raw data from which profits are calculated, and which form the basis of the *Trading Account* (we shall discuss this fully in Unit 5). For the present it is sufficient if you remember the following points about these items.

(a) *Purchases* and *sales* are opposites: one brings goods into the business to fill the shelves, the other removes them into the consumers' baskets.
(b) *Sales returns* and *purchases returns* are also opposites. The former brings back into the business goods formerly sold because for some reason the customer is dissatisfied with them. The latter removes goods from the business because of defects, and returns them to the supplier.
(c) *Opening stock* is an asset—at least it is on the first day of the year. It may be sold by the end of that day, or the next day. It is a rather special item. *Closing stock* is similarly rather special, and does not appear on the books at all: it is found by stock-taking.

Now practise drawing up Trial Balances by doing Exercises Set 6.

4.5 Exercises Set 6. Drawing up Trial Balances

1. Prepare a Trial Balance from the following accounts, which appear in R. Fowler's books on 31 March 20..:

Discount allowed $26.45; capital $18 000.00; rates $250.00; office expenses $142.50; loan from M. Castle $15 000.00; stock in hand at 1 Jan. 20.. $600.00; sundry creditors $845.00; cash at bank $2470.55; plant and machinery $1750.00; returns inwards $45.50; trade expenses $248.50; Sales Account $11 560.00; purchases $6580.50; cash in hand $65.50; freehold property $32 000.00; sundry debtors $1225.50.

2. The following accounts in A. Dealer's books have balances on them at 30 April 20... You are asked to arrange them in Trial Balance form.

Sundry Debtors' A/cs	$2516.50	Office Salaries A/c	$3265.50
Sundry Creditors' A/cs	$4826.50	Light and Heat A/c	$104.40
Land and Buildings A/c	$43 000.00	Telephone A/c	$176.70
Plant and Machinery A/c	$11 550.00	Warehouse Wages A/c	$4595.50
Furniture and Fittings A/c	$825.00	General Expenses A/c	$295.50
Opening stock at		Rates A/c	$462.90
1 April 20..	$3266.00	Insurance A/c	$380.50
Cash A/c	$175.00	Drawings A/c	$2228.00
Bank A/c	$2475.00	Loan A/c (R. Thomas)	$11 000.00
Purchases A/c	$16 875.00	Capital A/c	$30 000.00
Sales A/c	$46 365.00		

3. The following accounts have balances on them in Jill Brown's ledger at 31 December 20... Draw up the Trial Balance as at that date.

Returns Inwards $175.50; Returns Outwards $195.90; Cash in hand $40.00; Machinery $2640.00; Salaries $6522.00; Audit Fee $27.50; Sales $37 261.40; Stock $4800.00; Telephone Expenses $245.20; Bank Overdraft $1706.00; Factory Wages $4676.00; Discount Received $27.50; Creditors $4726.50; Debtors $3871.60; Carriage Outwards $42.40; Bad Debts $165.60; Capital $25 000.00; Rent and Rates $240.00; Purchases $12 535.50; Commission Received $1864.00; Furniture $1300.00; Premises $33 500.00.

4. The following accounts have balances on them in Pat Fisher's books on 31 December 20... Draw up a Trial Balance from them.

Warehouse Wages $4850.00; Office Salaries $4750.00; Debtors $2462.50; Creditors $4861.50; Furniture and Fittings $3250.00; Commission Received $1755.00; Capital $34 000.00; Drawings $6500.00; Returns Outwards $75.00; Returns Inwards $250.00; Rent and Rates $1450.00; Light and Heat $600.00; Carriage In $48.50; Carriage Out $72.60; Opening stock at 1 January 20.. $2575.00; Cash in hand $42.50; Cash at bank $1664.60; Sales $27 404.70; Purchases $11 160.50; Motor Vehicles $4420.00; Land and Buildings $25 000.00; Loan from bank $1000.00.

5. From the following figures draw up the Trial Balance of Irene Cooper as at 31 December 20..:

Purchases A/c $37 000.00; Sales A/c $96 000.00; Purchases Returns A/c $194.50; Sales Returns A/c $2 004.00; Stock A/c at 1 January 20.. $8 850.50; Warehouse Wages $16 250.90; Warehouse Expenses $456.00; Discount Allowed A/c $236.50; Discount Received A/c $479.80; Light and Heat A/c $1 198.40; Travelling Expenses A/c $434.50; Repairs A/c $518.50; Rent Paid A/c $2 450.00; Rent Received A/c $1 150.00; Commission Received A/c $2 185.55; Furniture and Fittings A/c $2 650.00; Plant and Machinery A/c $13 840.70; Motor Vehicles A/c $6 825.50; Debtors' A/cs $4 675.50; Creditors' A/cs $12 133.00; Cash A/c $1 383.50; Bank A/c $4 718.35; Salaries A/c $19 900.00; Loan from Bank Finance Ltd $1 000.00; Drawings A/c $7 750.00; Capital A/c $18 000.00.

6. Prepare a Trial Balance as at 31 December 20.. from the following ledger accounts of David Cann, exporter of manufactured goods:

	$		$
Goodwill (asset)	5 000.00	Stock at 1 January	4 450.00
Bad Debts	426.00	Postage	656.50
Commission Received	1 285.00	Office Expenses	275.50
Motor Vehicles	6 750.00	Bank Loan	20 000.00
Furniture	3 450.00	Capital	31 516.50
Premises	43 800.00	Rates and Insurance	1 450.50
Warehouse Wages	11 150.00	Light and Heat	1 276.80
Discount Received	24.50	Purchases	38 572.60
Creditors	1 284.00	General Expenses	8 240.60
Debtors	2 562.00	Cash in hand	248.00
Carriage In	82.00	Machinery	11 250.00
Returns In	141.00	Office Salaries	12 376.00
Returns Out	60.50	Sales	97 987.00

4.6 Revise and Test 4. The Trial Balance

Cover the page with a sheet of paper; then read one question at a time.

Answers	*Questions*
—	**1.** What is a Trial Balance?
1. It is a list of all the balances on the ledger accounts, with all the debit balances on the left-hand side and all the credit balances on the right-hand side.	**2.** When do we take out a Trial Balance?
2. On the last day of the month usually.	**3.** Why do we do it?
3. To check up on the accuracy of our book-keeping and find out if we've done all the double entries correctly.	**4.** How can you tell if the book-keeping is correct?
4. If the two columns, the debit column and the credit column balance (i.e. come to the same total) then probably the double entries have been done correctly.	**5.** Why can't we be sure?
5. Because some errors don't show up on the Trial Balance. These are explained later.	**6.** What types of accounts will we find in the list of debit balances?
6. a) Three Trading Account items; b) the assets of the business; c) the losses of the business; d) the drawings taken by the proprietor.	**7.** What are the three Trading Account items?
7. The opening stock, the Purchases Account, and the Sales Returns Account.	**8.** What types of accounts will we find in the list of credit balances?

8. a) Two Trading Account items; b) the liabilities of the business; c) the profits of the business; d) the proprietor's capital. (This is of course a liability, but rather a special liability because it will only be cleared when the business ceases to trade.)	**9.** What are the two Trading Account items?
9. The Sales Account and the Purchases Returns Account.	**10.** What is special about Trading Account items?
10. They are used in the Trading Account at the end of the year to work out the 'Gross Profit' of the business (see Revise and Test 5 for a full explanation).	**11.** One Trading Account item is not on the Trial Balance. Why?
11. Because it is the closing stock. We only know that figure when we do a stock-taking, and bring it on to the books as we work out the Gross Profit.	**12.** When does a computer produce a Trial Balance?
12. Whenever we ask it to do so at any time.	**13.** Why doesn't the computer make many errors?
13. Because the program writers build in validation programs which check each batch of documents being entered. If the entries don't make a proper double-entry the computer rejects the batch.	**14.** Go over the page again until you are sure you understand the Trial Balance.

Please note. The next three Revise and Test exercises on pages 72, 81 and 95, are about the Final Accounts of a business. They have to be based, like all Final Accounts, on a Trial Balance of the books of the business concerned. To make the figures realistic these three Revise and Test exercises are based on the Trial Balance of Rosemary Larkin below.

Trial Balance of Rosemary Larkin as at 31 December 20..

	Dr.	*Cr.*
	$	$
Opening Stock at 1 January 20..	7800	
Purchases	46500	
Sales		150000
Purchases Returns		1250
Sales Returns	3250	
Salaries	30250	
Lighting and Heating	425	
Equipment and Fittings	13250	
Carriage Outwards	834	
Carriage Inwards	1150	
Bad Debts	180	
Office Stationery	2000	
Discount Allowed	760	
Discount Received		850
Rent, Rates and Insurance	17295	
Motor Vehicles	9250	
Cash in Hand	430	
Sundry Creditors		4264
Sundry Debtors	3085	
Balance at Bank	9150	
Drawings	12850	
Capital at start of year		18990
Warehouse Wages	19240	
Warehouse Expenses	7855	
Rent from Sub-tenant		5200
Loan from Helpful Bank		5000
Total	$185554	$185554

Note: The closing stock-taking found that the valuation of closing stock was $11200.

UNIT 5

Accounting to Final Accounts Level. 2. The Gross Profit on Trading

5.1 What is Profit?

Once the Trial Balance is properly understood the Final Accounts of a business may easily be prepared and the profits for the year discovered. We must now consider carefully the question, 'What is profit?'

Profit has already been defined as the reward for entering into business activity. The sole trader or partners who set up a small business, and the shareholders who contribute the capital for companies, are running certain risks. They immediately lose the enjoyment and use of their funds, which are now tied up in the business; they may eventually lose their capital if the enterprise fails. Profit is their reward for surrendering the use of their money, and for running the risks of business life.

To determine the profit it is necessary to find the difference between the costs of the enterprise and its earnings. This is an involved process with many hidden difficulties, since different ideas exist as to what are the true costs and what are the true earnings. We shall be discussing these difficulties more fully later. Here we are interested in simpler ideas.

First we need to find the rough profit of the business, which in accounting is called the *gross profit*; this means the 'overall' profit, without deductions of any sort. The best definition of gross profit is:

gross profit = sales − cost of sales

We shall now follow a simple example through in four stages to find a perfect gross profit figure.

5.2 Finding the Gross Profit: Stage 1

Sales less Purchases

A shopkeeper sells a bicycle to Mrs Jones for her son's birthday present. She pays $82.00 for it. The bicycle cost the shopkeeper $45.50. The gross profit, which is found in the *Trading Account*, would be discovered as shown below. The amount paid for the goods (the purchase price) is set against the amount received for them (the sale price) and the difference between the two is the gross profit.

Trading Account L205

	$		$
Purchases		Sales	82.00
(cost of sales)	45.50		
Gross profit	36.50		
	$82.00		$82.00

(*Note:* The gross profit will be transferred to the Profit and Loss Account, discussed in Unit 6.3, so that its double entry appears there.)

5.3 Finding the Gross Profit: Stage 2

(a) Net Sales less Net Purchases

Unfortunately the example shown above is too simple, for it overlooks several difficulties that are met in all businesses. First, we often find that some of the goods we sell are returned to us, so that the sales figure on our Sales Account must usually have some *sales returns* (*returns in*) deducted from it to arrive at the true sales figure. Similarly we often return goods we have purchased which for some reason are unsatisfactory: these are known as *purchases returns* (*returns out*). It follows that a normal Trading Account will have both sales returns and purchases returns deducted from the appropriate sides, to give us the *net sales* and *net purchases* figures. (The word 'net' comes from the French, and means 'clean' or 'clear'. Net sales are therefore 'clear sales' and net purchases are 'clear purchases'—free of any returns.)

If we take slightly more sensible figures than the single items shown above—for example, the figures given in the Trial Balance in Unit 4.2—we have a Trading Account on 31 December 20.. like this:

Trading Account for month ending 31 December 20.. L205

20..		$	$	20..		$
31 Dec.	Purchases	6400.00		31 Dec.	Sales	11865.50
	Less Purchases returns	460.00		31 Dec.	*Less* Sales returns	65.50
	Net purchases (cost of sales)		5940.00		Net sales (turnover)	11800.00
	Gross profit		5860.00			
			$11800.00			$11800.00

Notes:

(i) The heading to the Trading Account always includes a phrase 'for month (or any other period) ending' followed by the date. This is because we are working out the gross profit for a period of time, not just for a single day. In this example it is the gross profit for the month of December that we are calculating.

(ii) The word 'turnover' or 'net turnover', is often used for the net sales figure. The *turnover* of a business is a very important figure in accounting, since every purchaser of a business, and every bidder in the takeover of a company, considers the turnover of the business very seriously before deciding what the price should be.

(iii) The gross profit is once again the difference between the sales and the cost of sales, but we now have more accurate figures for both these items, since returns have been taken into account on both.

(iv) Notice that the purchases-less-returns figures have been positioned a little towards the left of the page. This style is adopted to enable stock to be taken into account, as we shall see in Stage 3.

(v) The gross profit is transferred to the Profit and Loss Account.

(b) Double Entries and the Trading Account

Two points are of importance in following the double entries in a Trading Account. They are the style in which the Trading Account is presented, and the need to 'close off' revenue accounts.

(i) Good style and the Trading Account The Trading Account, like every other account, must observe the rules of double entry. We cannot debit the Trading Account unless we credit some other account at the same time, and we cannot credit the Trading Account unless we debit some other account. The Trading Account is not just *any* ledger account, however; it is one of the two *Final Accounts*, which are only made out once a year to determine the profits of the business. It follows that *good style* on the Trading Account becomes extremely important. By 'good style' we mean a clear presentation of how the profits were achieved. We therefore, while sticking to the rules of double entry, adopt a few variations in a stylish Trading Account. These variations will be explained as they are introduced.

(ii) The 'closing-off' of expense accounts and receipts accounts Consider the Trading Account above. It has had the entry 'Purchases $6 400.00' entered on the debit side, and the entry 'Sales $11 865.50' entered on the credit side. Clearly neither of these entries can be made unless equal and opposite entries are made in the accounts named. The effect of these entries is to 'close off' the Purchases Account and the Sales Account and leave them with no balances at all; the accounts are cleared into the Trading Account. Before closing off, the accounts looked like this:

Purchases Account L27

		$			
20..					
	Sundry purchases	6 400.00			

Sales Account L28

					$
			20..		
				Sundry sales	11 865.50

After closure, they appear thus:

Purchases Account L27

		$			$
20..			20..		
			31 Dec.	Transfer to Trading Account	
	Sundry purchases	$6 400.00			$6 400.00

Sales Account L28

		$			$
20..			20..		
	Transfer to Trading A/c	$11 865.50		Sundry sales	$11 865.50

The chief point to note here is that when the Final Accounts are prepared we have to close off any accounts that are transferred to them. These accounts, which are either expenses (losses of the business) or receipts (profits of the business) cease to have any balances on them, and consequently disappear from the Trial Balance as soon as they are absorbed into the 'final' account concerned.

(iii) Good style and the 'returns' entries on the Trading Account Let us repeat both the points explained above by considering the purchases returns and sales returns entries. On the Trial Balance (Unit 4.2) we see that these accounts have balances as follows:

Purchases Returns Account L29

		$	20..		$
				Sundry returns	460.00

Sales Returns Account L30

20..		$			
	Sundry returns	65.50			

The entry necessary to clear the Purchases Returns Account is clearly a debit entry, thus:

Purchases Returns Account L29

20..		$	20..		$
31 Dec.	Transfer to Trading A/c	$460.00		Sundry returns	$460.00

We would therefore expect the double entry in the Trading Account to appear on the credit side:

Trading Account L205

	$		$
Purchases	6400.00	Purchases Returns A/c	460.00

Instead we improve the style in the Trading Account by deducting the purchases returns from the purchases figures on the debit side. *To deduct something from the debit side is the same as adding it to the credit side.* We then have:

Trading Account L205

Purchases	6400.00			
Less Purchases returns	460.00			
Net purchases		$5940.00		

The advantage is that we are now able to see clearly what we actually did purchase, that is, the net purchases figure. Similarly, on the credit side, we are able to bring out clearly that very important figure, net turnover, thus:

Trading Account L205

	$		$
Purchases	6400.00	Sales	11865.50
Less Purchases returns	460.00	*Less* Sales returns	65.50
Net purchases	$5940.00	Net turnover	$11800.00

We are now ready to proceed to Stage 3 in the discovery of the gross profit figure—the question of stock.

5.4 Finding the Gross Profit: Stage 3

(a) The Question of Stock

We have still not arrived at a perfect figure for the cost of sales, since in real life we rarely sell everything that we purchase in the trading period. Instead we still have in stock at the end of the year (or whatever period for which we are trying to discover the profits) some of the goods purchased. Clearly we must take away from the net purchases figure any *closing stock* which we have not yet sold, and this stock will become the *opening stock* for the new period just about to begin. It must therefore be added to the purchases of the new period when the time comes to decide the profits of that period.

Before looking at the Trading Account with opening stock and closing stock, we must make one point about the *valuation of stock*. This is a subject of some controversy in the world of accounting, since different accountants might place different values upon the stock in hand. In one celebrated take-over bid the accountants of the two firms differed about the valuation to be placed upon the stock by as much as £4 million. These matters are discussed later (see Unit 21.1), but for the present we will just say that before the Trading Account can be worked out we must first count the stock to find the number of units in hand, then value each line of goods at cost price and finally multiply this figure by the number of units to find the total value of that line of goods in stock. (The number of people who actually do the stock-taking varies; in a small business one person can do the job, whereas in a big firm like a supermarket a large staff is needed to count stocks of possibly 10000 different lines on the shelves.)

The Trial Balance we are using (see Fig. 4.1 on page 54) shows an opening stock figure of $1200.00, and a closing stock figure of $1300.00. Using these figures we now find that the Trading Account looks like this:

Trading Account for month ending 31 December 20.. L205

20..		$	$	20..		$
31 Dec.	Opening stock		1200.00	31 Dec.	Sales	11865.50
	Purchases	6400.00			*Less* Returns	65.50
	Less Returns	460.00			Net sales (turnover)	11800.00
	Net purchases		5940.00			
	Total stock available		7140.00			
	Less Closing stock		1300.00			
	Cost of stock sold		5840.00			
	Gross profit		5960.00			
			$11800.00			$11800.00

The notes on page 67 explain this example.

Notes:

(i) The positioning of the purchases-less-returns figure makes a very clear presentation of the account. As in real life the goods actually purchased are added to the stock in hand, giving 'total stock available' during the month of $7 140.00. When the unsold stock is deducted from this we arrive at the cost of the stock sold. What was purchased for $5 840.00 was sold for $11 800.00, earning a profit of $5 960.00.

(ii) The phrase 'cost of stock sold' has been used here instead of 'cost of sales'. The reason is made clear in Stage 4 (Unit 5.5).

(iii) The double entry for the gross profit is in the Profit and Loss Account.

(iv) Of course, had trading been difficult it would have been possible to have made a gross loss, not a gross profit. In that case the gross loss would appear on the other side of the Trading Account, because the figure for the cost of stock sold would have been larger than that for the net sales.

(b) Double Entries for Stock Account

The stylish Trading Account shown above has required some adaptation of double entry, similar to the adaptations made in bringing out the net purchases and net sales figures. Let us consider the Stock Account carefully. On the Trial Balance the Stock Account appears with a date written by it: 'Stock Account (at 1 December 20..)'. Here it is.

Stock Account L49

20..	$
1 Dec. Opening balance	1 200.00

Notes:

(i) The opening balance was found at the stock-taking at the end of the previous trading period and it does not vary during the trading period.

(ii) Any stock that is purchased is not entered in Stock Account, but in Purchases Account. (If firms do keep 'running' Stock Accounts they are only memorandum accounts kept for their own convenience in doing quick stock-taking checks.)

To clear the Stock Account to the Trading Account is a simple double entry, like this:

Stock Account L49

20..	$	20..	$
1 Dec. Opening balance	1 200.00	31 Dec. Trans. to Trading A/c	1 200.00

Trading Account L205

20..	$
31 Dec. Opening stock	1 200.00

The Stock Account is now clear, and disappears, for a few minutes, from the Trial Balance. However, it immediately reappears as a different figure, because we need now to bring the stock-taking figure—just discovered by our stock-takers—on to the books. The 'closing stock' figure in this case is $1 300.00. Clearly this is an asset, and must come on the debit side of the Stock Account. The double entry must be a credit entry in the Trading Account on 31 December 20... Here it is, by strict double entry, although not in good style:

Stock Account L49

20..		$	20..		$
1 Dec.	Opening balance	1 200.00	31 Dec.	Trans. to Trading A/c	1 200.00
20..		$			
1 Jan.	Trading Account	1 300.00			

Trading Account for month ending 31 December 20.. L205

20..		$	$	20..		$
31 Dec.	Opening stock		1 200.00	31 Dec.	Sales	11 865.50
	Purchases	6 400.00			*Less* Returns	65.50
	Less Returns	460.00				
					Net sales (turnover)	11 800.00
	Net purchases		5 940.00		Closing stock	1 300.00
	Total stock available					13 100.00
			7 140.00			
	Gross profit		5 960.00			
			$13 100.00			$13 100.00
					Gross profit	5 960.00

The entry in the Stock Account is dated for the first day of the new trading period, and the Stock Account will now reappear on the Trial Balance—*but at a new figure.*

It would be much better style (because it would bring out clearly the 'cost of stock sold' figure) to transfer the closing stock over to the debit side *and deduct it.* Once again the deduction of an item from the debit side is the same as adding it to the credit side. We have adapted the double-entry system, but it is a good double entry just the same. This gives us a Trading Account as shown already, on page 66.

5.5 Finding the Gross Profit: Stage 4

(a) Trading Expenses

A great many expenses are incurred in the course of business, such as rent, light and heat, advertising, postage and telephone expenses. We shall see shortly that most of these expenses are deducted from the gross profit in an account called the Profit and Loss Account. However, some of these expenses are looked upon as being so directly connected with the actual trading activities that they are deducted from the profits in the Trading Account. (Later on we shall also see that manufacturing expenses are similarly deducted in a Manufacturing Account.) The items treated as Trading Account items may be divided into two groups:

(i) those expenses that are best looked upon as an additional cost of our purchases—the commonest of these are 'carriage in' and 'customs duty on imported purchases';
(ii) those expenses that are truly an expense involved in the trading activities, such as warehouse wages and warehouse expenses.

The former (i) should really be added to purchases before the returns are deducted—for example:

	$	$
Purchases	6400.00	
Add Carriage in	30.00	
	6430.00	
Less Returns	460.00	
		5970.00

The point here is that if we pay either 'carriage in' or 'customs duty on purchases', the goods really cost us both the purchase price on the invoice and the expenses incurred in bringing the goods to us. The true cost of the purchases above is $6430.00, not $6400.00.

The latter group of expenses (ii) are added to the 'cost of stock sold' to give the final figure for the cost of sales.

When all these matters have been attended to we may confidently say we have reached as accurate a gross profit figure as is possible. Here is such a Trading Account.

Trading Account for month ending 31 December 20.. L205

20..		$	$	20..		$
31 Dec.	Opening stock		1 200.00	31 Dec.	Sales	11 865.50
	Purchases	6 400.00			*Less* Returns	65.50
	Add Carriage in	30.00				11 800.00
		6 430.00				
	Less Returns	460.00				
			5 970.00			
	Total stock available		7 170.00			
	Less Closing stock		1 300.00			
	Cost of stock sold		5 870.00			
	Warehouse wages	600.00				
	Warehouse expenses	256.00				
			856.00			
	Cost of sales		6 726.00			
	Gross profit		5 074.00			
			$11 800.00			$11 800.00

(b) Double Entry and the Expense Accounts

In each case as we transfer these items to the Trading Account the double entry closes off the expense account concerned, leaving the account clear, thus:

Carriage Inwards Account L36

20..		$	20..		$
	Sundry cash items	30.00	31 Dec.	Transfer to Trading A/c	30.00

Warehouse Wages Account L37

20..		$	20..		$
	Sundry cash items	600.00	31 Dec.	Transfer to Trading A/c	600.00

Warehouse Expenses Account L38

20..		$	20..		$
	Sundry cash items	256.00	31 Dec.	Transfer to Trading A/c	256.00

Notes:

(i) The use of the word 'sundry' indicates that in fact there may have been several entries making up the figure shown (which is the total expense for the trading period under consideration).

(ii) The closing-off of these accounts removes them automatically from the Trial Balance—since there is no longer a balance on any of them.

You should now prepare several Trading Accounts in the style shown above, using the information given in Exercises Set 7.

5.6 Exercises Set 7. The Trading Account

1. At the end of her trading year, on 31 December 20.., Nina Hudson has the following balances on her accounts: opening stock $825.00; purchases $40 785.00; sales $92 725.00; purchases returns $615.00; sales returns $725.00. A check on her stock in hand gives a total for closing stock of $1 295.00. Prepare her Trading Account and discover the gross profit for the year.

2. At the end of his trading year, on 30 June 20.., I. Brunel has the following balances on his accounts: sales $47 250.00; purchases $22 520.00; sales returns $1 120.00; purchases returns $1 520.00. Opening stock had been $1 500.00 on 1 July the previous year. Stock-taking revealed a closing stock figure of $2 370.00. Prepare his Trading Account and hence calculate his gross profit for the year.

3. When Terry Turner closes his books for the year on 31 March 20.. he has the following balances on his accounts: purchases $66 275.00; sales $184 000.00; purchases returns $1 275.00; sales returns $2 500.00; opening stock $17 280.00; warehouse wages $23 400.00. Stock-taking revealed a closing stock of $14 180.00. Prepare his Trading Account and thus find his gross profit.

4. On 31 March 20.. J. Metcalfe has the following balances on his books: opening stock $12 500.00; purchases $105 000.00; carriage inwards $500.00; sales $175 200.00; sales returns $3 700.00; purchases returns $1 800.00; warehouse wages $13 500.00; warehouse expenses $1 500.00. The closing stock is found to be $14 700.00. Prepare his Trading Account and find the gross profit of his business.

5. Angela Miller's accounts show the following balances, among others, at 31 March 20.. when she prepares her Trial Balance. Prepare her Trading Account and discover the gross profit of her business. Sales $85 700.00; purchases $38 440.00; sales returns $255.50; purchases returns $262.75; carriage in $130.00; opening stock $2 350.50; warehouse wages $22 565.00; trade expenses $1 370.35. The closing stock is found to be $2 535.40.

6. When the Trial Balance of G. Poole's books is prepared on 30 June 20.. the following balances are found to exist. Use them to prepare his Trading Account and hence discover the gross profit of his business. Opening stock $15 750.00; purchases $105 002.00; sales $196 000.00; purchases returns $1 280.50; sales returns $2 500.00; customs duty on imported purchases $620.00; carriage in $150.00; warehouse wages $21 650.70; warehouse expenses $3 752.30; warehouse redecoration $1 249.60. The closing stock is found to be $16 726.60.

5.7 Revise and Test 5. The Trading Account (based on the Trial Balance of Rosemary Larkin (see page 60)

Cover the page with a sheet of paper; then read one question at a time.

Answers	*Questions*
—	**1.** What is the Trading Account?
1. It is the first part of the 'Final Accounts' of a business, in which we work out the gross profit of the business at the end of the trading period, usually one year.	**2.** How is the account headed?
2. Trading Account for year ended 31 December 20... Of course the trading year could end at any time; for instance at the anniversary of start-up.	**3.** What is the simplest way of looking at Gross Profit?
3. It is the difference between cost price (the purchases figure) and selling price (the sales figure). So, in its simplest form:	

Trading Account for year ended 31 December 20..

	$		$
Purchases	46 500	Sales	150 000
Gross Profit	103 500		
	$150 000		$150 000

(*Note:* To find the gross profit you take the purchases figure from the sales figure.)

Answers	*Questions*
	4. Why is this too simple?
4. Because some purchases are returned for various reasons (wrong colour, size, type, etc.) and some sales are returned (customer dissatisfied).	**5.** So how should we adjust for this?

5. **Trading Account for year ended 31 December 20..**

	$		$
Purchases	46500	Sales	150000
Less Purchases Returns	1250	*Less* Sales Returns	3250
Net purchases	45250	Net Sales (net turnover)	146750
Gross Profit	101500		
	$146750		$146750

(*Note:* To find the gross profit figure take the Net Purchases figure from the Net Sales).

6. Why is net turnover an important figure?

---

6. Because when businesses are bought and sold the turnover figure tells us exactly how big a business we are buying, and therefore how much to pay for it.

7. Why is the Trading Account in 5 above still not good enough?

---

7. Because it doesn't take 'stock' into account.

8. The Stock Account is a strange account. In what way?

---

8. It is opened up on the first day of the financial year and then doesn't change until we do a stock-taking on the last day of the year.

9. What about all the stock we buy and sell as the year goes by?

---

9. Stock bought during the year is called 'purchases'. Stock sold during the year is called 'sales'.

10. What happens in real life to the opening stock in the Stock Account?

---

10. It is sold in the first few days of the new year and becomes 'sales'. It is replaced by lots more purchases which also become sales but eventually some of the purchases made in the last few weeks of the year will be left unsold on the last day and become 'Closing Stock'.

11. So now bring these stocks into the Trading Account.

11. We do this on the debit side only:

		$		$
Opening stock		7800	Sales	150000
Add Purchases	46500		*Less* Sales Returns	3250
Less Returns	1250			
		45250	Net sales (Net turnover)	146750
Total stock available		53050		
Less Closing stock		11200		
Cost of stock sold		41850		
Gross Profit (deducting the cost of stock sold from the Net Sales of $146750		104900		
		$146750		$146750

12. What else do we need to include in the Trading Account?

---

12. Some expenses are trading expenses: Carriage In (an increase really in the cost of the Purchases), and Warehouse Expenses and Warehouse Wages.

13. How will these fit into the Trading Account?

---

13. The Carriage In increases the Purchases figure and the others are losses of the business on the debit side.

Trading Account for year ended 31 December 20..

		$		$
Opening Stock		7800	Sales	150000
			Less Sales Returns	3250
Add Purchases	46500			
and Carriage in	1150		Net Sales (Net turnover)	146750
	47650			
Less Purchases Returns	1250			
		46400		
Total stock available		54200		
Less Closing stock		11200		
Cost of stock sold		43000		
Warehouse wages		19240		
Warehouse expenses		7855		
Cost of sales		70095		
Gross profit		76655		
		$146750		$146750

Note: To find the Gross Profit take the Cost of Sales from the net turnover.

UNIT 6

Accounting to Final Accounts Level. 3. The Net Profit of the Enterprise

6.1 Taking Account of Expenses and Receipts

(a) Expenses

In Unit 5 certain expenses of the business—carriage in, warehouse wages and warehouse expenses—were deducted from the profits of the business. Most of the expenses of the business, particularly the items—usually known as *overheads*—such as rent, rates, insurance and telephone expenses, are deducted from the profits in the Profit and Loss Account. It is usual to arrange them in some logical order, which may be appropriate to the type of business concerned. A common choice is to group them under three headings: administrative expenses, financial expenses and selling and distribution expenses.

(b) Receipts

Similarly, where a business earns fees, commissions or rents of any kind these receipts are brought into the profit calculations as part of the Profit and Loss Account.

6.2 Updating the Trial Balance

Before seeing how this is done we must update the Trial Balance that is being used as the basis of our calculations. The Trading Account prepared in Unit 5 has resulted in the closing of many accounts, which consequently have disappeared from the Trial Balance. We are therefore left with a smaller list of balances. The Trial Balance shown in Fig. 4.1 (see Unit 4.2) has now become:

Trial Balance of D. Webster as at 31 December 20..

Accounts	*Dr.*	*Cr.*	*Notes*	
	$	$		
Light and Heat	128.50		Loss	
Repairs	65.50		Loss	
Rent	150.00		Loss	
Discount Allowed	242.50		Loss	
Discount Received		132.50		Profit
Commission Received		112.00		Profit
Land and Buildings	28750.00		Asset	
Furniture and Fittings	4250.00		Asset	
Motor Vehicles	6500.00		Asset	
Sundry Debtors	650.50		Asset	
Sundry Creditors		2430.50		Liability
Plant and Machinery	2880.00		Asset	
Cash	164.75		Asset	
Bank	2047.25		Asset	
Drawings (D. Webster)	620.00		Special asset	
Mortgage on Premises		22000.00		Liability
Loan (Finance Co.)		1000.00		Liability
Capital (D. Webster)		17000.00		Special liability
Stock (at 31 Dec. 20..)	1300.00		Asset	
Trading (gross profit)		5074.00		Special liability
	$47749.00	$47749.00		

Notes:

(i) The stock has changed to the new stock figure. It can also be correctly described as an asset, because this time it really does describe the actual goods on the shelves; it is a real account, not a nominal account.

(ii) The Trading Account balance is a special type of liability, because it is owed to the owner of the business, just like the capital he originally contributed.

6.3 The Profit and Loss Account

The Profit and Loss Account is very simply prepared, for there are fewer special points of style than in the Trading Account. Once again, the heading 'Profit and Loss Account' is followed by a phrase showing the period for which we are calculating the profits—in this case, it is the month of December.

The first item to be transferred is the gross profit, which is transferred from the Trading Account. Then the various expenses are transferred to the debit of the Profit and Loss Account, and the various receipts are transferred to the credit side. When totalled, the difference between the two sides is the profit (or loss) of the business. Using the modified Trial Balance above as the source of our figures we may prepare the Profit and Loss Account as follows:

Profit and Loss Account for month ending 31 December 20.. L206

20..		$	20..		$
	Light and Heat A/c	128.50		Gross profit	5074.00
	Repairs A/c	65.50		Discount Received A/c	132.50
	Rent A/c	150.00		Commission Received A/c	112.00
	Discount Allowed A/c	242.50		Total profits	5318.50
	Total expenses	586.50			
	Net profit	4732.00			
		$5318.50			$5318.50

Notes:

(i) The net profit is transferred to the proprietor's Capital Account.

(ii) Had the expenses on the debit side been greater than the profits on the credit side there would have been a net loss, and the balancing figure (the 'Net loss') would have appeared on the credit side.

6.4 Double Entries in the Expenses and Receipts Accounts

As these items are transferred into the Profit and Loss Account the double entries in every case will be in the various accounts named, and will result in the closure of these accounts. They will be left without any balance, and consequently will disappear from the Trial Balance. The accounts are closed off as follows:

Light and Heat Account L8

		$			$
20..			20..		
	Sundry items	128.50	31 Dec.	Transfer to P & L A/c	128.50

Repairs Account L9

		$			$
20..			20..		
	Sundry items	65.50	31 Dec.	Transfer to P & L A/c	65.50

Rent Account L10

		$			$
20..			20..		
	Sundry items	150.00	31 Dec.	Transfer to P & L A/c	150.00

Discount Allowed Account L11

		$			$
20..			20..		
	Sundry items	242.50	31 Dec.	Transfer to P & L A/c	242.50

Discount Received Account L12

		$			$
20..			20..		
31 Dec.	Transfer to P & L A/c	132.50		Sundry items	132.50

Commission Received Account L13

		$			$
20..			20..		
31 Dec.	Transfer to P & L A/c	112.00		Sundry items	112.00

You should now prepare several Profit and Loss Accounts in the style shown in Unit 6.3.

6.5 Exercises Set 8. Profit and Loss Accounts

1. Prepare the Profit and Loss Account from Linda Lawrence's books, for the year ending 31 December 20... Figures are as follows: Trading A/c balance (gross profit) $12 755.00; Rent and Rates A/c $1 850.00; Light and Heat A/c $1 230.50; Office Salaries A/c $4 945.00.

2. Prepare the Profit and Loss Account of William Sandon, for the year ending 31 March 20... His Trial Balance shows: gross profit $18 655.00; Rent and Rates A/c $2 560.00; Light and Heat A/c $426.00; Commission Received A/c $2 065.00; Office Salaries A/c $7 956.00; Rent Received A/c $1 240.00; Telephone Expenses A/c $636.50; Sundry Expenses A/c $132.50; Postage A/c $425.50.

3. Prepare from the following list of balances the Profit and Loss Account of M. Chesterfield for the year ending 30 June 20..:

	$
Gross profit	78 561.75
Rent Paid	2 865.50
Rent Received	525.25
Office Salaries	9 589.50
Office Expenses	2 361.00
Office Light and Heat	854.60
Advertising Expenses	7 965.50
Interest on Loans	450.00
Interest on Bank Overdraft	65.50
Entertainment of Visitors	2 725.50

4. From the following figures, prepare Lucy Burton's Profit and Loss Account for the year ending 31 December 20..:

	$
Gross profit	22 840.00
Rent and Rates	2 800.00
Office Expenses	1 440.00
Lighting and Heating	640.00
Discount Received	260.00
Commission Received	480.00
Loan Interest	400.00
Salaries	5 664.00
Discount Allowed	400.00
Advertising Expenses	886.00
Transport Costs	2 106.00
Rent Received	860.00

5. From the following particulars prepare the Trading Account and the Profit and Loss Account of Derek Lucerne, for the year ending 31 March 20..:

	$
Opening stock at 1 April 20..	3521.10
Purchases	9101.00
Sales	27033.20
Sales Returns	33.67
Purchases Returns	24.25
Closing stock	3171.30
Discount Received	254.00
Discount Allowed	334.50
Insurance	108.30
Office Expenses	853.50
Printing and Stationery	651.76
Rent and Rates	1885.00
General Expenses	1649.80
Telephone Expenses	951.00
Office Salaries	5261.10
Light and Heat	849.20

6. From the following particulars taken from Barbara Grant's records prepare the Trading Account and Profit and Loss Account for the year ending 31 December 20.., using such figures as you consider appropriate.

	$		$
Capital	72000.00	Returns Inwards	350.00
Rent and Rates	1000.00	Returns Outwards	1500.00
Purchases	46550.00	Cash in hand	100.00
Sales	82500.00	Machinery	45050.00
Stock at 1 January 20..	12000.00	Stock at end of year	11500.00
Bad Debts	1150.00	Land and Buildings	36500.00
Carriage Outwards	1300.00	Office Salaries	9450.00
Debtors	8000.00	Telephone Expenses	750.00
Creditors	4550.00	Bank Overdraft	1650.00

6.6 Revise and Test 6. The Profit and Loss Account

The figures in this revision exercise come from the Trial Balance on page 60. Cover the page with a sheet of paper; then read one question at a time.

Answers	*Questions*
—	**1.** What is the Profit and Loss Account?
1. It is that part of the Final Accounts where we work out the net profit of the business.	**2.** What does 'net' profit mean?
2. Clean profit, from the French verb *nettoyer*—to clean.	**3.** How does the Profit and Loss Account start?
3. With the gross profit, brought down from the Trading Account, on the right-hand side. Very rarely, where a trader hasn't even made a gross profit, the gross loss will be brought down on the left-hand side.	**4.** How does this gross profit turn into a net profit?
4. We deduct all the expenses of the business, rent, rates, wages, etc. on the left-hand side and thus leave only the clean profit.	**5.** Does anything else come in the Profit and Loss Account.
5. Some other profits, such as Discount Received, Rent Received (from a sub-tenant), Commission Received, etc. We might even have a profit on the sale of an asset.	**6.** Why should this come in the Profit and Loss Account, it is more like a capital gain?
6. No. Over the years we are allowed to depreciate our assets each year as one of the losses of the business. If, at the end of the lifetime of the asset, we make a profit on it, it means we deducted too much depreciation in earlier years. The profit has to be brought in to the Profit and Loss Account as a revenue profit.	**7.** Produce the Profit and Loss Account for the exercise on page 60. Remember the Gross Profit was \$76 655, as calculated at the end of Unit 5.

7. **Profit and Loss Account for year ending 31 December 20..**

	$		$
Salaries	30250	Gross Profit	76655
Lighting & Heating	425	Discount Received	850
Carriage Outwards	834	Rent from sub-tenant	5200
Bad debts	180		
Office Stationery	2000	Total profits	82705
Discount allowed	760		
Rent, rates and insurance	17295		
	51744		
Net profit	30961		
	$82705		$82705
		Net profit	30961

8. Why do we bring down the net profit on to the right hand side?

---

8. If we don't it looks as if the account is clear. It isn't, it still has the net profit on it and this belongs to the proprietor. So the balance is a liability owed to the owner(s) of the business and all liabilities have credit balances.

9. Supposing in the example in 7 above the gross profit had only been $26655 so that the overall result was a loss. How would the account have looked?

---

9. The total earnings would have fallen to $32705 and there would have been a loss of $19039. This would have finished up as a balance on the debit side. The end of the account would have looked like this:

		Total profits	32705
Total expenses	51744	Net loss	19039
	$51744		$51744
Net loss	19039		

10. What happens to this loss?

---

10. It goes to the debit side of the proprietor's Capital Account. He/she has been living off his/her capital. If this continues next year the trader will probably go out of business.

11. Go over the page again until you are sure of all the answers.

UNIT 7

Accounting to Final Accounts Level. 4. The Balance Sheet of the Business

7.1 The Idea of a Balance Sheet

A *Balance Sheet* is a list of balances outstanding on the accounts after the Trading Account and Profit and Loss Account have been completed. We have already seen that as these two accounts are prepared, a number of other accounts are cleared, and the Trial Balance is therefore left with only a few accounts. Most of these are either assets or liabilities, but we do have one special asset, the Drawings Account (the proprietor's temporary debts to the business), and a special liability, the Capital Account (the amount of money contributed by the proprietor to the business). There is also now another special liability: the Profit and Loss Account. This shows the profits earned during the year and these, of course, belong to the proprietor. Soon we shall see how these special items are dealt with, and how a Balance Sheet, or list of assets and liabilities, can be drawn up.

This list of assets and liabilities is very important, because it forms the basis on which businesses are bought and sold. A new owner, anxious to purchase an existing business, needs to know what assets are being purchased, and what liabilities are being incurred. The Balance Sheet helps a purchaser to judge what is a fair price for the business being acquired. The purchase price will be the value of the assets acquired less the total of the liabilities incurred, but in practice an additional payment for the *goodwill* of the business will also be paid. (Goodwill is dealt with later, in Unit 22.11(e).) Here it is sufficient to note that the Balance Sheet, provided it is prepared from honest figures, is a *statement of the affairs of the business* which enables a purchaser to judge a proper purchase price.

Before preparing a Balance Sheet, let us clarify what happens to the special items mentioned above.

7.2 The Appropriation of Profits

The owner of the business *appropriates the net profit*. The verb 'appropriate' means 'take possession of'. Since the whole purpose of the business is to make profit, the owner takes possession of the profits which are added to his or her Capital Account. This does not necessarily mean that the profits are actually taken out as money. If some of the profit is taken out by the owner in money this is called *drawings*, and the amounts are recorded in the Drawings Account (see Unit 4.3). The balance of undrawn profit remains in the business and enables the business to 'grow'. The transfer of net profit to the Capital Account is effected by double entries like those shown below, closing off the Profit and Loss Account.

Capital Account (D. Webster) L1

		$
20..		
1 Dec.	Balance	17000.00
31 Dec.	Profit and Loss A/c	4732.00

Notes:

(i) The double entry for the transfer of the profit is of course in the Profit and Loss Account.

(ii) Obviously, if the result of the year's work was a net loss, the loss would appear on the debit side.

In partnerships, the profits in the Profit and Loss Account are appropriated by the partners in the manner laid down in the partnership agreement; in limited companies they are appropriated by the shareholders by resolution of the company as proposed by the directors at the annual general meeting. This requires a slightly more sophisticated treatment than that shown above, which makes it clear, however, that at the end of the trading period the owner's capital has increased by the amount of net profit made during that period. (If there had been a net loss the result would have been a reduction in the capital by the amount of the net loss.)

7.3 Closing the Drawings Account

The sums withdrawn by the owner of the business, usually in cash but sometimes in the form of goods, are debited to Drawings Account throughout the trading period. They are often looked upon as capital withdrawn from the business, but it is better to regard them as withdrawals in expectation of profits. A prudent owner limits drawings to the amount of profit he/she can reasonably expect to make in the trading period. To exceed this figure would be to consume capital—an undesirable state of affairs. Whether the owner is prudent or imprudent, however, drawings (collected in the Drawings Account) are transferred to the Capital Account as a debit item, to reduce the balance on that account. Here is the double entry:

Drawings Account (D. Webster) L9

20..			$	20..			$
7 Dec.	Bank		155.00	31 Dec.	Capital Account		620.00
14 Dec.	Bank		155.00				
21 Dec.	Bank		155.00				
28 Dec.	Bank		155.00				
			$620.00				$620.00

Capital Account (D. Webster) L1

20..			$	20..			$
31 Dec.	Drawings A/c		620.00	1 Dec.	Balance		17 000.00
31 Dec.	Balance	c/d	21 112.00	31 Dec.	Profit and Loss A/c		4 732.00
			$21 732.00				$21 732.00
				20..			$
				1 Jan.	Balance	B/d	21 112.00

The final situation is that the owner's Capital Account has increased by the difference between the net profit made in the period and the drawings made from the business in the period.

7.4 The Residual Trial Balance

The Trial Balance of D. Webster's books, originally including all the ledger accounts (see Unit 4.2) and subsequently reduced by the closure of the accounts absorbed into the Trading Account and the Profit and Loss Account, has now been further reduced by the closure of the Profit and Loss Account and the Drawings Account. We are left with a residue of accounts which cannot be closed, *but which must be carried on into the next trading period.* All these accounts are either assets or liabilities and form the raw data from which a Balance Sheet may be prepared. Here is this residual Trial Balance of D. Webster's books:

Trial Balance of D. Webster's books as at 31 December 20..

Accounts	*Dr.*	*Cr.*	*Notes*	
	$	$		
Land and Buildings	28750.00		Asset	
Furniture and Fittings	4250.00		Asset	
Motor Vehicles	6500.00		Asset	
Sundry Debtors	650.50		Asset	
Sundry Creditors		2430.50		Liability
Plant and Machinery	2880.00		Asset	
Cash	164.75		Asset	
Bank	2047.25		Asset	
Mortgage on Premises		22000.00		Liability
Loan (Finance Co.)		1000.00		Liability
Capital (D. Webster)		21112.00		Liability
Stock (at close)	1300.00		Asset	
	$46542.50	$46542.50		

Before displaying this information in Balance Sheet form it is necessary to explain the historical development of the Balance Sheet, from its origin in the sixteenth century.

7.5 The History of the Balance Sheet

Simon Stevin of Bruges first devised what he called a statement of affairs of a business early in the sixteenth century, using the data provided by the residue of the Trial Balance such as is given in Unit 7.4. The name 'statement of affairs' is still used in book-keeping today (see Unit 26.3) but the more modern term is 'Balance Sheet', since it is a list of the outstanding balances on the ledger accounts.

As may be seen in the Trial Balance above, the asset accounts all have debit balances, and the liabilities all have credit balances. It would therefore have been logical to display the balances like this.

Balance Sheet as at 31 December 20..

	$		$
Assets	46542.50	Liabilities	46542.50

Unfortunately Stevin reversed the sides, thus:

Balance Sheet as at 31 December 20..

	$		$
Liabilities	46542.50	Assets	46542.50

There was no sensible reason for doing this—indeed, it was positively misleading—but as a statement of affairs is not part of double-entry book-keeping, no one could say that it was 'wrong'; it was just illogical.

The Companies Act passed by the British Parliament in 1856 stated that a Balance Sheet should be prepared for every company at the end of its financial year in the style shown in the Schedule to the Act. This Schedule showed a Balance Sheet in exactly the style laid down by Simon Stevin three centuries before. In obeying the Act accountants established the British practice, later copied by Commonwealth and Colonial countries, of displaying the Balance Sheet in Stevin's way. Belgium, Stevin's own country, and other continental countries, as well as the United States of America, have long abandoned Stevin's illogical display and always present their Balance Sheets logically.

Fortunately, harmonization of accounting practices in the European Economic Community has led Parliament to enact formats for the Balance Sheet which conform with the European style, with assets stated first (on the left-hand side) and liabilities stated on the credit side, as in the actual accounts. For printing reasons some accountants prefer to produce a Balance Sheet in vertical style, and this format also appears in Schedule 4 of the Companies Act 1985. In this textbook assets are shown on the left-hand side, and liabilities on the right-hand side, in the correct manner. (You may still meet the illogical style in older textbooks, however.)

7.6 Marshalling the Assets

It is a principle of modern accounting that the accountant should arrange the accounts in such a way that anyone reading them—providing they have some understanding of accounts—can immediately appreciate the important aspects of the business, and be able to assess the firm's true position. In former times a chief preoccupation of some accountants was to hide the true state of affairs from interested parties. This was particularly undesirable with limited companies, since innocent shareholders were often unable to discover weaknesses in the business until too late, and were left with worthless shares on their hands. Today the Companies Act 1985 requires auditors to certify that in their opinion the accounts do give 'a true and fair view' of the business.

One of the ways in which a clear picture can be presented is by dividing the assets into separate classes. Here we shall consider the two chief types: *current assets* and *fixed assets*.

(a) Current Assets

These are sometimes called *circulating assets*, as they are assets which are continually being turned over. The word 'current' comes from the French word *courant*, meaning running. Fig. 7.1 illustrates the way in which stock which has been manufactured or purchased for resale is marketed and sold, either for cash or on credit terms. The cash received (whether immediately or later) is then used to purchase further stock for resale.

The current assets from the Trial Balance in Unit 7.4 may therefore be listed as follows:

Current assets:	$
Stock	1300.00
Sundry Debtors	650.50
Cash at bank	2047.25
Cash in hand	164.75
	4162.50

Equally well they could have been presented as follows:

Current Assets:	$
Cash in hand	164.75
Cash at bank	2047.25
Sundry Debtors	650.50
Stock	1300.00
	4162.50

The two alternative presentations are discussed later (see Unit 7.8).

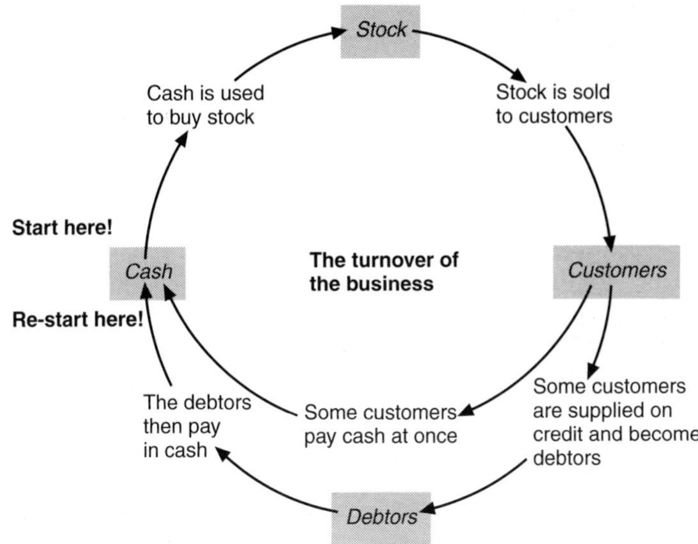

Fig. 7.1 Circulating or current assets

(b) Fixed Assets

These are assets which are not 'turned over' and sold at a profit, but are 'fixed' in the business and retained over a very long period. They are often called *capital assets* (see Unit 17.2(a)), since they form part of the permanent capital equipment in use. The longest-lasting item is land, which may be said to be eternal. Plant and machinery last many years, while assets like motor vehicles last only a few years.

The fixed assets listed in the Trial Balance in Unit 7.4 may be shown like this, with the longest-lived asset first:

Fixed assets:	$
Land and Buildings	28 750.00
Plant and Machinery	2 880.00
Furniture and Fittings	4 250.00
Motor Vehicles	6 500.00
	42 380.00

Or they may be grouped in the opposite order, as follows:

Fixed assets:	$
Motor Vehicles	6 500.00
Furniture and Fittings	4 250.00
Plant and Machinery	2 880.00
Land and Buildings	28 750.00
	42 380.00

These alternative presentations are discussed later (see Unit 7.8).

7.7 Marshalling the Liabilities

Just as the arrangement of the assets in clearly defined groups is helpful in presenting a simple picture to the public, a clear division of the liabilities is also helpful. There are three groups to whom any business owes funds.

(i) The owner (or owners) who expects eventually to be repaid the capital originally contributed, plus any profits retained in the business over the course of the years. The amounts owing to the owner are contained in the Capital Account, but by convention it is usual to display the capital at the start of the trading period, adding the net profit and deducting the drawings as already explained in Units 7.2 and 7.3. This enables anyone studying the Balance Sheet to see the profits earned in the trading period.

(ii) Long-term creditors, who have usually made a special contract with the owner of the business, and whose repayment terms are specified in the contract. Examples are those who lend money for mortgages and personal loans. We call such liabilities *long-term liabilities*.

(iii) Short-term creditors who may expect to be paid almost at once (certainly within one year). These liabilities are called *current liabilities*. The commonest Balance Sheet items of this sort are creditors and bank overdrafts.

We can present the liabilities in the Trial Balance in Unit 7.4 as follows:

	$	$
Capital (at start):		17000.00
Add Net profit	4732.00	
Less Drawings	620.00	
		4112.00
		21112.00
Long-term liabilities:		
Mortgage on Premises	22000.00	
Loan A/c (Finance Co.)	1000.00	
		23000.00
Current liabilities:		
Creditors		2430.50
		$46542.50

These items could also have been presented in the reverse order. As shown above they are presented in the *order of permanence*. The reverse order would be the *order of liquidity*.

7.8 The Order of Permanence and the Order of Liquidity

When a Balance Sheet is arranged in the order of permanence, the most enduring item is entered first. Then successive items are positioned in the list in decreasing order of permanence, finishing up with cash in hand, which is a perfectly 'liquid' item. *Liquid* in business means 'available in cash form', so that land, which is difficult to turn into cash—because it must be 'conveyed' by deed to a new owner—is illiquid, while stock is more liquid, since it can be sold without any formal transfer.

Some businesses, to whom liquidity is very important, arrange their Balance Sheets in the order of liquidity. The best examples are the banks. Ask a major bank for its published accounts, available free to anyone interested, and note the order of liquidity used. Most manufacturing businesses, with many capital assets of a very permanent nature, use the order of permanence, while small traders are free to choose whichever presentation they prefer.

Figs 7.2 and 7.3 present the Balance Sheet of D. Webster in both forms, to display the alternative presentations. Compare the two. Note that a Balance Sheet always has the date clearly indicated, in the same way as a Trial Balance. Don't confuse the phrase 'as at 31 December 20..', used on Trial Balances and Balance Sheets, with the phrase 'for year ending 31 December 20..', used on Trading Accounts and Profit and Loss Accounts. Remember, a Trial Balance or a Balance Sheet is only true for a single moment in time—the next day everything starts to change—so 'as at 31 December 20..' is a correct description of its situation. Gross profits and net profits are not earned in a single moment but over a period of time; we usually calculate them over a period of one year.

Balance Sheet of D. Webster as at 31 December 20..

	$	$		$	$
Fixed assets:			Capital:		
Land and Buildings		28750.00	At start		17000.00
Plant and Machinery		2880.00	*Add* Net profit	4732.00	
Furniture and Fittings		4250.00	*Less* Drawings	620.00	
Motor Vehicles		6500.00			4112.00
		42380.00			21112.00
Current assets:					
Stock	1300.00		Long-term liabilities:		
Sundry Debtors	650.50		Mortgage on Premises	22000.00	
Cash at bank	2047.25		Loan A/c (Finance Co.)	1000.00	
Cash in hand	164.75				
		4162.50			23000.00
			Current liabilities:		
			Creditors		2430.50
		$46542.50			$46542.50

Fig. 7.2 A Balance Sheet with assets and liabilities listed in order of permanence

Balance Sheet of D. Webster as at 31 December 20..

	$	$		$	$
Current assets:			Current liabilities:		
Cash in hand		164.75	Creditors		2430.50
Cash at bank		2047.25	Long-term liabilities:		
Sundry Debtors		650.50	Loan A/c (Finance Co.)	1000.00	
Stock		1300.00	Mortgage on Premises	22000.00	
		4162.50			23000.00
Fixed assets:			Capital:		
Motor Vehicles	6500.00		At start	17000.00	
Furniture and Fittings	4250.00		*Add* Net profit 4732.00		
Plant and Machinery	2880.00		*Less* Drawings 620.00		
Land and Buildings	28750.00				
		42380.00		4112.00	
					21112.00
		$46542.50			$46542.50

Fig. 7.3 A Balance Sheet with assets and liabilities listed in order of liquidity

You should now draw up several balance sheets from the exercises given below, presenting them in good style, and in the order indicated in the question.

7.9 Exercises Set 9. The Balance Sheet of a Business

1. Prepare a Balance Sheet from the following information drawn from R. Long's books. He presents his Balance Sheet in the order of permanence.

Trial Balance (R. Long) as at 31 December 20..

	Dr.	*Cr.*
	$	$
Cash in hand	1 000.00	
Cash at Bank	9 000.00	
Stock at close	10 000.00	
Land and Buildings	40 500.00	
Office Equipment	4 500.00	
Creditors		4 500.00
Debtors	2 000.00	
Motor Vehicles	12 000.00	
Capital (at start)		47 000.00
Drawings	12 500.00	
Net profit		15 000.00
Bank loan		25 000.00
	$91 500.00	$91 500.00

2. Prepare John Triton's Balance Sheet in the order of permanence from the Trial Balance given below.

Trial Balance (J. Triton) as at 31 December 20..

	Dr.	*Cr.*
	$	$
Cash in hand	150.00	
Cash at bank	6 850.00	
Stock at close	4 500.00	
Debtors	1 600.00	
Motor Vehicles	5 000.00	
Land and Buildings	40 000.00	
Office Equipment	2 000.00	
Plant and Machinery	13 000.00	
Capital (at start)		43 000.00
Net profit		8 000.00
Mortgage on Premises		25 000.00
Creditors		1 850.00
Drawings	4 750.00	
	$77 850.00	$77 850.00

3. Prepare Tricia North's Balance Sheet from the Trial Balance given below, arranging the items in the order of liquidity.

Trial Balance (T. North) as at 31 December 20..

	Dr.	*Cr.*
	$	$
Cash in hand	36.50	
Cash at bank	2548.50	
Trade debtors	1036.50	
Stock at close	1245.00	
Short-term investments	400.00	
Motor Vehicles	3500.75	
Furniture and Fittings	2515.55	
Plant and Machinery	4400.00	
Land and Buildings	23000.00	
Creditors		997.20
Mortgage on Premises		10000.00
Capital		20185.00
Bank loan		3000.00
Drawings	4750.00	
Net profit for year		9250.60
	$43432.80	$43432.80

4. Prepare M. Twain's Balance Sheet in the order of liquidity from the figures given below in his Trial Balance.

Trial Balance (M. Twain) as at 31 March 20..

	Dr.	*Cr.*
	$	$
Cash in hand	138.50	
Cash at bank	4720.50	
Debtors and creditors	1434.25	1919.25
Closing stock	2500.00	
Motor Vehicles	7675.50	
Furniture and Fittings	2565.50	
Land and Buildings	19000.00	
Mortgage on Premises		14000.00
Capital		21765.00
Drawings	4500.00	
Profit and Loss A/c balance		4850.00
	$42534.25	$42534.25

7.10 Revise and Test 7. The Balance Sheet

The figures used in this revision exercise come from the Trial Balance of Rosemary Larkin's business, on page 60. Cover the page with a sheet of paper then read one question at a time.

Answers	*Questions*
—	**1.** What is a Balance Sheet?
1. It is a snapshot of the affairs of a business at a given moment in time. Usually the moment chosen is 23:59 on the last day of the financial year.	**2.** What does it consist of?
2. A list of all the balances on all the accounts of the business at that time. They will be assets or liabilities.	**3.** Why can't they be nominal accounts—losses or profits?
3. Because we will just have worked out the profits of the business, and in doing so we will have transferred all the losses and profits to the Final Accounts (the Trading Account and the Profit and Loss Account). There will be no balances on the nominal accounts.	**4.** How do we head the Balance Sheet?
4. Balance Sheet as at 31 December 20... But of course you can take out a Balance Sheet on any day of the year—for example on the anniversary of the start-up date of the business.	**5.** What is the best way to draw up a Balance Sheet?
5. With the assets on the left and the liabilities on the right.	**6.** Why do we often see them the other way round?
6. Because of a mistake made in the Companies Act 1856. It shows how conservative accountants are!	**7.** What other points are there to know about presentation?

7. We can list the items in the order of permanence or in the order of liquidity. With the order of permanence the most permanent asset (land and buildings) is shown first and the most liquid asset (cash) is shown last. In the order of liquidity the order is reversed, cash first and land and buildings last.

8. Which presentation is used by most small businesses?

8. The order of permanence.

9. Show the Balance Sheet for the set of Final Accounts on page 60.

9.

Balance Sheet as at 31 December 20..

	$	$		$	$
Fixed Assets			*Capital*		
Equipment and Fittings		13 250	At start		18 990
Motor Vehicles		9 250	*Add* Net Profit	30 961	
		22 500	*Less* Drawings	12 850	
					18 111
					37 101
Current Assets					
Closing stock	11 200		Long Term Liabilities		
Debtors	3 085		Loan		5 000
Cash at Bank	9 150		Current Liabilities		
Cash in Hand	430		Creditors		4 264
		23 865			
		$46 365			$46 365

Now go over the page again until you are sure of all the answers.

UNIT 8

Accounting to Final Accounts Level. 5. Exercises to Final Accounts Level

8.1 Introduction

You are now ready to carry out some consolidating work to ensure that you have fully assimilated the arguments and ideas developed in the first seven Units. You should now be able to carry out the following accounting activities:

(i) make double entries in the ledger accounts for every type of transaction;
(ii) extract a Trial Balance of the ledger and, if the sides do not agree, check the double entries until agreement is achieved;
(iii) prepare from the Trial Balance a set of Final Accounts, i.e. a Trading Account and a Profit and Loss Account, closing off in the process all the nominal accounts in the ledger;
(iv) prepare a Balance Sheet, in good style, from the remaining accounts, the *real accounts* and the *personal accounts*, i.e. the residue of the Trial Balance.

You should now prepare several sets of records from the opening of the accounts right through to the Balance Sheet. You will find it helpful first to look at the specimen exercise in accounting to Final Accounts level in Unit 8.2.

8.2 A Specimen Exercise

R. Brown starts in business on 1 June 20.. contributing these assets: motor vehicles $5 530.00; furniture and equipment $3 650.00; cash in hand $230.00; cash at bank $3 980.00; stock $830.00. Open the ledger accounts to record these items. The following transactions then take place. Record them by double entries.

1 June	Purchases postage stamps, $21.20 in cash, and goods for resale, $478.00, on credit from T. Jones.
2 June	Purchases scales for use in shop, $115.00 cash. Purchases goods for resale, $736.50 cheque.
5 June	Cash sales $999.50. Pays cleaning expenses, $45.00 cash.
8 June	Postage $10.75 cash. Purchases on credit from R. Freedom goods for resale, $925.95.

10 June	Sells on credit to I. Slade goods valued at $595.50.
12 June	Cash sales $2 150.60. Pays into bank $1 200.00.
15 June	Purchases on credit from T. Jones goods for resale $1 285.50.
16 June	Postage $11.25 cash. Pays A. Builder cash for shelving $136.00.
19 June	Cash sales $488.75. Pays insurance by cheque $124.50.
22 June	Pays T. Jones by cheque $478.00.
24 June	Pays rates for half-year to Urban District Council $278.50, cheque.
26 June	Cash sales $2 195.25.
29 June	Postage $2.25 cash.
30 June	Cash sales $864.75. Pays into bank from cash till $3 150.00.

Extract a Trial Balance as at 30 June 20... Then prepare Trading and Profit and Loss Accounts for the month, and a Balance Sheet as at 30 June 20... The closing stock was valued at $1 144.00.

Model Answer: Part 1

Entering the opening items in the ledger accounts we have these entries:

Motor Vehicles Account L1

20..		$
1 Jun. Capital	L6	5 530.00

Furniture and Equipment Account L2

20..		$
1 Jun. Capital	L6	3 650.00

Cash Account L3

20..		$
1 Jun. Capital	L6	230.00

Bank Account L4

20..		$
1 Jun. Capital	L6	3 980.00

Stock Account L5

20..		$
1 Jun. Capital	L6	830.00

Capital Account (R. Brown) L6

			20..		$
			1 Jun. Sundry asset a/cs	L1–5	14 220.00

Notes:

(i) Each asset has been debited in an account.
(ii) The entry in the Capital Account—to save making several entries—is simply the total value of the assets contributed by the proprietor, R. Brown.
(iii) The folio numbers indicate where the other half of a particular double entry is to be found.

Model Answer: Part 2

Continuing with the transactions that took place in June, we have the following set of accounts. Work through the set, and make sure you follow each double entry.

Motor Vehicles Account L1

20..		$
1 Jun. Capital	L6	5 530.00

Furniture and Equipment Account L2

20..		$
1 Jun. Capital	L6	3 650.00
2 Jun. Cash	L3	115.00
16 Jun. Cash	L3	136.00

Cash Account L3

20..		$	20..		$
1 Jun. Capital	L6	230.00	1 Jun. Postage	L7	21.20
5 Jun. Sales	L10	999.50	2 Jun. Furniture and Equipment	L2	115.00
12 Jun. Sales	L10	2 150.60	5 Jun. Cleaning Expenses	L11	45.00
19 Jun. Sales	L10	488.75	8 Jun. Postage	L7	10.75
26 Jun. Sales	L10	2 195.25	12 Jun. Bank	L4	1 200.00
30 Jun. Sales	L10	864.75	16 Jun. Postage	L7	11.25
			16 Jun. Furniture and Equipment	L2	136.00
			29 Jun. Postage	L7	2.25
			30 Jun. Bank	L4	3 150.00
			30 Jun. Balance	c/d	2 237.40
		$6 928.85			$6 928.85
30 Jun. Balance	B/d	2 237.40			

Bank Account L4

20..		$	20..		$
1 Jun. Capital	L6	3 980.00	2 Jun. Purchases	L8	736.50
12 Jun. Cash	L3	1 200.00	19 Jun. Insurance	L14	124.50
30 Jun. Cash	L3	3 150.00	22 Jun. T. Jones	L9	478.00
			24 Jun. Rates	L15	278.50
			30 Jun. Balance	c/d	6 712.50
		$8 330.00			$8 330.00
30 Jun. Balance	B/d	6 712.50			

Stock Account L5

20..		$
1 Jun. Capital	L6	830.00

Capital Account (R. Brown) L6

				20..			$
				1 Jun.	Sundry asset a/cs	L1–5	14 220.00

Postage Account L7

20..			$				
1 Jun.	Cash	L3	21.20				
8 Jun.	Cash	L3	10.75				
16 Jun.	Cash	L3	11.25				
29 Jun.	Cash	L3	2.25				

Purchases Account L8

20..			$				
1 Jun.	T. Jones	L9	478.00				
2 Jun.	Bank	L4	736.50				
8 Jun.	R. Freedom	L12	925.95				
15 Jun.	T. Jones	L9	1 285.50				

T. Jones Account L9

20..			$	20..			$
22 Jun.	Bank	L4	478.00	1 Jun.	Purchases	L8	478.00
30 Jun.	Balance	c/d	1 285.50	15 Jun.	Purchases	L8	1 285.50
			$1 763.50				$1 763.50
				1 July	Balance	B/d	1 285.50

Sales Account L10

				20..			$
				5 Jun.	Cash	L3	999.50
				10 Jun.	I. Slade	L13	595.50
				12 Jun.	Cash	L3	2 150.60
				19 Jun.	Cash	L3	488.75
				26 Jun.	Cash	L3	2 195.25
				30 Jun.	Cash	L3	864.75

Cleaning Expenses Account L11

20..			$				
5 Jun.	Cash	L3	45.00				

R. Freedom Account L12

				20..			$
				8 Jun.	Purchases	L8	925.95

I. Slade Account L13

20..			$				
10 Jun.	Sales	L10	595.50				

Insurance Account L14

20..			$				
19 Jun.	Bank	L4	124.50				

Rates Account L15

20..			$				
24 Jun.	Bank	L4	278.50				

Model Answer: Part 3

If we tidy up the accounts where necessary by balancing off those that have items on both sides, and total (in pencil) those that have two or three entries on one side only, the Trial Balance may be extracted like this:

Trial Balance (R. Brown) as at 30 June 20..

	Dr.	*Cr.*
	$	$
Motor Vehicles Account	5530.00	
Furniture and Equipment Account	3901.00	
Cash Account	2237.40	
Bank Account	6712.50	
Stock Account	830.00	
Capital Account		14220.00
Postage Account	45.45	
Purchases Account	3425.95	
T. Jones Account		1285.50
Sales Account		7294.35
Cleaning Expenses Account	45.00	
R. Freedom Account		925.95
I. Slade Account	595.50	
Insurance Account	124.50	
Rates Account	278.50	
	$23725.80	$23725.80

Model Answer: Part 4

Using the closing stock figure given, $1144.00, the Trading Account, Profit and Loss Account and Balance Sheet can be prepared.

Trading Account for month ending 30 June 20..

	$		$
Opening stock	830.00	Sales	7294.35
Purchases	3425.95		
Total stock available	4255.95		
Less Closing stock	1144.00		
Cost of stock sold	3111.95		
Gross profit	4182.40		
	$7294.35		$7294.35

Profit and Loss Account for month ending 30 June 20..

	$		$
Postage	45.45	Gross profit	4182.40
Cleaning Expenses	45.00		
Insurance	124.50		
Rates	278.50		
Total expenses	493.45		
Net profit	3688.95		
	$4182.40		$4182.40

Balance Sheet of R. Brown as at 30 June 20..

		$		$	$
Fixed assets:			Capital:		
Furniture and Equipment		3901.00	At start	14220.00	
Motor Vehicles		5530.00	*Add* Profit	3688.95	
		9431.00			17908.95
Current assets:			Current liabilities:		
Closing stock	1144.00		R. Freedom	925.95	
I. Slade	595.50		T. Jones	1285.50	
Cash in bank	6712.50				2211.45
Cash in hand	2237.40				
		10689.40			
		$20120.40			$20120.40

Two sets of exercises follow. Set 10 provides examples of transactions by sole traders to help you master accounting to Final Accounts level. Set 11 provides several Trial Balances, from which you may achieve real facility in the preparation of Final Accounts. You will need to draw up many accounts as you work through them; although it is not recommended (since it wastes time in examinations) you may use continuous-balance accounts if you wish. The first four questions in Exercises Set 10 have disregarded VAT. Questions 5 and 6 do involve VAT, to puzzle your brains a bit more. The VAT rate used is 10 per cent.

8.3 Exercises Set 10. Accounting to Final Accounts Level

1. On 1 July 20.. Ken Todd starts in business with capital of $1 500.00 which he banks. He then buys by cheque a market stall (Stall and Equipment Account), $125.00; goods for resale, $234.00; and equipment $112.50. His transactions are as follows (note that VAT has been disregarded in this exercise):

2 July	Cash sales $136.00. Purchase of goods for resale $68.00 cash. Wages of assistant in cash $10.00.
3 July	Cash sales $242.00. Purchase of goods for resale $126.50 cash. Electric light connection fee $12.00 cash. Tip to dustman $1.00 cash.
4 July	Cash sales $193.00. Purchase in cash of goods for resale $121.50. Wages of assistant $10.00 cash.
5 July	Cash sales $284.00. Purchase by cheque of goods for resale $116.50. Wages of assistants $20.00 cash. Banked $250.00.
6 July	Cash sales $262.50. Wages of assistants $20.00 cash. Todd takes $100.00 from cash box as personal drawings.

Record the above items, extract a Trial Balance as at 6 July 20.. and from it prepare a Trading Account and Profit and Loss Account for the week, and a Balance Sheet as at that date. Stock at the close was valued at $117.50. Wages are to be charged to Profit and Loss Account.

2. On 1 July 20.. Emma Carr starts in business with capital of $2 500.00, which she banks. She then buys by cheque a market stall (Stall and Equipment Account), $175.00; goods for resale $320.00; and equipment $67.50. Her transactions are as follows, disregarding VAT:

2 July	Cash sales $284.00. Purchase in cash of goods for resale $218.00. Wages of assistant $12.00 cash.
3 July	Cash sales $242.00. Purchase in cash of goods for resale $136.50. Electric light fee $20.00 (cash). Tip to dustman $1.00 (cash).
4 July	Cash sales $413.00. Purchase by cheque of goods for resale $185.00. Wages of assistant $12.00 cash. Paid to bank $400.00.
5 July	Cash sales $294.00. Purchase in cash of goods for resale $162.50. Wages of assistants $17.50 cash.
6 July	Cash sales $264.00. Wages of assistants $17.20 cash. Carr takes $140.00 as personal drawings from cash.

Record the above items, extract a Trial Balance as at 6 July 20.. and from it prepare a Trading Account and Profit and Loss Account for the week, also a Balance Sheet as at that date. Stock at the close was valued at $434.00. Wages are to be charged to Profit and Loss Account.

3. On 1 March 20.. M. Tapley starts in business with assets as follows: cash in hand $1 150.00; cash at bank $3 830.00; premises $36 250.00; motor vehicle $3 720.00; and furniture and fittings $1 380.00. Enter these opening items, then record the following transactions for the first two weeks of March. Balance such accounts as require it, prepare a Trial Balance and a full set of Final Accounts. Advise Tapley whether he should continue in business. (The closing stock was valued at $148.00. Wages are to be charged to Profit and Loss Account. Disregard VAT.)

1 March	Purchases goods for resale by cheque $272.00. Purchases goods for resale on credit from Wholesale Suppliers Ltd, $325.00.
2 March	Postage $6.50 cash. Entertainment of commercial traveller $4.75 cash. Purchases fittings $124.50 by cheque.
3 March	Sells goods on credit to M. Jones $142.50. Pays telephone connection charge $32.50 cash.
4 March	Purchases answering machine for cash $124.00. Purchases goods for resale by cheque $234.80.
5 March	Cash sales for week $263.00. Pays to bank $400.00. Pays wages of assistants $87.50 in cash. Drawings for self, cheque $240.00.
8 March	Jones pays $40.00 on account in cash. Purchases goods for resale on credit from W. Grossmith $340.00.
9 March	Sells goods on credit to M. Jones $62.30.
11 March	Pays motor vehicle expenses $25.00 cash.
12 March	Cash sales for week $430.00. Pays to bank $180.00. Pays wages of assistants $87.50 in cash. Drawings for self, cheque $240.00.

4. On 1 May 20.. R. Quilp starts in business with assets as follows: cash in hand $150.00; cash at bank $2 350.00; premises $33 500.00; motor vehicle $5 650.00; and furniture and fittings $3 240.00. Enter these opening items, then record the following transactions for the first two weeks of May. Now:

a) balance such accounts as require it, and
b) prepare a Trial Balance and a full set of Final Accounts. Then advise Quilp whether he should continue in business. (The closing stock was valued at $2 472.00. VAT should be disregarded.)

1 May	Purchases goods for resale by cheque $342.00. Purchases goods for resale on credit from Wholesale Suppliers Ltd, $1 465.50.
2 May	Travelling $21.25 cash. Entertainment of finance house representative $12.40 cash. Purchases goods from Universal Shop Suppliers on credit $1 380.00.
3 May	Sells goods on credit to M. Freeman $268.50. Pays for improvements to premises (Premises Account) cheque $400.00.
4 May	Purchases goods for resale in cash $124.50. Sells goods on credit to M. Wilde $125.40.
5 May	Cash sales for week $1 385.00. Pays to bank $1 000.00. Pays wages $113.50 cash. Drawings for self, cheque $150.00.
8 May	Purchases goods for resale, cash $138.50. Purchases goods on credit from Wholesale Suppliers Ltd, $1 525.50.
9 May	Sells goods on credit to M. Freeman $295.65.
11 May	Pays Wholesale Suppliers Ltd on account $800.00 by cheque.
12 May	Cash sales for week $1 620.00. Banks $1 000.00. Pays wages of assistants $113.50 cash. Drawings for self, cheque $150.00

5. David Bingham starts in business on 1 April 20.. with the following assets: motor vehicles $3 530.00; furniture and fittings $1 275.00; premises $43 800.00; cash in hand $524.50; and cash at bank $3 725.50. At this date the VAT Account was clear. Open the ledger accounts to record these items, also the following transactions:

1 April	Purchases stock for resale by cheque, $1 500 plus VAT $150. Buys electronic till $255.00 plus VAT $25.50, by cheque.
2 April	Purchases goods for resale, on credit from T. Lines, $755.00 plus VAT $75.50. Purchases shelving and equipment $170.00 plus VAT $17.00 by cheque.
6 April	Cash sale $165.50 plus VAT $16.55. Travelling expenses $21.25 cash.
8 April	Sells goods on credit to R. French $255.00 plus VAT $25.50. Buys goods (for resale) at auction of a bankrupt's property, $65.50 plus VAT $6.55, by cheque.
10 April	Purchases fax machine $432.50 plus VAT $43.25 cash. Purchases stationery $85.50 plus VAT $8.55 cash.
12 April	Sells goods on credit to T. Tozer, $942.50 plus VAT $94.25. Purchases goods for resale, $240.00 plus VAT $24.00 by cheque.
13 April	Cash sales $1 238.25 plus VAT $123.82. Banks $1 000.00 from till.
16 April	Pays wages $142.00 in cash.
20 April	Cash sales $1 167.00 plus VAT $116.70. Purchases goods for resale on credit from T. Lines $185.50 plus VAT $18.55.
23 April	Pays fares $2.25 in cash.
27 April	Cash sales $1 245.50 plus VAT $124.55. Pays $1 000.00 into bank.
29 April	Recorded letter $1.25 cash. Pays for repairs $71.65 plus VAT $7.16 cash.
30 April	Draws cash for personal use by cheque $660.00. Pays wages $142.00 cash. Pays T. Lines $75.00 by cheque, on account.

Extract a Trial Balance as at 30 April 20.. and from the Trial Balance prepare a Trading Account and Profit and Loss Account for the month ending 30 April, and a Balance Sheet as at that date. (Closing stock was valued at $916.00.) Wages are to be dealt with in the Profit and Loss Account.

6. Anna Day starts in business on 1 August 20.. with the following assets: motor vehicles $4650.00; furniture and fittings $1230.00; premises $54200.00; cash in hand $235.00; and cash in bank $3475.00. Open the ledger accounts to record these items, also the following transactions:

1 August	Purchases stock for resale by cheque $1250.00 plus VAT $125.00. Purchases in cash second-hand electronic weighing machine $68.00 plus VAT $6.80.
2 August	Purchases goods for resale, on credit from R. Lyons $275.00 plus VAT $27.50. Purchases computer from Keystriker Ltd, on credit $1485.00 plus VAT $148.50.
6 August	Cash sales $884.75 plus VAT $88.48. Postage $2.25 cash. Pays telephone connection fee, $42.50 plus VAT $4.25 by cheque.
8 August	Cleaning materials $32.55 plus VAT $3.26 cash. Sales on credit to Mowler Tooth and Co $442.50 plus VAT $44.25.
10 August	Repairs to window fitting $12.25 plus VAT $1.22 cash.
12 August	Pays for electric fittings and installation $36.80 plus VAT $3.68 cash.
13 August	Cash sales $1172.50 plus VAT $117.25. Pays into bank $1150.00.
16 August	Purchases goods for resale on credit from R. Lyons $160.00 plus VAT $16.00.
20 August	Cash sales $2163.80 plus VAT $216.38. Pays into bank $1800.00.
22 August	Pays wages to casual worker $23.25 in cash.
23 August	Pays cash for fittings bought at bankruptcy sale $27.50 plus VAT $2.75.
27 August	Cash sales $2236.50 plus VAT $223.65. Pays $3200.00 into bank.
29 August	Recorded letter $0.85 cash. Sells on credit to R. White goods $55.00 plus VAT $5.50.
30 August	Pays cash wages $77.50. Draws cash for personal use by cheque $400.00. Pays for advertisement by cheque $32.10 plus VAT $3.21. Pays by cheque to Keystriker Ltd, $1633.50.

Extract a Trial Balance as at 31 August 20.. and from the Trial Balance prepare a Trading Account and Profit and Loss Account for the month ending 31 August 20.. and a Balance Sheet as at that date. (Closing stock was valued at $155.50.) Wages are to be dealt with in the Profit and Loss Account.

8.4 Exercises Set 11. Final Accounts from a Trial Balance

1. Andrew Davies's Trial Balance at 31 December 20.. shows the following balances. Prepare from them Trading and Profit and Loss Accounts for the year ending 31 December 20.., and a Balance Sheet as at that date.

	Dr.	*Cr.*
	$	$
Purchases Account	35 840	
Sales Account		59 726
Purchases Returns Account		1 840
Sales Returns Account	726	
Opening stock (1 January 20..)	2 000	
Sundry Expenses Account	1 426	
Rent and Rates Account	850	
Light and Heat Account	230	
Discount Allowed Account	285	
Discount Received Account		465
Land and Buildings Account	24 500	
Furniture and Fittings Account	1 380	
Motor Vehicles Account	3 750	
Debtors	495	
Creditors		1 295
Drawings	4 500	
Capital		15 656
Cash in hand	200	
Cash at bank	2 800	
	$78 982	$78 982

Closing stock was valued at $1 780 on 31 December 20...

2. Penny Robinson's Trial Balance at 31 March 20.. shows the following balances. From this Trial Balance prepare a Trading Account and Profit and Loss Account for the year and a Balance Sheet as at that date.

	Dr.	*Cr.*
	$	$
Purchases and Sales	30250	61155
Sales Returns and Purchases Returns	1355	650
Opening stock (1 April 20..)	2175	
Warehouse Wages	8135	
Warehouse Expenses	2108	
Sundry Expenses	4640	
Selling Expenses	11255	
Interest Paid	215	
Discount Allowed and Received	172	88
Commission Received		1255
Cash in hand	450	
Cash at bank	2950	
Premises	23240	
Motor Vehicles	4850	
Fixtures and Fittings	1430	
Debtors and Creditors	1555	1795
Drawings	5950	
Capital		31487
Loan from A. Colleague		4300
	$100730	$100730

Closing stock was valued at $2250 on 31 March 20...

3. Gordon Ford's Trial Balance is given below as it was drawn up on 31 December 20... From it you are asked to prepare a Trading Account and a Profit and Loss Account for the year ending 31 December 20.. and a Balance Sheet as at that date.

	Dr.	*Cr.*
	$	$
Purchases and Sales	31 800	67 550
Sales Returns and Purchase Returns	1 550	800
Opening stock (as at 1 January 20..)	1 850	
Carriage In	240	
Warehouse Expenses	7 895	
Rent, Rates and Insurance	1 725	
Light, Heat and Fuel	1 480	
Petrol and Oil	854	
Motor Vehicle Repairs	726	
Cleaning Expenses	872	
Repairs and Redecorations	234	
Commission Received		285
Fees Received		1 245
Land and Buildings	35 000	
Furniture and Fittings	3 840	
Fork-lift Trucks	4 220	
Debtors and Creditors	2 425	1 385
Mortgage on Premises		13 000
Interest Paid	420	
Drawings	6 850	
Capital		22 716
Cash in hand	150	
Cash at bank	4 850	
	$106 981	$106 981

Closing stock was valued at $2 000 on 31 December 20...

4. Bob Maycock's Trial Balance is given below as it was drawn up on 31 December 20... From it you are asked to prepare a Trading Account and a Profit and Loss Account for the year ending 31 December 20.., and a Balance Sheet as at that date.

	Dr.	*Cr.*
	$	$
Purchases and Sales	35725.50	71246.50
Sales Returns and Purchases Returns	246.50	425.50
Opening stock (as at 1 January 20..)	1850.75	
Carriage In	235.75	
Warehouse Expenses	6425.25	
Rent, Rates and Insurance	1136.50	
Light, Heat and Fuel	749.75	
Petrol and Oil	1235.25	
Motor Vehicle Repairs	462.50	
Cleaning Expenses	448.50	
Repairs and Redecorations	230.65	
Commission Received		1175.50
Fees Received		1250.00
Land and Buildings	46250.00	
Furniture and Fittings	6385.80	
Fork-life Trucks	6485.50	
Debtors and Creditors	3247.35	2656.50
Mortgage on Premises		24000.00
Interest Paid	336.50	
Drawings	6450.00	
Capital		18148.05
Cash in hand	25.00	
Cash at bank	975.00	
	$118902.05	$118902.05

Closing stock was valued at $3000.00 on 31 December 20...

5. From the following Trial Balance of Alison Brewis's books prepare a Trading Account and Profit and Loss Account for the year ending 31 March 20.., also a Balance Sheet as at that date.

	Dr.	*Cr.*
	$	$
Purchases and Sales	27246	64725
Sales Returns and Purchases Returns	725	1266
Carriage In	180	
Carriage Out	325	
Opening stock at 1 April 20..	4650	
Rent and Rates	1420	
Insurance	148	
Light and Heat	1630	
Discount Allowed and Discount Received	725	86
Commission Paid and Commission Received	1095	2469
Salaries	25854	
Debtors and Creditors	2760	4600
Land and Buildings	26750	
Furniture and Fittings	6250	
Motor Vehicles	4480	
Drawings	16625	
Cash in hand	138	
Cash at bank	12745	
Loan from R. Petworth		25000
Capital		35600
	$133746	$133746

Closing stock was valued at $5450 on 31 March 20...

6. From the following Trial Balance of E. London's books prepare a Trading Account and Profit and Loss Account for the year ending 31 December 20.., and a Balance Sheet as at that date.

	Dr.	*Cr.*
	$	$
Purchases and Sales	42 580.50	125 624.30
Sales Returns and Purchases Returns	1 624.30	580.50
Opening stock at 1 January 20..	2 000.00	
Carriage In	120.50	
Warehouse Wages (Trading Account)	9 480.50	
Warehouse Expenses (Trading Account)	1 338.75	
Light and Heat	240.50	
Rent and Rates	1 248.00	
Telephone Expenses	486.55	
Insurance	148.50	
Selling Expenses	22 726.30	
Motor Vehicle Expenses	641.55	
Travellers' Salaries	13 865.25	
Office Salaries	11 585.50	
Rent Received from Sub-tenant		840.00
Land and Buildings	41 250.00	
Furniture and Fittings	6 870.50	
Plant and Machinery	13 150.00	
Drawings	4 650.00	
Debtors and Creditors	842.00	1 736.00
Cash in hand	142.70	
Cash at bank	4 150.00	
Mortgage		17 250.00
Bank Loan		1 000.00
Capital		32 111.10
	$179 141.90	$179 141.90

Closing stock was valued at $2 500.00 on 31 December 20...

8.5 Revise and Test 8. A Special Note

It was not felt necessary to include a Revise and Test page for this unit.

UNIT 9

Books of Original Entry.
1. Journals and Day Books

9.1 Documents, Day Books and the Ledger

We have seen that the main book of account is the ledger, and that we can keep accounts by making entries directly into the ledger accounts, so long as we use the double-entry system correctly, and debit and credit the right accounts appropriately.

The real-life sequence of events is usually a little more complex than this, however.

(a) The first record of a transaction is a *document* such as an invoice, a debit note, a credit note, a cheque, a petty cash voucher and so on. (All these documents will be discussed in the next few Units.)

(b) The next stage is to record the documents in a *day book* in chronological order, as they occur day by day. The chief day book is the *Journal* (the name is simply the French word for 'day book'), but this is often split up into a Purchases Day Book, a Sales Day Book and so forth.

(c) The day book records are *posted* (transferred) from the day book into the *ledger*.

It is possible—though at the cost of some loss of clarity—to leave out the day book stage altogether. There are also some quick ways of doing the day book work, such as the use of simultaneous entries (making the day book entries and ledger entries at the same time—see Unit 15) or using a computer, which also allows us to make both the entries at once.

9.2 The Journal

The Journal is the most important of the subsidiary books. 'Subsidiary' means 'giving additional help to': the Journal gives additional help to the ledger, which is the main book of account. Journal paper is ruled like this:

Date	Details	Folio	Debit column (in which the accounts to be debited are listed)	Credit column (in which the accounts to be credited are listed)

At one time there was only one Journal, where all original entries were made. These entries were then transferred into the ledger accounts, a process known as 'posting the day book to the ledger'. Later a great many of the routine entries in the Journal were removed and put into specialized day books, such as the Purchases Day Book and the Sales Day Book. This left the Journal with only the more unusual items in it and it became known as the *Journal Proper*, to distinguish it from the specialized journals which had only one type of entry—for example, purchases invoices in the Purchases Day Book. Each Journal entry includes a short explanation, called the *narration*, starting with the word 'Being', to remind the accountant of the circumstances.

J1

20..			$	$
11 Jan.	Motor Vehicles A/c Dr.	L5	6270.50	
	Danehole's Garage	L7		6270.50
	Being new motor vehicle D1756AJN purchased at this date			

The above Journal entry, when posted to the ledger accounts, produces the following entries:

Motor Vehicles Account L5

20..			$				
11 Jan.	Danehole's Garage	J1	6270.50				

Danehole's Garage Account L7

				20..			$
				11 Jan.	Motor Vehicles	J1	6270.50

The use of the Journal Proper is dealt with more fully later in this book (see Units 12 and 13).

9.3 Trading Businesses—Goods for Resale

One of the commonest business activities is the purchase of goods for resale at a profit. This is the activity known as *trade*; it comprises *wholesale trade* which may also involve importing and exporting, and *retail trade*. Another business activity, *manufacturing*, also requires the purchase of raw materials and components, and these are eventually resold as part of the finished product that is being manufactured.

It follows that purchases of goods and sales of goods are repeatedly taking place in such firms. In business, however, the words 'goods', 'purchases' and 'sales' have special meanings.

Goods refers to items forming part of the stock in trade of a firm, which are purchased to be resold at a profit. A firm may purchase other items for use in the business, but they are not purchases of 'goods'. They may be purchases of *assets*, which will last a long time, or purchases of *consumables*, which only last a short time, being used up in the business. For example, a draper purchases sheets, pillow cases or towels as goods for resale, but he or she would buy a cash register for use in the business as an asset, and paper bags and wrapping paper as consumables. Filing cabinets, word processors and calculators would be goods to a supplier of office equipment, but capital assets to everyone else. To a garage, cars are goods since they form part of the stock in trade; to everyone else they are assets, recorded in the Motor Vehicles Account.

Purchases refers to the purchase of goods for resale, and not to the purchase of assets or consumables. The Purchases Account therefore only contains purchases of goods for resale. It is an *error of principle* to record purchases of assets and consumables in the Purchases Account.

Sales refers to sales of goods which have formed part of the stock in trade of the business. Sales of other items, such as worn-out or obsolete assets or assets surplus to requirements, are not 'sales' in the accounting meaning of that word. It would again be an error of principle to record sales of assets in the Sales Account.

9.4 The Invoice

(a) Characteristics of an Invoice

An invoice is a document for the sale of goods, made out by the seller and used to inform the buyer of the type, number, price and value of the goods supplied. There may be as many as twenty copies of an invoice, but more usually three, four or five are sufficient. While it may not actually form the contract between the two parties to the transaction, it is very good evidence of the contract and is often produced in court in cases where disputes over contracts for the sale of goods are being decided. It should have the following details:

(i) the names and addresses of both parties to the contract;
(ii) an exact description of the goods, including the number, unit price and total value of the consignment;

(iii) the terms and conditions of sale, or a reference to the place where the terms and conditions of sale may be discovered.

It often carries the letters E&OE, which stand for 'errors and omissions excepted'. This is an old-fashioned practice, which recognizes the legal maxim that written evidence cannot be varied by oral evidence. It was formerly thought that a mere slip of the pen, or a typist's error, would have to be honoured if the invoice itself was the contract. Thus if an invoice concerning a machine valued at $1 000.00 was incorrectly made out for $100.00, the seller might have been bound to sell at the lower figure. However, the case of Webster *v.* Cecil (1861) decided that a mere slip of the pen may be corrected, so that the letters E&OE are not strictly necessary now.

A typical invoice is illustrated in Fig. 9.1.

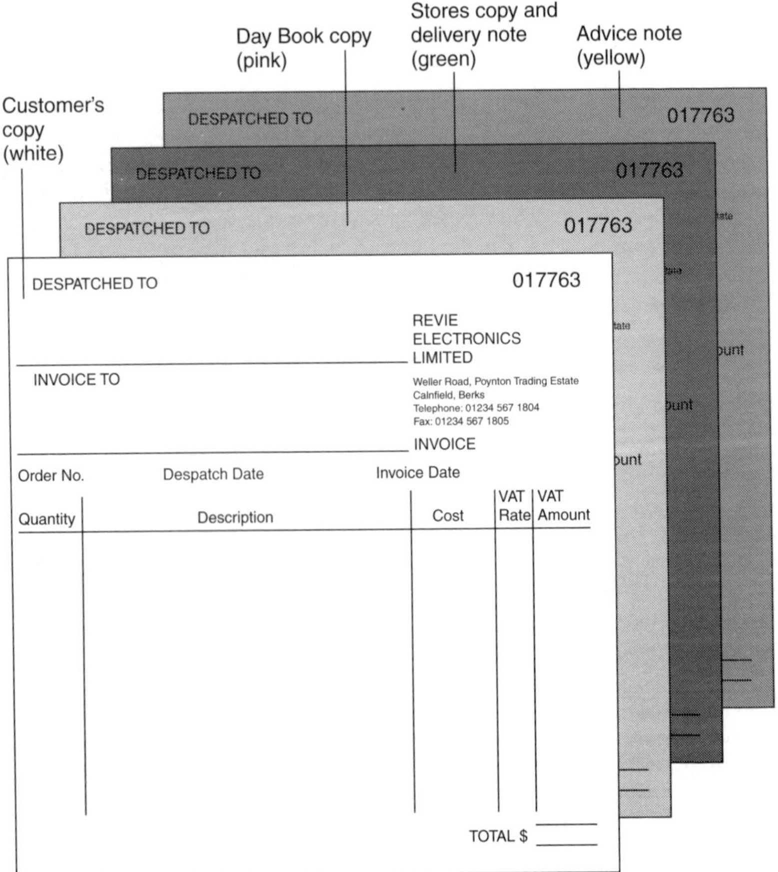

Fig. 9.1 An invoice with a four-copy distribution

(b) Distribution of Invoices

The *top copy* always goes to the purchaser, and becomes his or her accounting record, entered—with any other purchases invoices—in the *Purchases Day Book.*

The *second copy* stays with the seller, and becomes his or her accounting record, entered—with any other sales invoices—in the *Sales Day Book.*

The *third and fourth copies,* often called the *delivery note* and the *advice note* are sent down to the seller's dispatch department. Goods are obtained for dispatch from the Stock Department, and the advice note is packed in the parcel with the goods for the customer's information. The delivery note is then used by the courier to obtain a signature from the customer acknowledging delivery of the goods in sound condition.

The *fifth copy,* if there is one, is often used as a *file copy* or *representative's copy.* It informs the representative, about to call on a customer, that the previous order for that customer has been fulfilled by Head Office.

(c) Trade Discount

A *discount* is a reduction in price. Frequently a type of discount called *trade discount* is given to traders. The granting of trade discount has developed because it often happens that it is more convenient for all those concerned with a product to think of it in terms of the final price to the consumer. Thus a vacuum cleaner manufacturer may turn out two models—a standard model at $60.00 and a *de luxe* model at $90.00. Although the manufacturer does not sell the cleaners to retailers at these prices—because these are the final prices to the consumer—it is convenient to invoice them to the retailer at this value. Such an invoice might read:

		$
8 *de luxe* vacuum cleaners at $90.00 each	=	720.00
Less trade discount 40%	=	288.00
		$432.00

A high rate of trade discount has been granted to the retailer in this case. Trade discount tends to be high when goods are expensive and slow-moving, and low when the turnover is more rapid. This discount represents the profit to which the retailer is entitled, and may be defined as follows:

> *Trade discount is a reduction made in the catalogue price of an article to enable the retailer to make a profit.*

It is *not* given on ordinary trade items such as groceries, where the profit margins are fixed by the retailer. Trade discount does *not* enter the ledger accounts, but may be recorded in the day books—for example, in the Purchases Day Book in Fig. 9.2 (on page 120) trade discount has been given on the Scandinavian quilt.

(d) Debit Notes

It sometimes happens that an invoice is incorrectly made out, understating the value of the transaction. When this occurs it is usual to correct the error by sending a *debit note* to the customer. This document is treated exactly like an invoice, and is entered in the day books in the same way. (For the correction of an error in the opposite direction—overstating the transaction's value—see Unit 9.10(a).)

(e) Value Added Tax

In Unit 1.6 we mentioned that Value Added Tax (VAT) is payable on supplies of goods and services. The tax is imposed on consumers when they purchase goods, but is collected at every point at which value is added along the chain of production, distribution and trade. Suppose a customer buys a $100 coffee table from a furnishing store and VAT at 10% is added, making $110 in all. The trader has received $100 for his/her business activity, but has also collected $10 tax for the Government. This is payable to HM Customs and Excise, but the trader does not pay over the full $10 to the Customs. This is because, when purchasing the coffee table from a wholesaler for $80 the trader paid VAT on it of 10% = $8, making $88 in all.

The trader's Output Tax (collected from the customer) was $10.
The Input Tax was $8 (paid to the wholesaler)
The amount due to HM Customs is Output Tax − Input Tax = $10 − $8 = $2

Actually all the trader has to pay to HM Customs is the tax on the value he/she has added. The table which cost $80 was sold for $100. Value Added = $20. Tax on the value added is 10% of $20 = $2.

The full story of how the $10 tax reaches HM Customs is as follows:

The retailer paid HM Customs $2, as we have seen. The wholesaler sold the table for $80 + VAT, after buying it from the manufacturer for $60 + VAT = $66. Tax due; input tax $6; output tax $8.

Output Tax − Input Tax = $8 − $6 = $2 payable to HM Customs

The manufacturer sold the table for $60 + VAT after buying a walnut tree from A. Farmer for $30 + VAT = $33. Output Tax = $6; Input Tax = $3.

Output Tax − Input Tax = $6 − $3 = $3 payable to HM Customs

A. Farmer sold the tree (a gift of nature) for $30 + VAT = $33. He/she had no input tax to pay.

Output Tax $3 − Input Tax $0 = $3 payable to HM Customs

so the $10 paid by the purchaser was paid to Customs in four parts: $2 + $2 + $3 + $3 = $10. It is not important to know the details of how the VAT system works, but you do need to understand how the output and input tax are found in the accounting system. This is explained in the sections that follow.

VAT rates change from time to time but in this book a rate of 10 per cent has been assumed throughout.

9.5 The Purchases Day Book

During the nineteenth century the volume of goods produced in fields and factories rose and it became clear that the Journal was inadequate as the sole book of original entry. Too many clerks wanted to make entries in the same book at the same time. It became easier to have a separate book for the commoner activities, like purchases and sales. Not only that, but the use of these special journals, or day books, was simplified. Instead of making a double entry for every invoice, the clerk would make only a single entry at that time, leaving the double entry until the end of the month. For example, in the Purchases Day Book, every invoice entered was for purchases. Each required a credit entry in the supplier's account (the supplier had given goods) and a debit entry in the Purchases Account (the Purchases Account had received goods). There was little point in making the second of these entries in the Purchases Account separately for each entry. A simpler way was to add up the whole book at the end of the month, and make one entry of the total figure in the Purchases Account. The two columns of the Journal (see Unit 9.2) were no longer needed, and the inner column became merely an addition column for invoices with several items on them. With the introduction of Value Added Tax an extra column was inserted to catch the VAT input tax. The last column became the important one, showing how much should be credited to each supplier's personal account, and the total of the book on the last day of the month showed the total to be debited to Purchases Account. An example is shown in Fig. 9.2.

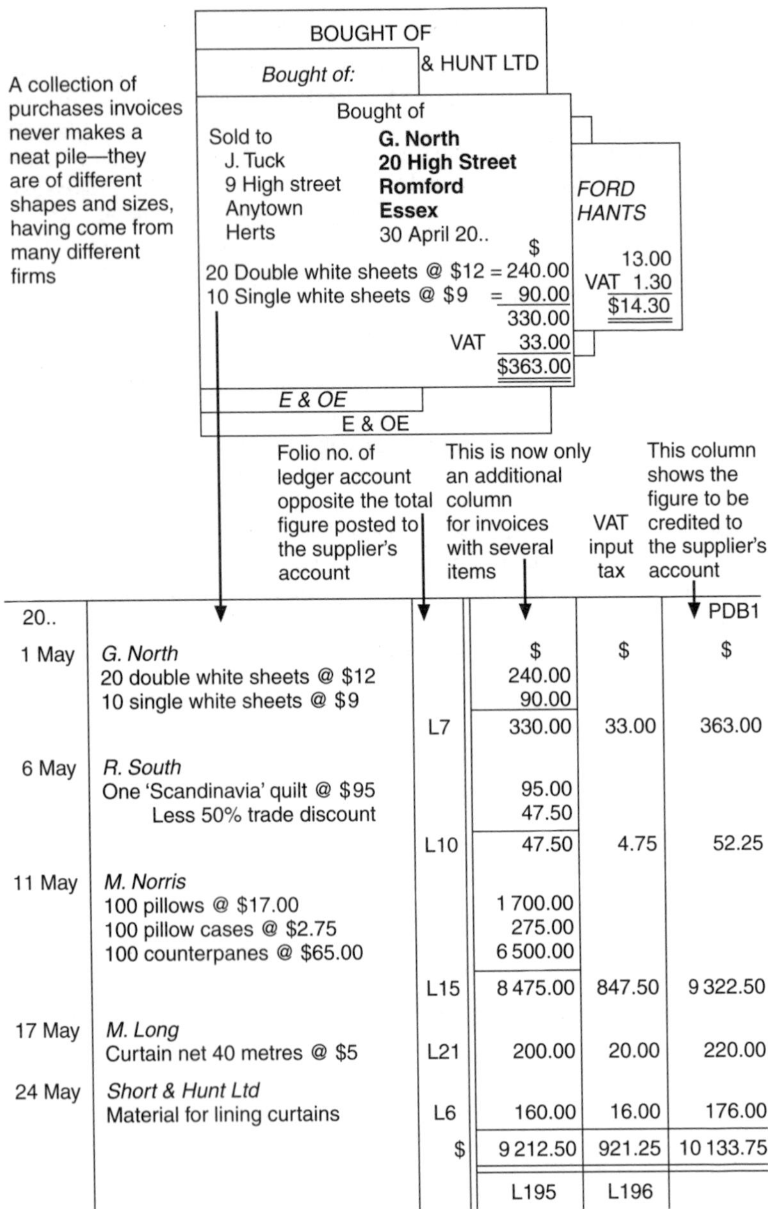

20..					PDB1
			$	$	$
1 May	*G. North* 20 double white sheets @ $12 10 single white sheets @ $9		240.00 90.00		
		L7	330.00	33.00	363.00
6 May	*R. South* One 'Scandinavia' quilt @ $95 Less 50% trade discount		95.00 47.50		
		L10	47.50	4.75	52.25
11 May	*M. Norris* 100 pillows @ $17.00 100 pillow cases @ $2.75 100 counterpanes @ $65.00		1 700.00 275.00 6 500.00		
		L15	8 475.00	847.50	9 322.50
17 May	*M. Long* Curtain net 40 metres @ $5	L21	200.00	20.00	220.00
24 May	*Short & Hunt Ltd* Material for lining curtains	L6	160.00	16.00	176.00
		$	9 212.50	921.25	10 133.75
			L195	L196	

Fig. 9.2 The Purchases Day Book: the total 'net of VAT' purchases are debited in L195, the Purchases Account; the total input tax is posted to the debit side of L196, the VAT Account; the individual items in the column on the far right are posted to the credit side of the creditors' accounts

Posting the Purchases Day Book to the Ledger

When posted to the ledger, the entries would be as shown below. In each case the supplier is credited (credit the giver) and the firm whose books are being kept is debited with the total 'net of VAT' purchases in the Purchases Account. The input tax total is debited in the VAT Account. These two debit entries make up the double entry for *all* the entries in the suppliers' accounts.

G. North Account L7

			20..		$
			1 May Purchases	PDB1	363.00

R. South Account L10

			20..		$
			6 May Purchases	PDB1	52.25

M. Norris Account L15

			20..		$
			11 May Purchases	PDB1	9322.50

M. Long Account L21

			20..		$
			17 May Purchases	PDB1	220.00

Short and Hunt Ltd Account L6

			20..		$
			24 May Purchases	PDB1	176.00

Purchases Account L195

20..		$			
31 May Sundry creditors	PDB1	9212.50			

VAT Account L196

20..		$			
31 May Sundry creditors	PDB1	921.25			

Now you will find it useful to practise one or two entries in the Purchases Day Book, using the examples given in Exercises Set 12.

9.6 Exercises Set 12. The Purchases Day Book

1. Enter the following items in the Purchases Day Book of M. Sibthorpe, and post the book to the ledger accounts. Total the book on 31 May 20...

1 May	F. Ball sells Sibthorpe 3 sets of golf clubs @ $142.50 per set ($427.50). VAT is $42.75. (Total $470.25.)
2 May	B. Bannerman sells Sibthorpe 20 badminton sets @ $21.55 each ($431.00) and 20 comeback tennis trainers @ $12.25 each ($245.00). VAT is $67.60. (Total $743.60.)
11 May	R. Downs supplies Sibthorpe with 100 golf balls @ $0.95 each ($95.00). VAT is $9.50. (Total $104.50.)
17 May	P. Roberts supplies Sibthorpe with 40 leather footballs @ $7.80 each ($312.00) and 200 plastic footballs @ $0.85 each ($170.00). VAT is $48.20. (Total $530.20.)
24 May	G. Wright supplies Sibthorpe with 200 'Homesocca' games @ $12.35 each ($2470.00). VAT is $247. (Total $2717.00.)

2. Enter the following items in the Purchases Day Book of R. Beech, and post the book to the ledger accounts. Total the book on 31 May 20...

1 May	M. Benton sells Beech 5 sets of 'Home Painter' equipment @ $5.50 per set ($27.50). VAT is $2.75. (Total $30.25.)
3 May	D. Cade sells Beech 20 drums of paint @ $4.85 each ($97.00) and 20 litres thinners @ $1.65 per litre ($33.00). VAT is $13.00. (Total $143.00.)
14 May	S. Carter supplies Beech with 100 rolls wallpaper @ $2.55 each $255.00). VAT is $25.50. (Total $280.50.)
27 May	D. Cade supplies Beech with 40 tins white gloss paint @ $4.60 each ($184.00) and 200 plastic paint trays @ $0.45 each ($90.00). VAT is $27.40. (Total $301.40.)
29 May	G. Wright supplies Beech with 100 rolls wallpaper @ $1.85 each ($185.00). VAT is $18.50. (Total $203.50.)

3. Kim Lawson is invoiced for the following goods by the suppliers shown. Record them in her Purchases Day Book and post to the ledger accounts. Total the book on 31 January 20...

4 January	R. Davy supplies 12 Barracuda fish tanks @ $13.20 each ($158.40). VAT is $15.84. (Total $174.24.)
10 January	K. Adcock supplies 12 mini-tank aeration pumps @ $4.55 each ($54.60). VAT is $5.46. (Total $60.06.)
13 January	M. Bridger supplies assorted tropical fish, valued at $98.50, and sub-marine landscape features (24 sets) @ $2.85 per set ($68.40). VAT is $16.69. (Total $183.59.)
21 January	D. De'ath supplies garden fish tanks valued at $184.50. VAT is $18.45. (Total $202.95.)
23 January	R. Lawrence supplies freshwater fish valued at $72.50 and weed (assorted) valued at $6.00. VAT is $7.85. (Total $86.35.)

9.7 The Sales Day Book

Like the purchase of goods for resale, the sale of goods is an everyday transaction. A single invoice typist may type as many as one hundred invoices every day and will, in addition, separate the top copy from each set and send it to the customer, who will enter it in his or her Purchases Day Book. The third and fourth copies will be sent down to the dispatch department for processing. The second copy becomes the Accounts Department copy, for entry into the Sales Day Book. Fig. 9.3 shows the entries in this book, which are in the identical form to those made in the Purchases Day Book. The pile of invoices is neater, however, since this time they have not come from many different firms but are all from our own, and therefore identical in shape, size and colour.

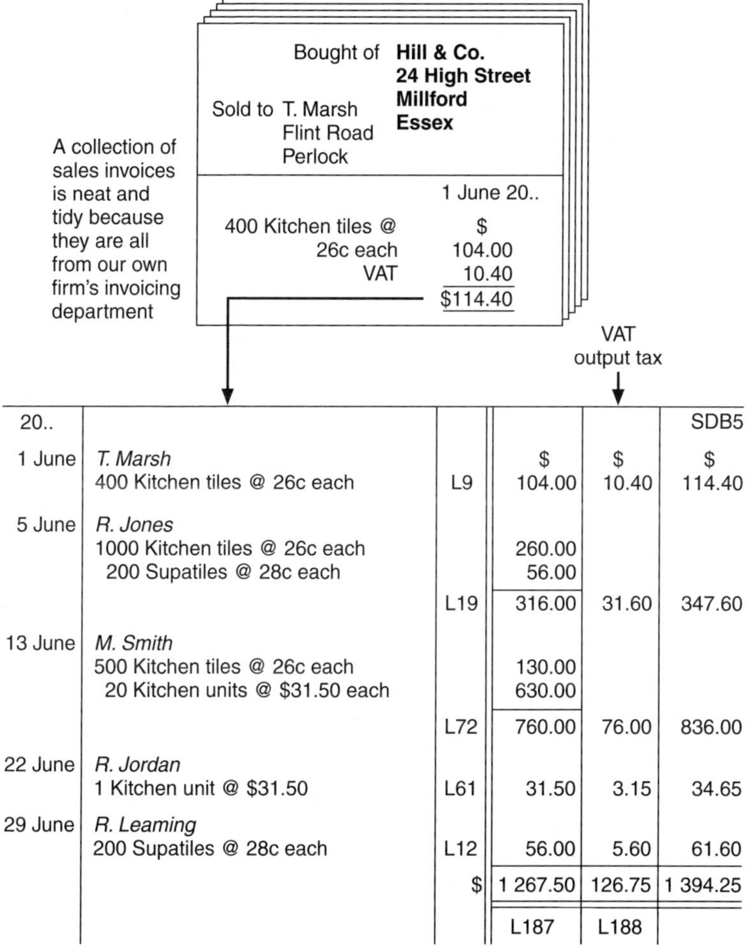

20..					SDB5
1 June	*T. Marsh* 400 Kitchen tiles @ 26c each	L9	$ 104.00	$ 10.40	$ 114.40
5 June	*R. Jones* 1000 Kitchen tiles @ 26c each 200 Supatiles @ 28c each		260.00 56.00		
		L19	316.00	31.60	347.60
13 June	*M. Smith* 500 Kitchen tiles @ 26c each 20 Kitchen units @ $31.50 each		130.00 630.00		
		L72	760.00	76.00	836.00
22 June	*R. Jordan* 1 Kitchen unit @ $31.50	L61	31.50	3.15	34.65
29 June	*R. Leaming* 200 Supatiles @ 28c each	L12	56.00	5.60	61.60
		$	1 267.50	126.75	1 394.25
			L187	L188	

Fig. 9.3 The Sales Day Book

Posting the Sales Day Book to the Ledger

When the Sales Day Book is posted to the ledger, each customer is debited with the goods he or she has received (debit the receiver) and the firm whose books are being kept is credited with the sales figure. The VAT Account is credited with the output tax, which must be accounted for to the Customs and Excise Department.

T. Marsh Account L9

Date	Details	Folio	$
20..			
1 June	Sales	SDB5	114.40

R. Jones Account L19

Date	Details	Folio	$
20..			
5 June	Sales	SDB5	347.60

M. Smith Account L72

Date	Details	Folio	$
20..			
13 June	Sales	SDB5	836.00

R. Jordan Account L61

Date	Details	Folio	$
20..			
22 June	Sales	SDB5	34.65

R. Leaming Account L12

Date	Details	Folio	$
20..			
29 June	Sales	SDB5	61.60

Sales Account L187

Date	Details	Folio	$
20..			
30 June	Sundry debtors	SDB5	1 267.50

VAT Account L188

Date	Details	Folio	$
20..			
30 June	Sundry debtors	SDB5	126.75

Notice that every customer has been debited with the goods invoiced to him or her, becoming a debtor for that amount. The total of the 'net of tax' items on the Sales Day Book, posted to the Sales Account on the credit side, and the VAT credited in the VAT Account together make up the double entry for all the entries made in the debtors' personal accounts. The folio numbers of these two entries in the Sales Day Book are usually written below the total figure, to mark their posting to the ledger at the end of the month.

You should now do some Sales Day Book entries as shown in this section. Exercises Set 13 gives three for you to try.

9.8 Exercises Set 13. The Sales Day Book

1. R. Hall, who is in the timber trade, supplies the following customers in May 20..:

1 May	R. Whitechurch is supplied with 2 chicken sheds at $145.50 each ($291.00). VAT is $29.10. (Total $320.10.)
13 May	M. Lamb is supplied with 'Peep-proof' garden fencing—20 × 2-metre panels at $9.50 per panel ($190.00) and 3 × 1-metre panels at $4.50 per panel ($13.50). VAT is $20.35. (Total $223.85.)
17 May	R. Marshall is supplied with a lean-to greenhouse frame $113.50. VAT is $11.35 (Total $124.85.)
19 May	R. Shaw buys 12 kits for garden sheds at $63.80 per kit ($765.60). VAT is $76.56. (Total $842.16.)
27 May	M. Lever buys 4 chicken sheds at $145.50 ($582.00). VAT is $58.20. (Total $640.20.)

Enter these items as invoices in Hall's Sales Day Book and post them to the ledger accounts so that a proper double entry is achieved.

2. Sue Thomas is in the catering trade. During June 20.. she caters for the following functions, supplying goods as shown. Enter the invoices in her Sales Day Book and post it to the ledger to achieve a proper double entry. VAT has to be added to all invoices at 10 per cent.

4 June	M. Allen (wedding)	
	200 assorted sandwiches @ 45c each	= $90.00
	400 pastries @ 25c each	= $100.00
	1 three-tier cake	= $60.00
11 June	R. Cross (golden wedding)	
	400 bridge rolls @ 10c each	= $40.00
	300 assorted sandwiches @ 45c each	= $135.00
	300 pastries @ 25c each	= $75.00
	1 single-tier cake	= $25.00
24 June	R. Diamond Ltd (annual conference of sales representatives)	
	200 filled rolls @ 24c each	= $48.00
	200 sandwiches @ 45c each	= $90.00
	500 pastries @ 25c each	= $125.00
	Decorated *petits fours*	= $20.00

3. R. Larch is a nurseryman wholesaling plants to shops in his locality. He invoices the following sales in April 20... Enter these invoices in Larch's Sales Day Book and post them to the ledger to achieve a proper double entry. VAT has to be added to all invoices at 10 per cent.

2 April	Garden Traders Ltd, 25 boxes antirrhinums @ $2.00 per box ($50.00); 25 boxes salvias @ $2.25 per box ($56.25).
9 April	Fine Gardens Co., 200 boxes dahlias @ $1.80 = $360.00
21 April	Green, Finger & Co., 100 boxes each of dahlias @ $1.80 ($180.00), salvias @ $2.25 ($225.00), lobelia @ $2.00 ($200.00), mesembryanthemums @ $2.00 ($200.00), and alyssum @ $1.75 ($175.00).
28 April	Garden Traders Ltd, 50 boxes alyssum @ $1.75 ($87.50), and 50 boxes lobelia @ $2.00 ($100.00).

9.9 Returns

Any trading business that supplies goods to customers must inevitably at times receive back goods which for some reason are unsatisfactory to the customer. Contracts for the sale of goods cannot be cancelled at the customer's whim; this would constitute *breach of contract.* Goods may however be returned if there is some genuine complaint as to matters such as their quality, colour or size. A trader may also allow a customer to return goods which he or she has decided are not required, if it is felt that the customer's goodwill in the future is worth more than the loss of profit on this particular transaction. A further reason for returns is the movement of empty containers and crates which are charged out to the customer when goods are dispatched, on the understanding that they are returnable when empty.

Whenever goods or containers are returned, for whatever reason, the appropriate document is the *credit note.*

9.10 Credit Notes

A credit note is a business document which is made out whenever one person returns goods to another. The credit note is made out by the original supplier of the goods, after the returned goods have come back to his or her warehouse. Credit notes are always printed in red, to distinguish them from invoices. Like an invoice, a credit note constitutes written evidence of the returns transaction, and may be produced in the courts in the event of a dispute over the contract.

Credit notes are also used in the following circumstances:

(a) where an error has been made on an invoice, resulting in an *overcharge.* Clearly the excessive charge made must be cancelled in some way. The simplest method is to issue a credit note, even though no returns have actually been made.

(b) where goods are damaged in some minor way, as a method of making the customer an allowance on the goods. Thus a piece of furniture which has been scratched in transit might not merit return to the factory. The protesting customer is greeted with a suggestion that it be repolished, and an allowance against the invoice price is suggested. The customer may be quite happy to carry out the work, because he is paying less money. The allowance is made by sending the customer a credit note for the agreed sum. A second copy of this credit note is kept for the use of the accounts department. There are fewer copies of credit notes than of invoices.

9.11 The Purchases Returns Book

Credit notes sent to us by suppliers, to whom we have returned goods or containers, are entered into the Purchases Returns Book. This is a day book ruled exactly like the Purchases Day Book (Fig. 9.4).

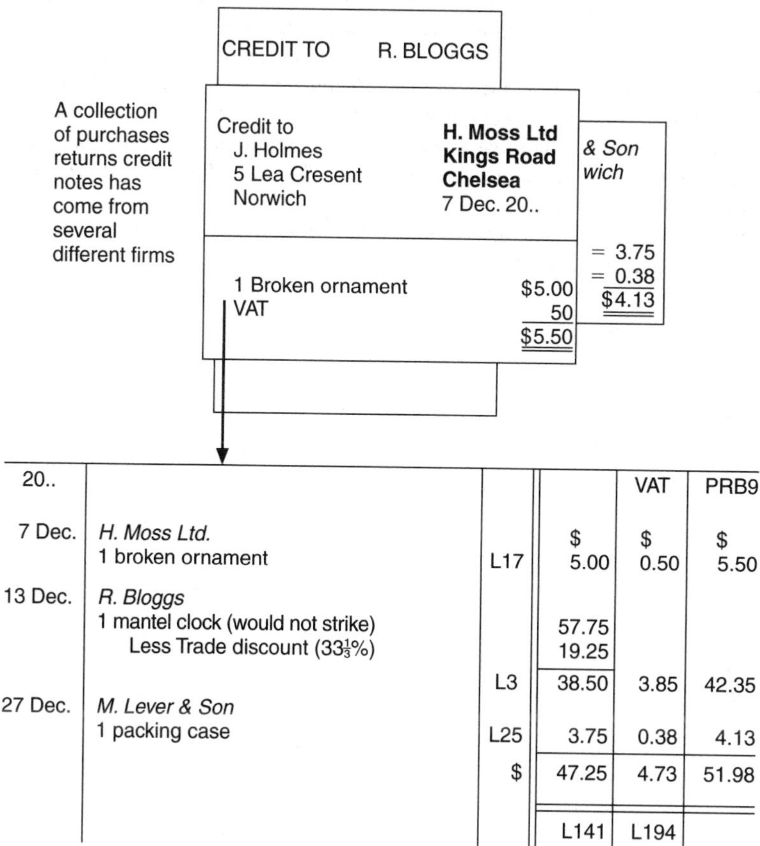

20..				VAT	PRB9
7 Dec.	*H. Moss Ltd.* 1 broken ornament	L17	$ 5.00	$ 0.50	$ 5.50
13 Dec.	*R. Bloggs* 1 mantel clock (would not strike) Less Trade discount (33⅓%)		57.75 19.25		
		L3	38.50	3.85	42.35
27 Dec.	*M. Lever & Son* 1 packing case	L25	3.75	0.38	4.13
		$	47.25	4.73	51.98
			L141	L194	

Fig. 9.4 Entering credit notes in the Purchases Returns Book

(a) Returns at Catalogue Price

As already pointed out (see Unit 9.4) goods are often invoiced at catalogue price, trade discount being deducted to give the retailer his/her margin of profit. This may result in difficulties when goods are returned, since they may be returned at their nominal catalogue price. If a supplier charges a customer *only* the 'trade discount' price but gives credit on the full retail price, the customer will make a profit on the returned item. Care should be taken to deduct trade discount, where this is appropriate.

(b) Posting the Purchases Returns Book to the Ledger

When the Purchases Returns Book is posted to the ledger, the suppliers who have received back the unsatisfactory items are debited (debit the receiver) and the Purchases Returns Account is credited. The firm whose ledger is being kept, our firm, has given these items back and must be credited with their value. The VAT on these items, which was part of our input tax, is not to be reclaimed and will be credited to VAT Account. These two credit entries form the double entry for the debit entries in the suppliers' accounts. The ledger accounts are shown here with the suppliers having supplied goods (on the credit side) since it would be unrealistic to talk about returning goods where nothing has been purchased.

H. Moss Ltd Account L17

		$			$
20..			20..		
7 Dec. Purchases Returns	PRB9	5.50	4 Dec. Purchases	PDB4	155.00

R. Bloggs Account L3

		$			$
20..			20..		
13 Dec. Purchases Returns	PRB9	42.35	3 Dec. Purchases	PDB4	337.50

M. Lever and Son Account L25

		$			$
20..			20..		
27 Dec. Purchases Returns	PRB9	4.13	17 Dec. Purchases	PDB4	48.50

Purchases Returns Account L141

					$
			20..		
			31 Dec. Sundry creditors	PRB9	47.25

VAT Account L194

					$
			20..		
			31 Dec. Sundry creditors	PRB9	4.73

Now you should practise entering groups of credit notes in the Purchases Returns Book, and posting the entries to the ledger.

9.12 Exercises Set 14. The Purchases Returns Book

1. Gill Lutterworth is in business as a retail draper. She receives the following credit notes from suppliers in May 20. .:

4 May	Lustre Colour Ltd—one set of ready-manufactured curtains (colour faded) $27.50. VAT is $2.75. (Total $30.25.)
11 May	C. E. Montrose—returned sheets 3 sets @ $12.25 per set (faulty design pattern) $36.75. VAT is $3.68. (Total $40.43.)
29 May	E. A. Phillips—returned curtain lining material (damaged by water in transit) $35.50. VAT is $3.55. (Total $39.05.)

Enter the credit notes in Miss Lutterworth's Purchases Returns Book and post to the appropriate ledger accounts.

2. E. S. Oliver is a garage proprietor. During July 20. . he receives the following credit notes from suppliers:

7 July	Miniparts Ltd—one set of chrome-plated mudguards (chrome imperfect) $28.75. VAT is $2.88. (Total $31.63.)
22 July	Accessories Ltd—one chronometer $28.95 (defective mechanism) and one oil pressure gauge (engine mounting badly machined) $14.25. VAT is $4.32. (Total $47.52.)
30 July	Battery Wholesale Supply Co. Ltd—one 12-volt battery (leaking) $14.35. VAT is $1.44. (Total $15.79.)

Enter the credit notes in Oliver's Purchases Returns Book and post the entries to the appropriate ledger accounts.

3. C. Hosking is in the confectionery trade and during June 20. . receives the following credit notes. Enter them in his Purchases Returns Book and post the entries to the appropriate ledger accounts.

1 June	Seager's Sweet Co.—one jar bullseyes @ $7.50 (suspected contamination with noxious fluid). VAT is $0.75. (Total $8.25.)
13 June	The Liquorice Allsorts Co.—empty jars and tins $3.45. VAT is $0.34. (Total $3.79.)
14 June	Read's Liqueur Chocolates Ltd—one box liqueur chocolates damaged in transit $2.55. VAT is $0.26. (Total $2.81.)
27 June	Seager's Sweet Co.—empty jars and tins $3.20. VAT is $0.32. (Total $3.52.)

9.13 The Sales Returns Book

When a firm receives goods returned from a dissatisfied customer, it draws up a credit note and sends off the top copy to the customer. The second copies of all the credit notes are used to complete the accounting records in the books of the seller, who has now received back the goods returned. As shown in Fig. 9.5, the credit notes form a neat pack because they are all prepared by the same firm, the seller. Entries are exactly similar to those for the Purchases Returns Book, but the postings are different. The customers' accounts are credited, and the Sales Returns Account is debited with the total returns for the month. The VAT Account is debited with the value of the VAT.

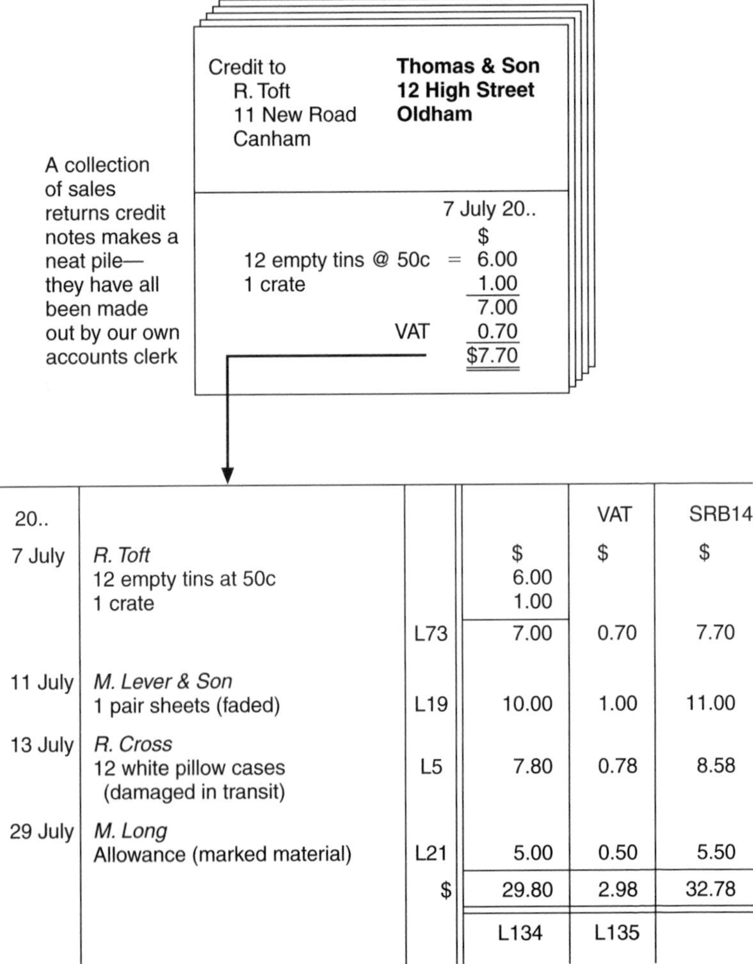

20..				VAT	SRB14
7 July	*R. Toft*		$	$	$
	12 empty tins at 50c		6.00		
	1 crate		1.00		
		L73	7.00	0.70	7.70
11 July	*M. Lever & Son*				
	1 pair sheets (faded)	L19	10.00	1.00	11.00
13 July	*R. Cross*				
	12 white pillow cases (damaged in transit)	L5	7.80	0.78	8.58
29 July	*M. Long*				
	Allowance (marked material)	L21	5.00	0.50	5.50
		$	29.80	2.98	32.78
			L134	L135	

Fig. 9.5 Entering credit notes in the Sales Returns Book

Posted to the ledger the entries appear as follows:

R. Toft Account L73

		$			$
20..			20..		
1 July Sales	SDB6	27.50	7 July Sales Returns	SRB14	7.70

M. Lever and Son Account L19

		$			$
20..			20..		
3 July Sales	SDB6	116.60	11 July Sales Returns	SRB14	11.00

R. Cross Account L5

		$			$
20..			20..		
12 July Sales	SDB8	77.55	13 July Sales Returns	SRB14	8.58

M. Long Account L21

		$			$
20..			20..		
20 July Sales	SDB15	72.05	29 July Sales Returns	SRB14	5.50

Sales Returns Account L134

		$
20..		
31 July Sundry debtors	SRB14	29.80

VAT Account L135

		$
20..		
31 July Sundry debtors	SRB14	2.98

You should now practise entering credit notes in the Sales Returns Book, using Exercises Set 15.

9.14 Exercises Set 15. The Sales Returns Book

1. Tess Cratchett is a wholesaler supplying goods to customers in the domestic appliances field. In June 20.. she issues the following credit notes. Enter them in her Sales Returns Book and post the entries to the appropriate ledger accounts.

4 June	Pram Centre Co. One 'Slumbercot', damaged in transit, $24.50. VAT is $2.45. (Total $26.95.)
6 June	E. Proctor and Co. Ltd. One coach-built pram, wheels strained, $43.45 and one pram basket, damaged by paint in transit, $3.00. VAT is $4.64. (Total $51.09.)
16 June	R. Rudd. One electric toaster, faulty switch, $13.25. VAT is $1.32. (Total $14.57.)
27 June	T. W. Russell. One 'Vacumetric' vacuum cleaner, motor burnt out, $84.65. VAT is $8.46. (Total $93.11.)

2. Paul Luscombe supplies toys to retailers. During January 20.. the following were credited by him for goods returned. Record these credit notes in his Sales Returns Book and post the entries to the appropriate ledger accounts.

4 January	Macaulay and Co. One train set, motor mechanism faulty, $38.25. VAT is $3.82. (Total $42.07.)
11 January	Petersen and Co. One 'Hobbyhorse' scooter and trailer, painting defective, $27.25. VAT is $2.72. (Total $29.97.)
19 January	T. Barr. A set of twelve boxes of bricks, contents incorrectly packed, $18.58. VAT is $1.86. (Total $20.44.)
29 January	T. R. Portray Ltd. One train set, motor mechanism faulty, $28.25. VAT is $2.82. (Total $31.07.)

3. A. Robens is a supplier of office equipment. Record the following credit notes in his Sales Returns Book for the month of February 20.. and post to the ledger to achieve a correct double entry for the month.

1 February	T. MacAndrew and Co. Ltd returned goods as follows: one typist's chair $35.50 (metalwork rough), one filing cabinet (lock faulty) $79.75. VAT is $11.52. (Total $126.77.)
4 February	R. Robertson returned a cabinet (wrong colour) $83.95. VAT is $8.40. (Total $92.35.)
14 February	M. Loach returned crates charged to him at $5.50. VAT is $0.55. (Total $6.05.)
25 February	R. Ingrams returned a filing cabinet (lock faulty) $79.75 and metal trays (swivel mechanism faulty) $15.50. VAT is $9.52. (Total $104.77.)

9.15 Revise and Test 9. Business Documents for Purchases and Sales

Cover the page with a sheet of paper; then read one question at a time.

Answers	*Questions*
—	**1.** Why are business documents important?
1. Because every activity and every transaction starts with a business document (or its electronic equivalent).	**2.** What are the chief documents?
2. a) invoices; b) debit notes; c) credit notes; d) statements; e) cheques; f) receipts; g) petty cash vouchers; h) formal legal documents, such as hire purchase documents, contracts, mortgages, etc.	**3.** Why are invoices, debit notes credit notes and statements the most common documents?
3. Because they document the purchases and sales of goods and services; transactions which happen millions of times a day.	**4.** What is an invoice?
4. An invoice is a business document which is made out whenever one person sells goods to another.	**5.** Is it a legal document?
5. No, but it may be used as evidence of a contract of sale.	**6.** How many copies are there?
6. Usually three, four, or five.	**7.** Name the five possible copies, and the places they go to.

7. Top Copy, sent to purchaser, who puts it in his/her Purchases Day Book; Second Copy, goes to Accounts Dept. to go in Sales Day Book; Delivery Note, goes to stores and is taken by carman for signature on delivery; Advice Note, goes to stores to be wrapped with goods so that purchaser can check them; Representative's Copy, goes to commercial traveller who took the order.	**8.** How long do we keep invoices?
8. Six years.	**9.** Why six years?
9. Because the Statute of Limitations says if six years expire from the time an ordinary contract is made, then legal action cannot be taken.	**10.** What must an invoice have on it?
10. a) Names and addresses of both parties; b) exact description of goods; c) value of goods; d) terms and conditions of sale; e) it often has E&OE; f) VAT details.	**11.** What does E&OE mean?
11. Errors and Omissions Excepted	**12.** Why is this put on the invoice?
12. Because otherwise a genuine mistake or omission would perhaps not be able to be corrected.	**13.** What is a debit note?
13. It is a business document which is made out whenever an invoice has an undercharge on it, to correct the undercharge. It is treated just like an invoice.	**14.** What else could it be used for?
14. To charge carriage or insurance	**15.** What is a Credit Note?

15. It is a business document made out whenever a buyer returns goods to a seller.	**16.** Who makes it out, and when?
16. The seller makes it out when the goods return to his premises.	**17.** What safety device prevents anyone mistaking a Credit Note for an invoice?
17. A Credit Note is always made out in red and may be printed with the red ribbon on the typewriter.	**18.** How many copies are made out?
18. Two copies.	**19.** Where do they go?
19. One copy is sent to the debtor who returned the goods; he/she enters it in the Purchases Returns book. The other copy is kept by the seller and entered in his/her Sales Returns Book.	**20.** Why might a debtor return goods?
20. a) Because they were damaged on arrival; b) because they were the wrong size, colour, or type; c) not up to sample; d) not up to specification; e) goods sent 'on approval' and not required.	**21.** Can the buyer return the goods because he/she has decided after all that they are not wanted?
21. No. This would be a breach of contract.	**22.** Why else do we send someone a Credit Note (two reasons)?
22. a) If an invoice is incorrect, having been overstated, a Credit Note will put it right; b) if goods are not satisfactory, the buyer may agree to have them at a cheaper price instead of returning them. This is called 'an allowance' and it is made by sending him/her a Credit Note.	**23.** How many questions did you get right out of 22? Go over the page several times.

UNIT 10

Books of Original Entry.
2. The Three-column Cash Book

10.1 Cash Account and Bank Account

The simplest accounts that we have considered so far are perfectly satisfactory for keeping a record of transactions with debtors and creditors, or a record of assets purchased or expenses paid. Any clerk usually has access to the ledger and performs a variety of entries in it as and when required. But with two accounts—the Cash Account and the Bank Account—it is much less desirable to permit everybody in the office to make entries. These accounts are very vulnerable, and a skilled clerk might make entries which would enable him or her to extract either cash or cheques for personal use. Such losses are called *defalcations*. To prevent such losses it is usual to remove the Cash Account and the Bank Account from the ledger and put them instead into a special book called a cash book. The person appointed to keep this book is called the *cashier* and is generally a mature and trusted member of staff. This book is the *book of original entry* for all payments and receipts, whether in cash or by cheque.

As a further safeguard against defalcations, it is a common practice to insure the firm against theft by the cashier. This type of insurance is called a *fidelity bond* (fidelity means faithfulness) and is usually taken out for a considerable sum such as $10 000.

10.2 The Three-column Cash Book

If the Cash Account and Bank Account are to be in use frequently throughout the day as cash and cheques are entered, there is little point in having them on separate pages with a consequent need to turn over from one account to another continually. It is much better to have them set out side by side and have both accounts visible at once. This will enable the cashier to make entries as they occur in the appropriate account without the need to turn over when the items dealt with change from cash to cheques, or vice versa. At the same time a third column can be added in which cash discount allowed or cash discount received can be recorded. Fig. 10.1 shows such a ruling, which is called a 'three-column cash book'. You should obtain a supply of this type of paper from a stationer. It is best to buy a small booklet, rather than a loose-leaf pad, since loose-leaf paper of this sort is very inconvenient unless a proper binder is available. When opening the booklet the first page is only half a page of a three-column cash book—leave this blank, and start on the following page.

Consider the entries shown in Fig. 10.1, and the notes on the pages that follow.

(a) Debit Side

(Money or cheques being received by the business of B. Jones.)

1 May. Opening balances. Note that there are two opening balances because there are two accounts, side by side on the page. Both may be written on the same line, and the folio number J1 indicates that the entry has come from the Journal Proper.

1 May, etc. Cash sales. Every day the till has been cashed up, and the cash sales figure entered into the cash column. These are the daily takings of the business.

1 May. R. Miles. Clearly R. Miles must have been a debtor, who has paid Jones $54.75. The entry of $2.88 in the discount column indicates that the total amount of his debt was really $57.63, but Jones allowed him discount of 5 per cent. This is known as a *settlement discount*. Similar entries also occur on 2, 3, 4 and 5 May, but only some are given discount.

2 and 5 May. Two *contra entries*. First consider the entry of $580.00, *which appears on both sides of the book*. On the debit side, $580.00 is received by the Bank Account from the Cash Account. On the credit side $580.00 is given by the Cash Account to the Bank Account. Clearly these two entries are connected—money is taken out of the till and banked for safe keeping—but the Cash Account and the Bank Account are affected in opposite ways. The name *contra entries* is given to these entries (*contra* is Latin for 'opposite') since the two entries appear opposite one another, and a letter 'C' is inserted in both folio columns. This is the only place in the accounts where both halves of a double entry are visible on the same page, for it is the only place where two ledger accounts appear side by side.

Sometimes, of course, the contra entry is of the opposite type: we need at times to withdraw funds from the bank to ease a shortage of cash. This might happen on days when wages are paid, or when the proprietor needs cash to attend sales or auctions. On these occasions a cheque is presented at the bank and the cash required is withdrawn. The effect on the cash book would be the opposite of the entry shown on 2 May, the Bank Account being credited and the Cash Account debited.

The entry of $1 250.00 on 5 May is exactly similar to the entry of $580.00 on 2 May.

Three-column Cash Book (B. Jones)

CB1

Dr. Date	Details	Folio	Discount allowed	Cash A/c	Bank A/c	Date	Details	Folio	Discount received	Cash A/c	*Cr.* Bank A/c
20..			$	$	$	20..			$	$	$
1 May	Opening balances	J1		37.50	4050.00	1 May	Signwriters Ltd	L15			116.30
1 May	Sales	L5		342.80		1 May	Cash purchases	L19		124.50	
1 May	R. Miles	L29	2.88		54.75	1 May	M. Lodge	L37			73.85
2 May	Sales	L5		362.60		1 May	Soloman and Co.	L26			161.50
2 May	P. Marchant	L30			47.95	2 May	Hedell and Co.	L38	7.06		134.20
2 May	Cash	C			580.00	2 May	Bank	C		580.00	
3 May	R. Marshall	L31	2.00		38.00	2 May	Postage	L16		22.50	
3 May	M. Runes	L32	0.60		11.40	3 May	Cash purchases	L19		112.25	
3 May	Sales	L5		425.80		3 May	M. Liversy	L39	6.67		126.75
4 May	Lomax Ltd	L33		7.70		4 May	R. Sterling	L40			31.40
4 May	Sales	L5		235.50		4 May	Repairs	L20		43.50	
5 May	Coral and Co.	L34	2.50		47.50	4 May	Travelling expenses	L21		16.25	
5 May	Sales	L5		1640.80		4 May	M. Rostov	L41	12.28		233.25
5 May	Cash	C			1250.00	5 May	Bank	C		1250.00	
						5 May	Drawings	L131			140.00
						5 May	Wages	L22		117.50	
						5 May	Balances	c/d		786.20	5062.35
			$7.98	$3052.70	$6079.60				$26.01	$3052.70	$6079.60
			L48						L49		
8 May	Balances	B/d		786.20	5062.35						

Fig. 10.1 A three-column cash book

(b) Credit Side

(Money or cheques being paid out by B. Jones.)

1 May.	Signwriters Ltd were paid by cheque an amount of $116.30.
1 and 3 May.	On each of these occasions goods were purchased for cash.
1, 2, 3 and 4 May.	Various creditors were paid by cheque. Some of them gave discount since Jones had paid promptly.
2, 4 and 5 May.	Payments for postage, repairs, travelling expenses and wages were made in cash.
5 May.	Jones, the proprietor, drew a cheque (Drawings) for his own use.
5 May.	The cash book was totalled, and the balances discovered and carried down ready to start the next week's records. The till would also be checked to ensure that the cash balance was in fact correct in the till.

Notice that when the cash book columns are totalled, no balance is struck on the discount columns, which are not accounts but only *memorandum columns*.

10.3 Double-Entry and the Three-column Cash Book

Throughout this book, we always try to think in double-entry terms, since this is the basic principle behind accounting. In practice, however, cashiers and book-keepers specialize in particular aspects of the work, and do not stop what they are doing to go and make the other half of a double entry. For example, the cashier may have over a hundred cheques in the post each morning. He records them one after the other in the cash book—two or three pages of entries, perhaps. He then sends George—the messenger—down to the bank with the paying-in book and the cheques. He also calls Ann—a trainee accountant—and asks her to 'post the cash book' for him. So Ann is the one who actually carries the cash book upstairs to the offices where the various ledgers are, and posts the ledger.

So, although you should always think in double entries, don't make the mistake of imagining that every debit entry is immediately followed by a credit entry. The accountant will have devised a system which ensures that these double entries are always done, but in a way which is economical of effort in the office.

The posting of the three-column cash book is illustrated in Fig. 10.2. Note especially that all items on the debit side of the cash book are posted to the credit side of the accounts, except the total of the Discount Allowed Account, while all items on the credit side of the cash book are posted to the debit side of the accounts, except the total of the Discount Received Account. An explanation of this is given in Unit 10.4, but first you should look at the ledger postings from the three-column cash book shown in Fig. 10.1.

The ledger entries from the debit side of the cash book are as follows:

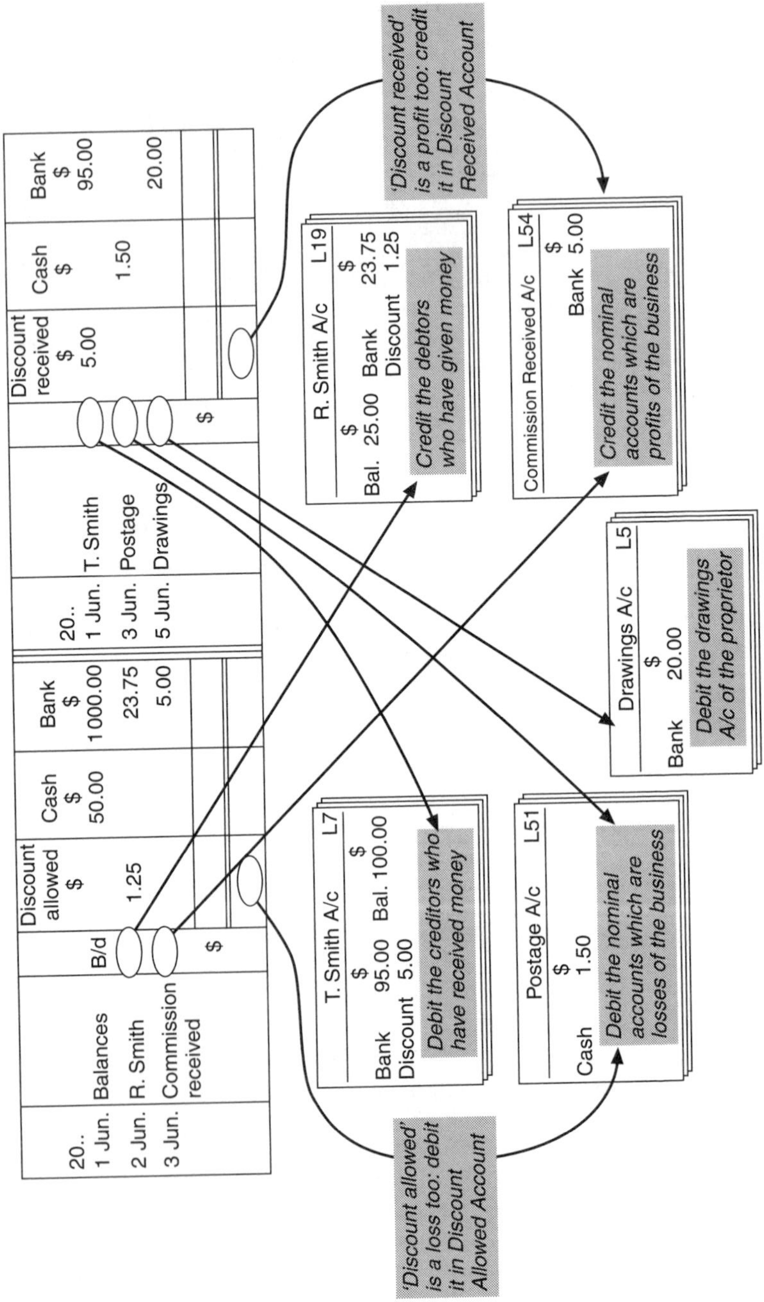

20..			Discount allowed $	Cash $	Bank $	20..			Discount received $	Cash $	Bank $
1 Jun.	Balances	B/d		50.00	1000.00	1 Jun.	T. Smith		5.00		95.00
2 Jun.	R. Smith		1.25		23.75	3 Jun.	Postage			1.50	
3 Jun.	Commission received				5.00	5 Jun.	Drawings				20.00
		$						$			

Fig. 10.2 Posting the three-column cash book

Sales Account L5

			20..			$
			1 May	Cash	CB1	342.80
			2 May	Cash	CB1	362.60
			3 May	Cash	CB1	425.80
			4 May	Cash	CB1	235.50
			5 May	Cash	CB1	1 640.80

R. Miles Account L29

20..			$	20..			$
30 April	Balance	B/d	57.63	1 May	Bank	CB1	54.75
				1 May	Discount Allowed	CB1	2.88

The accounts of P. Marchant, R. Marshall, M. Runes, Lomax Ltd and Coral and Co. will be similar.

Discount Allowed Account L48

20..			$
5 May	Sundry debtors	CB1	7.98

The ledger postings from the credit side of the cash book are as follows:

Signwriters Ltd Account L15

20..			$	20..			$
1 May	Bank	CB1	116.30	30 April	Balance	J1	116.30

The accounts of M. Lodge, Soloman and Co., Hedell and Co., M. Liversy, R. Sterling and M. Rostov will be similar.

Purchases Account L19

20..			$
1 May	Cash	CB1	124.50
3 May	Cash	CB1	112.25

The Postage Account, Repairs Account, Travelling Expenses Account and Wages Account will be similar.

Drawings Account L131

20..			$
5 May	Bank	CB1	140.00

Discount Received Account L49

			20..			$
			5 May	Sundry creditors	CB1	26.01

10.4 Why the Totals of the Discount Accounts do not Change Sides

One of the commonest causes of an incorrect Trial Balance is the mis-posting of the totals of the Discount Allowed and Discount Received Accounts. These are the only two accounts which are *not* posted from the cash book to the opposite side of the nominal accounts. The explanation is as follows.

Consider the entries in the example above relating to R. Miles's payment of $54.75, in full settlement of his account of $57.63, on 1 May 20... The double entries are as follows:

Debit entry in cash book:	*Credit entry* in Debtors Ledger
$54.75 (Bank A/c)	(R. Miles A/c): $54.75 cash
	$2.88 discount

Clearly this is not a proper double entry, because the entry in the cash book of $2.88 in the Discount Allowed column is only an entry in a memorandum column. It is not an entry in an account. Therefore, to correct this lack of a proper double entry we need an entry on the debit side of some account. As we can see in Unit 10.3, the double entry is achieved when we *debit* the Discount Allowed Account with $7.98, which is the total of the discounts allowed during the week, and includes the $2.88 allowed to R. Miles. This debit is a loss of the business.

The complete double entry therefore is as follows:

Debit entry:	*Credit entry* in R. Miles A/c:
$54.75 in the Bank A/c	$54.75 cash
$2.88 in the Discount Allowed A/c (part of the $7.98)	$2.88 discount

Similarly the Discount Received Account must be *credited* with the profit made when discounts are received for prompt payments.

10.5 Documents and the Three-column Cash Book

The documents chiefly connected with the cash book are the cheque, the statement and the receipt.

(a) Cheques

A cheque is defined as *an unconditional order in writing addressed to a banker, signed by the person giving it, requiring the banker to pay on demand a sum certain in money either to the bearer of the cheque, or to a particular named person, or to that person's order.*

In the cheque illustrated in Fig. 10.3, A. Trader is instructing the banker to pay R. T. Jenkins the sum of $40.00, or order. This is an 'order' cheque, which means that if R. T. Jenkins cares to do so, he can pass the cheque on to a third person, after ordering the bank to pay that third person by writing 'Pay A. N. Other, signed R. T. Jenkins' on the back of the cheque.

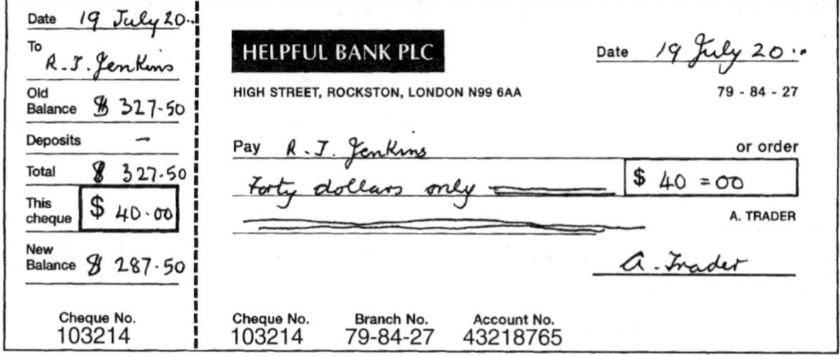

Fig. 10.3 An open cheque and its stub

The number of cheques (and electronic movements of funds) is enormous. At the time of writing in London alone 8.4 million transactions are cleared every day, at a total value of £5700 million (roughly $8500 million). In view of the likelihood of errors creeping in, the Cheques Act 1957 gives certain protections to the paying banker and the collecting banker. Most of the legal aspects of cheques need not concern us here, but it is important to consider the distinction between 'open' cheques, 'crossed' cheques, 'account payee' cheques and 'special crossings'.

(i) Open cheques The cheque in Fig. 10.3 is an open cheque – it has no crossing (see below). An open cheque may be cashed over the counter of a bank, so it is difficult to stop a thief from enjoying the proceeds of a stolen one.

(ii) Crossed cheques have two parallel lines drawn or printed across them. Traditionally the words 'and Co.' were inserted between the lines, but this is no longer necessary for the crossing to be legally valid. Such a cheque is said to be 'crossed generally', and the effect of the crossing is to make the cheque payable only through a banker for entry into a bank account. There is no restriction on a simple crossed cheque as to the account into which it must be paid. Thus a cheque sent to Mrs Brown, who does not have a bank account, may be paid into T. Smith's account if she *endorses* the cheque over to him (that is, if she writes on the back of it 'Please pay T. Smith' and signs her name). Since 1992 it is usual to write the words 'A/c Payee' or 'A/c Payee Only' between the lines. Under the Cheques Act 1992 such cheques are only valid between the parties and cannot be paid into any account except the payee's own account. If such a cheque is presented at the bank for the credit of another account, it will be refused. This change in the law has reduced the theft of cheques.

(iii) Special crossings Here the bank is named between the crossing lines, and the cheque may only be cleared into an account at the named bank. This is called a 'special crossing'.

These crossings are illustrated in Fig. 10.4.

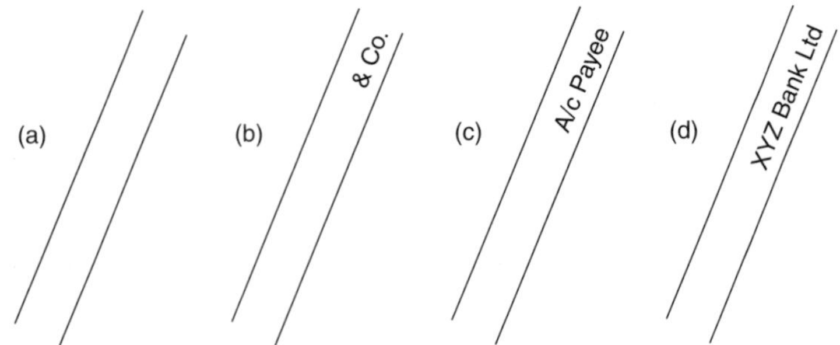

Fig. 10.4 Cheque crossings: (a), (b), (c) general crossings; (d) a special crossing

(b) Bank Statements

Each month banks send a statement to each customer showing all the transactions that have taken place in their account during the previous month. These are computerized statements in 'running-balance style' (see Section 2.9).

The arrival of the monthly statement gives the cashier a chance to check the Cash Book against the Bank Statement and investigate any discrepancy. This is called 'Bank Reconcilation' and is fully explained in Unit 16.

Bank statements are not sent out on the last day of each month, because the banks have millions of statements to process. They therefore use a procedure called 'cyclical billing' in which about 5% of statements are sent out each day. If you ask your bank for a monthly statement, you might find that it arrives on the ninth day of the month, and on the ninth day of each month thereafter.

(c) The Paying-in Book

When cheques are received from debtors they have to be paid into the bank. Most firms receive a number of cheques each day and it is customary to pay them in the same day unless banking is particularly difficult, as in some country areas. The opportunity is generally taken to pay in cash takings at the same time. A paying-in book, supplied free of charge by the bank, usually contains about fifty perforated paying-in slips and either duplicate copies or stubs on which the details may be written. A typical slip is shown in Fig. 10.5. The list of cheques paid in is made out on the back of the slip and the total only is then carried overleaf to the front of the form.

The bank cashier will check the cheques and the total, check the cash paid in, and stamp and initial both the slip and the carbon copy (or stub). The slip will be retained by the bank. The paying-in book, with the receipted copy, will be returned to the person lodging the cheques with the bank, who will take it back to the firm's cashier.

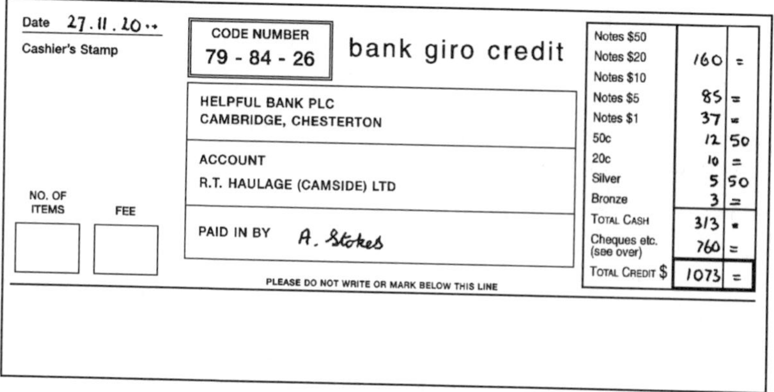

Date 27.11.20..
Cashier's Stamp

CODE NUMBER
79 - 84 - 26

bank giro credit

HELPFUL BANK PLC
CAMBRIDGE, CHESTERTON

ACCOUNT
R.T. HAULAGE (CAMSIDE) LTD

NO. OF ITEMS

FEE

PAID IN BY A. Stokes

PLEASE DO NOT WRITE OR MARK BELOW THIS LINE

Notes $50		
Notes $20	160	=
Notes $10		
Notes $5	85	=
Notes $1	37	=
50c	12	50
20c	10	=
Silver	5	50
Bronze	3	=
TOTAL CASH	313	=
Cheques etc. (see over)	760	=
TOTAL CREDIT $	1073	=

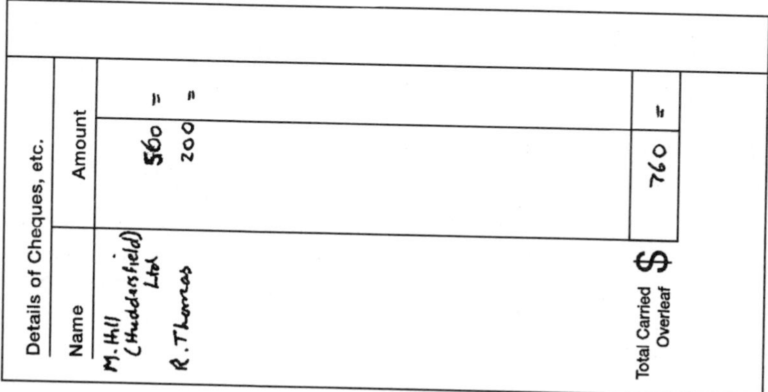

Details of Cheques, etc.

Name	Amount
M. Hill (Huddersfield) Ltd	560 =
R. Thomas	200 =
Total Carried Overleaf $	760 =

Fig. 10.5 A paying-in slip (both sides)

(d) The Cheque-book Stub

Where a cheque is made out and torn out of a cheque-book to be sent to the payee the sender requires a record of the amount paid. This is provided by the completion of a stub, which is left in the cheque-book (see Fig. 10.3).

(e) Receipts

At one time a receipt was made out for every sum of money paid, as proof of payment. Every debtor is entitled to demand a receipt but under the Cheques Act 1957 the cheque itself, if stamped 'paid' by the banker, is a receipt for the money. This has rendered many receipts unnecessary, although a debtor is still legally entitled to demand one. Most firms who receive payments by cheque do not send a receipt unless specifically requested to do so.

Where a receipt is required it is usual to use a receipt book. The top copy of the receipt is perforated and is generally backed by adhesive. After it has been written out and carbon-copied on to the page below, the top copy is torn off and stuck to the bill or invoice presented with the payment. This is proof of payment by the debtor, and can be produced as evidence in a court of law.

A typical receipt is shown in Fig. 10.6.

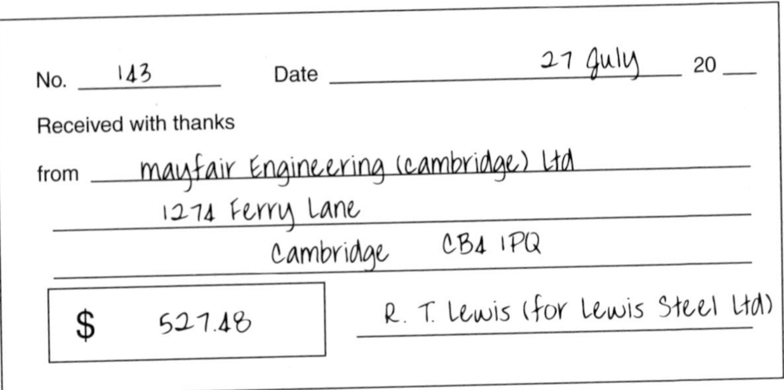
No. 143 Date 27 July 20__

Received with thanks

from Mayfair Engineering (Cambridge) Ltd
1274 Ferry Lane
Cambridge CB4 1PQ

$ 527.48

R. T. Lewis (for Lewis Steel Ltd)

Fig. 10.6 A receipt for payment rendered

10.6 VAT and the Cash Book

Some of the entries in the cash book are affected by VAT, in particular cash sales and cash purchases. Since we must collect VAT from our customers, all sales tickets are marked up inclusive of VAT, and the takings in the tills are always made up partly of sales and partly of VAT. To recognize this, we must write in 'Cash sales plus VAT' in the details column of the three-column cash book and, when posting this to the ledger, we must take the sales to the credit side of Sales Account and the VAT element to the credit side of VAT Account.

To calculate the VAT element in cash sales, we must use the *VAT fraction*—a very important concept. The VAT fraction is the proportion of the total price paid which consists of VAT. For instance, if a company fixes its price for a product at \$100 and VAT is charged at a rate of 10 per cent, the VAT payable when the product is sold is \$10 and the total paid by the customer is \$100 + \$10, or \$110. The VAT fraction in this case is \$10 ÷ £110, or one-eleventh, that is, at this rate of VAT the total VAT payable is one-eleventh of the total sales of VAT-rated goods. The VAT fraction is worked out similarly for any other rate of VAT.

VAT paid on cash purchases is handled in the same way as that on cash sales, but of course the postings will be to the debit side of VAT Account and Purchases Account. VAT also affects some expense accounts, such as those for repairs and office expenses. Question 5 in the exercises in Unit 10.8 is designed to give you practice in handling VAT in the cash book.

10.7 Cash Flow

The term *cash flow* refers to the way in which liquid funds (money) move in and out of the business; it is important that this flow is kept under control so that funds are always available to meet requirements. Stocking up with goods to meet busy periods brings about heavy cash flows out of the business, while at times of heavy selling the buying function may be reduced to a minimum so that cash flows into the business are greater than outgoings.

Part of this inflow consists of the profits we are making, but whether these profits are available in cash form depends upon the uses to which the cash flows are put. If we have surplus cash available and decide to use it to purchase motor vehicles we may find later that there are no funds to pay out as profits. It is wise to plan ahead with a *cash forecast*, using two columns for each month, a *'budget' column* and an *'actual' column*. An example is shown below.

Cash flow	*January*		*February*		*March*	
	Budget	*Actual*	*Budget*	*Actual*	*Budget*	*Actual*
	$	$	$	$	$	$
1. Cash balance (cash and bank)	3580		10630		−2140	
Receipts:						
2. Sales in cash	12500		9800		13600	
3. Debts collected	3150		2350		3220	
4. Other receipts	420		420		420	
5. Extra capital contributed	–		–		1000	
6. Total receipts (add 2–5)	16070		12570		18240	
7. Total cash available (1 + 6)	19650		23200		16100	
Payments:						
8. Payments for business stock	5340		8500		9200	
9. Wages	2420		2420		2450	
10. Other payments	660		580		580	
11. Capital items	–		13240		–	
12. External payments (add 8–11)	8420		24740		12230	
13. Drawings	600		600		600	
14. Total payments	9020		25340		12830	
15. Final cash balance (7–14)	+$10630		*Deficit* −$2140		+$3270	

Note: Bring in new capital $1000. Ask for bank overdraft $1500.

Clearly, 'other payments' and 'capital items' could be given in greater detail. Time lags have to be taken into account, especially on such matters as 'debts collected' and 'payments for business stock'. It is usual to plan six months ahead, and roll the plan forward every two months.

When the actual receipts and payments are made the figures can be inserted in the 'actual' column. They can then be compared with the budget, and the difference accounted for. An excess payment for business stock might be explained by a favourable opportunity which arose due to another trader's bankruptcy. It might have to be explained by higher prices, and the budgets in the months ahead might need to be adjusted, and a check made on selling prices to ensure that these higher costs were passed on to consumers wherever possible.

Wherever possible *cash flow smoothing* should be carried out. This means that where regular payments fall due at a time of year when general expenditure is heavy, we should see if some of them can be moved to another part of the year when funds are readily available. Thus annual payments for items such as car tax, insurance premiums and pension fund contributions can be moved around by agreement with the organization concerned. To move your motor vehicle insurance to a different time of year, for example, requires only a letter to the insurance company and agreement on an interim payment to provide cover for the few months before the annual payment is paid again on the rearranged date. Similarly new capital expenditure can be scheduled so that payment becomes due at the best time for payment from the business's point of view.

10.8 Exercises Set 16. The Three-column Cash Book

1. Enter the following in D. Swann's cash book (ledger postings are not required):

20..	
1 March	Swann has balances as follows: cash $72.50, bank $1 550.75. Pays A. Driver his account, $100.00 less 5 per cent discount, by cheque.
2 March	Pays R. Jones $38.00 by cheque, receiving $2.00 discount off the account.
3 March	Pays travelling expenses $13.25 (cash) and rates to District Council $214.75, by cheque.
4 March	Pays carriage inwards $21.55 cash. R. Hope pays by cheque $4.75. Gives him discount $0.25.
5 March	Cash sales $903.55. Banks from till $700.00 (contra entry). Pays wages to part-time helper, cash $48.50.

Balance off the cash book on 5 March and bring the balances down ready for business on 8 March 20...

2. Enter the following in D. Hunter's three-column cash book. Invent suitable folio numbers but do not post the entries to the ledger accounts.

20..	
1 May	Balances: cash $28.55, bank $275.65. Pays R. Benjamin $6.50 in cash. Pays postage $4.25 in cash.
2 May	R. Long pays his account of $80.00, which was overdue, in full by cheque.
3 May	Pays rent $125.00 by cheque. Pays M. Morgan's account $72.00 less 5 per cent cash discount by cheque.
4 May	Draws cash from bank for office use, $50.00. Cash purchases $45.00.
5 May	D. Lester sends a cheque for $85.50, being settlement in full of his debt of $90.00. Cash sales for the week $1 275.50. Banks $880.00 for safe keeping. Pays wages in cash $127.50 and postage $11.15. Balances off the books and brings the balances down ready for the next week's work on 8 May.

3. B. Gale's cash book is a three-column cash book. Make the following entries in it for the week shown below. Then balance the book and bring down the balances. Invent suitable folio numbers, but do not draw up the ledger accounts.

20..	
11 November	Balances in hand: cash $672.65, bank $4 250.50. Buys goods for resale, cash $236.50.
12 November	R. Levis pays cash $9.75 in full settlement of her account of $10.00. Pays L. Robbins cheque, $42.75. Receives discount, $2.25.
13 November	Pays for meter hire and connection charges in cash, $37.50 (Light and Heat Account). Sundry expenses $9.42, postage $6.85, both in cash.
14 November	Draws cash from bank for office use $80.00. Receives from D. Delderfield cheque for $92.62 in full settlement of $95.00.
15 November	Pays wages in cash $135.00. Pays for fuel oil in cash $47.50. Pays postage $12.50 cash.

4. Elizabeth Stapleton has a three-column cash book. On 1 December 20.. she has $25.00 in her cash till, but is overdrawn at the bank by $326.55. Open her cash book with these balances (one will be a credit balance) and enter the following items:

20..

1 December	She receives a loan from the bank of $500.00.
2 December	R. Hopkinson is paid $42.56 by cheque, in full settlement of his account of $44.80. M. Giles pays $39.00 to Mrs Stapleton, by cheque in full settlement of a debt of $40.00. Mrs Stapleton withdraws $80.00 from the bank for the cash till. She also pays for repairs to a window, $15.35, in cash.
3 December	R. Lawton pays $117.00 cheque to Mrs Stapleton. The balance of his account, $3.00, is treated as cash discount. M. Glyndeborne, a creditor, is paid $27.25 in cash. Mrs Stapleton pays by cheque $25.60 for stationery, and train fares in cash $13.35.
4 December	Mrs Stapleton purchases goods for resale, $129.50, by cheque. She also pays by cheque $95.00 P. Roche's account of $100.00—the rest is discount.
5 December	She draws a cheque for drawings $80.00, pays wages in cash $64.60. Cash sales for the week total $1 275.00. She banks $850.00 from the cash till, for safe keeping.

Balance off the cash book and bring down the balances. Invent suitable folio numbers, but do not post the entries to ledger accounts.

5. W. Allen's three-column cash book has balances on 15 July 20.. of $5.00 cash and $1 047.15 at the bank. Enter these balances, and the items shown below. Balance off the cash book and bring down the balance. Then post the cash book to the ledger accounts. VAT has been included in this exercise (see Unit 10.6 above).

15 July	Pays postage $4.35 cash. M. Long pays by cheque $23.75 in full settlement of his account for $25.00. Draws $200.00 from Bank Account for office use.
16 July	Purchases in cash of goods for resale $132.50 plus VAT $13.25, travelling expenses $8.50 in cash.
17 July	Allen pays M. Treegrove by cheque $128.70. Also postage $4.85 in cash and repairs $24.25 in cash of which VAT is $2.20. R. Lightfoot clears his account of $200.00 by cheque for $195.00.
18 July	M. Hudson is paid by cheque $28.50, discount received $1.50. R. Thomas pays his account $35.65 by cheque.
19 July	Cash sales $2 112.75, which includes VAT of $192.07. R. Johnson is paid $42.75 by cheque after deducting $2.25 discount from his account. Allen draws $80.00 for personal use from the Bank Account. Wages paid, $96.50 in cash. Banks $1 800.00 from till.

6. Rule up a suitable paying-in slip (similar to Fig. 10.5) and complete it with the following details:

17 December 20.. paid in as follows: 3 × $50 notes, 17 × $20 notes, 18 × $10 notes, 23 × $5 notes, 78 × $1 notes, 56 × 50c coins, 24 × 20c coins, silver $11.80, bronze $4.50. Cheques from M. Lark $273.27 and T. Raisin $34.75.

7. Rule up a suitable paying-in slip (similar to Fig. 10.5), date it for 24 July 20.., and complete it with the following details:

Cheques: M. Smith $38.82, T. Growmore $173.75, M. Lucas $299.75, R. Bugg $133.20. Cash: 23 × $20 notes, 45 × $10 notes, 127 × $1 notes and $15.00 bronze coins.

8. Rule up a blank cheque form with stub (similar to Fig. 10.3). Use it to settle a debt to R. Gould, for $2 632.60, less 5 per cent settlement discount. Instruct the bank to pay R. Gould, or order, the sum required. Use your own name as signature and the date you do the exercise as the date. The old balance on the cheque-book was $3 271.94.

9. Rule up a blank cheque form with stub (similar to Fig. 10.3). Make it out to settle a debt of $610.53, less 5 per cent settlement discount. Instruct the bank to pay M. Loughborough, or order, the sum required. Use your own name as signature and the date you do the exercise as the date. The old balance on the cheque-book was $495.42, but an overdraft has been sanctioned.

10. The following estimates of Tom Smith's cash flow are available for the month of January. Work out a cash flow budget for the month and hence find the balance at the end of the month.

Cash in hand $250; cash at bank $5 250; cash sales $8 648; credit sales $5 240; debts to be settled by customers in the month—previous periods $3 842; one-quarter of this month's credit sales is also expected to be paid in the month; commission received $320; cash purchases $5 260; payments to creditors for business stock in previous periods $2 426; wages $876; capital expenses (buying assets) $1 520; rates $320; drawings $600.

11. The following estimates of Peter Jones's cash flow are available for the month of August. Work out a cash flow budget for the month and determine the balance at the end.

Cash in hand $245; cash at bank $5 384; cash sales $12 756; credit sales $5 960; debts to be settled by customers in the month—previous periods $2 386; one-quarter of this month's credit sales is also expected to be paid in the month; rent received $240; cash purchases $4 580; payment to creditors for business stock $1 241; wages $1 385; capital expenses (buying assets) $1 416; rates $256; drawings $800.

10.9 Revise and Test 10. The Three-column Cash Book

Cover the page with a sheet of paper; then read one question at a time.

Answers	*Questions*
—	**1.** Why do we take the Cash Account and the Bank Account out of the Ledger?
1. a) Because they are busy accounts; b) because they are vulnerable.	**2.** What do we call the theft of money by a trusted employee?
2. Embezzlement.	**3.** What is the missing money called?
3. A defalcation.	**4.** What insurance policies cover this risk?
4. Fidelity bonds.	**5.** Why are there three columns on each side of the Three-column Cash Book?
5. a) One for the Cash Account; b) one for the Bank Account; c) one for the Discount column.	**6.** Do the Discount columns form an account?
6. No. They are only memorandum columns.	**7.** What type of accounts are the Cash Account and Bank Account?
7. They are both real accounts.	**8.** What is the rule for these accounts?
8. a) Debit increases in value; b) credit decreases in value.	**9.** What is a Contra Entry in the Cash Book?
9. A Contra Entry is one where both the debit and credit entries appear on the page at once, one in the Cash Account and one in the Bank Account.	**10.** Can a Contra Entry like this appear anywhere else in the ledger?
10. No—because this is the only place where two accounts are written side by side.	**11.** How do we post the Cash Book to the Ledger?

---

11. a) Everything on the debit side of the Cash Account and Bank Account is posted to the credit side of an account in the Ledger;
b) everything on the credit side of the Cash Account and Bank Account is posted over to the debit side of the Ledger.

12. Is there anything that does not change sides?

---

12. Yes. The totals of the Discount Allowed column and Discount Received column do not change sides.

13. What are the three kinds of Discount?

---

13. Cash Discount, Settlement Discount and Trade Discount.

14. What are Cash Discount and Settlement Discount?

---

14. Amounts deducted from a purchase or a statement paid promptly.

15. When should a debtor pay his/her debts?

---

15. When the period of credit expires, which is usually at the end of the month.

16. What do we call it if debtors do not pay when they should?

---

16. A breach of 'Good Faith'.

17. What are the usual rates of discount?

---

17. $2\frac{1}{2}\%$ and 5%.

18. Suppose you owe $50.00 and receive a statement that allows 5% discount. What do you do?

---

18. Write on the statement below the

total figure	= 50.00
Less 5% Cash Discount	= 2.50
Cheque enclosed	$47.50

and send a cheque for $47.50.

19. What do 'Terms Cash Net' or 'Terms Strictly Nett' mean?

---

19. They mean that no Cash Discount is allowed.

20. What is Trade Discount?

20. It is a reduction in the catalogue price of a branded good to enable the retailer to make a profit when he/she sells at this catalogue price.

21. What are the usual rates of Trade Discount?

---

21. 10–45% are quite common.

22. When is the rate of Trade Discount small?

---

22. When the turnover is rapid, i.e. chocolates, cigarettes.

23. When is it large?

---

23. When the items are slow-moving, i.e. furniture.

24. Why is it large with these items?

---

24. To enable the retailer to cover overhead expenses of a longer period.

25. Who writes the Trade Discount on the invoice?

---

25. The supplier before he sends it out.

26. Does cash discount go in the books?

---

26. Yes. It is entered in the Cash Book and posted to the Ledger.

27. Does Trade Discount go in the books?

---

27. It is entered in the Day Book but is *never* posted to the Ledger.

28. Is there a Trade Discount Account?

---

28. No. It never goes in the Ledger.

29. Go over the page again if necessary.

UNIT 11

Books of Original Entry.
3. The Petty Cash Book

11.1 The Imprest System

There are many minor items of expenditure in any office which are too trivial to justify an entry in the main cash book. It would interrupt the cashier's work to be asked for money for bus fares, postage and other small items. At the same time all such expenditures must be honestly and accurately accounted for. The solution is to appoint a *petty cashier*, who will be responsible for paying for all such minor items, recording them in the *petty cash book*. Usually it is convenient to appoint the person in charge of the mail as petty cashier.

The petty cash book is kept on the *imprest system*, which is a system whereby a certain sum of money is advanced for a particular purpose. The sum advanced will be deemed adequate for the purpose, say $50.00 or $100.00 for a week, depending on the needs of the business. The cashier credits the cash book with this amount and it is debited in the petty cash book. The petty cashier then pays the money out as the need arises for postage stamps, travelling expenses and so on, and at the end of the week balances the book and takes it to the cashier for checking. The cashier then 'restores the imprest', making it up again to the original sum.

Advantages of the Imprest System

The advantages of the imprest system are as follows:

(a) It saves the time of the chief cashier, who is a busy person with heavy responsibilities.

(b) It trains young staff to be responsible about money and accurate in accounting for it.

(c) The sum impressed is small, and unlikely to prove much of a temptation either to the person in charge of it or to others in the office.

(d) It enables a great saving to be effected in the posting of small items to the ledger accounts, since it uses an analysis system which collects these small items together into weekly or monthly totals. These are then posted to the ledger accounts. Individual items such as small payments to creditors are entered in a column headed 'Ledger accounts'.

11.2 The Petty Cash Book

This may be described as an extension of the three-column cash book. It is clearly a part of the double-entry system, for the sums debited into it from the cash book are then credited out for the various purposes required. The items spent thus become either losses or (if spent on durable items) assets of the business. As such, in both cases, they become debits in the respective accounts. An example of the petty cash book is given in Fig. 11.3, and explained in the notes facing it (pages 158–9). Please read these now.

11.3 The Petty Cash Voucher

Every transaction has its original document, which is entered in the book of original entry and leads to postings in the ledger accounts. For the petty cash book this takes the form of a *petty cash voucher* (Fig. 11.1)—these vouch for (declare to be honest) the expenditure concerned, and usually have to be signed by some authorized person. Wherever possible, the voucher should be supported by evidence from outside the business that the expenditure has been made—for example, a bus ticket, a till receipt (Fig. 11.2) or a receipt for a registered letter. All such items are carefully preserved and pasted or clipped to the vouchers; the petty cashier or the member of staff concerned must make sure that the voucher carries enough detail for it to be understood by the staff member who authorizes or checks the payments. The vouchers are numbered and filed in numerical order for subsequent inspection by senior members of the staff or by the auditors.

Petty Cash Voucher Folio PCV19
Date 27 July 20..

For what required	AMOUNT $	c
Train fares to London	11	20
Train fares to Beccles	9	35
	$ 20	55

Signature K. T. Roberts

Passed by A. A. Kenningham

Fig. 11.1 A petty cash voucher

HAWKINS LTD
STATIONERS AND PRINTERS
BARCHESTER
VAT No. 999-9999-99

12 FEB 20..

Envelopes	1	1.17	
Paper clips	1	35	
Treasury tags	1	1.05	
Tippex fluid	1	86	
Pencils 2	@ 21c	42	
		3.85	TL
		10.00	AT
		6.15	CH

Fig. 11.2 Documentary support for a petty cash outlay

11.4 Posting the Petty Cash Book to the Ledger

As shown in Fig. 11.3, every item on the debit side of the petty cash book must appear in the credit side of an account elsewhere, while every credit entry must be debited to some loss, or some asset account. Considering these postings, the debit side has only three items, two of them receipts of imprest money from the chief cashier. Each must have its credit entry elsewhere.

The credit entry for the original imprest will be in the Bank Account, while the money for the telephone call, and any other sums received at any time by the petty cashier, are entered as credit entries in the account affected. For example, the sums received for staff private telephone calls are credited to Telephone Expenses Account, reducing the losses suffered on this account.

Telephone Expenses Account L5

20..			$	20..			$
31 Mar.	Bank	CB27	172.50	4 Apr.	Petty cash receipt	PCB5	1.24
30 June	Bank	CB36	166.45	10 July	Petty cash receipt	PCB9	1.31
30 Sept.	Bank	CB54	171.90	3 Dec.	Petty cash receipt	PCB27	0.48

The credit entries on the petty cash book are debited into the accounts concerned. Now you can see how useful the analysis system is for collecting together the tiny disbursements for postage, travelling expenses and so on. These items are posted to the debit side of the 'loss' accounts concerned, while the items in the special column headed 'Ledger accounts', which cannot be posted as one figure, are posted separately to their ledger accounts, the folio number being inserted in the folio column alongside each amount posted.

Although VAT has been disregarded in Fig. 11.3 a single extra column could be used to collect it together and carry it to the VAT Account.

You should now try some of the exercises given below. You will need to rule up petty cash paper, unless you buy paper that is already ruled.

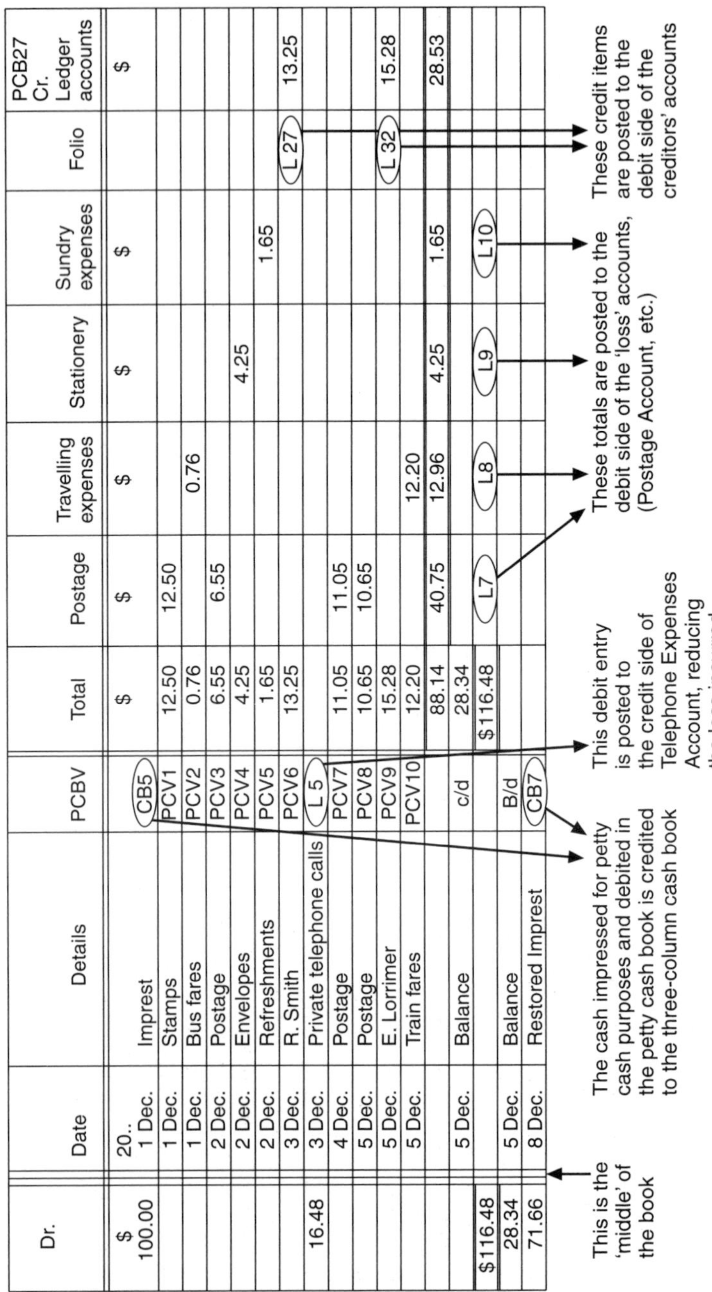

Dr.	Date	Details	PCBV	Total	Postage	Travelling expenses	Stationery	Sundry expenses	Folio	PCB27 Cr. Ledger accounts
$	20..			$	$	$	$	$		$
100.00	1 Dec.	Imprest	CB5							
	1 Dec.	Stamps	PCV1	12.50	12.50					
	1 Dec.	Bus fares	PCV2	0.76		0.76				
	2 Dec.	Postage	PCV3	6.55	6.55					
	2 Dec.	Envelopes	PCV4	4.25			4.25			
	2 Dec.	Refreshments	PCV5	1.65				1.65		
	3 Dec.	R. Smith	PCV6	13.25					L 27	13.25
16.48	3 Dec.	Private telephone calls	L 5							
	4 Dec.	Postage	PCV7	11.05	11.05					
	5 Dec.	Postage	PCV8	10.65	10.65					
	5 Dec.	E. Lorrimer	PCV9	15.28					L 32	15.28
	5 Dec.	Train fares	PCV10	12.20		12.20				
				88.14	40.75	12.96	4.25	1.65		28.53
	5 Dec.	Balance	c/d	28.34						
$116.48				$116.48	L7	L8	L9	L10		
28.34	5 Dec.	Balance	B/d							
71.66	8 Dec.	Restored Imprest	CB7							

This is the 'middle' of the book
The cash impressed for petty cash purposes and debited in the petty cash book is credited to the three-column cash book
This debit entry is posted to the credit side of Telephone Expenses Account, reducing the loss incurred
These totals are posted to the debit side of the 'loss' accounts, (Postage Account, etc.)
These credit items are posted to the debit side of the creditors' accounts

Fig. 11.3 The petty cash book (for simplicity's sake VAT has been disregarded)

Notes on Fig. 11.3

(a) The pages are not divided down the centre since very few entries refer to money received. Hence the debit side is reduced, in most rulings, to a single money column, or perhaps a date column, details column and money column. In the ruling shown, the details are written in the right-hand column for both sides of the book, but cash received is placed over on the debit side.
(b) The chief item received is the original imprest, $100.00. Other items include the money paid by staff for private telephone calls. Sales of brochures and similar small items are recorded in this way in some firms.
(c) Moneys disbursed are recorded on the credit side and then analysed out into a number of analysis columns which serve as collection columns for a large number of small items. Thus all the postage is collected together in the 'postage' column.
(d) Certain payments cannot be added together in this way; for example, the payments to Smith and Lorrimer must be posted to the personal accounts of these creditors. Similarly the purchase of any small asset for office use would be posted to Office Equipment Account. A special column at the end headed 'Ledger accounts', which has a folio column alongside, enables these items to be posted separately to their respective accounts.
(e) When the petty cash book is balanced off, a line is drawn right across the figures on the credit side, and all the columns are added up. Then the analysis columns *only* are closed with a double line, the total column being left open. The analysis columns are cross-totted, to check that they total the same as the total column. If they do not, the error must be discovered.
(f) The balance of cash in hand can now be calculated by taking the total spent from the total received. The answer to this calculation should be the sum of money left in the petty cash till. This is inserted in the credit column, the book is balanced off and the balance brought down.
(g) The book and the till are then presented to the cashier, who checks the petty cashier's work and restores the imprest by refunding the money paid out, less any sums recovered for items such as private phone calls. The restored imprest gives the petty cashier, for the new week, the sum the management has authorized to be advanced each week. It would be bad accounting practice to give a further $100.00 since this would raise the sum in the care of the petty cashier to $128.34, which is more than this management deems necessary for this particular function.
(h) The postings are explained in Unit 11.4 below.

11.5 Exercises Set 17. The Petty Cash Book

1. State briefly what you would do if you were asked to check the accuracy of the entries in a firm's analytical petty cash book kept on the imprest system.

2. What are the advantages of a petty cash book kept on the imprest system? Explain how the various entries are posted to the ledger accounts, using as illustrations the following items:

(a) the total of the analysis column headed 'Postage';
(b) an entry in the ledger accounts column reading 'L. Shire $4.25';
(c) the entry on the debit side which reads 'restored imprest';
(d) an entry on the debit side reading 'staff purchases $4.25'.

3. Using petty cash paper open D. Benson's petty cash book on 7 April 20.., with an initial balance of $4.35. Then enter the cash given to the petty cashier by the proprietor to restore the imprest to $60.00, and the following transactions:

7 April	Pays postage $2.22 and bus fares $0.64; pays R. Collins's Account $4.32.
8 April	Receives from a member of staff $0.75 for a private telephone call; pays postage $3.36, stationery $4.20.
9 April	Pays postage $2.24, train fares $4.65; gives dustman $0.50.
10 April	Purchases letter scales for post department $11.27; pays office cleaner $9.25, also cleaning materials $5.00.
11 April	Pays postage $2.49; buys cakes for typist's birthday $3.28.

The petty cash book has analysis columns for postage, travelling expenses, office cleaning expenses, stationery and sundry expenses, and a ledger accounts column where payments to creditors, or for the purchase of assets, are recorded. Balance the book at the end of the week, ready to present to the proprietor for checking. Invent suitable folio and petty cash voucher numbers.

4. Enter the following items in R. Norris's petty cash book which has five columns, for postage, fares, office sundries, repairs and ledger accounts. Invent sensible folio numbers and petty cash voucher numbers.

20..	
15 July	Draws petty cash imprest $50.00; pays postage $3.50.
16 July	Pays fare $1.28; buys ball of string $0.80; pays plumber to clear drain $12.75, and a creditor, T. Bright, $4.75.
17 July	Pays postage $1.55; buys stationery $6.50; buys cleaning materials $3.25.
18 July	Pays R. Jones $4.45; members of staff pay $29.35 for private telephone calls; pays fares $1.16.
19 July	Pays fares $2.35; pays for repairs to door $12.85; pays M. Knight $3.25; pays postage $2.50.

Balance the book and restore the imprest to $50.00.

5. a) Kate Jobling runs her office petty cash on the imprest system, giving the petty cashier a basic imprest of $60.00. The book has five columns for postage, travelling expenses, cleaning, sundry expenses and ledger accounts. Enter the following items, balance off the book at the end of the week and restore the imprest.

20..	
19 March	Balance on book $12.00; imprest restored by proprietor; postage $4.45; bus fares $2.65.
20 March	Pays postage $3.36; a debtor, Tom Jones, calls in and pays a small account $1.35, which the petty cashier accepts and for which he gives a receipt; fares $2.15.
21 March	Postage $4.05. Envelopes and wrapping paper $3.23. Soap and detergents $1.65.
22 March	Pays M. Brogan $3.75. Purchases spirit lamp for postal clerk $3.50 (Office Equipment Account).
23 March	Postage stamps $1.25. Cleaner's wages $25.00.

b) Explain the postings to be made for the entries on 20 March.

11.6 Revise and Test 11. The Petty Cash Book

Cover the page with a sheet of paper; then read one question at a time.

Answers	*Questions*
—	**1.** What does 'petty' mean?
1. Small or unimportant.	**2.** What system is used for Petty Cash?
2. The Imprest System.	**3.** What is an Imprest?
3. A sum of money set aside for a particular purpose.	**4.** What are the advantages of the Imprest System?
4. a) It saves bothering the main cashier; b) little risk, and little temptation; c) trains young staff; d) saves time on posting to the Ledger because of the analysis columns; e) is easily checked.	**5.** Where is the 'middle' of a page in a Petty Cash Book?
5. Set towards the left-hand side of the page.	**6.** Why is this done?
6. Because the petty cashier doesn't often receive money.	**7.** When does he/she receive money?
7. a) When he/she draws the Imprest from the cashier; b) when members of staff pay for telephone calls, etc.	**8.** Why does the credit side need more room than in an ordinary Cash Book?
8. Because there are extra analysis columns.	**9.** What is the point of these analysis columns?
9. To collect together similar minor expenses and to make it possible to post the total each week in only one posting per column.	**10.** Why is the end column different?

10. Because where postings are to either Personal or Real Accounts they must be kept separate. Only expenses for the Nominal Accounts can be added together.	**11.** How do you finish off a Petty Cash Book?
11. a) Add the columns, then add across to check the work; b) find the balance, check that the till is right, balance the books and bring down the balance; c) ask the cashier to restore the Imprest.	**12.** What is the document for which the Petty Cash Book is the Book of Original Entry?
12. The Petty Cash Voucher.	**13.** Where should a Petty Cash Voucher come from ideally?
13. From outside the business.	**14.** As we post the Petty Cash Book what must we write on it?
14. The folio numbers of the ledger accounts to which the expenses have been posted.	**15.** Go over the page again if necessary.

UNIT 12

Books of Original Entry.
4. The Journal Proper

12.1 Opening Journal Entries

Whenever a business is established, the first Journal entry made is the contribution of the proprietor, in the form of capital. This contribution may be in money form, but more often it consists of a variety of assets, some cash, a balance at the bank, premises, motor vehicles and so on. The new business may also already have a few debtors or creditors, for varying amounts.

Let us look at an example.

Example

R. Grimshaw sets up in business on 1 July 20.., with the following assets: cash in hand, \$25.00; cash at bank \$156.00; premises \$12 500.00; furniture and fittings \$2 850.00; motor vehicle \$3 400.00. He has a creditor, Long Loans Ltd, for \$1 500.00. Draw up the Journal entry and open the ledger accounts.

In preparing this Journal entry the assets are listed, and totalled as shown below. The liabilities are then set beside them.

Assets:		*Liabilities:*	
	\$		\$
Cash	25.00	Long Loans Ltd	1 500.00
Bank balance	156.00		
Premises	12 500.00		
Furniture	2 850.00		
Motor vehicles	3 400.00		
	\$18 931.00		\$1 500.00

The assets and liabilities of any business must always balance, yet clearly this is not so here. What is missing? The answer is the Capital Account. We must always calculate the Capital Account and include it in the Journal entry. The calculation is:

		\$
Total assets	=	18 931.00
Less Amounts financed by external creditors	=	1 500.00
Capital	=	\$17 431.00

We can now write the complete opening Journal entry for Grimshaw's new business and open the ledger accounts, as shown in Fig. 12.1.

Although opening entries are usually done on the first day a business starts they are also necessary at other times. For example, a business that has not kept proper records of its affairs may change to using the double-entry system. The first stage of such a change is to open the necessary accounts from an opening Journal entry.

You should now practise several opening entries, using Exercises Set 18 (Unit 12.2).

					J1
20..				$	$
1 July	Cash	Dr.	L1	25.00	
	Bank	Dr.	L2	156.00	
	Premises	Dr.	L3	12 500.00	
	Furniture and Fittings	Dr.	L4	2 850.00	
	Motor Vehicles	Dr.	L5	3 400.00	
	Long Loans Ltd		L6		1 500.00
	Capital Account		L7		17 431.00
	Being assets and liabilities at this date			$18 931.00	$18 931.00

Cash Account L1

20..			$
1 July	Capital	J1	25.00

Bank Account L2

20..			$
1 July	Capital	J1	156.00

Premises Account L3

20..			$
1 July	Capital	J1	12 500.00

Furniture and Fittings Account L4

20..			$
1 July	Capital	J1	2 850.00

Motor Vehicles Account L5

20..			$
1 July	Capital	J1	3 400.00

Long Loans Ltd Account L6

20..			$
1 July	Capital	J1	1 500.00

Capital Account L7

20..			$
1 July	Sundry assets	J1	17 431.00

Fig. 12.1 An opening Journal entry posted to the ledger accounts

12.2 Exercises Set 18. Opening Journal Entries

1. Ruth Marshall sets up in business on 1 October 20.., with a capital of $1 000.00, in cash, which she puts into the bank. Record this opening Journal entry and post it to ledger accounts opened for the purpose.

2. Mike Tyler sets up in business on 1 February 20.., with the following assets: cash in hand $24.00; cash at bank $125.00; premises $22 500.00; motor vehicles $3 472.00 and office equipment $1 350.00. Calculate his capital, and draw up the opening Journal entry. Give a suitable narration.

3. Rosemary Lucas sets up in business on 1 May 20.., with the following assets: cash in hand $48.00; cash at bank $225.00; premises $33 800.00; motor vehicles $5 740.00 and office equipment $2 520.00 Calculate her capital and draw up the opening Journal entry. Give a suitable narration.

4. Stephen Thompson sets up in business on 1 April 20.., with the following assets and liabilities: cash in hand $82.00; cash at bank $1 156.00; premises $32 958.00; plant and machinery $6 440.00; stock $3 650.00. He has two debtors R. Lyons $276.50 and A. Moore $550.50. His only creditor, Lyle Finance Co., is owed $4 268.50. Draw up an opening Journal entry showing the total capital contributed. Post the opening entry to the ledger accounts.

5. Steptoe's son, having completed his education at a local technical college, is about to join his father in the family business. He persuades the old man, who has never kept proper books of account, to agree to this practice in future. Draw up the opening Journal entry for Steptoe and Son on 1 July 20.., the senior partner to have $25 000.00 of the capital allocated to him. The following assets and liabilities exist: cash in hand $85.00; cash at bank $1 876.00; premises and yard $32 800.00; stock of scrap materials $2 185.00; motor vehicles $3 650.00; scales and other equipment $542.50. Debtors: A. Scrapiron $1 285.00, B. Ragdealer $155.50. A bill for motor vehicle repairs is owing to A. Welder $125.00.

12.3 'Bad' Debtors

Whenever a businessman supplies customers on credit, the person supplied becomes a *debtor* of the business. Clearly no one gives credit to customers that are considered unreliable, and when asked to supply goods in this way a trader usually takes up references from other suppliers, or from the customer's bankers. If these references prove satisfactory the trader will then allow goods to be supplied on credit.

It may happen, though, that debtors who have been good customers in the past may find themselves in unforeseen difficulties. Sickness of the proprietor may affect the business, or a change in the general prosperity of the area may affect the purchasing power of the business's customers. A debtor who for some reason cannot meet his/her obligations is called a 'bad' debtor and the debt is spoken of as a 'bad' debt. A bad debt must be written off, a process which requires a Journal entry of some sort. There are three possibilities:

(a) a debt may be entirely bad;
(b) a debt may be partially bad—some settlement being arrived at by which part payment only is received;
(c) a debt written off at an earlier date may be recovered.

These three aspects of bad debts are dealt with below.

12.4 A Debt which is Entirely Bad

On 1 August R. Jones is a debtor for the sum of $50.00. He is found to have left the country, and it is decided to write the debt off as bad.

The solution is to clear the debtor's account by writing it off to Bad Debts Account. A simple Journal entry would be made, thus:

				J5
20..			$	$
1 Aug.	Bad Debts Account Dr.	L21	50.00	
	R. Jones Account	L57		50.00
	Being bad debt written off after discovering that Jones had left the country			

The ledger accounts would appear as shown below. Note that the debtor's account is marked clearly (in red ink) BAD DEBTOR to prevent any further credit being made available.

R. Jones Account L57

20..			$	20..			$
17 May	Sales	SDB1	50.00	1 Aug.	Transfer to Bad Debts A/c	J5	50.00

BAD DEBTOR

Bad Debts Account L21

20..			$
1 Aug.	R. Jones	J5	50.00

12.5 A Debt which is Partially Bad

Sometimes a debtor may make an arrangement with the creditors whereby a certain sum is made available in full settlement of the debt. This is called a *composition* with the creditors, i.e. a voluntary agreement to settle the debt by paying a proportion only. In other cases the debtor will be bankrupted, his or her assets seized and sold for the benefit of the creditors, and the proceeds shared up among them. In both these circumstances the sums received will be debited in the Bank Account or Cash Account, the unpaid portion being written off to Bad Debts Account. For example, suppose that P. Rossiter is adjudged bankrupt on 5 July 20.., and a payment of 10 cents in the $1.00 is authorized from the funds available after the sale of his assets. We are his creditors for $40.00. Here is the Journal entry for this matter.

					J5
20..				$	$
5 July	Bank Account	Dr.	CB7	4.00	
	Bad Debts Account	Dr.	L21	36.00	
	P. Rossiter Account		L69		40.00
	Being bad debt written off at this date on payment by Official Receiver of $4.00 in full settlement				

Posted to the ledger, the accounts would look like this:

Cash Book (bank columns only) CB7

20..			$
5 July	P. Rossiter	J5	4.00

Bad Debts Account L21

20..			$
5 July	P. Rossiter	J5	36.00

P. Rossiter Account L69

20..			$	20..			$
20 April	Sales	SDB5	40.00	5 July	To Bank and Bad Debts	J5	40.00

BAD DEBTOR

12.6 A Bad Debt Recovered

When a debtor's account has been cleared off and the debtor has ceased to trade, the debtor's account will be removed from the ledger and will be stored in a file of 'dead' accounts. Suppose such a debtor wishes to clear his/her name by paying up the debt with interest. The payment will be most acceptable, but there is little point in reviving the 'dead' account. Instead the unexpected profit may be recorded on a special Bad Debts Recovered Account, or on the credit side of the Bad Debts Account where it will offset any bad debts that occur this year. Note that no entry at all is made in the debtor's 'dead' account.

For example, M. Lucas, whose debt of $54.00 was written off last year, pays $56.70 in cash in full settlement on 4 August 20.., being the sum of $54.00 due, plus interest at 5 per cent for one year. Here is the Journal entry for this transaction.

				J1
20..			$	$
4 Aug.	Cash Account Dr.	CB197	56.70	
	Bad Debts Recovered Account	L72		54.00
	Interest Received Account	L73		2.70
	Being M. Lucas's bad debt recovered with interest at 5 per cent per annum			

Posted to the ledger accounts, these entries would now appear as follows:

Cash Book (Cash Account only) CB197

20..			$
4 Aug.	Bad debt recovered and interest recd.	J1	56.70

Bad Debts Recovered Account L72

20..			$
4 Aug.	Cash Account	J1	54.00

Interest Received Account L73

20..			$
4 Aug.	Cash Account	J1	2.70

Mr Lucas has now honoured his debt and it is possible he may wish to do business with us again. If his account is still 'live' in the ledger and has not been archived, we should write a note on the account: 'Debt honoured in full, restored as a bona fide customer'.

Suppose, however, that we do our accounting by computer, and that we are asked for a credit reference on Mr Lucas. If we simply print out his account there is a danger that the enquirer might be told that Lucas is a bad debtor. To avoid this, it would be safer to reopen the account, restoring both the debt and the interest on the debt to M. Lucas's Account. The credit entries shown in L72 and L73 would not alter, except that the wording would change to 'M. Lucas's Account' in each case. The cash book entry for $56.70 would be posted to M. Lucas's Account, and thus show that he has paid the debt with interest.

Now try the following exercises.

12.7 Exercises Set 19. Bad Debts

1. R. Porter, who owes your firm $50.40, dies tragically in a fire at a local cinema. It is decided to write the debt off as a gesture of sympathy to his family. Do the Journal entry dated 19 July 20.. and post it to the ledger.

2. Anne Oldlady owes you $35.00. She is unable to pay, and an Aged Persons Charitable Association asks you to agree to a payment of half the sum in full settlement of her debt. You agree to the composition, and they pay by cheque. Do the Journal entry dated 2 October 20.. and post it to the ledger.

3. Carnival Productions (Westlake) Ltd are debtors for goods supplied for $34.50. They are insolvent, and the liquidator pays $0.80 in the $1.00 by cheque. Show the Journal entry dated 11 July 20.. and post to the ledger accounts.

4. A. Partner, whose debt of $30.00 was written off five years ago, sends a payment of $38.28 cash on 8 December 20.. representing payment in full with 5 per cent compound interest. Record the payment in the Journal Proper and post the entry to the ledger accounts.

5. A. Sloman sends postal orders on 1 June 20.. for $113.00, being a debt of $100.00, interest $5.00 and legal expenses $8.00. The debt (which was written off one year ago) is thus fully recovered, as are the legal charges incurred. The postal orders are paid into the bank. Draw up a suitable Journal entry and post it to the cash book and the ledger.

12.8 Revise and Test 12. The Journal Proper

Cover the page with a sheet of paper; then read one question at a time.

Answers	*Questions*
—	**1.** What is the Journal Proper?
1. It is the day book which records the basic facts about all the more difficult transactions which take place.	**2.** Which transactions don't go in the Journal Proper?
2. Routine transactions on buying, selling and supplying goods and services.	**3.** Where do these routine transactions go?
3. In the Purchases Day Book, the Sales Day Book, the Purchases Returns Book and the Sales Returns Book.	**4.** List the types of entry that go in the Journal Proper.
4. a) Opening entries (to start a new business or a new year); b) bad debts; c) purchase of assets; d) sale of worn-out assets; e) depreciation entries; f) dishonoured cheques; g) correction of errors; h) formal documents, like leases, mortgages, hire purchase transactions, etc.	**5.** What does each Journal entry finish with?
5. A narration, beginning with the word 'Being'. For example 'Being bad debt written off at this date.'	**6.** What is significant about every Journal entry?
6. It will be a perfect double entry in almost every case.	**7.** What is an Opening Journal Entry?
7. An entry made on the very first day of a new business to get the accounts open and ready for business.	**8.** What are the rules for making an Opening Journal Entry?

8. a) List all the assets brought in by the proprietor. They will all be debited in the asset accounts (including any Cash or Bank balances in the three-column Cash Book; b) list any liabilities. These will be creditors (either trade creditors [for goods] or financial creditors [for capital]); c) take the total liabilities from the total assets and you find the capital of the proprietor. This is the capital value of the assets provided by the proprietor and it is credited to Capital Account; d) when the Opening Journal Entry is posted to the Ledger and the Cash Book the accounts are all opened and trading can begin.	**9.** What is the Journal Entry for a bad debt?
9. Debit Bad Debts Account to record the loss. Credit the debtor's account to clear the account off our books.	**10.** What is the Journal entry for a partially Bad Debt?
10. Debit Cash Account (or Bank Account) with the money coming in. Debit Bad Debts Account with the part lost. Credit the debtor's account with the full amount to clear it from the books.	**11.** What is the entry for a Bad Debt recovered?
11. Debit the Cash or Bank Account with the money that comes in. Credit the Bad Debts Recovered A/c with the amount of the debt. If any interest or legal charges were also recovered credit Interest Received Account or Legal Charges Recovered Account.	**12.** Go over the page again until you are sure of all the answers.

UNIT 13

Books of Original Entry. 5. More on the Journal Proper

13.1 The Purchase of Fixed Assets

Fixed assets are items purchased for use in the business which bring it some benefit and increase its profit-making capacity, *on a long-term basis*. Items with a short life, such as stationery and postage stamps, are called *consumables* and are *current assets*. The dividing line between the two is drawn at a lifetime of one year. Items that last longer than a year are regarded as fixed assets of the business; common examples are land and buildings, furniture and fittings, plant and machinery, motor vehicles and computers.

13.2 Recording the Purchase of Fixed Assets

When fixed assets are purchased it is usual to enter the purchase in a Journal entry, which is then posted to the ledger. The rules are:

(a) Always debit the asset account (for it has received value).
(b) Any VAT charged on the asset is input tax, which can be reclaimed by businesses (except for VAT paid on motor cars) and should therefore be debited in the VAT Account.
(c) Credit *either:*
   (i) Cash Account, if cash was paid for the asset, *or*
   (ii) Bank Account, if the asset was paid for by cheque, *or*
   (iii) the supplier, if the asset was supplied on credit, the account being payable at a later date.

As with opening Journal entries (see Unit 12.1) it is usual to include a short explanation of the entry, or narration. In the narration of a Journal entry about the purchase of assets it is helpful to record any details which could be used to help prove ownership at some future date. Computers and cars, for example, are often stolen, and if stolen goods are recovered their identity may need to be established. Here is an example of such an entry:

					J1
20..				$	$
15 Jan.	Furniture and Fittings Account	Dr.	L77	232.50	
	VAT Account	Dr.	L143	23.25	
	Sheer Beauty Ltd		L85		255.75
	Being the purchase on credit of a showcase for the foyer (Ref No. stl/50 874)				

Posted to the ledger, the accounts would read as follows:

Furniture and Fittings Account L77

20..			$				
1 Jan.	Balance	B/d	875.00				
15 Jan.	Sheer Beauty Ltd	J1	232.50				

VAT Account L143

20..			$				
15 Jan.	Sheer Beauty Ltd	J1	23.25				

Sheer Beauty Ltd Account L85

				20..			$
				15 Jan.	Furniture and Fittings	J1	255.75

You should now try some ‘purchase of asset’ entries from the exercises that follow.

13.3 Exercises Set 20. The Purchase of Fixed Assets

1. R. Lever is in business as a stationer. On 1 Jan. 20.. he purchases twelve Bettaview display cabinets at a total invoice price of $2 156.00 (of which $196.00 was VAT), paying by cheque. The serial numbers of the cabinets are A1856 to A1867. Record the purchase in Lever's Journal Proper, and post the entry to the ledger accounts.

2. Mollie Robertson is in business as an accountant. On 16 July 20.. she purchases from Olivetti Ltd a computer valued at $1 375.00 plus $137.50 VAT, on the usual monthly credit terms. Record this entry in her Journal Proper. The reference number of the machine is E1/20785. Post the entry to the ledger accounts.

3. A. Printz is an exporter to the European market. On 1 August 20.. he purchases a motor vehicle for roll-on, roll-off services to Holland and Germany. The price is $29 500.00 plus $2 950.00 VAT, payable on monthly credit terms to Heavy Autos Ltd. The vehicle number is W1456 AJH, and the VIN (Vehicle Identification Number) is JN1000 B1100527. Record the purchase in Printz's Journal Proper, and post to the ledger.

4. Sally Debbotista is in the silverware trade. On 31 May 20.. she purchases a security vehicle, registration number W2957AJH, for transporting goods to clients' premises. It costs $17 656.00 plus $1 765.60 VAT. Half is paid at once by cheque and the balance at the end of the month. It is supplied by Special Motors Ltd. Record the entries in the Journal Proper.

Note: From this point in the book onwards, '.00' will be omitted from all round figures. It will only appear in displayed text where fractions of $1 (i.e. cents) need to be shown.

13.4 The Principles of Depreciation

Every capital asset, that is, every purchase resulting from capital expenditure, wears out as the years go by. This is usually referred to as 'fair wear and tear', a decline in value of the asset as it renders service to the business. People who own motor vehicles know how lucky they are if they last longer than five years of steady wear and tear. By the end of that time repair bills begin to increase and breakdowns are more frequent. Sooner or later the inconvenience arising from the vehicle's uncertain behaviour leads to a decision to replace it.

The accounting term for this declining value of assets is *depreciation*. The principles that underlie depreciation may be listed as follows.

(a) *Every year should carry a proper share of the burden of business expenses*, and these expenses should clearly include capital losses incurred through fair wear and tear. Only if a year carries its full share of the losses of the business shall we arrive at a correct profit figure.

(b) *These losses should be spread evenly over the lifetime of the asset.* Occasionally, however, there are very good reasons for not doing so. For example, where a machine was only used in the manufacture of a particular article, and the number of articles made varied from year to year, there might be some case for depreciating the machine according to the use made of it in a particular year. It is much more usual to equalize the charges made.

(c) *The assets must be correctly valued on the Balance Sheet.* If we do otherwise, the Balance Sheet does not give a 'true and fair view' of the assets of the business as required by law for limited companies. Although there is no such legal requirement for sole traders and partnerships, it is still desirable that assets should be accurately valued on their Balance Sheets as well.

The ways in which these principles are carried into effect vary slightly from one accountant to another, but the following solutions are common.

(i) We can credit the asset account with the amount of the depreciation (to reduce the asset to its true value) and debit this amount (the loss in value due to fair wear and tear) direct to the Profit and Loss Account—thus taking the loss into account. The disadvantage of this method is that the Profit and Loss Account has a debit entry for each type of asset.

(ii) We can credit the asset account with the amount of the depreciation and debit this amount in a Depreciation Account, which then collects the depreciation for all the various fixed assets in the one account. The Depreciation Account is then cleared to the Profit and Loss Account by a single closing Journal entry when the final accounts of the business are being compiled.

(iii) A third method, particularly used for companies but also adopted by accountants for other firms, is explained in Unit 13.10.

Whichever of the three solutions is used, losses caused by depreciation must appear eventually as losses on the Profit and Loss Account.

13.5 The Methods of Depreciation

There are several different methods of depreciation used in business, some of which are very elaborate and difficult to calculate. Here we will consider the three commonest methods in use. These are:

- the 'equal-instalment' method, or 'straight-line' method;
- the diminishing-balance method;
- the revaluation method.

13.6 The Equal-instalment Method

With this method, the asset is written down in value each year by the same amount, the sum being calculated by the use of a formula, as follows:

$$\textit{depreciation charge} = \frac{\textit{cost price of the asset} - \textit{estimated residual value}}{\textit{estimated lifetime in years}}$$

Imagine that a machine costs $10 000, and that a further $2 500 is needed to erect it into position and install access features for the product it is to process. It is estimated to have a working life of ten years, and at the end of the time it will fetch $1 500 on sale to scrap dealers. The depreciation charge on the basis of the formula given above will be ($12 500 − $1 500) ÷ 10 = $1 100 per annum.

The asset will appear on the books as follows:

Machinery Account L167

20.. (year 1)		$	20..			$
1 May New machine		10 000	30 April Depreciation A/c			1 100
1 May Installation etc.		2 500	30 April Balance		c/d	11 400
		$12 500				$12 500
20.. (year 2)		$	20..			$
1 May Balance	B/d	11 400	30 April Depreciation A/c			1 100
			30 April Balance		c/d	10 300
		$11 400				$11 400
20.. (year 3)		$				
1 May Balance	B/d	10 300				

and so on over the years, until

20.. (year 10)		$	20..			$
1 May Balance	B/d	2 600	30 April Depreciation A/c			1 100
			30 April Balance		c/d	1 500
		$2 600				$2 600
20.. (year 11)		$				
1 May Balance	B/d	1 500				

At this point steps will be taken to dispose of the machine.

The Depreciation Account in year 1, for example, would record the depreciation for machinery as shown below (together with several other items on which depreciation had been deducted). The total depreciation would then be cleared to the Profit and Loss Account, reducing the profits for the year by the amount of loss suffered due to 'fair wear and tear'.

Depreciation Account L295

20..		$	20..		$
30 April	Machinery	1 100	30 April	Profit and Loss A/c	4 681
30 April	Motor Vehicles	1 342			
30 April	Fixtures and Fittings	385			
30 April	Office Equipment	1 854			
		$4 681			$4 681

Advantages and Disadvantages of the Equal-instalment Method

(i) Advantages

1. It is easy to understand, and the calculations are simple.
2. The valuation of the asset appearing on the Balance Sheet each year is reasonably fair, and complies with the Companies Act's requirements in the vast majority of cases.

(ii) Disadvantages

1. If a further machine is purchased, the amount now required to be written off needs to be recalculated (with a percentage method of depreciation such as the diminishing-balance method discussed below, this is not necessary).
2. The charge to the Profit and Loss Account increases over the years, for in the first year or two repairs will be uncommon, but as the machine gets older it will require more frequent attention. Suppose that in year 1 the repairs cost $80, and in year 8 they cost $650. The charge against the Profit and Loss Account in year 1 totals $1 180 and in year 8 it is $1 750.

Both these criticisms are overcome by the use of the diminishing-balance method.

13.7 The Diminishing-balance Method

Under the diminishing-balance method a fixed percentage of the diminishing value of the asset is written off each year; for example, the depreciation percentage might be agreed at 20 per cent and one-fifth of the value at the start of the year be written off each year. The calculations involved in deciding the correct percentage are outside the range of our study here, but in the Machinery Account just considered they work out to about 19 per cent. Taking 20 per cent as a more convenient figure, you will see that this is one-fifth of the diminishing value of the asset, a much larger percentage than was written off under the equal-instalment method. The actual deductions, however, come to about the same figure over the full lifetime of the asset, because the percentage deduction is being calculated only on the diminishing balance, and consequently the amount written off gets less every year. The figures over the ten-year period are shown below. As you see, the balance has come down lower than the residual value of $1 500. This is because the deductions were made at an approximate rate of 20 per cent, instead of the more precise figure of 19 per cent.

Machinery Account L167

20..	(year 1)		$	20..			$
1 May	New machine		10000	30 April	Depreciation A/c		
1 May	Installation, etc.		2500		(20%)		2500
				30 April	Balance	c/d	10000
			$12500				$12500
20..	(year 2)		$	20..			$
1 May	Balance	B/d	10000	30 April	Depreciation A/c		2000
				30 April	Balance	c/d	8000
			$10000				$10000
20..	(year 3)		$	20..			$
1 May	Balance	B/d	8000	30 April	Depreciation A/c		1600
				30 April	Balance	c/d	6400
			$8000				$8000
20..	(year 4)		$				
1 May	Balance	B/d	6400				

and so on over the years until

20..	(year 10)		$	20..			$
1 May	Balance	B/d	1678	30 April	Depreciation A/c		336
				30 April	Balance	c/d	1342
			$1678				$1678
20..	(year 11)		$				
1 May	Balance	B/d	1342				

Advantages and Disadvantages of the Diminishing-balance Method

(i) Advantages

1. It gives a more even charge against the profits, since the decreasing charges for depreciation each year cancel out the increasing charges for repairs. Thus the charges shown in the example above over ten years might be as follows:

		$
Year 1	Depreciation	2 500
	Repairs (say)	80
	Charge to Profit and Loss Account	$2 580

		$
Year 10	Depreciation	336
	Repairs (say)	2 200
	Charge to Profit and Loss Account	$2 536

   Of course this is only a very 'rough and ready' way of equalizing the charge to Profit and Loss Account, but it is better than the previous method from this point of view.
2. No recalculation is necessary when further assets are purchased.
3. Except for assets with a very short life, it better reflects the fact that, for many items, the annual loss of value is greatest in the early years of their lives.

(ii) Disadvantages

1. The percentage figure to be deducted each year is difficult to calculate (although there is an accepted formula).
2. For assets with a very short life, the percentage figure is so high that it becomes ridiculous. Thus, an asset with a life of two years only would need to be written off by 99 per cent to remove it from the books in two years. Thus a $1 000 machine would be reduced by $990 in the first year—leaving a $10 balance, and 99 per cent of that, $9.90, would be written off in year 2. Clearly this is not a very sensible percentage, and in particular it gives an unsatisfactory balance sheet value at the end of year 1. The asset would appear on the books after half its useful life at one-hundredth of its original value. This hardly gives a 'true and fair view' of the asset as required by the Companies Act.

13.8 The Revaluation Method

Sometimes it is impossible to treat a particular kind of asset in the ways outlined. For example, in farm accounting a Herd Account cannot be depreciated in a regular way at all. Animals are maturing, bearing young, changing and declining as the years ago by. It is ridiculous to say that a cow has depreciated 10 per cent in the year, especially if she has borne two calves. Similarly certain engineering tools are very expensive to make, but their value cannot be said to decline in use, and indeed they may even appreciate in value. Examples are the very expensive presses for stamping out plastic articles. These may cost $5 000 or $10 000 to produce, but if well cared for will last for a long time.

At the end of a year we have to decide whether these items have or have not depreciated. The best solution is to *revalue* them. A valuer (preferably an independent one) is asked to appraise them and give a figure for their value. The difference in value can then be taken into account, or the better method is to write off the whole of the old value to Profit and Loss Account and bring in the whole of the new value as a profit. Consider the following example.

Example

Farmer Giles's Herd Account shows a value on his books at the start of his financial year, 1 September 20.., of $12 785. On 31 August the herd is valued at $13 980. Record this in his Journal and post to the appropriate accounts.

Date	Particulars	Folio	$	J27 $
20..				
31 Aug.	Profit and Loss Account Dr.	L192	12 785	
	Herd Account	L73		12 785
	Being valuation of herd at start of year transferred to Profit and Loss Account at this date			
31 Aug.	Herd Account Dr.	L73	13 980	
	Profit and Loss Account	L192		13 980
	Being new valuation of herd at close of year brought on to books as an asset at this date			

Herd Account

Date	Particulars	Folio	$	Date	Particulars	Folio	$
20..				20..			
1 Sept.	Balance	J1	12 785	31 Aug.	Profit and Loss A/c	J27	12 785
1 Sept.	Profit and Loss A/c	J27	13 980				

Profit and Loss Account L192

Date	Particulars	$	Date	Particulars	$
20..			20..		
31 Aug.	Herd Account	12 785	31 Aug.	Herd Account	13 980

An alternative method would have been to find the increased value—in this case $1 195—and enter it to the debit of Herd Account and the credit of Profit and Loss Account.

13.9 The Amortization of Leases

When a lease on property is obtained, it is usually granted for a term of years. This phrase includes fractions of a year, so that some leases may only be weekly or monthly leases. Special considerations enter into the use of property in this way. If a lease is for ten years when it is obtained, usually on payment of a lump sum, it will only have nine years to run one year after purchase, eight years to run two years after purchase, and so on. In the final year the tenant must either move out, or renew the lease. The old leasehold rights are said to have died, and can only be brought to life by a new agreement. Clearly we ought to recognize the gradual dying away of the leasehold rights over the course of the lifetime of the lease and this is called *amortization* (from the French word *mort*—dead).

Amortization is simply a special case of the equal-instalment method of depreciation, there being no residual value on the lease. The amortization charge is found by the formula

$$\textit{amortization charge} = \frac{\textit{original cost of lease}}{\textit{lifetime of the lease}}$$

It would simply be entered into Depreciation Account, after a simple Journal entry, thus:

					J25
				$	$
20..					
31 Dec.	Depreciation Account	Dr.	L86	250	
	Lease Account		L155		250
	Being amortization of one year's life of a twenty-year lease				

Depreciation Account L86

			$				
20..							
31 Dec.	Lease A/c	J25	250				

Lease Account L155

			$				$
20..				20..			
1 Jan.	Bank A/c (Lease purchase)	J5	5000	31 Dec.	Depreciation A/c	J25	250
					Balance	c/d	4750
			$5000				$5000
31 Dec.	Balance	B/d	4750				

Note: The depreciation shown on the Depreciation Account (L86) will of course be cleared to the Profit and Loss Account with other depreciation items, to take account of the loss suffered by the amortization of the lease during the year.

13.10 Depreciation and the Companies Acts 1985–89

These British Acts, which consolidate the Companies Acts 1948–81, attempt to ensure that an investor, considering whether to invest in a company, shall have available all the information needed to make a wise decision. One unsatisfactory aspect of company accounts before 1948 was that there was no need to show whether the assets listed were new, or old and worn-out. The Acts require that assets are shown 'at cost—less the total depreciation to date'. Thus the plant and machinery shown below reveals to the investor that it is largely obsolete equipment.

Fixed assets:	*At cost*	*Less depreciation*	*Present value*
Plant and machinery	$100 000	$96 000	$4 000

To assist in making these figures available, it is usual, instead of writing down the asset on the asset account each year, to leave it on the asset account at its original cost. The depreciation deducted is collected in a Provision for Depreciation Account, and is only deducted from the asset account when the asset is finally disposed of. Here are the entries from the accounts referred to above.

Plant and Machinery Account L2

20..		$
1 Jan. Bank A/c	CB5	100 000

Provision for Depreciation on Plant and Machinery Account L73

			$
Yr. 1	Depreciation A/c	J5	16 000
Yr. 2	Depreciation A/c	J9	16 000
Yr. 3	Depreciation A/c	J16	16 000
Yr. 4	Depreciation A/c	J25	16 000
Yr. 5	Depreciation A/c	J33	16 000
Yr. 6	Depreciation A/c	J38	16 000

You should now work through some of the exercises in depreciation that follow.

13.11 Exercises Set 21. Depreciation

1. Mills Ltd purchased a machine by cheque for $1 500 on 1 January 20... Its probable working life was estimated at ten years and its probable scrap value at the end of that time as $200. It was decided to write off depreciation by equal annual instalments over the ten years. Show the Machinery Account for the first two years.

2. A. Thompson purchased a machine by cheque for $2 800 on 1 January 20... Its probable working life was estimated at eight years and its probable scrap value at the end of that time was $400. It was decided to write off depreciation by equal annual instalments over the years. Show the Machinery Account for the first three years.

3. T. Brown started business on 1 January 20.. and on that date purchased machinery by cheque for $3 000. He decided to close his books each year at 31 December and to depreciate machinery by 10 per cent of the original cost for each year of use, placing the depreciation in a Provision for Depreciation Account and assuming a scrap value of nil at the end of the life of the machines.

On 1 July of the following year he purchased by cheque another machine for $600. You are asked to show

a) the Machinery Account as it would appear in the ledger from 1 January;
b) the Provision for Depreciation Account for years 1 to 3 inclusive;
c) how this asset would appear in the Balance Sheet at 31 December of year 3.

4. On 1 January 20.. Philippa Wye bought a machine for $1 800 by cheque. It was decided to write off depreciation by the diminishing-balance method, at 25 per cent per annum. Show the Machinery Account for the first two years.

5. John Mainway started business as a haulage contractor on 1 January 20... He bought one new lorry for $12 000 by cheque. His business expanded, and on 1 July 20.. of the following year he purchased lorry number 2 for $14 000. On 1 October of the next year he purchased lorry number 3, also for $14 000.

At the end of year 4, he engaged an accountant to prepare Final Accounts for each of his four years in business. You are required to write up his Motor Lorries Account allowing for depreciation at the rate of 20 per cent of original cost per annum (i.e. on the fixed-instalment method).

Your calculations, showing how the figure for depreciation each year is reached, must be shown separately underneath the account.

6. On 1 January of year 1 Tom Smith, a haulage contractor, purchased four motor lorries for $12 400 each by cheque. At the end of each year depreciation is provided for at the rate of 20 per cent per annum on the straight-line method, this depreciation being recorded in a separate Provision Account.

A fifth vehicle was purchased on 1 July of year 3 for $14 700 (cheque) and a sixth on 1 April of year 4 for $16 400 (cheque).

Show the Motor Lorries Account and the Provision for Depreciation Account for the years 1, 2, 3 and 4, and the Balance Sheet entry on 31 December, year 4.

7. Marketing Ltd provides for depreciation of its machinery, at 20 per cent per annum on the diminishing-balance system. This depreciation is calculated by reference to the number of months during which the machines are in use. It is carried to a special Provision Account.

On 31 December 20. . the machinery consisted of three items, purchased as under:

On 1 January, year 1	Cost $3 000 cheque
On 1 July, year 2	Cost $12 400 cheque
On 1 October, year 3	Cost $6 400 cheque

Show the entry in the firm's ledger for the Machinery Account and the Provision for Depreciation Account for the three years. All calculations should be shown.

8. A. Manufacturer had the following new machine in his factory at 1 January 20. . (year 1):

	Cost
Machine No. 1	$5 600

He purchases the following machines on the dates indicated, by cheque.

		Cost
Machine No. 2	Mar. 1, year 2	$12 400
Machine No. 3	Apr. 1, year 2	$13 200
Machine No. 4	Aug. 1, year 3	$11 800
Machine No. 5	Dec. 1, year 3	$11 700

Depreciation is written off at the rate of 24 per cent per annum on cost to the nearest $1, new machines being depreciated from the date of purchase.

Show the Machinery Account and the Provision for Depreciation on Machinery Account for the three years, together with your calculations. Show also the Balance Sheet entry on 31 December, year 3, for the fixed asset Machinery Account.

13.12 The Sale of Worn-out Assets

When an asset comes to the end of its useful life, it is disposed of at the best price it will fetch. The useful life of an asset may come to an end for several reasons. It may break down, and be sold for scrap. It may be constantly needing attention, so that production is interrupted and it becomes cheaper to buy a new machine. It may have been rendered obsolete by more modern devices, so that although it is still in good working condition a newer model will raise productivity.

Practically always there will be some final adjustment to the Profit and Loss Account as the asset is disposed of. At the time of the sale we shall have the asset on the books at a known *book value*. This value may be the value on the asset account, if depreciation has been written off the asset from time to time so that the diminishing balance of value only is left; alternatively, if the procedure laid down by the Companies Acts 1985–89 (see Unit 13.10) is being used, the book value of the asset will be the value on the asset account *less* the depreciation written off to date in the Provision for Depreciation Account. At the time of sale there are three possibilities:

(a) The book value of the asset at the time of sale may be greater than the price we can obtain for it. For example, suppose that a van is valued at $800 on the Motor Vehicles Account but the most the garage will give us as trade-in value is $430. Clearly we have under-estimated the depreciation over the years and the extra $370 will have to be written off as a loss. It is usual to debit it to the Sale of Vehicles Account.
(b) The book value of the asset may be exactly the same as the sum offered by its purchaser. This is rather unlikely; it means our estimates of profit over the years have been exactly right. No final adjustment is necessary.
(c) The book value of the asset may be less than the actual value on the day of disposal. This frequently happens, because some firms follow a policy of reducing assets to a very nominal value of $1. When finally disposed of, even for scrap, most machinery and equipment will fetch more than $1. Some readjustment of profit is made on disposal to take account of the overdepreciation in earlier years. Examples of these three situations are given below, with the appropriate Journal entries.

The rules for these entries are:

(i) Always remove the asset completely from the asset account. This means that the asset account must be credited with the book value. If a provision account has been used this has to be done in two stages. The asset will still be on the asset account at the original cost price, and has to be removed by crediting the asset account. The depreciation will be on the credit side of the Provision for Depreciation Account, and has to be removed by debiting the provision account with the correct amount of depreciation.

(ii) Debit the Cash Account (or the Bank Account) with any cash (or cheque) received. If the person purchasing the old asset is not paying at once but only in the usual course of business (i.e. at the end of the month), debit him or her as debtor for the amount due.

(iii) Adjust the Profit and Loss Account by taking the profit on sale, or the loss on sale, to a suitable account, such as the Sale of Machinery Account. This will be cleared to Profit and Loss Account in due course.

Examples 1, 2 and 3 below have been done without using a Provision for Depreciation Account. Example 4 shows what has to be done when a Provision for Depreciation Account is used.

Example 1: Asset Overvalued on the Books

T. Hodges has a motor vehicle valued on 1 November 20.. at $250. He disposes of it to a friend at the best price he can get, $180 in cash, on that day. Show the Journal entry.

					J1
20..				$	$
1 Nov.	Cash Account	Dr.	CB1	180	
	Sale of Vehicles Account	Dr.	L72	70	
	Motor Vehicle Account		L8		250
	Being sale of motor vehicle SJN375 at this date for the best price obtainable				

Example 2: Asset Valued Correctly on the Books

R. Bines has a sewing machine valued at $5 on the Small Machines Account. She disposes of it for cash to an employee at that figure. Show the Journal entry on 1 July 20...

					J1
20..				$	$
1 July	Cash Account	Dr.	CB1	5	
	Small Machines Account		L15		5
	Being sale of sewing machine S12745 at book valuation to Miss R. Jones (employee)				

Example 3: Asset Undervalued on the Books

M. Blanchflower has a Mobilmix cement mixer valued on his books on 30 June at $180. He disposes of it on that date in exchange for a stock of motor-vehicle tyres valued at $300. Show the Journal entry on 30 June 20...

				J1
			$	$
20..				
30 June	Motor Vehicle Spares Account Dr.	L27	300	
	Plant and Machinery Account	L5		180
	Sale of Machinery Account	L72		120
	Being exchange of Mobilmix cement mixer for spare tyres at this date			

Example 4: Use of a Provision for Depreciation Account

On 1 January, year 1, Tom Green, a haulage contractor, purchased four motor lorries for $19 600 each, by cheque. At the end of each year depreciation is provided for at the rate of 20 per cent per annum on the original cost, this depreciation being recorded in a separate Provision Account.

One of these vehicles was sold on 1 January, year 4, for $5 000 paid by cheque. A new lorry is purchased the same day for $22 500, by cheque.

Show the appropriate ledger accounts for the years 1, 2, 3 and 4, and the Journal entry concerning the sale of the asset.

First, the Motor Lorries Account is debited with the value of the vehicles purchased on 1 January, year 1 ($78 400). No other entries need to be made on this account until the sale of one of the vehicles on 1 January, year 4.

Each year the depreciation is written off and credited to Provision for Depreciation on Motor Lorries Account ($15 680 for each of the first three years).

When we sell the lorry on 1 January, year 4, we must take the following actions:

(a) remove the original cost ($19 600) from the Motor Lorries Account;
(b) remove from the Provision for Depreciation Account that part of the depreciation which has been written off this particular vehicle (in this case three years' depreciation at $3 920 per year = $11 760);
(c) adjust for any discrepancy on the realized price of the old vehicle. As the vehicle still has a value on the books of $19 600 – $11 760 = $7 840, and we are able to sell it for only $5 000, there is a loss on sale of the vehicle of $2 840. This sum, identified as 'loss on sale of motor lorry', will be taken to the debit side of the Profit and Loss Account at the end of the year.

The Journal entry for this and the ledger accounts are shown below.

					J56
20..				$	$
1 Jan.	Bank Account	Dr.	CB57	5000	
	Provision for Depreciation Account	Dr.	L28	11760	
	Sale of Motor Lorry Account	Dr.	L59	2840	
	Motor Lorries Account				19600
	Being loss on sale of motor lorry at a price below its book value				

Motor Lorries Account L27

20..	(year 1)		$	20..	(year 4)		$
1 Jan.	Bank	CB5	78400	1 Jan.	Bank and Provision for Depreciation	J56	19600
20..	(year 4)				Balance	c/d	81300
1 Jan.	Bank	CB177	22500				
			$100900				$100900
20..	(year 5)		$				
1 Jan.	Balance	B/d	81300				

Provision for Depreciation on Motor Lorries Account L28

20..	(year 4)		$	20..	(year 1)		$
1 Jan.	Motor Lorries Account	J56	11760	31 Dec.	Depreciation	J5	15680
31 Dec.	Balance	c/d	51540	20..	(year 2)		
				31 Dec.	Depreciation	J27	15680
				20..	(year 3)		
				31 Dec.	Depreciation	J54	15680
				20..	(year 4)		
				31 Dec.	Depreciation	J73	16260
			$63300				$63300
				20..	(year 5)		$
				1 Jan.	Balance		51540

Sale of Motor Lorry Account L59

20..	(year 4)		$
1 Jan.	Motor Lorries Account	J56	2840

Now try the following exercises on the disposal of worn-out assets. (For simplicity's sake, VAT has been disregarded.)

13.13 Exercises Set 22. The Disposal of Assets

1. Jenny Kelleher owns a motor vehicle, H1785TRS, valued on the books at $850 on 31 December 20... She is approached by a fellow-trader who wishes to purchase it at that figure. The offer is accepted. Do the Journal entry for the transaction, which is settled by cheque.

2. A. Hancock is a retail tobacconist who has an electronic till surplus to requirements. On 31 July 20.. it is valued on his books at $145. He disposes of it, for cash, to A. Streetseller at the book valuation. Do the Journal entry for the transaction.

3. D. Heywood runs a boutique and is about to undertake a major redesign of her premises. On 1 February 20.. she disposes of fixtures and fittings, valued at $300 on her books, to A. Junkbuyer for $85 cash. Show the Journal entry required.

4. J. Scaggs, a grocer, disposes of premises which have become inconveniently situated, due to the introduction of a one-way system, for $12800. They were valued at $13250 on her books. Payment was by cheque. Do the Journal entry necessary to record this transaction on 1 August 20...

5. Allen Motors Ltd have premises at a particularly valuable corner site. These premises are valued on their books at 31 August 20.. at their original cost price of $10000. On this date they sell the premises for $88000, recording the increased value, caused by a rise in land values, in a special account called Site Appreciation Account. Do the Journal entry, and show the ledger accounts. The sale price of $88000 was settled by cheque.

6. A motor vehicle, valued on John Briggs' books at $480, was sold on 1 June 20.. for $630 cash. Show the Journal entry required to record this transaction.

7. On 1 January, year 2, Roadfast Ltd have one vehicle on their books, valued at its original cost of $12400, from which $3100 has been written off to a separate Provision for Depreciation on Motor Vehicles Account. On 1 July of year 2 a second vehicle is purchased for $14000 and on 1 October, year 3, a third vehicle is purchased for $18500. On 1 January, year 4, the first vehicle is disposed of for $4800, and replaced by another vehicle costing $18500. All vehicles are paid for by cheque. Depreciation is written off each 31 December at 25 per cent per annum on the original cost (correct to the nearest $1). You are asked to show
   a) the Motor Lorries Account from the start of year 2 to the end of year 4;
   b) the Provision for Depreciation on Motor Lorries Account for the same period;
   c) the Journal entry for the disposal of the vehicle in January of year 4, together with your calculations for this, and the ledger entries;
   d) the Balance Sheet entry at the end of year 4.

8. On 1 January, year 1, Toolroom Services (Upton) Ltd is set up with machines worth $38000, all purchased by cheque. On 1 April a further machine is purchased for $5200 (cheque) and on 1 October a further machine is purchased for $28600 (cheque). Depreciation is written off each 31 December at 20 per cent per annum on cost and taken to a special Provision for Depreciation on Machines Account. On 1 July, year 2, one machine which cost $12500 on 1 January, year 1, is disposed of for $4800 (cheque) and replaced by a new machine costing $15600, also paid for by cheque. You are asked to show

a) the Machinery Account for years 1 and 2;
b) the Provision for Depreciation on Machinery Account for years 1 and 2;
c) the calculations for the sale of the machine on 1 July, year 2 and the Journal entry and ledger entries that followed;
d) the Balance Sheet entry for machinery as at 31 December, year 2.

13.14 Revise and Test 13. More about the Journal Proper

Cover the page with a sheet of paper; then read one question at a time.

Answers	*Questions*
—	**1.** What is the Journal entry for the purchase of an asset?
1. Always debit the asset account. Credit cash (if you paid cash) or bank (if you paid by cheque) or the creditor if payment is delayed until a different date.	**2.** When we record the purchase of an asset what do we usually include in the Journal entry?
2. Any information that will identify the asset (serial number, car registration number, etc.).	**3.** What is the Journal entry for the depreciation of an asset?
3. Debit Depreciation Account to record the loss to the business (loss by fair wear and tear). Credit the asset account to reduce the book value of the asset.	**4.** There is another way to do it to meet the requirements of the Companies Acts. What is it?
4. Debit Depreciation Account as before. Leave the asset account alone (keep it on the books at the full value) but: Credit a Provision for Depreciation Account).	**5.** What does this enable us to do?
5. We can always tell the original cost (it is on the Asset Account). From this we can deduct the depreciation to date (it is on the Provision for Depreciation Account). The Companies Act requires us to show the asset at cost, less depreciation to date, to give the net value.	**6.** What are the three common ways to calculate depreciation?
6. a) Equal instalment (Straight Line) method; b) diminishing Balance Method; c) revaluation method.	**7.** Explain the Straight Line method.

7. Take off a fixed amount each year based on the formula:

$$Depreciation = \frac{Original\ cost - Residual\ value}{Life\ of\ the\ asset\ (in\ years)}$$

8. Explain the Diminishing Balance Method.

---

8. Write off a fixed percentage (say 20%) of the diminishing balance each year.

9. What is the advantage of this method?

---

9. It equalizes the charges over the years.
Year 1 Big depreciation charge—small repairs bill.
Year 5 Small depreciation charge—larger repair bills.

10. What is the revaluation method?

---

10. You revalue the assets each year.
Useful for agriculture—flocks and herds. In a bad year the herd value will fall—depreciation. In a good year the herd will grow—appreciation.

11. What is the journal entry for the disposal of an asset?

---

11. It depends on what we get on disposal.
The rule is:
Always credit the asset account with the book value (to clear the asset off the books); always debit the proceeds in Cash Account or Bank Account.

Note:

1. If the debit entry is more than the credit entry we made a Profit on Sale—credit the profit in 'Sale of Asset Account'.
2. If the credit entry is more than the debit entry we made a loss on sale—debit the loss in 'Sale of Asset Account'.

12. Go over the page until you are sure of all the answers.

UNIT 14

Limitations of the Trial Balance

14.1 Errors not Disclosed by the Trial Balance

One of the chief reasons for drawing up a Trial Balance of the accounts is to discover whether there are any mistakes of double entry in the month's work. When the Trial Balance does balance, we usually assume that the accounts have been carefully prepared, and we can go on to the next month's work without any problems. If it is the end of the financial year, we prepare a set of Final Accounts from the Trial Balance, and determine the profit for the period.

In fact there are five classes of error that do not show up on a Trial Balance, either because they affect both sides in the same way or because they affect the same side in opposite ways, so that—for example—the debit column is increased by $5 by one error and decreased by $5 by the other. As a result the errors pass unnoticed, yet they are quite likely to be revealed later—possibly by angry telephone calls from customers or sarcastic letters from business associates. A correct Trial Balance is therefore often said by accountants to give only a *prima facie* proof of accuracy. *Prima facie* means 'at a first look'; a second look, later, may reveal one of these errors.

The five classes of error are:

- original errors,
- errors of omission,
- errors of commission,
- compensating errors, and
- errors of principle.

(a) Original Errors

These are errors in the original documents, or errors made in copying those documents into the book of original entry. For example, an incorrect figure may be copied from the invoice to the Purchases Day Book and, from there, posted to the credit side of the ledger account of the supplier and to the debit side of the Purchases Account. Clearly it will not show up on the Trial Balance. Both sides will be wrong, by the same amount.

A good way to reduce original errors is to take each day's bundle of invoices (or credit notes, or whatever the documents are) and pre-list them with an add-listing machine. Then, when the total entries have been made in the day book, the increase in the day book total should be the same as the pre-list. If not, an error in copying may have been made. It is particularly helpful if different people do the pre-listing and the entering into the day books.

(b) Errors of Omission

Sometimes a document is left out altogether, and omitted completely from the accounting records. Perhaps it blew out of the window one blustery day. Clearly it does not reach any account at all. The Trial Balance balances, and everyone feels pleased—but when the creditor who is waiting to be paid finally rings the accountant to ask why the debt has not been settled, there will be embarrassment all round.

(c) Errors of Commission

The word 'commission' means 'authority to do something'. An error of commission is a faulty performance of one's duty, and such errors are quite common. Most of the errors by junior members of the accounting staff are errors of commission. For example, where two debtors have the same name and initials it is quite easy to post a debt to the wrong account, so that Mr D. Smith of Harrow is debited with goods supplied to Mr D. Smith of Henlow. The Trial Balance does not distinguish between these two gentlemen, the total of 'debtors' is correct; but Mr D. Smith of Harrow will write a sarcastic letter when he is asked to settle the account, and Mr D. Smith of Henlow will wonder if he is ever going to be asked to pay for the goods he has already enjoyed.

(d) Compensating Errors

Sometimes the Trial Balance agrees, but in fact two quite separate errors of the same amount have been made. This is often true of addition errors, say \$1 or \$10 or \$100 errors. If two similar arithmetical slips are made, one affecting an account on the debit side and one affecting an account on the credit side, the Trial Balance will be wrong twice over, but it will appear—*prima facie*—to be correct.

(e) Errors of Principle

This type of error is caused by a failure to appreciate the *principles of accounting* which this book is designed to outline. It amounts to a misconception of the double-entry system, and it most commonly occurs as a failure to appreciate the difference between *capital* and *revenue expenditure*. A full discussion of this is given later, in Unit 17, but a simple example would be as follows.

Mr A's clerk receives an invoice for the purchase of an asset and, instead of making an entry in the Journal Proper, enters it in the Purchases Day Book. It follows that the asset is not recorded on the debit side of an asset account, but instead is recorded on the debit side of Purchases Account. The credit entry of course would be in the creditor's account and would be correct. The Trial Balance would agree, and appear to be correct, but in fact a serious error of principle has been made. In due course the error on Purchases Account will increase the cost of goods sold in the Trading Account and thus reduce the profits. Mr A will therefore be given a false impression of the profitability of the business. Also, since the asset is understated, the Balance Sheet will give a false view of the position of the business.

Errors of principle thus offend against two fundamental rules of accounting:

(i) the accountant should always bring out a true net profit of the business;
(ii) the accountant should always display a true and fair view of the business in the Balance Sheet.

14.2 When a Trial Balance does not Agree

When a Trial Balance does not agree, how shall we resolve the difficulty? Clearly there must be some mistake in the double entries. The question is, where? The following procedure will help to discover it fairly quickly.

(a) Add up the Trial Balance again—it may be just an arithmetical error. If this does not solve the problem then proceed to (b).
(b) Take one side from the other to discover the amount of the error. (Of course this may be the result of twenty different mistakes, but there is just the chance that only one error is present.) Suppose it is an error of $45.50. Someone may recall 'Ah, now that is the valuation we placed upon the motor vehicle sold to the caretaker as surplus to requirements. We agreed to deduct it from his wages over the next six months. Have we forgotten to make him a debtor?' And of course we have! If no one can recall an item of this amount we proceed to (c).
(c) Divide the error in half. Half of $45.50 is $22.75. Is there an item of $22.75 which has been put on the wrong side of the Trial Balance? If so it will make one side $22.75 too large and the other side $22.75 too small. The result will be an apparent error of twice the amount concerned. If there does not seem to be a figure of this amount proceed to (d).

(d) In certain accounting systems it is usual to keep *control accounts*, or *total accounts*, which check up on certain parts of the ledger. This is quite a complex idea, and it is explained in Unit 30. If a control account system is in use, or if one can be built up quickly from the total figures, it will eliminate areas where no mistake exists, and bring out areas where there are mistakes. This reduces the total amount of checking necessary.

(e) The only remaining thing to do is to check every entry that has been made throughout the month to ensure that a correct double entry has taken place. This is a long and laborious process. Now you can see why a Trial Balance is extracted at least once a month. It is bad enough to have to look through a month's entries. To go through a whole year's entries would be insufferably tedious.

14.3 Suspense Accounts

Suppose that it proves impossible to get the books correct, even though hours of work have been devoted to the task. The only solution is to open up a *Suspense Account.* This is a general name for any account where we hold a balance until we decide what to do with it. In this case we have a Suspense Account holding a 'difference on books' figure. Clearly the mistake will be explained sooner or later, probably as a result of some letter of complaint.

Some firms take the view that it is a waste of time looking for an error on the Trial Balance—whatever the mistake, the explanation will turn up one day. Therefore, they argue, it is simpler just to enter the difference in a Suspense Account and carry on with next month's work. The only difficulty here is that if it is the end of the year, the balance must appear on the Balance Sheet as 'difference on books'. That is not a happy thing for any accountant to have to admit.

The creation of a Suspense Account is quite simple. Suppose the debit side of the Trial Balance is greater than the credit side by $50. A Suspense Account opened as shown below will immediately put the Trial Balance right. Of course it is a complete invention, but we expect to be able to remove it from the books in due course as the mistakes that caused it are discovered.

Suspense Account (Difference on Books) L181

			20..		$
			31 Dec.	Balance	50

14.4 The Correction of Errors

One of the commonest types of examining questions concerns the correction of errors. This may or may not involve using a Suspense Account. For example, if an error has been made on the books, and it is reported or discovered within a few days, we shall be able to get it right without having to open a Suspense Account. If the error has existed for some time, so that the end of a month arrives and it has not been discovered, a Suspense Account will be needed and any eventual correction that is made must now involve the Suspense Account as well as the account containing the error.

When correcting errors there is no simple rule. We must discover the nature of the error, and do whatever it is necessary to do to put the matter right. Let us look at a few examples.

Example 1: An Error of Commission

On 11 January 20.. we discover that T. Smith has been debited in error with goods sold to E. Smith, valued at $50. To correct this error we must remove the $50 from T. Smith's Account and enter it where it really belongs, in E. Smith's Account.

The Journal entry and the ledger accounts will be as follows:

					J11
20..				$	$
11 Jan.	E. Smith	Dr.	L56	50	
	T. Smith		L57		50
	Being correction of error whereby $50 was debited in T. Smith's account in error				

E. Smith L56

20..			$				
11 Jan.	T. Smith	J11	50				

T. Smith L57

20..			$	20..			$
1 Jan.	Balance	B/d	50	11 Jan.	E. Smith	J11	50

Example 2: An Error of Principle

Thomas Hudson's book-keeper has entered an invoice for the purchase of office furniture from the Guardian Furnishing Co. in the Purchases Day Book, and has posted the entry to the ledger accounts. Correct this error with a Journal entry and show the ledger postings. The amount concerned was $240, and the mistake was discovered on 12 July 20...

Here the situation is as follows:

(a) The Purchases Account has been debited with the total of the Purchases Day Book which includes this $240—in other words, it is overstated by $240.
(b) The account of the Guardian Furnishing Co. has been credited with $240. This entry is of course correct.

The error of principle is that the Purchases Account has been debited with $240 when it ought to be the asset account that is debited, i.e. Furniture and Fittings Account.

To correct the error we must debit Furniture and Fittings Account and credit Purchases Account. The Journal entry and the ledger accounts will then look like this:

				J8
20..			$	$
12 July	Furniture and Fittings Account Dr.	L21	240	
	Purchases Account	L31		240
	Being correction of error of principle in which the purchase of an asset was treated as purchases of goods for resale			

Purchases Account L21

20..			$				$
30 June	Sundry purchases	PDB1	4075	12 July	Furniture and Fittings Account	J8	240

Furniture and Fittings Account L31

20..			$
1 Jan.	Balance	B/d	2800
12 July	Purchases Account	J8	240

Example 3: An Arithmetical Error

It often happens that a slip in arithmetic results in a difference on the books, and it is nearly always a single-sided error. For example, a careless addition of the Sales Day Book which results in a total that is wrong by $50 will not necessarily affect any account other than the Sales Account to which this total is posted. It is most unlikely that the same error would be made elsewhere, and if it was it would be quite separate, even if it resulted in a compensating error (see Unit 14.1(d)).

The problem arises as to how we should correct a single-sided error of this sort. Two solutions are as follows:

(a) We can physically cross out the incorrect total posted to Sales Account, and replace it by the correct figure. In such circumstances it is wise to initial the error, or better still, to sign your full name against it. This explains the untidiness in the book-keeping and allocates responsibility for the error, or for its correction. Clearly this sort of annotation of the accounts should not be carried out by an office junior without the approval of the accountant or chief clerk. Such an error would be corrected thus:

Sales Account L274

20..			$
31 Jan.	Sundry debtors	SDB5	~~4850~~
		G. M. Whitehead	4800

(b) We can do a single-sided Journal entry. This is rather unusual but it is the only kind of entry that can be made, since only one account is affected. The Journal entry and account would be as follows:

					J5
20..				$	$
6 Feb.	Sales Account	Dr.	L274	50	
	Being a single-sided correction of an arithmetical error				

Sales Account L274

20..			$	20..			$
6 Feb.	Correction of error	J5	50	31 Jan.	Sundry debtors	SDB5	4850

14.5 Clearing a Suspense Account

When a Suspense Account has been opened, the errors that caused it to be made out will gradually come to light as the business receives complaints from aggrieved persons who have been over- or under-charged. When these errors are corrected, it will usually be possible to remove some, or all, of the Suspense Account balance. Consider the following example.

Example

An accountant finds the Trial Balance on 31 January 20.. to be $43.50 in excess on the debit side. A Suspense Account is opened to correct the Trial Balance, but later is cleared by the following discoveries:

(a) Furniture purchased for $85.00 was entered properly in the cash book but posted to Furniture Account as $58.00.
(b) A balance due to R. Tomlinson for $79.00 had been omitted from the Trial Balance, although Tomlinson's account was perfectly correct.
(c) Bank charges of $8.50 had been entered in the cash book, but not posted to the nominal account.

Make the Journal entries and show the final Suspense Account.

The Trial Balance had to be corrected by putting a balance of $43.50 on the credit side, thus:

Suspense Account L272

			20..			$
			31 Jan. Balance			43.50

(a) Here the Furniture Account has been under-debited by $27.00 ($85.00 – $58.00). We must debit Furniture Account with $27.00 and credit Suspense Account with $27.00, like this:

					J6
20..				$	$
27 Feb.	Furniture Account	Dr.	L5	27.00	
	Suspense Account		L272		27.00
	Being correction of an error where furniture purchased for $85.00 was entered as $58.00				

Furniture Account L5

20..		$		
28 Jan. Bank	CB7	58.00		
27 Feb. Suspense Account	J6	27.00		

Suspense Account L272

			20..		$
			31 Jan. Balance		43.50
			27 Feb. Furniture Account	J6	27.00

(b) Here we have a single-sided correction. There is nothing wrong with Tomlinson's Account, but it has not been entered on the Trial Balance, where it would have been in the credit column. Its omission has resulted in the Suspense Account being $79.00 bigger on the credit side than necessary. But there isn't as much as $79.00 on the Suspense Account, so how can we say it is $79.00 too big? The only explanation must be that a further undiscovered error has still to be revealed. The correction for item (b), which is to debit Suspense Account with $79.00, is shown below:

				J6
			$	
20..				
28 Feb.	Suspense Account Dr.	L272	79.00	
	Being correction of Suspense Account due to an omission from the Trial Balance			

Suspense Account L272

			$				$
20..				20..			
28 Feb.	Correction of error	J6	79.00	31 Jan.	Balance		43.50
				27 Feb.	Furniture Account	J6	27.00

(c) Here Bank Charges Account has not been debited with $8.50. If we debit it with $8.50 and credit Suspense Account, we shall finally clear the Suspense Account. This tells us that the errors have now all been discovered, and this final correction is shown below. Note that as this error was not discovered until 4 March, the Suspense Account would have been balanced off and tidied up at the end of February when the February Trial Balance was prepared.

				J7
			$	$
20..				
4 Mar.	Bank Charges Account Dr.	L42	8.50	
	Suspense Account	L272		8.50
	Being correction of error in which bank charges were not posted to Bank Charges Account			

Bank Charges Account L42

			$
20..			
4 Mar.	Suspense Account	J7	8.50

Suspense Account L272

			$				$
20..				20..			
28 Feb.	Correction of error	J6	79.00	31 Jan.	Balance		43.50
				27 Feb.	Furniture Account	J6	27.00
				28 Feb.	Balance	c/d	8.50
			$79.00				$79.00
1 Mar.	Balance	B/d	$8.50	4 Mar.	Bank Charges	J7	$8.50

14.6 Exercises Set 23. Limitations of the Trial Balance

1. There are several types of error not disclosed by the Trial Balance. List them, and give an example of each of two different types.

2. 'An agreed Trial Balance is only *prima facie* proof of accurate accounting records.' Explain this statement fully.

3. What procedures should be followed if a Trial Balance fails to agree? List the measures you would take in logical order, and explain them.

4. 'If an item is placed on the wrong side of a Trial Balance it causes an error of twice its value.' Explain this statement, using an actual example of a Trial Balance which had the Discount Allowed Account listed as a credit balance of $14.98. Invent suitable totals for the Trial Balance to demonstrate your reasoning.

5. Correct, by Journal entries, the following entries which have been made in the ledger of R. Taylor. Date the entries 30 September 20...

(a) $18 received from P. Dark had been posted to the account of D. Park.
(b) $40 expended by the trader on her own expenses had been posted to the Office Expenses Account.
(c) $10 received in respect of the sale of some bookcases from the office had been posted to the Sales Account. The book value of the bookcases was exactly $10.

6. Correct, by Journal entries, the following entries which have been made in the ledger of A. Trader. Date the entries 31 May 20...

(a) $28 paid to D. Montgomery had been posted to the account of D. Montmorency.
(b) $65 expended by the trader on office furniture had been posted to the Office Expenses Account.
(c) $10 discount allowed had been posted to the credit side of the Discount Account.

7. Show, by means of Journal entries, how the following errors would be corrected in the books of M. Bines. Date all items 30 June 20...

(a) Machinery valued at $1 600 purchased on credit from Machinery Ltd had been debited to Purchases Account.
(b) When paying A. Rosner, a creditor, Bines had deducted $7.50 as discount. Rosner had disallowed this discount.
(c) Depreciation of $80 on machinery had been credited to Fixtures and Fittings Account.

8. Correct by Journal entries the following errors:

(a) A purchase of furniture valued at $120 was debited in Furnishing Co. Ltd's account instead of in Furniture and Fittings Account. The mistake was discovered on 5 July 20...

(b) A lorry recorded in the books of R. Lamperter was valued at $220. It was sold on 4 August 20.. by Lamperter to R. Gould and Co. for $175, but the Motor Vehicles Account was only credited with $175 instead of the full book value. The error was discovered on 8 August 20...

(c) A machine was purchased for $2 000 from Lucas Engineering Ltd, but the invoice was not passed through the books at all. On 12 July 20.., six months later, it was agreed with the managing director of Lucas Engineering Ltd that a cheque would be sent in full at once, and with 5 per cent interest per annum added.

9. (a) What is a Suspense Account?

(b) On 30 April 20.. R. Whistler decides to open a Suspense Account with a debit balance of $45, because he cannot discover the error on his books. On 17 May it is found to be due to a failure to post a cheque for $45 paid to a creditor R. Lawson from the cash book to his account. Show the Journal entry clearing the Suspense Account and the Suspense Account itself.

10. On 31 August 20.. R. Hull's Trial Balance failed to agree, the debit side being $42.50 greater than the credit side and consequently he opened a Suspense Account. The errors proved to be as follows:

(a) The total of discount allowed for one week of $8.50 had not been posted to the appropriate account.

(b) A debtor R. Day had paid his account, $51.00 in full, but this had not been credited to his account.

Show

(i) the Journal entries to correct these errors, and

(ii) the Suspense Account after the corrections had been completed. Invent sensible dates in September for these corrections.

11. On 30 September 20.. R. T. Crafty extracted a Trial Balance. The debit side of the Trial Balance totalled $18 150.85, and the credit side $17 887.80. Crafty opened a Suspense Account for the difference. During October he discovered the following errors, which accounted for the difference:

(a) The total of the Purchases Day Book for the month of September, $5 479.00, had been posted to the Purchases Account as $5 749.00.

(b) The 'discount received' column in the cash book had been wrongly totalled and posted to the Discount Received Account as $55.14 instead of $57.19.

(c) A cheque $76.42 paid for light and heat had been posted to the Light and Heat Account as $67.42.

(d) A credit note sent to S. Gilbert for $16.50 had been entered in the Sales Returns Book as $15.60 and posted to Gilbert's Account as that figure.

Draw up the Suspense Account, inventing suitable dates in October.

14.7 Revise and Test 14. The Limitations of the Trial Balance

Cover the page with a sheet of paper; then read one question at a time.

Answers	*Questions*
	1. What is a Trial Balance?
1. It is a list of all the accounts that have balances on them.	**2.** When is it taken out?
2. At least once a month.	**3.** What do we take it out for?
3. To discover whether the book-keeping has been carefully done.	**4.** What will happen if we have done our book-keeping properly?
4. The Trial Balance will balance—that is the debit balances will exactly equal the credit balances.	**5.** Is the agreement of the Trial Balance conclusive evidence that the books are correct?
5. No—only *prima facie* evidence.	**6.** Why is it not quite conclusive?
6. Because five types of errors do not show up on the Trial Balance.	**7.** What are these five types of errors?
7. a) Original errors; b) errors of omission; c) errors of commission; d) errors of principle; e) compensating errors.	**8.** Explain each of these in turn.

8. Original errors are errors in the original documents to be recorded; errors of omission occur when we leave something out altogether; errors of commission are errors where we make a slip in doing the work, i.e. enter an item for D. Brown in G. Brown's account; errors of principle are errors where we do not understand our basic principles of book-keeping, i.e. Purchases of Assets treated as Purchases of Goods; compensating errors are errors that compensate for one another, i.e. a $10.00 adding up mistake on each side.	**9.** What do you do if a Trial Balance does not agree?
9. a) Add it up again in case we've made a slip; b) see if anyone remembers an amount for the difference, say $48.00; c) if this doesn't help, divide by 2 and see if $24.00 is on the wrong side; d) if this doesn't help, check the extractions to the Trial Balance from the Ledger; e) if this doesn't help, take out Control Accounts on the Sales and Purchases Ledgers; f) if this doesn't help, check everything; g) if we still haven't found the mistake, open up a Suspense Account.	**10.** Go over this again until you are perfectly sure of it all.

UNIT 15

Short Cuts on Day Book Entries

15.1 The Problems with Day Book Entries

While the full system of double-entry records we have described gives a perfect system of accounting, it has to be admitted that it involves a great deal of work. Whenever a system requires entries to be made in one book and then posted to another, it is subject to two criticisms: first, that work is being duplicated unnecessarily and, second, that there is a chance that errors will be made.

There are four main ways of overcoming these problems. These are:

- simplified 'one-book' systems;
- slip systems;
- simultaneous records systems;
- computerized systems.

In this Unit we will look briefly at the first three of these systems. The use of computers in accounting is referred to in Unit 18.3.

15.2 Simplified 'One-book' Systems

These use an abbreviated double-entry system, which is produced in book form, with each page designed to carry one week's records. They normally allow for 53 weeks in the year (every few years we need to use a fifty-third week) and there are summaries at the back of the book which are really the ledger entries. They are extremely helpful for small businesses—the whole year's records appear on about 60 pages of paper only. One of these is the Simplex System, run by George Vyner Ltd, Freepost, Holmfirth, Huddersfield HD7 2RP, United Kingdom.

15.3 Slip Systems

A slip system of book-keeping avoids making entries in day books and journals by using the actual basic documents as the source of information for making entries in the ledger. We are used to this system in banks, for example, where the customer makes out a slip of paper (the paying-in slip) each time money has to be entered into his or her account, or writes another slip of paper (a cheque) for making payments out of the account; these slips of paper are all the bank needs to make entries in the customer's account. Similarly, the invoices we enter in the Purchases Day Book and the Sales Day Book could easily be used to make entries in the accounts of debtors and creditors. The usual procedure is to 'batch up' a group of invoices every day, clipping them together with a stapling machine and attaching a slip of paper from an add-listing machine which totals the value of the purchases (or sales) for the day, and the VAT charged.

Suppose we imagine fifteen sales invoices going out to fifteen customers. The duplicate copies will be batched up, clipped together and totalled on an add-listing machine. We now debit each debtor with the value of the goods received, recording the invoice number in case we need to refer to it later and crediting Sales Account with the value of the sales for the day, as shown on the add-list. We also credit VAT Account with the tax charged to customers, which is of course output tax payable to the Customs and Excise Department. The batch of invoices is then filed away in a binder—usually a month's invoices are bound together. This gives a fairly sound collection of invoices which can be turned up if we need to check any detail at a later date.

15.4 Simultaneous Records Systems

The principle of these systems, which depend upon the use of carbon paper or carbonless copy paper to produce the simultaneous records required, is that any group of documents and records which are related, and carry the same information, might as well be produced at the same time. It is usual to limit the system to three or four related sets of records. There are many such related groups of documents required in business. Some of the most useful are listed below, and a Sales Ledger system and a wages system are described in Units 15.5 and 15.6 respectively:

(a) The Sales Ledger system:
  (i) the statement placed on top of
  (ii) the ledger card placed on top of
  (iii) the Sales Day Book sheet.

(b) The Purchases Ledger system:
  (i) the remittance advice note placed on top of
  (ii) the ledger card placed on top of
  (iii) the Purchases Day Book sheet.

(c) Payments by bank giro credit:
   (i) the credit slip placed on top of
   (ii) the bank list placed on top of
   (iii) the payments cash book.
(d) Wages and salaries systems:
   (i) the employee's tax and earnings card placed on top of
   (ii) the payroll sheet and
   (iii) the employee's pay slip.
(e) The stock records system:
   (i) the stock record card placed on top of
   (ii) the stock control sheet.
(f) Income tax records system:
   (i) the P11 form (tax deducted in year) placed on top of
   (ii) the P60 form (certificate of tax deducted) placed on top of
   (iii) the P35 form (total tax deducted from all employees).

In each case the system used provides a plastic posting board sufficiently large to take the largest of the documents conveniently, with a row of studs or other mechanical or magnetic devices to hold the sheets in position. The posting board illustrated in Fig. 15.1 is manufactured by Safeguard Systems (Europe) Ltd, Duchy Road, Crewe CW1 6ND, United Kingdom, Telephone 01270 500921.

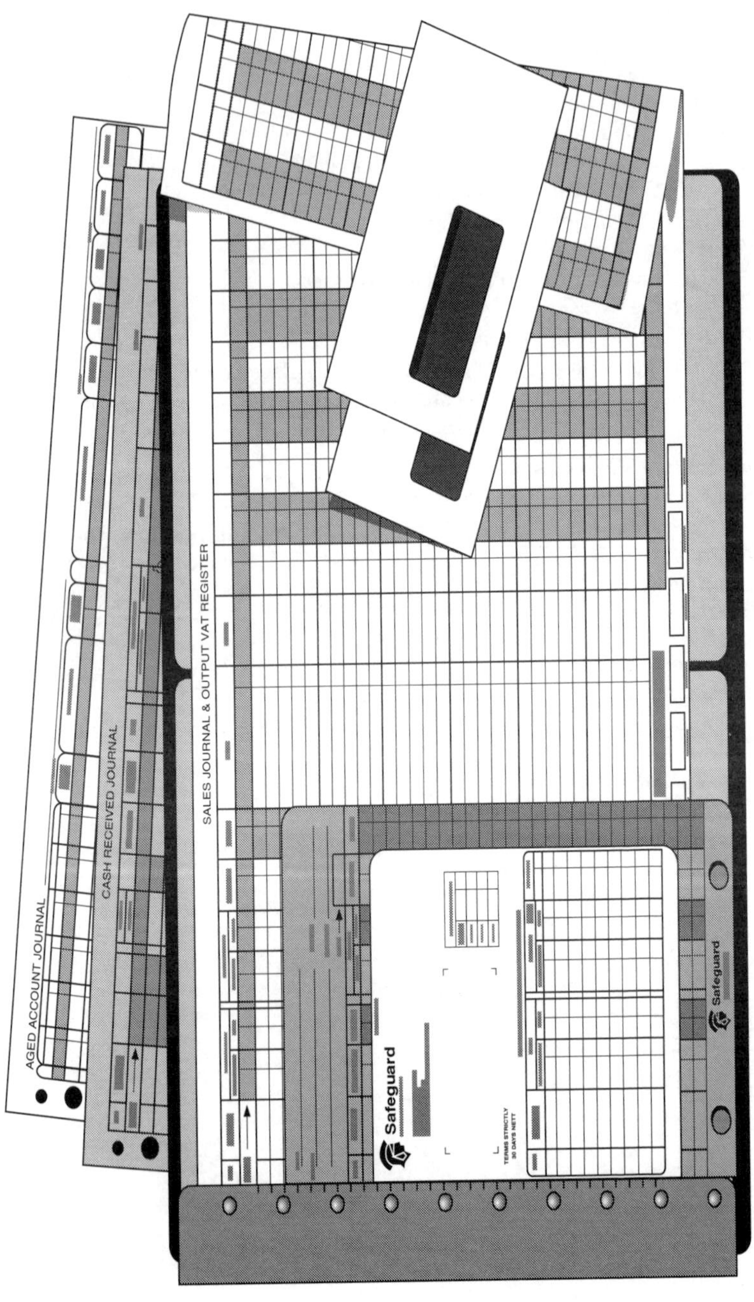

Fig. 15.1 Simultaneous records: the Sales Ledger (courtesy of Safeguard Systems (Europe) Ltd)

15.5 A Sales Ledger System with Simultaneous Entries

Here the important record is the *ledger card* of the customer, which is kept in a posting tray designed so that a particular ledger card can be found quickly by the posting clerk, who is said to 'pull' them from the system.

Kept with the ledger card is the monthly statement which is renewed every month as the previous month's statement is dispatched to the customer. The posting clerk 'pulls' the statement with the ledger card and assembles them on the posting board, together with the appropriate sheet from the Sales Day Book, which is kept in loose-leaf sheet form.

(a) Procedure

(i) The Sales Day Book form is laid on the posting board, its left-hand margin held to the board by two projecting studs.

(ii) The posting clerk 'pulls' the appropriate ledger card and statement from the posting tray and positions them, with carbon paper if used, so that the next clean line of each is against the next clean line of the Sales Day Book form. The statement is on top.

(iii) Details of the invoice are then entered on the statement and simultaneously copied on to the ledger card and day book below them.

(iv) The updated ledger card and statement are then returned to the posting tray, and the posting clerk selects the next card and statement to be updated.

(v) There are many different rulings of such day book forms, but the one shown here is helpful in providing control account records and departmental records in the analysis columns on the right of the day book sheet.

(vi) At the end of the page a check can be made on the entries in the following ways (take Fig. 15.1, where invoices are being posted, as an example):

1. The total of the debit column should be the same as the total of the invoice pre-list (an adding-machine total pinned to the batch of invoices to be posted).
2. The total of the old balances, added to the total of the debits entered, should equal the total of the new balances.
3. The control account columns should cross-tot to the total of the debits entered.
4. The departmental columns should cross-tot to the total of the debits entered.

(b) Advantages of the System

(i) All three records—statement, ledger card and day book—are prepared simultaneously.
(ii) No posting errors can be made since the entries in all three records are identical (the statement and the day book entries are copies of the ledger card).
(iii) Errors that might not show up until the Trial Balance stage are revealed on the day they occur if the checks and controls devised by the system planners are implemented.
(iv) By careful use of the analysis columns provided, an efficient control of business trends can be achieved. For example, where a particular department handles seasonal goods, its sales can be encouraged by increasing the floor space or shelf space allocated to the department at appropriate times.
(v) Statements are ready for dispatch at the end of the month without any work other than the actual mailing activities.

15.6 Simultaneous Records Wages Systems

The essential requirements of a wages records system are as follows:

(i) A permanent payroll record This must show who was paid on each pay-day, the amount of each person's gross pay, pensions deductions (if any), other deductions and the net pay. Totals are required of the gross pay, net pay, tax payable, National Insurance contributions payable and other deductions payable. This record, although part of the accounts of the firm, must be confidential since staff usually dislike other employees knowing how much they earn, regarding their pay as a private matter.

(ii) Permanent individual records These must be prepared for each member of staff to show a complete record of pay received, tax and other items deducted, statutory sick pay and so on. Such a record can be produced for discussion in the event of a dispute with the employee without the employee seeing other people's confidential records, as would happen if the complete payroll had to be produced.

(iii) Individual wages slips Each pay-day a slip must be included in the wage packet to show how much money has been paid, either in cash in the wage packet or by bank giro credit to the employee's bank account.

These three requirements can be met by using a 'three-in-one' records system. One of the simplest, which is used each week for the pay records of millions of people all over the world, is the Kalamazoo system.

(a) The Kalamazoo Wages System

The three records mentioned above are prepared in the Kalamazoo system as follows:

(i) The clerk uses a flat plastic board called a copywriter; it gives a good writing surface and carries a series of studs at the top, on which the special stationery supplied can be positioned. All the stationery used is punched with holes along the top edge of the paper, and when these holes are located on the studs the paper is held firmly. The first piece of stationery is a sheet of ten overlapping *pay advice slips*.

(ii) The second piece of stationery is a *payroll* sheet, which has columns on it sufficient to take ten sets of wages details. This is fitted on the studs so that the ten columns exactly cover the ten wages slips.

(iii) The third piece of stationery, which is changed each time a column is used, is the *individual pay record*. One of these is used for each employee, and contains fifteen columns, enough to record wages for fifteen weeks. When this individual pay record is positioned on the studs the next unused column on the individual pay record lies exactly over the next unused column on the payroll and the next unused pay advice slip. The week's pay can then be inserted, using the detailed lines provided. These lines, with some imaginary entries inserted, read as shown in Fig. 15.2.

Pay Advice

Week or Mth. No.	Date	14	10.7.

	Details	£	p
Earnings	A	200	80
	B	5	00
	C		
	D		
	E		
	SSP	29	60
	SMP		
	Gross Pay	235	40
	Superannuation	=	=
	Gross Pay less Superannuation	235	40
	Gross Pay to date for Tax Purposes	3859	60
	less Tax Free Pay	1633	40
K code	plus Additional K Code Pay	=	=
	Taxable Pay to Date	2226	20
	Tax Due to Date	584	20
K Codes	Tax Refund		
	Tax Due this Period		
	Regulatory Limit		
	Tax not collected due to Reg. Limit		
Deductions	Tax	34	40
	*N.I. Contribution (Employee)	12	90
	1 CHARITY (DR B.)		50
	2 T. U.	3	20
	3		
	4		
	5		
	Total Deductions	51	00
	Net Pay	184	40
	F SUBSISTENCE ALLOWANCE	84	20
	Total Amount Payable	268	60
	N.I. Contribution (Employer)	12	90
	N.I. Total (Employer and Employee)	12	90
	G		
	*Contracted-Out Contbn. incl above		
	Earn. on which E'ees contbn. pyble.		
	Earn. on which E'ees contbn. at CO Rate pyble.		

Your Pay is made up as shown above

K. E. MILLER

Fig. 15.2 A Kalamazoo pay advice slip

Fig. 15.2 shows how the wages payable are clearly displayed, and that the method of arriving at the net pay is simple to follow. Note the following:

(i) The earnings codes A to E refer to various types of pay. Thus A represents basic pay, B perhaps overtime earnings, C piecework payments, D bonuses, and so on.
(ii) Statutory sick pay (SSP) is paid in certain circumstances by the government to people who have been unable to work because of illness. The employer pays it to the employee at government-approved rates, and then reclaims the money from the tax collected from other employees. Statutory Maternity Pay (SMP) is a similar type of payment.
(iii) The figure for 'gross pay to date for tax purposes' is found by adding last week's figure to this week's pay.
(iv) The figures for tax deductions are found by using the tables supplied by the Inland Revenue.
(v) Extra lines are provided to suit the particular needs of some employers—for example, lines F and G might be used by employers needing to pay travelling or lodging allowances as well as net pay.
(vi) If required, stationery can be supplied in sets of fifteen, rather than ten.

The pay advice slips are torn off as each set is completed and with a single fold are ready for insertion into the pay envelopes—together with the cash itself if payment is to be made in cash. If payment is by bank giro credit, just the pay advice slip is inserted into the envelope. An extra column on the payroll sheet enables the total figures for the set of pay packets, and a coin summary if necessary, to be prepared. The payroll sheets and personal record sheets can be filed away in a special case, which is lockable and portable. One side of this case is detachable, and becomes the copywriter surface on which the records are prepared.

This simple, self-contained system provides a full record of wages for tax, National Insurance and statutory sick pay purposes and also for meeting the needs of both the employer and the employee.

(b) The Taxation of Wages—PAYE

As far as employees are concerned, the British tax system is a *pay-as-you-earn* system, usually abbreviated to PAYE. This is by far the most convenient system for the ordinary employee, since there is no need to save money in order to pay income tax. Instead, the tax and various other deductions are removed before the pay packet is prepared and the 'net pay' taken home is the residue which is available for the employee's own use. There have been many suggestions for reform of the tax system, but over the years PAYE has proved an efficient, cheap method of collection. It is based upon the following arrangements.

(i) Code numbers Every employee is given a *code number*, which is calculated on the allowances to which he or she is entitled. These will include a personal allowance and may also include allowances for children or a dependent relative and for the services of a son or daughter or a housekeeper, and perhaps other small allowances for hardship cases such as blindness. From these allowances a code number is calculated: a person with heavy responsibilities has large allowances and hence a high code number, a person with few responsibilities has a low code number and is taxed more heavily. Any change in circumstances (for example non-payment of tax on interest on savings, or other income outside employment) can result in a change of code number to collect the tax due.

(ii) Tax tables These are prepared by the Inland Revenue and issued to employers. By consulting the tax table, the employer can determine exactly how much tax should have been deducted by that week in the year. He can then compare this figure with the total tax paid already up to the previous week. The difference must be the amount that is to be deducted from this week's pay packet. If a change of circumstances has resulted in a change of code number, the tables might indicate that the employee has already paid more tax than the total figure that is due this week. This means that a refund is due to the employee, and it is put at once into the pay packet.

The total sums deducted from pay for taxation are paid each month by the employer to the Inland Revenue authorities, after allowing for any statutory sick pay or similar payments made to employees.

(iii) Other important tax records The P45 form is given to employees who change employment. The new employer can only deduct the correct tax if information is supplied by the old employer about the amount deducted to date and the total earned in the old employment. This information is supplied by the old employer on a P45 given to the employee when leaving the job.

The P60 is a form given to all employees at the end of the tax year. It shows the total pay received, the tax deducted, the National Insurance and other payments made and the net pay. It is widely used as part of the social security system, and should be kept by the employees in case they, or their family, wish to claim certain state benefits.

15.7 Exercises Set 24. Simultaneous Records and Wages Calculations

1. What is the meaning of the term 'simultaneous records'?

2. What are the advantages of keeping a record of sales by simultaneous records methods?

3. Write a few lines about the following income tax matters:
a) code numbers;
b) form P45;
c) gross pay, taxable pay and net pay;
d) form P60.

Answer the following questions correct to the nearest cent.

4. Paul Jones is paid a basic wage of $4.20 per hour for a basic 40-hour week: the first five hours in excess of this are paid at time and a quarter and any further hours are paid at time and a half. During the week ending 15 June 20.., he worked a total of 47½ hours and received in addition to his basic pay and overtime a productivity bonus of $10.

His deductions for the week were:

Company pension fund	5% of his gross wage
National Insurance	10% of his gross wage
Income tax	25% of all earnings in excess of $160 per week
Holiday and Welfare Fund	$2.00 per week

You are required to:
a) Calculate his gross pay for the week ending 15 June 20...
b) Show the amount of each deduction and calculate his take-home pay for the same period.

5. Annemarie Jarvis is paid a basic wage of $3.50 per hour for a basic 37½-hour week: the first six hours in excess of this are paid at time and a quarter and any further hours are paid at time and a half. During the week ending 5 May 20.., she worked a total of 46½ hours and received in addition to her basic pay and overtime a productivity bonus of $8.

Her deductions for the week were:

Company pension fund	5% of her gross wage
National Insurance	10% of her gross wage
Income tax	25% of all earnings in excess of $150 per week
Voluntary savings deduction	$2.00 per week

You are required to:
a) Calculate her gross pay for the week ending 5 May 20...
b) Show the amount of each deduction and calculate her take-home pay for the same period.

6. Complete wages advice slips in the style of Fig. 15.2 for the four employees shown in the table below. (In a real Wages Office you would need to look up some of the information in the tax tables supplied by the Inland Revenue to all employers. Here the information is given to you.)

Employee	(i)	(ii)	(iii)	(iv)
Name	A.A.K.	M.T.	R.A.S.	M.G.
Code no.	135	150	435	186
Week	1	15	21	34
Date	12 Apr. 20..	19 Jul. 20..	30 Aug. 20..	29 Nov. 20..
Earnings A	166.50	107.50	136.50	204.80
Earnings B	4.55	23.23	8.40	17.24
Gross pay	?	?	?	?
Superannuation	8.55	6.50	7.24	11.10
Gross pay for tax purposes (a)	?	?	?	?
Gross pay to date for tax purposes (last week's figure + (a))	?[1]	1890.20	2935.30	7529.20
Free pay[2]	26.14	435.30	1760.43	1222.30
Taxable pay to date	?	?	?	?
Tax due to date[2]	40.80	436.20	352.20	1891.80
Tax paid up to last week	—	396.50	368.50	1852.70
Tax	?	?	?	?
N.I. contribution[3] (b)	15.90	11.76	13.04	19.98
Charity	0.50	0.50	0.25	—
Total deductions (c)	?	?	?	?
Net pay ((a) − (c))	?	?	?	?
Refunds (if any)	?	?	?	?
Total amount payable	?	?	?	?
N.I. contribution (employer)[3] (d)	17.87	13.66	15.14	23.20
N.I. total ((b) + (d))	?	?	?	?

[1] Remember that this is week 1.
[2] Information taken from the Inland Revenue's tax tables.
[3] Information taken from National Insurance tables.

Note: The Kalamazoo wages system is widely used, but it is difficult to imitate it in a textbook exercise. The company makes stationery available at reasonable prices for educational purposes and schools and colleges wishing to purchase a small supply should approach the Education Department of Kalamazoo Ltd, Mill Lane, Northfield, Birmingham B31 2RW. For the purpose of this exercise it is suggested that pay advice slips similar to Fig. 15.2 should be ruled up.

15.8 Revise and Test 15. Short Cuts on Day Book Entries

Cover the page with a sheet of paper. Then uncover one question at a time.

Answers	*Questions*
—	**1.** What is the problem with day book entries?
1. They make an awful lot of work and give us very little benefit except that our loose documents have now been recorded in books and are therefore more secure.	**2.** What can go wrong in this recording process?
2. It is easy to make mistakes as we copy the details into the books. Copying is a boring procedure.	**3.** What are the alternatives to keeping day books?
3. a) Simplified one-book-only systems (with the documents being filed in a lever arch file); b) slip systems (such as banks use—cheques and paying-in slips, direct debits and credits); c) simultaneous records systems (where our record is carbon copied onto other records simultaneously); d) computerized records.	**4.** Which is the most widely used 'one-book' system?
4. The Simplex System supplied by George Vyner Ltd, of Huddersfield, United Kingdom.	**5.** How does it work?
5. It has a place for everything, and we put everything in its place (receipts, payments, bank lodgements, trade expenses and overheads).	**6.** Where are simultaneous records used?

6. Anywhere where two or three records fit together—for example:
 a) statement on top of debtors ledger on top of Sales Day Book;
 b) remittance advice note on top of creditors ledger on top of Purchases Day Book;
 c) payslip on top of employee's earnings card on top of payroll sheet.

7. What is the Kalamazoo system?

7. The most widely used of wages simultaneous records.

8. What about computerized records?

8. They are now the most widely used short-cut system.

9. Go over the list again until you are sure of all the answers.

UNIT 16

Bank Reconciliation Statements

16.1 Introduction

It frequently happens in business that two sets of figures should agree, but for some reason do not. For example, we might estimate that a certain profit should be made in a given period, but in fact we fail to achieve this expected profit. A good accountant would seek to *reconcile*—that is, to make compatible—the two sets of figures, examining the reasons for the discrepancy.

Perhaps the commonest of all such situations is the reconciliation of the Bank Account, as shown in our ledger, with the Bank Account in the bank's ledger, as shown when the bank sends us a *bank statement*. This is a computer printout showing the various transactions which have taken place between the bank and ourselves. We may have banked cheques or made withdrawals during recent weeks or months. The bank may have undertaken certain payments or collections on our behalf. The printout shows the bank's view of these matters, but we may need to reconcile its view with our own.

16.2 Practical Banking

When a bank agrees to permit a customer to open a current account by paying in an initial sum of money, and gives him or her a cheque-book so that payments may be made through the cheque system, it does not undertake to correspond with the customer every time a transaction takes place. Some banks hardly ever write to their customers at all, unless one of them fails to keep enough funds in the account to ensure that the bank will always be able to honour any cheques presented. Similarly, the customer never writes to the bank to tell the manager about a cheque that has been made out.

Most customers, however, are sent a statement of their bank account at regular intervals, on a 'cyclical billing' system. This means that the bank, to even out the flow of its work, sends out accounts to about 5 per cent of its customers every day. Suppose your account is made out to the ninth day of each month, you will receive your bank statement about two or three days after this date, every month. But when you see the bank statement it may come as a surprise if the statement differs from the Bank Account in the three-column cash book. There are several reasons why this may be so, and in practice the two accounts rarely show the same balance. The differences are always due to a lack of knowledge of what the other person has been doing. The reasons may be divided into three groups:

(a) differences arising from the bank's actions, about which we have not been notified;
(b) differences arising from the time-lag which is inevitable whenever cheques are sent in payment of debts, or are received and paid into the bank for clearing through the bankers' clearing house;
(c) errors either by the bank, or by our own cashier. Such errors are unlikely to occur frequently, because the banks usually institute careful checks on their figures, and a cashier is usually a responsible member of the staff. Inevitably though, mistakes do occur from time to time.

We will look more closely at the first two causes of difference.

(a) Differences due to Lack of Knowledge of the Bank's Actions

In certain circumstances the bank does not bother to inform us that it has taken money from, or has credited money to, our account. It expects us to discover from the statement that certain actions have been taken. Here are some of the most common.

(i) The removal of sums for bank charges, or for interest on overdrafts.
(ii) The payment of standing orders which we may have instructed the bank to pay. Most people remember to deduct these sums from the Bank Account if they are monthly payments, such as mortgage payments or payments for rates. The less frequent ones, such as annual contributions to charities, may be overlooked.
(iii) The payment of sums into the account through the bank giro system (now known as 'direct credits'). The commonest types of bank giro transfer are wages payments and transfers connected with investments. For example, the Bank of England, which manages the gilt-edged security market on behalf of the Treasury, prefers to pay interest on securities directly into the investor's bank account, rather than sending a cheque for the amount due. This direct credit will appear on the bank statement as a deposit, increasing the balance on the account.
(iv) The payment of sums by the bank as instructed by a *direct debit* or *debit transfer*. This is used in a similar way to a standing order—to pay money to a creditor—but this time it is the creditor who is allowed to ask the bank to debit our account. This is especially useful where the amount varies from year to year. As we do not know how much to pay, we cannot 'order' the bank to pay it. We therefore sign a letter of authority (a *mandate*) to permit the creditor to ask the bank for the amount of money required, and for the bank to debit our account with this sum. Subscriptions to professional bodies, which tend to change every year or two, are often paid in this way.

(v) The deduction of an agreed amount to repay a loan made by the bank at an earlier date (see Unit 16.5(b)). This is just a special case of the standing order.

When such items are discovered on a bank statement they must at once be entered in the Bank Account in the three-column cash book. They will increase the balance on the Bank Account (i.e. debit it) if they are receipts, and decrease the balance (i.e. credit the account) if they are sums paid away by the bank, or taken by the bank for services rendered.

(b) Differences due to Delays in the Cheque System

Imagine that we send a cheque for $50 to Angus McDowell, a farmer who lives at the other end of the country. Before we post the letter containing the cheque we shall credit the item in the Bank Account, which has given value, $50. It will probably be at least two days before that letter arrives, and when it does arrive Mr McDowall may find it difficult to get to the bank and pay it in. There will then be a further delay while the cheque is passed through head office in London, or through the clearing house if he banks with a different bank from ours. During this time-lag, our Bank Account will show that we have deducted the cheque from our available funds, but the bank will think that we still have this money. Sometimes, when a creditor puts a cheque in his pocket and forgets to pay it in, several months may pass before the two accounts agree on this point. *Neither of them is wrong*, and it would be a mistake to 'correct' them or take any action—we must simply wait for Mr McDowall to put the matter right by getting down to the bank in his local town and paying the cheque into his account. Such a situation would be explained in the bank reconciliation statement.

Now imagine we are going to the bank to collect a bank statement which the bank has already promised to prepare for us. Incidentally, while we are down there we will pay in those cheques that arrived this morning in the mail from customers. Before setting off we record these cheques in the Bank Account, on the debit side, and list them in the paying-in book. On arrival at the bank we greet the cashier, pay in the cheques and collect the bank statement. This bank statement will not be completely up to date, however, because the cheques just paid in will not appear upon it.

Again, we shall have to explain the differences between the Bank Account and the bank statement by a sentence or two in the bank reconciliation statement.

16.3 How to Prepare a Bank Reconciliation Statement

Consider the cash book (bank columns only) and the bank statement shown below.

A. Ryder—Cash Book (bank columns only)

20..		$	20..		$
1 Jan. Balance	B/d	494.24	2 Jan. T. Wilson	L72	71.65
5 Jan. Sales	L21	62.80	13 Jan. City Council	L33	30.50
12 Jan. Sales	L21	75.00	15 Jan. Cash	C	60.00
14 Jan. T. Bainbridge	L44	12.56	29 Jan. R. Long	L56	48.00
19 Jan. Sales	L21	35.00	31 Jan. Anne Employee	L5	120.00
26 Jan. Sales	L21	85.00	31 Jan. Balance	c/d	449.39
31 Jan. R. Loring	L57	14.94			
		$779.54			$779.54
31 Jan. Balance	B/d	449.39			

A. Ryder—Bank Statement
In account with Barminster Bank PLC

Date	*Details*	*Dr.*	*Cr.*	*Balance*
20..		$	$	$
1 Jan.	Bal. c/f			508.40
3 Jan.	101146	14.16		494.24
5 Jan.	Sundries		62.80	557.04
12 Jan.	Sundries		75.00	632.04
14 Jan.	101148	30.50		601.54
14 Jan.	Sundries		12.56	614.10
15 Jan.	101149	60.00		554.10
19 Jan.	Sundries		35.00	589.10
26 Jan.	Sundries		85.00	674.10
29 Jan.	101150	48.00		626.10
30 Jan.	Charges	4.55		621.55
30 Jan.	International Investors (credit)		12.80	634.35

The following points are of interest.

(a) The items which appear as debits on A. Ryder's cash book are credits on the bank statement. This appears confusing, but in fact it is only sensible, because the bank keeps its account with Ryder from its point of view and not from Ryder's. If Ryder has more cash in the bank (a debit entry in Ryder's cash book) it means the bank owes him more money, i.e. he is a creditor for a greater amount (a credit entry in Ryder's account in the bank).

(b) On 1 January the two accounts were different: Ryder thought he had $494.24 while the bank thought he had $508.40. Where there was a discrepancy to start with like this, it was clearly due to a time-lag on the account, and we should expect it to be cleared up at some time in the month under consideration. As we can see, the outstanding cheque was cleared up on 3 January when someone (a creditor) presented a cheque for payment. This made the two accounts agree.

(c) Ryder must now compare the two accounts to see which items are different. Looking down Ryder's debit column (and the bank statement credit column) we can see two differences.

(i) $14.94 from R. Loring was paid into the bank on the last day of the month. Clearly the bank have not yet credited Ryder with the value of this cheque. It is a 'time-lag' item and must be explained on the bank reconciliation statement.

(ii) $12.80 has been transferred by a firm called International Investors to Ryder's account. This must be a dividend on his investments and needs to be entered in his cash book—he was not aware that the bank had collected this money on his account.

Running our eyes down the credit side of Ryder's account (and down the debit column on the bank statement) we see that there are four further differences, of which one has already been referred to in (b) above. This leaves three further outstanding points. They are:

(iii) The cheque for $71.65 paid to T. Wilson on 2 January has not yet been presented by him for collection through the bankers' clearing house. This is a 'time-lag' item and will need to be explained on the bank reconciliation statement.

(iv) On 30 January the bank deducted $4.55 bank charges from Ryder's account. This needs to be entered in the cash book, since it is the first Ryder has heard about the bank's actions.

(v) On 31 January the cheque paid to Anne Employee, $120.00, has not yet been presented for payment. This is similar to Wilson's cheque in (iii) above.

The first thing to do is to bring the Bank Account up to date, by including items (ii) and (iv) above:

A. Ryder—Cash Book (bank columns only)

20..		$	20..		$
31 Jan. Balance	B/d	449.39	31 Jan. Bank charges		4.55
31 Jan. Dividends received		12.80	Balance	c/d	457.64
		$462.19			$462.19
1 Feb. Balance	B/d	457.64			

We are now ready to draw up the bank reconciliation statement. This requires us to start either with the cash book balance or the bank statement balance, and explain why it is in fact a perfectly good figure if the outstanding items are taken into account. We do this by working towards the other figure. Careful reading of the example below will make this explanation clear.

Bank Reconciliation Statement as at 31 January 20..

		$
Balance as per cash book	=	457.64
Deduct cheque paid in, not yet cleared		
R. Loring		14.94
(because the bank does not regard us as having yet received this money)		442.70
Add back cheques drawn but not yet presented for payment	$	
T. Wilson	71.65	
Anne Employee	120.00	
(because the bank regards us as still having this money)		191.65
Balance as per bank statement		$634.35

This statement reconciles the Bank Account with the bank statement, and we may therefore feel satisfied that no errors on the bank's or cashier's part have been made.

A neat copy of the bank reconciliation statement will be typed and filed away for reference purposes.

16.4 Exercise Set 25. Bank Reconciliation Statements

1. Enter in the Bank Account of Richard Lawrence's cash book, starting with the balance shown below, any item that needs to be entered. Then prepare a bank reconciliation statement from the following particulars:

	$
Cash at bank as per bank statement on 31 March 20. .	254.36
Cheques received and paid into the bank but not yet entered in bank statement	126.55
Cheques drawn and entered in the cash book but not yet presented to the bank	187.10
Direct debit for rates not yet entered in the cash book	115.40
On 31 March the bank column of the cash book showed a debit balance of	309.21

2. On 30 April 20. . Angus Grant's cash book showed a balance at the bank of $404.24 but at the same date the monthly statement from his bank showed a balance of $412.50.

The difference between the two balances was found to be due to the following:

(a) On 10 April a charge of $4.45 for foreign exchange commission had been made by the bank. Grant had forgotten to deduct this on his cash book.

(b) An annual subscription of $15.25 had been paid by direct debit on 25 April. This had also been overlooked by Grant.

(c) Cheques for $25.30 and $42.45 drawn in favour of D. Jones and T. Fortescue had not been presented for payment by them.

(d) A cheque for $39.79 from R. Sterling paid into the bank on 15 April had been returned marked 'Refer to Drawer'. No entry of this dishonour had been made in the cash book. (Note: credit the cash book with $39.79 to remove the money not received.)

You are asked

(i) to open Grant's cash book (bank columns only) on 30 April with the balance of $404.24,

(ii) to enter such items as need to be entered,

(iii) to balance off the cash book again and then, using this new balance, prepare a bank reconciliation statement as at 30 April 20. . for any remaining items.

3. On 31 March 20. . the balance in the bank account as shown in the cash book of Christine Roper was $485.00. On checking the cash book with the bank statement she discovered the following differences:

(a) Cheques credited in the cash book but not yet presented for payment, $142.00.

(b) The bank statement did not include cheques paid into the bank on 31 March, and debited in the cash book on that day, worth $137.50.

(c) The bank had charged her account with $8.25 charges, and had credited her account with $18.50, being a dividend received by the bank on her behalf. Neither of these items had been entered in the cash book.
(d) The bank statement balance was $499.75.

You are required
(i) to adjust the cash book balance, and
(ii) to reconcile the adjusted balance with the balance on the bank statement at 31 March 20...

4. Here are the Bank Account and bank statement of L. Roberts for the last week of June 20..

Cash Book (bank columns only)

			$				$
25 June	Balance	B/d	284.50	29 June	Knight		34.90
26 June	Jones		50.00	29 June	Harvey		72.60
28 June	Brown		110.25	29 June	Roach		5.55
29 June	Smith		35.45	30 June	Rudolfo		4.72
				30 June	Balance	c/d	362.43
			$480.20				$480.20
30 June	Balance	B/d	362.43				

Bank Statement as at 30 June 20..

Date	*Details*	*Dr.*	*Cr.*	*Balance*
		$	$	$
25 June	Balance			284.50
26 June	Sundries		5.00	289.50
28 June	Sundries		110.25	399.75
29 June	134134	34.90		364.85
29 June	Charges	4.30		360.55
30 June	Credit transfer (H. Neale)		42.60	403.15

You are asked a) to correct the cash book, bearing in mind that the cheque from Jones was really only $5.00, and b) to reconcile the new cash balance with the bank statement balance.

5. a) Your cash book shows a balance of $350. Cheques drawn but not presented total $135. What should be the balance according to your bank?
b) A standing order for $20 has not been entered in your cash book. If your bank statement shows a balance of $450, what should be the balance in your cash book before the standing order is recorded?
c) Your bank statement shows a balance of $700. Cheques drawn but not presented total $140. What should be the balance in your cash book?
d) A commercial traveller paid $150 into your account. His notification was lost in the post. If your bank statement shows a balance of $780, what should be the balance in your cash book?

6. Below are given the cash book and bank statement of a trader, D. Stevenson. You are required

a) to bring the cash book up to date, starting with the balance brought down on 1 July, and then

b) to prepare a statement reconciling the corrected cash book balance with the balance shown by the bank statement.

Note: It is helpful to point out that the opening balance on the Cash Book and the opening balance on the Bank Statement differ by $17.04.

Cash Book (bank columns only)

			$				$
24 June	Balance	B/d	600.00	25 June	Neil and Son		40.00
27 June	Cash		50.00	27 June	Riley		15.00
28 June	Lucas		8.15	28 June	Morris		10.12
30 June	Smithers		22.10	28 June	White		41.13
30 June	Jones		15.15	30 June	Balance	c/d	589.15
			$695.40				$695.40
1 July	Balance	B/d	$589.15				

Bank Statement

Date	*Details*	*Dr.*	*Cr.*	*Balance*
		$	$	$
24 June	Balance			617.04
25 June	127325	40.00		577.04
26 June	Sundries		50.00	627.04
26 June	127324	17.04		610.00
27 June	127326	15.00		595.00
28 June	Sundries		8.15	603.15
	Brown (Credit transfer)		10.00	613.15
30 June	Charges	5.25		607.90

7. At close of business on 28 February 20.., A. Trader's cash book showed a balance of $1 017.12, which did not agree with his bank statement, the following being sources of disagreement:

(a) Cheques issued but not presented: Green $115.10; Riley $237.50; Stokes $38.00.

(b) Lodgement 28 February not credited by bank: $185.15.

(c) Credit transfers not entered in the cash book: Boxer $5.75; Striker $16.60.

(d) A direct debit for $10.50, being a subscription to a trade association, had been paid by the bank but not entered in the cash book.

(e) A charge of $4.22 had been made by the bank for operating the account, but had not been entered in the cash book.

You are required to
(i) make such entries in the cash book as will result in the correct balance being shown,
(ii) prepare a statement accounting for the difference between your corrected cash book and the bank statement balance,
(iii) show on the statement required in (ii) the balance per the bank statement.

8. Set out below are the cash book (bank columns only) and bank statement of E. Hemingway for the month of January 20... You are asked to

(a) reopen the cash book with the balance of $992.13 and enter such items as have clearly not yet been entered (this will enable you to find a new balance as per cash book), and
(b) draw up a bank reconciliation statement as at 31 January, which reconciles your new cash balance with the bank statement balance.

Cash Book (bank columns only)

20..		$	20..		$
1 Jan. Balance	B/d	1 027.16	5 Jan. R. Palmer		14.18
13 Jan. Smith		16.18	7 Jan. Wages		118.10
13 Jan. Cash		54.10	19 Jan. T. Burton		7.12
27 Jan. Lovell		7.12	21 Jan. Wages		118.10
27 Jan. Cash		42.01	28 Jan. L. Mannheim		10.99
31 Jan. Whiteley		114.05	31 Jan. Balance	c/d	992.13
		$1 260.62			$1 260.62
31 Jan. Balance	B/d	992.13			

Bank Statement as at 31 January 20..

Date	*Details*	*Dr.*	*Cr.*	*Balance*
		$	$	$
1 Jan.	—			1 027.16
7 Jan.	145977	118.10		909.06
9 Jan.	145976	14.18		894.88
13 Jan.	Sundries		70.28	965.16
21 Jan.	145979	118.10		847.06
21 Jan.	HM Treasury Interest		12.15	859.21
24 Jan.	Bank charges	5.55		853.66
27 Jan.	Sundries		49.13	902.79
28 Jan.	145980	10.99		891.80

16.5 Double Entries and Bank Reconciliations

We have seen that it can sometimes happen that we haven't been fully aware of what the bank has been doing, so that a difference can arise between the balance in our Bank Account in the cash book and the balance in our account at the bank; and we have also seen how this can be corrected by making appropriate entries in the cash book. These will be posted to the ledger in the usual way, thus achieving double entries.

Where there is a possibility that a legal dispute might arise over the matter, however, we might feel that a clear record of a particular entry could be desirable. The commonest examples concern dishonoured cheques and bank loans.

(a) Dishonoured Cheques

When a customer pays by cheque, the cheque is debited in the cash book and credited to the customer's account. Very often the cheque is not for the full amount of the debt, since the customer deducts discount for paying promptly. Sometimes the cheque is returned by the bank, marked with the phrase 'refer to drawer'—in other words, 'ask the debtor why he has given you a cheque when he has no funds to cover it in his account'. Usually the debtor will then see his bank and arrange to have the cheque honoured at a subsequent presentation.

In the meantime the creditor should take action to *restore the debt, in full, to the debtor*. Clearly the customer has not paid, and the debt should be restored to his or her account. This requires not only the restoration of the value of the cheque, but discount as well, i.e. the value of the original debt, since the discount is not allowable now that the cheque has been dishonoured. The effect of this is to restore the full debt to the debtor's account, and at the same time recover the discount on the Discount Allowed Account. We shall not lose this discount now, as the debtor will have to pay in full. Remember, discount is only given to debtors who pay promptly. A typical Journal entry would be as follows:

					J7
20..				$	$
19 Jan.	A. Debtor	Dr.	L57	150.00	
	Bank Account		CB9		142.50
	Discount Allowed Account		L168		7.50
	Being dishonoured cheque returned marked 'refer to drawer' at this date				

These entries would then be posted to the account as follows (in each case the folio number J7 indicates the Journal entry—the other figures have been put in to make the account sensible and as it would appear in practice):

A. Debtor Account L57

20..		$	20..		$
1 Jan. Balance	B/d	150.00	15 Jan. Bank	CB5	142.50
19 Jan. Bank and Discount	J7	150.00	15 Jan. Discount Allowed	CB5	7.50

Cash Book (bank column only) CB9

			20..		$
			19 Jan. Dishonoured cheque A. Debtor	J7	142.50

Discount Allowed Account L68

20..		$	20..		$
8 Jan. Sundry discounts	CB3	142.50	19 Jan. A. Debtor	J7	7.50
15 Jan. Sundry discounts	CB5	138.65			

(b) Bank Loans

When a bank lends money to a customer it may do so in two ways. First it may *permit an overdraft*, which simply means that it will allow the customers to draw cheques to a greater value than the amounts paid in to his or her current account. Overdrafts are only intended to be short-term affairs, helping the customer to overcome a temporary shortage of cash. They may be recalled at any time, which means that the customer can be required to pay in the amount of the overdraft. It is most unlikely that the customer can do so (otherwise he or she would not be overdrawn) so where a bank calls in overdrafts, it may in fact have to formalize the overdraft by making a proper loan to the customer.

When a *bank loan* is arranged, the customer enters into a formal arrangement (i.e. signs an agreement) to borrow a sum of money and repay it over several years. The amount of the loan is then credited in the customer's current account (extinguishing an overdraft if one already existed) but another account, a Loan Account, is opened with the corresponding debit entry. Interest arrangements vary, but interest is often charged quarterly by deduction from the customer's current account, the customer discovering the deduction when a bank statement is sent. The customer needs to remember to keep sufficient funds in the current account to meet this interest as it falls due.

When a loan is made in this way it seems desirable to record it formally by means of a Journal entry, as in this example:

					J1
20..				$	$
1 Jan.	Bank Account	Dr.	CB95	2000.00	
	Bank Loan Account		L172		2000.00
	Being loan negotiated with Barminster Bank at this date, at 12 per cent over two years				

Posted to the ledger and the cash book the entries would be:

Cash Book (bank column only) CB95

20..		$			
1 Jan. Bank Loan	J1	2000.00			

Bank Loan Account L172

			20..		$
			1 Jan. Bank	J1	2000.00

The repayments on the loan would be deducted by the bank at the agreed dates, the customer crediting his cash book and debiting Bank Loan Account so that the loan is gradually extinguished. Such a bank loan, is, of course, a long-term liability on the Balance Sheet. Interest is deducted (as explained above) from the current account and when discovered on the bank statement it is credited in the Bank Account and debited to Interest Payable Account, thus:

Cash Book (bank column only) CB9

		20..		$
		31 Mar.	Interest on loan	60

Interest Payable Account L27

20..		$			
31 Mar.	Bank	60			

An alternative arrangement is for the interest charged to be added to the Loan Account, so that the outstanding balance is increased. When this is discovered on the loan statement it has to be credited to the Bank Loan Account and debited to Interest Payable Account:

Bank Loan Account L172

		20..		$
		1 Jan.	Bank	2000
		31 Mar.	Interest Payable A/c	60

Interest Payable Account L27

20..		$			
31 Mar.	Bank Loan A/c	60			

16.6 Exercises Set 26. Dishonoured Cheques and Bank Loans

1. On 4 May 20.. M. Dawson received a cheque from a debtor, P. Hawkins, for $120.25 in settlement of his debt of that sum. On 7 May the cheque was returned 'refer to drawer'. Show the Journal entry necessary to restore the debt to the debtor.

2. On 17 July M. Rookes pays B. Barnard a cheque for $38.50, in full settlement of his debt of $40.00. The cheque is passed through Barnard's cash book and is then paid into the bank. The cheque is returned marked 'refer to drawer' on 21 July 20... Show the Journal entry necessary to restore the debt to the debtor, and post it to the ledger account.

3. M. Kelley receives a cheque on 12 May 20.. from R. Boniface for $72.20, in full settlement of his account of $76.00. Kelley enters the cheque in his Bank Account, but it is returned dishonoured on 17 May 20... Show the Journal entry restoring the debt to the debtor, and post it to the relevant accounts.

4. On 15 December 20.. Dorothy Piggott arranges a loan with Midwest Bank PLC for $500, at 12 per cent, to be repaid over two years. Show the Journal entry in Dorothy Piggott's books, and the ledger accounts affected. (No entries about interest are necessary at present.)

5. On 8 April 20.. the Loamshire Quarry Co were overdrawn at the bank $231 729. The bank insisted on clearing this overdraft at once, but agreed to make a loan of $300 000 available at 11 per cent interest per annum, repayable over three years. This was agreed, and the accountant of the Quarry Co made an appropriate Journal entry. Show this Journal entry and post it to the ledger accounts affected. (Do not make any entries about interest.)

16.7 Revise and Test 16. Bank Reconciliation Statements

Answers	*Questions*
—	**1.** Why do we need to do a Bank Reconciliation?
1. Because our Bank Account in the Cash Book rarely agrees with our Bank Account at the bank, as shown on our Monthly Bank Statement.	**2.** Why is this?
2. a) Because we do things without telling the bank (like writing out cheques); b) because the Bank does things without telling us (like charging interest or paying direct debits); c) because there are time lags in the system, while cheques are cleared.	**3.** What is the first thing to do when trying to reconcile these different bank balances?
3. We can't go into the bank's system and put their records straight, but we can get our Cash Book right, so: a) check the Bank Statement to see if the bank has done anything we didn't know about; b) make an entry about each of the things we find in our Cash Book, so our Cash Book is now right.	**4.** What sort of things will we find?

4. a) Direct credits into our account— such as VAT refunds, tax refunds or payments by debtors who pay by BACS (Bankers Automated Clearance Service); b) direct debits out of our account; c) standing orders out of our account; d) bank charges.	**5.** Our Cash Book is now right— Why?
5. Because it knows everything we have done and everything the Bank has done. The Bank Account is still wrong.	**6.** Why?
6. Because time lags in the system mean it doesn't yet know what *we* have done.	**7.** Give examples of things the bank doesn't know.
7. a) It may not know that we have written cheques and sent them to our creditors; b) it may not know we have paid in cash and cheques for collection in the last day or so.	**8.** What do we do about these items?

8. We draw up the Bank Reconciliation Statement (see example below)

Bank Reconciliation Statement as at 3 January 20..

	$	$
Balance as per Cash Book (corrected figure)		1385.60
Deduct takings paid in on 3 January		
(*The Bank doesn't know we've paid them in*)		477.30
		908.30
Add back cheques drawn and sent to suppliers but not yet presented		
(*The bank thinks we've still got their money*)		
R. Jones	128.65	
M. Smith	63.40	
		192.05
Balance according to Bank Statement		$1100.35

UNIT 17

Capital and Revenue Expenditure and Receipts

17.1 Capital Items and Revenue Items

Years ago, the distinctions between capital and revenue expenditure, and between capital and revenue receipts, were not matters of much concern. Recently these distinctions have acquired great importance, because of high taxation and because tax systems are chiefly based upon the taxation of income. A businessman's income can only be determined if we calculate what he has received each year by way of fees, commissions and other business receipts, and set against these earnings the costs of achieving them. It becomes necessary to sort out what he has received this year from what he already had—the accumulated capital of an earlier period. A detailed study of taxation is not required in a book which is about the principles of accounting, but the concepts of capital and revenue expenditure, and capital and revenue receipts, are of fundamental importance to the determination of profits, and are necessary if 'correct' profit figures are to be found. You may wonder why the word 'correct' is written in quotation marks. The reason is that there is no one way of determining profit—there are many areas which are debatable, and many businessmen have gone to law with the Inland Revenue authorities, to determine the 'correct' way of determining profits. Often the distinction between capital and revenue expenditure has been at the centre of the discussion.

17.2 Capital and Revenue Expenditure

Whenever we spend money we receive something in return. These items may be classified as follows:

(a) Items which last a long time, and are used in the business over a period of years. These are called *fixed assets* or *capital assets* or capital expenditure. Examples are land and buildings, plant and machinery, fixtures and fittings, motor vehicles, leases on property, patent rights.
(b) Items which do not last a long time, but are quickly used for the benefit of the business and are then lost for all time. Examples are rent, light and heat, postage stamps, telephone calls, petrol and oil for motor vehicles. These are called *revenue items*, or revenue expenditure.
(c) Items which are purchased for resale, or purchased for manufacture before being resold. The whole purpose of many businesses is to manufacture a finished product from certain raw materials. Moreover the intention is to do so as quickly as possible, without taking years over the matter, so that all such items may be regarded as *revenue items*.
(d) Services, which are obtained in return for the money paid. These services are usually the result of contracts of service (employees) or contracts for services (outside contractors). Whichever they are, they may usually be regarded as relatively short term, and therefore be counted as *revenue items*.

It follows that the duration of use of an item—how long it lasts—is critical in deciding whether it is capital or revenue expenditure. The dividing line chosen is one year, because the Government claims its share of the rewards of any enterprise annually. Therefore the following definitions are appropriate:

- *Capital expenditure* is expenditure on items which last longer than a year, and which therefore have an enduring influence on the profit-making capacity of the business.
- *Revenue expenditure* is expenditure on consumable items, on services and on goods for re-sale. They last less than one year, and therefore only temporarily influence the profit-making capacity of the business.

In fact, at the end of any given year, there will be some revenue items which are still in hand and which will pass over to the new year, even though they were purchased in the previous year. These items have to be the subject of *adjustments* and are dealt with fully in Units 22.3 to 22.7.

The definitions above have been used to determine whether expenditures are capital or revenue, in the following examples quoted from an imaginary manufacturing firm:

Capital expenditure	*Revenue expenditure*
Purchase of a new factory	Wages for employees
Plant and machinery to equip the factory	Salary of factory manager
Office equipment (computers etc.)	Interest on money borrowed from bank
Goodwill payment on purchase of marketing area to assist disposal of new product	Raw materials purchases
	Office stationery, documents, etc.
	Repairs and redecorations (though management may decide to spread payment over several years)

17.3 Capital and Revenue Receipts

When a business receives money it may be a contribution by the proprietor, partners or shareholders towards the capital of the firm, in other words a *capital receipt.* Alternatively it may be a result of the firm's activity in the current period, part of its reward for offering goods or services to the public, such as payments received from customers and debtors for goods supplied, or fees received for services rendered. All such items are *revenue receipts*, and must be set against the revenue expenses in order to determine the profitability of the business for the period under discussion.

The only other kind of receipt is a receipt of money when a loan or a mortgage on property is arranged. This is like a contribution of capital to the business by someone outside the business, not the proprietor. It is regarded as a capital item, but the interest charged for the use of the money will be a revenue expense of the period in which it becomes due.

17.4 The Calculation of Profits—Revenue Accounts

We have already seen that capital expenditure and capital receipts do not enter into the calculation of business profits for taxation purposes. It is only the revenue expenditure and revenue receipts which are set against one another to discover the profit or loss of the period concerned. This, we already know, is done in the Trading Account and Profit and Loss Account of a business enterprise. Some businesses find the phrase 'Profit and Loss' distasteful or inappropriate, however. Thus doctors do not like to say 'We made a profit of $25.50 out of Farmer Brown's broken leg', and organizations like the Royal Automobile Club would not speak of 'making a profit out of the members'.

For these reasons, the following names have been devised over the years:

(a) *Revenue Account*—for a partnership of professional people such as lawyers, doctors, dentists, etc. This is the account where revenue expenditure will be set against revenue receipts to discover the excess of fees over expenses.

(b) *Trading and Profit and Loss Accounts*—for a business enterprise to discover profits over a period by setting revenue expenditure against revenue receipts.

(c) *Income and Expenditure Accounts*—for the accounts of a non-profitmaking body to determine the surplus, or deficit, contributed by the members.

These three names all refer to very similar accounts.

The importance of keeping proper accounts

For centuries it was the rule that it was not compulsory to keep books of account. Many people could not read and write, though they were surprisingly good at knowing the value of money, and what wages or change they were entitled to in money transactions. The tax authorities got over the difficulty of 'incomplete records' in the following way. They valued the business at the start of the year, and again at the end of the year. Suppose A. Trader's business is worth $100 at the start of the year and $6 100 at the end of the year. Clearly the extra wealth must have come from the profitable nature of his business. Not only this, but he has also lived through the year. The tax authorities will take the increased wealth of $6 000 and add on the trader's estimate of drawings for the year. Suppose he gave his wife $100 per week and had $25 for his own pocket. This makes drawings of $6 500 per year. Thus they would levy tax on earnings of $12 500.

Today in many countries incomplete records is not a satisfactory system. For example in the United Kingdom everyone is required to keep proper books of account. All records of receipts, payments, expenditure and income must be kept for six years, including all cheque book stubs, bank statements, documents and VAT records. There is a fine of up to £3 000 for failure to keep proper records. The aim is to arrive at a true earnings figure for the business. Our correct records, when we set revenue expenditure against revenue receipts will reveal our true profits.

17.5 Arriving at a 'True' Profit Figure

In order to arrive at a true profit figure we must obey the following rules:

(i) *Revenue expenditure*—ensure that the period under consideration carried every penny of loss that it should carry, but not a penny more.
(ii) *Revenue receipts*—ensure that the period under consideration is credited with every penny earned in the period, but not a penny more.

To ensure these rules are obeyed, we have to make certain adjustments. These adjustments are concerned with two ideas: the capitalization (even if only for a short while) of revenue expenditure and the 'revenue-ization' of capital expenditure (revenue-ization is an awkward and, strictly speaking, a non-existent word, here used to convey the idea of converting a capital item into a revenue item).

(a) The Capitalization of Revenue Expenditure

Sometimes we pay out money (revenue expenditure) for something which eventually becomes a capital asset. Thus we might employ our own workers to extend the factory canteen, for example, or to erect machinery and shelving, or belting systems. If we were to charge these expenses as a loss in the Profit and Loss Account, we should be making this year bear the entire loss for an asset that will last several years. To overcome this difficulty we capitalize the revenue expenditure, removing it from the 'loss' account and transferring it to an asset account. Consider the following example:

A. Shopkeeper is a builder's merchant. He also undertakes small contracts for householders in the area, employing six members of staff for the purpose. In February there is little work about, and he decides to use this labour force to redesign and redecorate the shop premises. The labour cost involved (that is, wages) is $1 245, and materials are used from stock at a cost of $1 450. The premises are calculated to increase in value by $5 000 as a result. Make the entries as at 28 February to capitalize this revenue expenditure.

How should Shopkeeper record these matters in his accounts? Clearly the wages will already have been debited in Wages Account and the materials will be debited in Purchases Account. What he has to do is to capitalize the revenue expenditure, changing it to a capital asset—premises—instead of two revenue losses—wages and purchases. In addition he has made a profit out of the work, since the premises are now believed to be worth $5 000 extra. This profit is to be treated as a capital profit, not a revenue profit, and will be credited to Appreciation of Buildings Account. The Journal entry will look like this:

				J111
20..			$	$
28 Feb.	Premises Account Dr.	L1	5000	
	Wages Account	L25		1245
	Purchases Account	L38		1450
	Appreciation of Buildings Account	L152		2305
	Being capitalization of revenue expenditure incurred in improving shop layout			

The ledger entries, assuming some imaginary figures already existing on the accounts, would be as follows:

Premises Account L1

20..		$			
1 Jan. Balance	B/d	26000			
28 Feb. Wages etc	J111	5000			

Wages Account L25

20..		$	20..		$
31 Jan. Cash	CB3	1280	28 Feb. Premises Account	J111	1245
28 Feb. Cash	CB17	1330			

Purchases Account L38

20..		$	20..		$
31 Jan. Sundry creditors	PDB11	4875	28 Feb. Premises Account	J111	1450
28 Feb. Sundry creditors	PDB16	3850			

Appreciation of Buildings Account L152

			20..		$
			28 Feb. Premises Account	J111	2305

(b) The 'Revenue-ization' of Capital Expenditure

'Revenue-ization' of capital expenditure—the idea that all capital assets eventually get written off to Profit and Loss Account over the years of their useful life—is just another way of describing the process of *depreciation*, discussed in Unit 13. We saw there that when we are attempting to calculate the profits of a trading period we must ensure that the Profit and Loss Account is debited with every penny of loss that it ought really to carry. If the trading period has used up some of the life of an asset, whether it is machinery, furniture, loose tools, patent rights, royalties owned or any other asset that is slowly consumed in the service of the business, then that asset must be depreciated by a 'fair' amount for the use made during the period concerned.

17.6 Doubtful Cases—Capital or Revenue Expenditure?

Sometimes it is difficult to decide whether an item should be treated as capital or revenue expenditure. Capital expenditure lasts longer than a year, and gives us something of long-term benefit to the firm. There are some expenses which seem to do the first, without doing the second. For example, repainting the premises usually lasts several years, but it only gives us a property that is restored to its original new condition—no extra value is really added, though the deterioration of the premises may be avoided. In such cases it is up to the accountant to decide what to do. Most accountants would probably feel that the considerable expenditure involved should be spread over more than one year—otherwise this year's profits will take a serious knock. Probably it would be a sound idea to capitalize the revenue expenditure and spread it out over this year and the next three years. To do this we could open a Repairs and Decorations Suspense Account, and write it off in four instalments. This account is shown below.

Repairs and Decorations Suspense Account L77

			$				$
20..				20..			
31 May	Bank Account	J15	600	31 Dec.	Profit and Loss Account	J29	150
				31 Dec.	Balance	c/d	450
			$600				$600
Next year				Next year			
1 Jan.	Balance	B/d	450	31 Dec.	Profit and Loss Account	J58	150
				31 Dec.	Balance	c/d	300
			$450				$450
Year 3				Year 3			
1 Jan.	Balance	B/d	300	31 Dec.	Profit and Loss Account	J98	150
				31 Dec.	Balance	c/d	150
			$300				$300
Year 4				Year 4			
1 Jan.	Balance	B/d	150	31 Dec.	Profit and Loss Account	J145	150
			$150				$150

17.7 Stock Losses

Some expenses need *not* be written off as losses of the business, because they will automatically be taken into account when we take stock. For example, if we suffer losses of stock due to accidental damage, or even due to pilfering by the staff or shoplifting by the customers, these losses need not be entered as losses in the Profit and Loss Account. They will automatically be picked up as losses when we count stock—they will not be there to count and so the stock-taking figure will be correspondingly lower than it should be. To enter such items a second time as losses would be to reduce the profits twice for the same loss.

Another example that has the same effect is losses of stock caused by perishable items that go bad. The spoiled items are disposed of and stocks reduced. There is no point in writing these off as losses; they will automatically reduce the stock figure. What we should do, though, is find out why the buyer concerned overbought—clearly it is bad buying to purchase perishable goods which are then left unsold. If you go to some shops late on a Saturday afternoon you will find them pushing the sales of perishable items like lettuces, tomatoes and bananas. Prices are reduced to dispose of goods likely to spoil over the weekend.

Some firms do run *perpetual inventory procedures*. These are systems where a team of specialist stock-takers is at work all the year round. Such firms deal with stock losses in rather a different way from smaller firms, and may not disregard the losses as explained above.

17.8 Exercises Set 27. Capital and Revenue Expenditure

1. Define capital expenditure and revenue expenditure. What is the importance of the distinction?

2. What is a capital receipt? What is a revenue receipt? The Inspector of Taxes for Alice Jones's area tells her that as her business was worth only $1 500 on 1 January of last year, and by 31 December it was worth $16 500, she must have made $15 000 profit in the year. Miss Jones had expanded her business by selling $4 000 of investments which were her personal property purchased many years earlier. She used the proceeds to re-equip the business. She now asks you to write a letter for her rejecting the tax inspector's suggestion. What would you say?

3. a) Writing about four or five lines on each, explain what is meant by
(i) capital expenditure,
(ii) revenue expenditure.
b) Give *two* examples of each type of expenditure.
c) A bull escapes in a crowded street market and blunders into a shop called 'Arts for All'. It breaks
(i) a display of china valued at $160, part of the stock to be sold,
(ii) the shop window, worth $125, which was unfortunately not insured.
Explain whether it would be necessary to write these items off as losses at the end of the financial year and give your reasons. The owner of the bull is insolvent and cannot pay any compensation.

4. State whether the following transactions of a youth centre should be classified as capital expenditure or revenue expenditure:

(a) the redecoration of the premises;
(b) the building of a new canteen;
(c) the building of an extension to the main hall;
(d) the purchase of soft drinks;
(e) the purchase of a music system for use in the centre.

5. Explain briefly the distinction between capital and revenue expenditure. State, with reasons, how you would classify each of the following two items:

(a) wages of own workers on building an extension to a firm's factory, and
(b) cost of rebuilding the wall of a factory.

6. The Newtown Players have recently enjoyed such success in their dramatic activities that they have been able to make purchases to improve their organization. As specified in the club rules, the treasurer regards all consumable and breakable items as revenue expenditure. Which of the following items would you regard as capital and which as revenue expenditure?

(a) erection of a theatre for club use;
(b) make-up for the next presentation;
(c) annual membership fee for the British Drama League;
(d) stage fittings, wings and pillars;
(e) flash powder for special effects;
(f) purchase of spotlights and dimmers;
(g) a club minibus for outside presentations;
(h) crockery for refreshment service;
(i) bar stocks;
(j) tickets for next performance.

7. M. Larkin has the following items of expenditure on his books for the year:

(a) wages paid to employees in warehouse, \$15 800;
(b) wages paid to some of the workers who agreed to assist in redesigning the warehouse layout during the firm's annual fortnight holiday closure, \$680;
(c) shelving and structural materials purchased for the redesigning programme, \$750;
(d) fork-lift trucks, \$4 850;
(e) purchases of goods for resale to stock warehouse after capacity had been increased, \$3 500.

Consider each of these items and state whether in your view it is capital expenditure or revenue expenditure. Then state whether the item would appear in the Trading Account, Profit and Loss Account or Balance Sheet.

8. The Linden Manufacturing Organization is setting up its own reprographic department. Write down the letters (a) to (j) to correspond with the items below, and write against them your opinion as to whether the item is capital or revenue expenditure:

(a) the purchase of a colour printer;
(b) white copier paper for the above;
(c) a word processor;
(d) a hand-operated ink duplicator;
(e) consumable items for the above machine;
(f) electricity bill for department;
(g) salary of the reprographic manager;
(h) supply of ink for offset litho machine;
(i) hiring charge for automatic overlay device;
(j) guillotine for trimming copies.

9. Your employer A. Decorator asks you to explain why a stock of wallpaper, which was thrown away as useless, has not been entered on the Profit and Loss Account as a loss. Justify your failure to write this item off. It had been damaged by rainwater after a skylight was accidentally left open.

10. A. Motor Manufacturer is retooling a section which produces batches of components for use on the main assembly line. It means closing the section for two weeks. To avoid laying off the workers involved, he asks them to agree to act as labourers in the installation and construction work going on. The following payments result from the re-equipment:

(a) purchase of machines $16 000 on credit from Power Tools Ltd;
(b) purchase of materials $1 450 on credit from Leigh Building Co.;
(c) wages of departmental staff for the fortnight $2 300;
(d) wages of craftsmen, electricians, builders, etc. employed on installation (these men are specialists employed in the plant) $1 580.

All these items, including the revenue items, are to be capitalized as part of the Machinery Account. Show the Journal entry required on 30 July 20...

11. Plastics Ltd employ their own maintenance staff on the extension of their canteen premises. The labour involved cost $1 580 and the materials cost $1 650. The value of the premises is increased by $5 000 as a result of the extension, the balance to be regarded as a capital profit and recorded in Appreciation on Buildings Account. Make the Journal entries necessary to record the above items in Plastics Ltd's records on 14 July 20...

12. a) Give three examples of capital expenditure that might be undertaken by a restaurant proprietor, and three examples of revenue expenditure that might be incurred by a garage owner.

b) Smart Wear Ltd spend $2 000 on redecorating their premises. They decide to regard this as lasting for five years, and to record it in a Decorations Suspense Account. At present $1 600 of it, which was paid as wages, is debited in Wages Account. The other $400, spent on materials, is included in Purchases Account after being posted there from the cash book. Do the Journal entry to capitalize this revenue expenditure at 31 August 20...

17.9 Revise and Test 17. Capital and Revenue Expenditure

Answers	*Questions*
—	**1.** What is capital expenditure?
1. Expenditure on assets which are purchased for long-term use in the business and are not to be resold except at the end of their life.	**2.** Name five capital assets.
2. a) Land and buildings; b) plant and machinery; c) furniture and fittings; d) motor vehicles; e) computers.	**3.** What are the ledger entries when we purchase assets?
3. a) Always debit the asset account b) Credit one of the following: (i) cash account if we pay cash; (ii) bank account if we pay by cheque; (iii) the creditor, if we obtain the assets on credit.	**4.** What is revenue expenditure?
4. Expenditure on items that only last the business a relatively short time, and are then used up completely.	**5.** Give examples.
5. a) Postage stamps; b) light and heat; c) telephone expenses; d) wages; e) carriage in; f) carriage out.	**6.** What are the ledger entries for revenue expenditure?

---

6. a) Debit the expense account—it becomes one of the losses of the business;
b) Credit:
(i) cash account if we pay cash;
(ii) bank account if we pay by cheque;
(iii) the creditor if the item was supplied on credit.

7. What is the boundary line in time between capital and revenue expenditure?

---

7. One year. Generally speaking, if an item lasts longer than one year it is a capital asset; if it lasts less than one year it is a revenue expense.

8. There are a few areas where we are not quite sure whether things are capital expenditure or revenue expenditure. What are they?

---

8. a) Things like redecorations. They are rather temporary, but may only be done every three years;
b) some revenue expenses result in the creation of capital items. These should be capitalized—as where our workers build an extension to the canteen.

9. What do we do with things like redecorations?

---

9. a) Capitalize the revenue expense—put it in an account such as the Decorations Suspense Account;
b) write off one-third of this each year in the Profit and Loss Account, so that each year carries a fair share of the cost.

10. What do we do about activities that increase the value of assets?

10. Capitalize the revenue expense. Suppose we buy a machine for \$20 000 and our own maintenance people build concrete platforms, supply electricity, etc. at a cost of \$1 000 for materials and \$4 000 for wages. We take the machine on the books at \$25 000 (debit Machinery Account) and credit the supplier \$20 000, Wages Account \$4 000 and Purchases Account \$1 000 (for the material used).	**11.** Why is it important to distinguish between capital and revenue expenditure (and also capital and revenue receipts)?
11. Because it is a rule in book-keeping that we must each year: a) work out our profits correctly so that we pay the correct amount of tax; b) produce a correct Balance Sheet, which gives a true and fair view of the business, its assets and liabilities.	**12.** Where do the revenue items come into this picture?
12. When we work out our profits—it is the revenue items that come in the Trading Account and the Profit and Loss Account.	**13.** And where do the capital items come into the picture?
13. They produce the Balance Sheet.	**14.** Go over the page again until you are sure of all the items.

UNIT 18

A Full Set of Accounts

18.1 From Original Entries to Final Accounts

We have now followed the accounting processes through the full range of accounting activities from the original entries for individual transactions to the final calculation of net profit and the preparation of a Balance Sheet at the end of the financial year. There are many further aspects of accounting to consider, but these only develop the basic principles as they are applied to different institutions—to partnerships, clubs, limited companies and public corporations.

Fig. 18.1 presents diagrammatically the complete development of double-entry accounting. There are six stages.

(a) Every transaction has its original document.
(b) These documents are posted into the books of original entry, which are:

- the Sales Day Book,
- the Sales Returns Book,
- the Purchases Day Book,
- the Purchases Returns Book,
- the Journal Proper,
- the Cash Book (which is also part of the ledger),
- the Petty Cash Book (which is an extension of the Cash Book and therefore also part of the Cash Account).

(c) These original entries are then posted to the ledger.
(d) A Trial Balance is extracted from the ledger.
(e) The Trial Balance is used to prepare a set of Final Accounts, i.e.

- a Trading Account,
- a Profit and Loss Account,
- a Balance Sheet.

Sometimes the first two are joined into a single Trading and Profit and Loss Account.

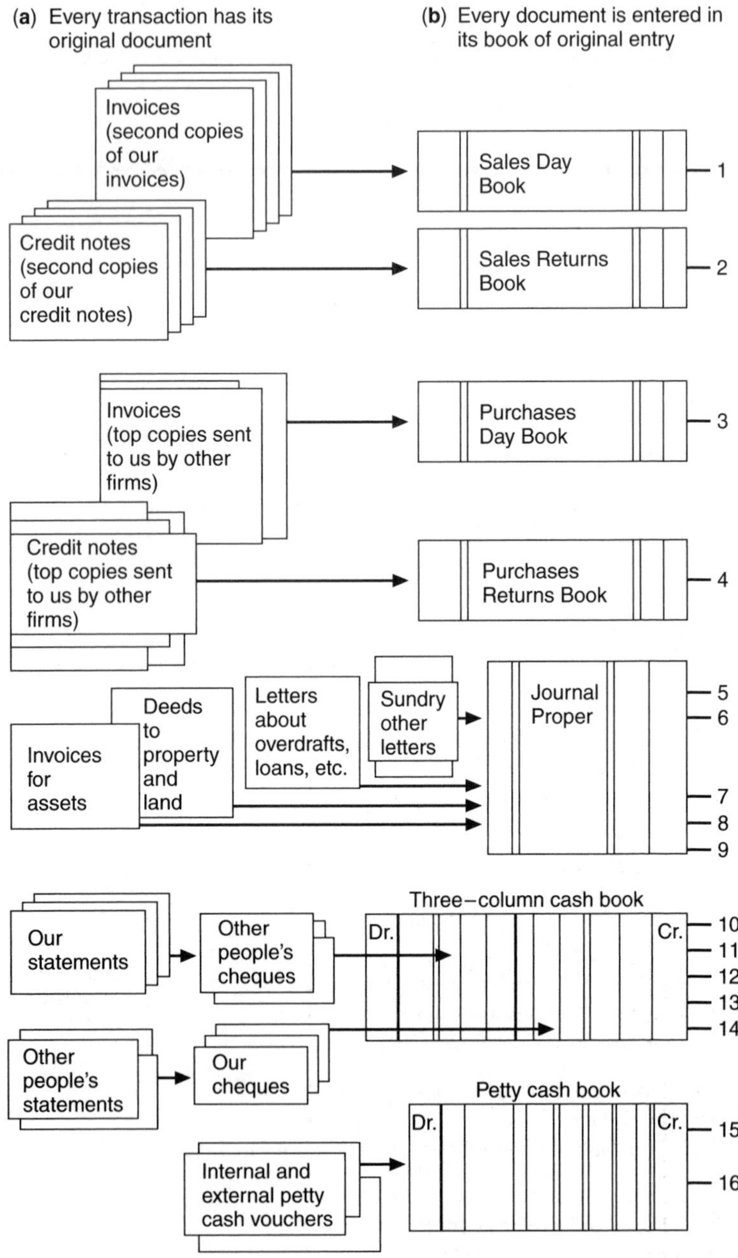

Fig. 18.1 Double-entry accounting: the Final Accounts can be adapted to suit the needs of other forms of business unit—partnerships, non-profit-making organizations, limited companies, public corporations and local and central authorities

(**c**) These books of original entry are posted to the ledger accounts (the three–column cash book and petty cash book are also part of the ledger)

(**d**) A Trial Balance is extracted from the ledger

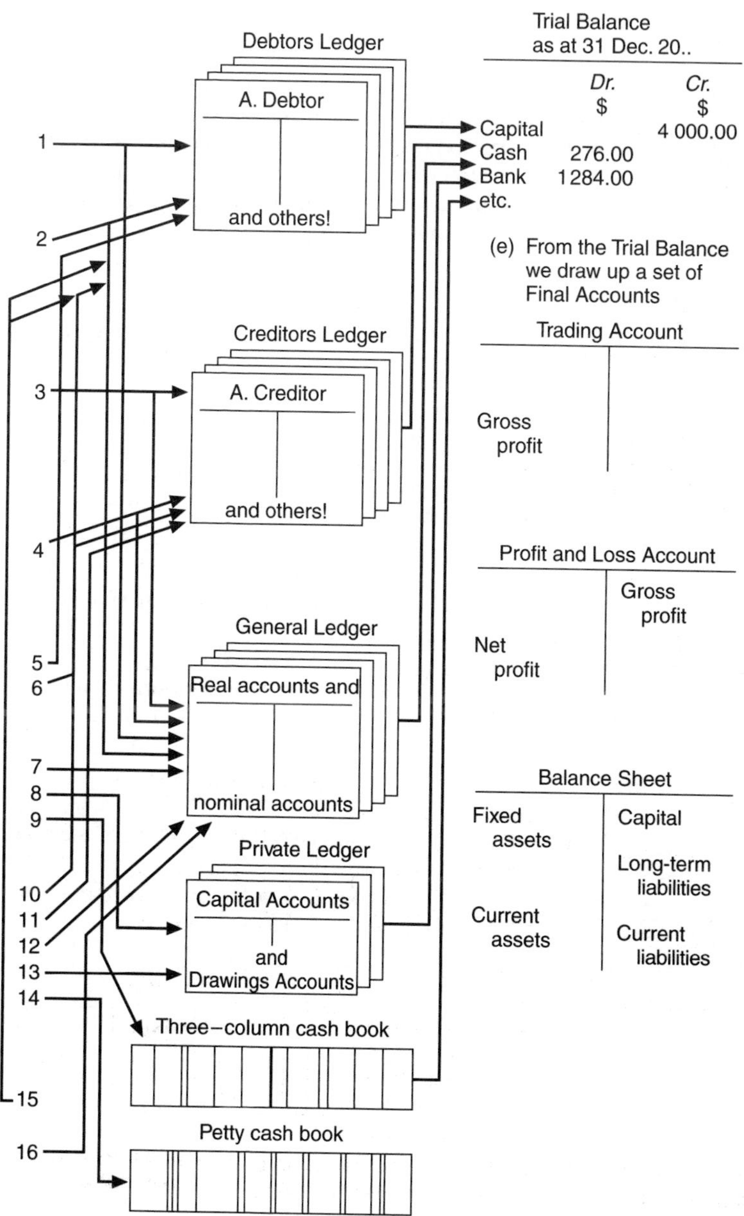

Trial Balance
as at 31 Dec. 20..

	Dr. $	*Cr.* $
Capital		4 000.00
Cash	276.00	
Bank	1 284.00	
etc.		

(e) From the Trial Balance we draw up a set of Final Accounts

(f) Finally these ideas are modified to meet the needs of particular business units such as partnerships, clubs, limited companies and other incorporated bodies like nationalized industries and the local and central government agencies. In particular, those ledger accounts which are of interest only to the proprietor(s) are removed to the Private Ledger (see Unit 23.4).

Follow the diagram through and make sure that you understand every part of it. Then try at least one, preferably several, of the exercises given at the end of this Unit. These will help you make sure that you know all that is required to keep the books of any sole trader enterprise, starting with original information about transactions and passing through all the stages to a Balance Sheet at the end of a financial period, which for our purpose here is taken to be one month.

18.2 A Model Exercise—Double-entry Accounting with a Full Set of Books

This model exercise shows you all the stages to be gone through when keeping a full set of books. The sequence of work is as follows:

(a) The starting point is the information given on pages 256 and 257.
(b) First an opening Journal entry is made (page 258).
(c) This is then posted to the three-column cash book (page 255).
(d) It is also posted to the ledger accounts (pages 258 and 259).
(e) Then the transactions are taken one at a time, and the decision taken as to which book of original entry each is entered in (pages 261–2). To help, an explanation is given in the 'Notes on Model Exercise'.
(f) When all transactions have been entered, the books of original entry are posted to the ledger (pages 258–60). Care is taken to total the Day Books and post them to Sales Account, Purchases Account and so on.
(g) The Trial Balance is extracted from the ledger after all the postings have been completed (page 262).
(h) The Trading Account, Profit and Loss Account and Balance Sheet are prepared from the Trial Balance (page 263).
(i) The accounts will be closed off for the end of the financial period when the final accounts are prepared, but to avoid confusion this has not been done in the sample exercise.

Note: Cash Book opposite
For convenience, this part of the exercise has been printed out of sequence. You should look at this illustration as instructed on page 258.

The three-column cash book

Dr. Date	Details	Folio	Discount allowed	Cash A/c	Bank A/c	Date	Details	Folio	Discount received	Cash A/c	*Cr.* Bank A/c
											CB5
20..			$	$	$	20..			$	$	$
1 Apr.	Balances	J1		25.50	2 450.00	7 Apr.	R. Grimes	L6	18.75		356.25
6 Apr.	Cash sales	L12/21		575.15		8 Apr.	Office expenses	L16/21		14.50	
19 Apr.	Cash sales	L12/21		1 230.15		14 Apr.	Fax machine	J1			258.50
30 Apr.	Cash sales	L12/21		1 245.25		16 Apr.	Salaries	L17			600.00
30 Apr.	Cash	C			2 100.00	22 Apr.	Drawings	L18		220.00	
						27 Apr.	Wages	L19		342.50	
						30 Apr.	Bank	C		2 100.00	
						30 Apr.	Balance	c/d		399.05	3 335.25
			—	$3 076.05	$4 550.00				$18.75	$3 076.05	$4 550.00
1 May	Balance	B/d		399.05	3 335.25				L20		

Model Exercise

On 1 April 20.. R. Marshall's books disclosed the following balances: cash in hand $25.50; cash at bank $2 450.00; furniture $4 250.00; stock $3 600.00; premises $36 500.00. Debtors M. Lupin $150.00, J. Jordan $130.00. Creditor R. Grimes $375.00.

Transactions for the month are as follows:

1 April	Sells to M. Tapley on credit goods $435.00, plus VAT $43.50.
3 April	Purchases on credit from R. Grimes, goods $390.00 less 15 per cent trade discount. VAT is $33.15.
6 April	Cash sales $575.15. Of this $52.29 is VAT.
7 April	Pays R. Grimes the sum due on 1 April by cheque, less cash discount 5 per cent.
8 April	Pays office expenses in cash $14.50. $1.32 of this is VAT.
9 April	Purchases goods on credit from R. Grimes $328.60, less 15 per cent trade discount. VAT is $27.93.
10 April	Receives a credit note from Grimes for goods returned, catalogue value $22.60. VAT is $1.92.
14 April	Purchases by cheque a mobile phone for office use $235.00 plus VAT $23.50.
16 April	Pays salaries by cheque $600.00.
17 April	Sends a credit note to M. Tapley for returns $65.00. VAT is $6.50.
19 April	Cash sales $1 230.15. VAT included in this is $111.83.
22 April	Marshall draws cash from till for his personal use $220.00.
25 April	Sells M. Lupin goods on credit $400.00, plus VAT $40.00.
27 April	Pays warehouse wages $342.50 in cash.
29 April	Sells goods to P. Brown on credit $524.50, plus VAT $52.45.
30 April	J. Jordan is bankrupt. Writes his account off as a bad debt. VAT of $11.82 can be recovered.
30 April	Cash sales $1 245.25, of which VAT is $113.20. Banks $2 100.00 from cash.

Note: Closing stock on 30 April is valued at $1 520.00.

Notes on Model Exercise

1 April	This is a Sales Day Book entry, with VAT.
3 April	This is a Purchases Day Book entry, with VAT.
6 April	Debit the cash sales in the Cash Account in the cash book. There is VAT here too.
7 April	Credit Bank Account and enter the discount in the discount column.
8 April	Credit the Cash Account with $14.50. VAT is to be taken into account when posting.
9 April	This is a Purchases Day Book entry, with VAT.
10 April	This is a Purchases Returns Book entry, with VAT.
14 April	A Journal Proper entry—purchase of an asset, with VAT.
16 April	Credit Bank Account in the cash book.
17 April	This is a Sales Returns Book entry, with VAT.
19 April	Debit the cash sales in the Cash Account. Take VAT into account when posting.
22 April	Credit the Cash Account with these drawings.
25 April	This is a Sales Day Book entry, with VAT.
27 April	Credit the Cash Account.
29 April	This is a Sales Day Book entry, with VAT.
30 April	This is a Journal Proper entry. The VAT on a bad debt can be recovered if the debtor is bankrupt.
30 April	Cash sales with VAT, followed by a contra entry in the cash book.

As the transactions are entered in the cash book and the day books these books will become as shown on pages 255 and 261–2. The extra Journal entries dealing with the more unusual items will be made as on page 258. Then the posting of these books into the ledger will give us the ledger accounts on pages 258–60. Note the treatment of VAT on cash sales and office expenses, as shown in the cash book and the ledger accounts.

From these ledger accounts, and from the cash book balances, the Trial Balance on page 262 will be prepared. From this Trial Balance, and using the closing stock figure given at the end of the model exercise, the Final Accounts shown on pages 263 will be prepared. Ledger entries to close the ledger accounts have not been shown.

The opening Journal entry

					J1
				$	$
20..					
1 April	Cash in hand	Dr.	CB5	25.50	
	Cash at bank	Dr.	CB5	2450.00	
	Furniture	Dr.	L1	4250.00	
	Stock	Dr.	L2	3600.00	
	Premises	Dr.	L3	36500.00	
	M. Lupin	Dr.	L4	150.00	
	J. Jordan	Dr.	L5	130.00	
	R. Grimes		L6		375.00
	Capital		L7		46730.50
				$47105.50	$47105.50
	Being assets and liabilities at this date				
14 April	Telephones Account	Dr.	L8	235.00	
	VAT Account	Dr.	L21	23.50	
	Bank Account		CB5		258.50
	Being purchase of mobile phone D/27 106 at this date				
30 April	Bad Debts Account	Dr.	L9	118.18	
	VAT Account	Dr.	L21	11.82	
	J. Jordan		L5		130.00
	Being bad debt written off at this date				

The three-column cash book.

See page 255.

The Ledger

Furniture Account L1

			$
20..			
1 April	Opening balance	J1	4250.00

Stock Account L2

			$
20..			
1 April	Opening balance	J1	3600.00

Premises Account L3

			$
20..			
1 April	Opening balance	J1	36500.00

M. Lupin Account L4

20..			$				
1 April	Opening balance	J1	150.00				
25 April	Sales	SDB10	440.00				

J. Jordan Account L5

BAD DEBTOR

20..			$	20..			$
1 April	Opening balance	J1	130.00	30 April	Bad debts	J1	130.00

R. Grimes Account L6

20..			$	20..			$
10 April	Returns	PRB7	21.13	1 April	Opening balance	J1	375.00
7 April	Cash	CB5	356.25	3 April	Purchases	PDB11	364.65
7 April	Discount	CB5	18.75	9 April	Purchases	PDB11	307.24
30 April	Balance	c/d	650.76				
			$1 046.89				$1 046.89
				1 May	Balance	B/d	650.76

Capital Account L7

				20..			$
				1 April	Opening balance	J1	46 730.50

Telephones Account L8

20..			$				
14 April	Bank	J1	235.00				

Bad Debts Account L9

20..			$				
30 April	J. Jordan	J1	118.18				

M. Tapley Account L10

20..			$	20..			$
1 April	Sales	SDB10	478.50	17 April	Returns	SRB4	71.50
				30 April	Balance	c/d	407.00
			$478.50				$478.50
1 May	Balance	B/d	407.00				

P. Brown Account L11

20..			$				
29 April	Sales	SDB10	576.95				

Sales Account L12

				20..			$
				30 April	Sundry debtors	SDB10	1 359.50
				6 April	Cash	CB5	522.86
				19 April	Cash	CB5	1 118.32
				30 April	Cash	CB5	1 132.05

Sales Returns Account L13

		$
20..		
17 April Sundry debtors	SRB4	65.00

Purchases account L14

		$
20..		
30 April Sundry creditors	PDB11	610.81

Purchases Returns Account L15

		$
20..		
30 April Sundry creditors	PRB7	19.21

Office Expenses Account L16

		$
20..		
8 April Cash	CB5	13.18

Salaries Account L17

		$
20..		
16 April Bank	CB5	600.00

Drawings Account L18

		$
20..		
22 April Cash	CB5	220.00

Wages Account L19

		$
20..		
27 April Cash	CB5	342.50

Discount Received Account L20

		$
20..		
30 April Sundry creditors	CB5	18.75

VAT Account L21

		$			$
20..			20..		
14 April Bank	J1	23.50	30 April Debtors	SDB10	135.95
30 April J. Jordan	J1	11.82	30 April Creditors	PRB7	1.92
30 April Debtors	SRB4	6.50	6 April Cash	CB5	52.29
30 April Creditors	PDB11	61.08	19 April Cash	CB5	111.83
8 April Cash	CB5	1.32	30 April Cash	CB5	113.20
30 April Balance	c/d	310.97			
		$415.19			$415.19
			20..		$
			1 May Balance	B/d	310.97

Notes on postings to the ledger:

You may wonder why the postings to the ledger are not in date order. The answer is that postings from the books of original entry to the ledger are done by different book-keepers whenever they get a free moment, and whenever the part of the ledger they require is available. We therefore cannot expect the entries to be in date order, for they will be made out of sequence. A book-keeper posting, say, the cash book will not know whether or not the colleague who keeps the Sales Day Book or the Journal Proper has any entries to make.

The Sales Day Book

20..			Details $	VAT $	SDB10 $
1 April	M. Tapley				
	Goods	L10	435.00	43.50	478.50
25 April	M. Lupin				
	Goods	L4	400.00	40.00	440.00
29 April	P. Brown				
	Goods	L11	524.50	52.45	576.95
			$1 359.50	$135.95	$1 495.45
			L12	L21	

The Sales Returns Book

20..			Details $	VAT $	SRB4 $
17 April	M. Tapley				
	Goods	L10	65.00	6.50	71.50
			$65.00	$6.50	$71.50
			L13	L21	

The Purchases Day Book

20..			Details $	VAT $	PDB11 $
3 April	R. Grimes				
	Goods		390.00		
	Less Trade discount		58.50		
		L6	331.50	33.15	364.65
9 April	R. Grimes				
	Goods		328.60		
	Less Trade discount		49.29		
		L6	279.31	27.93	307.24
			$610.81	$61.08	$671.89
			L14	L21	

The Purchases Returns Book

20..			Details	VAT	PRB7
10 April	R. Grimes		$	$	$
	Goods Returned		22.60		
	Less Trade discount		3.39		
		L6	19.21	1.92	21.13
			$19.21	$1.92	$21.13
			L15	L21	

The Trial Balance

Trial Balance as at 30 April 20..

	Dr.	*Cr.*
	$	$
Cash	399.05	
Bank	3 335.25	
Furniture	4 250.00	
Stock	3 600.00	
Premises	36 500.00	
M. Lupin	590.00	
R. Grimes		650.76
Capital		46 730.50
Telephones	235.00	
Bad Debts	118.18	
M. Tapley	407.00	
P. Brown	576.95	
Sales Returns and Sales	65.00	4 132.73
Purchases and Purchase Returns	610.81	19.21
Office Expenses	13.18	
Salaries	600.00	
Drawings	220.00	
Wages	342.50	
Discount Received		18.75
VAT		310.97
	$51 862.92	$51 862.92

The Final Accounts

Trading Account for month ending 30 April 20..

	$	$		$
Opening stock		3600.00	Sales	4132.73
Purchases	610.81		*Less* Returns	65.00
Less Returns	19.21			
Net purchases		591.60	Net turnover	4067.73
Total stock available		4191.60		
Less Closing stock		1520.00		
Cost of stock sold		2671.60		
Warehouse wages		342.50		
Cost of sales		3014.10		
Gross profit		1053.63		
		$4067.73		$4067.73

Profit and Loss Account for month ending 30 April 20..

	$		$
Bad debts	118.18	Gross profit	1053.63
Office expenses	13.18	Discount received	18.75
Salaries	600.00		1072.38
	731.36		
Net profit	341.02		
	$1072.38		$1072.38

Balance Sheet as at 30 April 20..

	$	$		$	$
Fixed assets:			Capital:		
Premises		36500.00	At start		46730.50
Furniture		4250.00	Net profit	341.02	
Telephones		235.00	*Less* Drawings	220.00	
		40985.00			121.02
					46851.52
Current assets:			Long-term liabilities		—
Stock	1520.00		Current liabilities:		
Debtors	1573.95		Creditors		961.73
Bank	3335.25				
Cash	399.05				
		6828.25			
		$47813.25			$47813.25

When working through this kind of complex exercise you will find that the crucial test of accuracy is whether the Trial Balance will balance or not. If it does not there is an error somewhere. For a procedure to follow when you are checking a Trial Balance that does not agree, see Unit 14.2.

18.3 Accounting by Computer

Today, computers are used in almost every aspect of business life, but they are especially useful in accountancy because many accounting activities are routine and repetitive—such as purchases, sales, payments for transactions, payroll activities, etc.—and computers can carry these out quickly and accurately. The power of a computer lies in this ability to perform certain simple functions (basically, adding and subtracting) immeasurably faster and more accurately than a human being can. Moreover, the computer does not get tired or careless towards the end of the day, and it does not forget or muddle up the instructions it has been given. It can thus cut out an enormous amount of repetitive drudgery and save a lot of time, which makes it a most useful tool for the accountant. But it cannot take over the role of the accountant; unless it is told exactly what it is to do it is completely helpless. In order to instruct it, and to make full use of its powers, the computer operator must thoroughly understand double-entry book-keeping to Final Accounts level.

The exercises at the end of this chapter, which you are about to attempt, cover the full activities of a business for one month. They therefore give you a chance to think about the sort of instructions that a computer operator must give to the computer, so that it can carry out all the procedures that a real business requires.

There are many software packages available for accounting by computer, and the suppliers will tell you that anyone can learn how to use them with only a few days' instruction. If you get the chance to use such software take it, and acquire the keyboard skills you need to operate the system. We cannot give an example here because all systems take account of local laws, taxation rules, etc., and consequently they all vary slightly. When you, or your college, purchase such software the manual supplied with it will tell you how to use it. Having studied *Success in Principles of Accounting* you should feel at home with the computer because you will understand what it is doing.

You should now try the exercises given in Unit 18.4 below.

18.4 Exercises Set 28. Accounting with a Full Set of Books to Final Accounts Level

VAT has been ignored in these exercises, except in Question 4.

1. Paul Brickhill had the following balances on his books on 1 May 20..: cash in hand \$212.00; cash at bank \$1 132.00; premises \$44 800.00; furniture \$2 450.00. Debtors R. Lyons \$256.50, B. Forte \$116.25. Stock \$4 450.00. Creditors M. Hague \$420.00, R. Wright \$270.00.

Make the opening Journal entry, post it to the cash book and the ledger and record the following transactions for the month in the books of original entry. Post these books to the ledger accounts and extract a Trial Balance. Use this Trial Balance to prepare a Trading Account and Profit and Loss Account for the month just ended and a Balance Sheet as at 31 May 20.., closing off the accounts for the year as you do so.

1 May	Cash sales \$642.50.
2 May	Sells goods on credit to R. Lyons \$236.50.
4 May	Loan from bank arranged \$1 500.00. (*Disregard interest.*)
5 May	Pays wages in cash \$69.30.
8 May	Cash sales \$2 262.50; banks \$2 000.00 from till.
10 May	Purchases goods on credit from M. Hague \$2 325.00.
11 May	Purchases fax machine for office use (reference no D/71258) by cheque \$255.00.
12 May	Pays wages in cash \$69.30; pays M. Hague's account as at 1 May, by cheque, less 5 per cent cash discount.
15 May	Buys goods on credit from R. Wright \$1 125.00.
16 May	R. Lyons pays his account as at 1 May, net, by cheque.
18 May	Sells goods on credit to B. Forte \$225.50.
19 May	Cash sales \$2 245.00; pays wages in cash \$69.30; banks \$2 000.00 from till.
22 May	Pays R. Wright by cheque the amount owing on 1 May, less 5 per cent cash discount.
23 May	Pays office expenses \$25.25 cash.
25 May	Sends credit note to B. Forte \$65.50—goods returned.
26 May	Cash sales \$1 448.50; pays wages in cash \$110.00.
29 May	Pays cash for goods to be resold \$337.50.
30 May	Pays office cleaning expenses \$37.25 cash; banks \$1 500.00 from till.
31 May	Cash sales \$749.50; draws for personal use from bank \$500.00.

Closing stock on 31 May was valued at \$3 300.00. Wages are to go in the Trading Account.

2. Mary Lawrence had the following balances on her books on 1 October 20..: cash in hand $327.00; cash at bank $4525.00; premises $29500.00; furniture $2850.00. Debtors M. Lowe $227.50, R. Lark $338.60. Stock $4500.00. Creditors M. Thomas $872.60, R. Peacock $462.50.

Make the opening journal entry, post it to the cash book and the ledger and record the following transactions for the month in the books of original entry. Post these books to the ledger accounts and extract a Trial Balance. Use this Trial Balance to prepare a Trading Account and Profit and Loss Account for the month just ended and a Balance Sheet as at 31 October 20.., closing off the accounts as you do so.

1 October	Cash sales $827.50.
2 October	Sells goods on credit to M. Lowe $385.50.
4 October	Purchases showcases on credit from Office Display Co. Ltd, $386.50.
5 October	Pays wages in cash $144.50.
8 October	Cash sales $936.50; banks $1200.00 from till.
10 October	Purchases goods on credit from M. Thomas $1428.75.
11 October	Purchases calculator for office use (reference no M/727a) by cheque $34.00.
12 October	Pays wages in cash $144.50.
15 October	Sells goods on credit to R. Lark $316.50.
16 October	Pays M. Thomas his account dated 1 October, less 5 per cent discount, by cheque.
18 October	R. Lark pays his account as at 1 October by a cheque for $321.67 (full settlement).
19 October	Cash sales $1172.75; pays wages in cash $144.50.
22 October	Purchases goods on credit from R. Peacock $1640.00.
23 October	Pays Peacock's account as at 1 October, net, by cheque.
25 October	Sends a credit note to M. Lowe $145.00, goods returned.
26 October	Cash sales $975.50; banks $1800.00 from till.
29 October	Pays for minor repairs $24.25 cash.
30 October	Pays office-cleaning expenses $37.50 cash.
31 October	Cash sales $838.50; draws for personal use from bank $420.00.

Closing stock on 31 October valued at $3400.00. Wages are to go in the Trading Account.

3. Martin Candler was in business as a fishmonger and his financial position on 1 July was as follows: cash in hand $438.50; cash at bank $3 250.00; stock $320.00; furniture and fittings $3 650.00. Debtors M. Truelove $415.75, R. Carter $321.60. Creditors M. Perkins $1 184.60. Make the opening Journal entry, enter the following transactions and, after tidying up such accounts as require it, prepare a Trial Balance as at 31 July 20... Then draw up a set of Final Accounts for the month and a Balance Sheet as at that date—bearing in mind that closing stock was valued at $165.00. Wages are to be entered in the Trading Account. Close off the accounts for the year.

1 July	Cash purchases $226.50; M. Truelove pays his account by cheque in full.
2 July	Purchases goods on credit from M. Perkins $468.50.
4 July	Pays M. Perkin's account at 1 July less 5 per cent discount, by cheque.
5 July	Cash sales for week $1 442.46; banks $1 120.00 for safe keeping.
8 July	Cash purchases $145.50.
9 July	R. Carter pays his account by cheque less 5 per cent cash discount.
11 July	Purchases new electronic scales for shop $228.40 on credit from Truecharge Ltd.
12 July	Cash sales for week $965.60; banks $700.00.
15 July	Cash purchases $236.85; pays for repairs to refrigerators $48.25 cash.
19 July	Cash sales for week $1 132.80.
22 July	Cash purchases $1 272.50; banks $650.00 from till.
23 July	Sells goods on credit to R. Carter $127.80.
24 July	Pays casual worker $25.00 cash.
25 July	Pays accountant's charge $98.40 by cheque.
26 July	Cash sales for week $1 224.26; banks $950.00 from till.
29 July	Cash purchases $140.45.
30 July	Paid casual workers $26.50 in cash.
31 July	Cash sales $865.20; drawings $620.00 by cheque.

4. On 1 March 20.. Paul Dombey's financial position was as follows: cash in hand $227.50; cash at bank $4056.50; stock $7500.00; land and buildings $43800.00; furniture and fittings $5425.00; plant and machinery $33250.50. Debtors M. Wyatt $272.80 and C. Dobson $216.50. Creditors C. Dickens $775.60. Open the books with an opening Journal entry, enter the following transactions in the correct books of original entry, post them to the ledger and extract a Trial Balance as at 31 March 20... Then draw up a full set of Final Accounts, bearing in mind that closing stock was $7650.00 on that date. Close off the accounts as you do so.

1 March	Buys a second-hand motor van on credit from Royal Motors Ltd for $2725 plus VAT $272.50.
2 March	Buys goods for resale at auction $453.50, by cheque. This includes $41.23 VAT.
2 March	Cash sales $976.50. This includes $88.77 VAT.
3 March	M. Wyatt returns goods valued at $115.50 plus VAT $11.55.
4 March	Buys goods from C. Dickens on credit, $472.75 plus VAT $47.28.
5 March	Pays cash for stationery $37.55 plus VAT $3.76, postage $33.25 and motor vehicle expenses $112.55 plus VAT $11.26.
6 March	M. Culver sold Dombey goods, value $548.50 on credit, plus VAT $54.85.
7 March	Pays C. Dickens's account as at 1 March, less 5 per cent cash discount, by cheque.
9 March	M. Wyatt pays his account as at 1 March, less discount 5 per cent, by cheque.
10 March	Cash sales $1189.50 including VAT of $108.14; banks $1500.00 for safe keeping.
13 March	Purchases desks and chairs for office use $468.00 plus VAT $46.80, by cheque.
17 March	Buys goods from C. Dickens on credit $285.50, plus VAT $28.55.
19 March	C. Dobson pays his account of $216.50 in full by cheque.
22 March	Pays motor vehicle expenses $215.50 in cash, plus VAT $21.55.
24 March	C. Dobson's cheque is returned dishonoured.
29 March	Pays salaries by cheque $685.00.
31 March	Drawings by cheque $420.00; sells M. Wyatt goods on credit $345.60, plus VAT $34.56.

18.5 Revise and Test 18. A Full Set of Accounts

Answers	*Questions*
—	**1.** What do we mean by a full set of accounts?
1. We mean the complete accounting records from the start of a trading period to the end of that period. It includes all the records of purchases, sales, returns, receipts, payments etc., right up to working out the profit at the end of the financial period.	**2.** How long is that in real life?
2. It is usually one year. In our exercises, and in examinations, it is usually one month.	**3.** List the parts of the work that you need to do.
3. a) The Opening Journal Entry to get the books open, and to start the Ledger Accounts; b) all the trading entries, purchases, sales and returns inwards and outwards; c) all the Cash Book entries (receipts and payments); d) posting all these books to the Ledger and taking out a Trial Balance. We must get the Trial Balance to balance; e) using the Trial Balance to find the gross profit, the net profit and the final Balance Sheet of the business.	**4.** In real life what would happen to all these records at the end of the year?

4. a) Sole traders would take the profit, and after paying taxation would enjoy the fruits of their labours; b) partners would share the profits in the agreed way and pay any taxes due, etc.; the same as sole traders; c) limited companies would transfer the profits to an Appropriation Account and the directors would decide what to do with them; d) the detailed records would be archived for at least six years and may then be disposed of.	**5.** What should a student do who has successfully completed two or three of these exercises?
5. Congratulate himself/herself and press on with the more difficult work in the rest of this book.	**6.** (A slight celebration is in order. You are now a book-keeper to Final Accounts level!)

UNIT 19

Columnar Books

19.1 Controlling a Business

At one time business competition was chiefly exercised in manufacturing, and people like Henry Ford, who developed new methods of working, planning and factory layout, became world-famous. More recently warehousing, distribution and retailing have come under careful scrutiny as businesses seek economies of operation in all these fields. Management itself has had to examine office practices to streamline documentation, and costing, financial and departmental controls have been instituted.

The basis of all control activities is the evaluation of figures collected about the activities of different departments and functions in the enterprise. Very often, estimates are prepared beforehand so that actual performances can be compared with estimated performances and any differences (known by the technical name 'variances') can be investigated. *Variance analysis* is one of the really important control techniques.

The collection of the figures required is a simple matter, provided management is prepared to adapt procedures and systems. The simplest adaptations are the addition of analysis columns to day books, cash books and so forth, to bring out the figures required. Today electronic tills and computerized accounting systems can be programmed to extract useful data as it is processed, and to present the *customer activity* in every area of business. This reveals which are the most popular lines and deserve the most shelf space, while less popular items are relegated to less accessible shelves. Seasonal variation patterns are quickly established and adjustments to marketing capacity can be planned to anticipate changes and ensure the greatest volume of sales.

19.2 Columnar Sales and Purchases Day Books

Where a business has a variety of lines which are marketed simultaneously, management will find it interesting to analyse sales on a product basis. This will reveal which lines sell best and can even lead to the preparation of Trading and Profit and Loss Accounts on each product. This may show that one product does not yield a profit at all, and should be discontinued, or raised in price.

Date	Details	Groceries	Green-groceries	Bread and cakes	Wines	Folio	Details	Sales net of VAT	VAT	Total
20..		$	$	$	$		$	$	$	$
1 Jun.	Roebuck and Co.									
	6 cases tomatoes		18.50				18.50			
	4 crates white wine				16.50		16.50			
						L27		35.00	1.65	36.65
2 Jun.	Lamont Ltd									
	5 sides bacon	32.80					32.80			
	5 crates beans	7.50					7.50			
	Loaves, etc			17.50			17.50			
2 Jun.	Frobisher Ltd					L13		57.80		57.80
	6 cases tomatoes		18.50			L8		18.50		18.50
	and so on throughout the month until									
30 Jun.	Lucas and Co.									
	Loaves, etc.			35.25		L91		35.25		35.25
		$3856.25	$725.55	$495.25	$866.25	L272		$5943.30	$217.94	$6161.24

Fig. 19.1 Extract from a columnar Sales Day Book

Fig. 19.1 illustrates a columnar day book of this sort. Notice the following points:

(a) The columns have not changed their function, and the end column still provides the figures to be posted to each customer's ledger account. The VAT column still collects together the output tax, but the 'sales net of tax' column now provides the figures to go to the Sales Account.
(b) The extra analysis columns must cross-tot to give the same total as the figure shown in the end column. These columns may be totalled by data-processing methods, or by registers on the accounting machine. Alternatively they may be added on an add-listing machine or a calculator.
(c) When posted to the ledger, the total figures may either be posted to separate accounts, such as a Sales of Groceries, Sales of Greengroceries and so on, or may be posted to a special columnar account using analysis ledger paper as shown in Fig. 19.2 (only the credit side of the account is shown).

Page centre

Date	Details	Groceries	Green-groceries	Bread and cakes	Wines	F	L272 Total
20..		$	$	$	$		$
30 Jun.	Sundry debtors	3856.25	725.55	495.25	866.25	SDB9	5943.30

Fig. 19.2 An analysed Sales Account (credit side only)

19.3 Columnar Cash Books

For control account purposes it is often convenient to know the total cash payments made by customers with names in a certain section of the alphabet. For example, a young clerk may be in charge of the A–E debtors ledger. A mistake may be made, perhaps several mistakes in the course of a month, and as a result the Trial Balance will fail to agree. If we can prepare an A–E Debtors Ledger Control Account, telling us what this section of the ledger should total at the end of the month, any error the clerk has made will be revealed before the figures are passed to the Trial Balance clerk. Part of the work of preparing such a control account is to draw up the figures of total cash paid by this group of debtors. This can be done if columnar 'Cash Received' Books are kept, either as part of the three-column cash book, or as *memorandum books* related to it. (A memorandum book is one that gives additional details of a particular group of transactions but is not itself part of the double-entry system.) Fig. 19.3 illustrates such a columnar ruling, giving control account figures for each sub-division of the ledger.

		A–E	F–L	M–S	T–Z	Folio	Discount	Cash	Bank
20..		$	$	$	$		$	$	$
1 Jun.	R. Marks			30.00			1.50		28.50
1 Jun.	M Evans	45.50					2.27		43.23
2 Jun.	P. Peters			46.50			2.32		44.18
2 Jun.	L. Toff				27.90			27.90	
2 Jun.	S. Marshall			13.25				13.25	
2 Jun.	R. Bones	14.65							14.65
3 Jun.	B. Wyvern				15.75		0.79		14.96
3 Jun.	S. Potter			46.00					46.00
	and so on throughout the month until								
30 Jun.	T. Helga		149.90				7.49		142.41
		$957.28	$1 056.42	$1 279.30	$820.70		$72.56	$184.72	$3 856.42

Fig. 19.3 A columnar Cash Received Book

19.4 Exercises Set 29. Columnar Books

1. Rule up a suitable Purchases Day Book in columnar form giving columns for furniture, soft furnishings and carpets. Insert three invoices, each having three items on the invoice. Total the columns and cross-tot to check your entries. Invent appropriate folio numbers.

2. Rule up a suitable analysis cash book for cash payments made, in which the payments made are analysed into two sections, the A–K and the L–Z creditors. Enter five items, at least two from each sub-division. Total and cross-tot the book to check its accuracy. All the creditors are to be paid by cheque and we receive cash discount of 5 per cent on all payments.

3. G. Jenkins is in business as a wholesale nurseryman. He deals in three main classes of goods: roses, trees and shrubs, and bulbs. Record the following invoices in a suitable Sales Day Book, analysed for these departments. VAT on all items supplied is payable at 10 per cent.

20..			$
13 June	B. Lobley purchases goods as follows:		
	100 assorted rose bushes	=	75.00
	100 assorted shrubs	=	50.00
	10 sacks bulk narcissi	=	75.00
18 June	R. Brown purchases goods as follows:		
	6 boxes crocuses	=	27.00
	12 roses (standards)	=	18.00
	3 boxes irises	=	13.50
27 June	B. Grant purchases goods as follows:		
	100 trees (cypresses)	=	225.00
	2 000 rose bushes	=	1 000.00
	2 000 assorted shrubs	=	800.00
30 June	G. Wakeman purchases goods as follows:		
	6 boxes crocuses	=	27.00
	100 shrubs (assorted)	=	50.00
	100 rose bushes	=	75.00

4. Rule up a special sheet of day book analysis paper, and record the following invoices in the columnar Purchases Day Book of the Pop Musical Co. This firm has three departments:

a) tapes and CDs, b) CD players and hi-fi, and c) musical instruments.

You should head the analysis columns accordingly. Rule off the Day Book on 30 April, inventing suitable folio numbers as if you had posted the Day Book to the ledger. VAT on all items purchased was at 10 per cent.

20..	
1 April	Bought from Musical Instruments Co. Ltd 6 guitars @ $38.50 each.
11 April	Bought from R. T. Lamb (Electrical) Ltd 12 CD players @ $55.25 each and 2 electronic keyboards @ $167.50 each.
19 April	Bought from Recording Ltd 200 CDs @ $2 each and 4 violins @ $47.50 each.
25 April	Bought from A. Dealer two saxophones @ $129 each.
30 April	Bought from R. K. Radios 2 hi-fi control panels @ $38.75 each.

19.5 Revise and Test 19. Columnar Books

Answers	*Questions*
—	**1.** What is meant by columnar books?
1. They are books with extra columns in them so that analysis work can be carried out to check up on the purchases, sales, returns, etc. to give a wider range of information.	**2.** Give examples.
2. We might analyse our sales to discover which of our products sell best, for example groceries, greengroceries, ladies fashions, menswear, etc. We might analyse our Cash Books to show receipts from A–E debtors, F–M debtors, N–S debtors and T–Z debtors. In a firm with 40 000 customers the Debtors' Ledger would be too much for one book-keeper, and this would enable four people to share the work.	**3.** How would a computer keep the same type of analysis?
3. By the use of codes. At the same time as the figures are entered the computer asks for the code, and items which are similarly coded will be collected together to give, for example, the customer activity in each product area.	**4.** What is the general accounting term for these activities which show how each part of the business is doing?
4. They are called 'Departmental Accounts'. (See Unit 29.)	**5.** Go over the page again if necessary.

UNIT 20

The Bank Cash Book

20.1 Introduction

The idea behind the bank cash book is the establishment of control over the movement of cash. Cash is easy to misappropriate, but the chances of misappropriation can be reduced by using a system which requires that all the cash received is paid at once into the bank. The sums paid in must agree exactly with the sums collected on the till rolls, etc., and any difference will be the subject of rigorous investigation. If any disbursement of cash is required it will be arranged through the imprest system, that is, through the petty cash system.

Sometimes, where businesses are open at hours when the banks have shut, it is necessary to pay the remainder of the day's takings in by the 'night safe' system. Managements adopting this policy regard the small charge made for the night safe service as well worth while in view of the extra control given to them over the cash received. The manager who has to bank the evening's takings before going home is less likely to be tempted to use them for his/her own ends, while premises which are known to have no cash in the tills are less likely to be burgled.

Fig. 20.1 shows a typical bank cash book.

20.2 Notes on the Bank Cash Book

(a) The Cash Account is not needed. No payments are made in cash except through the petty cash book on the imprest system, and all cash received is treated as if it was cheques and paid straight into the bank. It follows that the Cash Account columns can be used as details columns to collect together the daily transactions, and a total only will appear in the bank column. These daily totals are particularly useful on the debit side, since the total entered daily will appear on the bank statement at a later date as 'sundries' paid in. It is convenient to have this sundries figure in one total in the cash book.

(b) Daily takings are cashed up at the end of the day and paid in either through the night safe service or first thing the next morning.

(c) Since the petty cash book is now going to be used for all cash payments it is necessary to keep a reasonable sum in the petty cashier's till. It might also be necessary to cash the book up and restore the imprest rather more frequently.

Apart from these differences, the bank cash book is very similar to the three-column cash book.

Date	Details	Folio	Discount allowed	Details	Bank	Date	Details	Folio	Discount received	Details	Bank
			$	$	$				$	$	$
20..	Balance	B/d			1747.50	20..					
1 March	M. Smith	L15	1.30	24.70		2 March	District				
1 March	T. Grover	L27		36.25			Council	L77			346.50
1 March	Cash sales	L59		572.80		3 March	Lee and Co.	L13	5.00	95.00	
					633.75	3 March	Millward Ltd	L57		272.50	
2 March	T. Lark	L18	4.80	91.20		3 March	T. Harper	L53	0.75	14.25	
2 March	R. Parsons	L22	0.50	9.50		3 March	Petty cash	PCB7		100.00	
2 March	Cash sales	L59		748.50							481.75
					849.20	3 March	Balance	c/d			3466.45
3 March	R. Jones	L7	2.50	47.50							
3 March	P. White	L11		38.20							
3 March	E. Tucker	L28		14.95							
3 March	Cash sales	L59		963.60							
					1064.25						
			$9.10		$4294.70				$5.75		$4294.70
			L27						L29		
4 March	Balance	B/d			$3466.45						

Fig. 20.1 The bank cash book

20.3 Exercises Set 30. The Bank Cash Book

1. Write up F. Carver's bank cash book from the following information:

a) His balance at the bank at the close of business on 27 May 20.., according to his cash book, was $872.80.

b) The counterfoils of his paying-in book give the following details:

28 May	Total paid in $903.30, consisting of cash from sales $745.80, a cheque from B. Bath for $60.00, and a cheque from L. Poole for $97.50. Poole's cheque was accepted in full settlement of $100.00 owed by him.
30 May	Total paid in $644.15, consisting entirely of cash from sales.
31 May	Total paid in $780.50, consisting of cash from sales $739.00 and a cheque from H. Winton for $41.50.

c) The counterfoils of his cheque-book show:

28 May	J. Burner and Sons Ltd	$290.13
30 May	W. Thorley and Co.	$195.00
31 May	Petty cash	$126.15
	Self	$350.00
	Elton's Garage	$147.11

The cheque to Elton's Garage was for petrol, oil and maintenance of the delivery van for the previous month, and no previous record of this transaction had gone through the books.

The details columns of the cash book should indicate clearly which ledger account is to be debited or credited in respect of each entry. Rule off and balance the cash book as at the close of business on 31 May 20...

2. Gail Vyner, the proprietor of a trading business, banks all the business receipts daily and meets all but petty cash expenditure by cheque. You are required to write up her bank cash book from the following information:

(a) The balance at the bank at the close of business on 3 May 20.., according to the cash book, was $1 375.40.

(b) She drew four cheques in the remaining days of the week; the counterfoils of the business cheque-book show:

4 May	H. Moore and Sons	$472.11
	W. Blake and Co.	$95.00
5 May	Eastern Electricity	$119.10
6 May	Cash (self $120; petty cash $88.66)	$208.66

Note: The cheque to W. Blake and Co. was in full settlement of $100.00 owing to them, and the payment to Eastern Electricity was in prompt payment of their account for the last quarter's consumption of electricity.

(c) The counterfoils of her paying-in book give the following details:

4 May	Total paid in $496.77, consisting of shop takings $431.17, a cheque from J. Hart for $18.10 and a cheque from G. Farley for $47.50 (accepted in full settlement of $50.00 owed by him).
5 May	Total paid in $551.17, consisting entirely of shop takings.
6 May	Total paid in $790.45, consisting of shop takings $748.00 and a cheque from R. Nelson for $42.45.

In drawing up the cash book, see that the details column contains the name of the ledger account to which the posting is to be made in respect of each entry. Rule off and balance the cash book as at the close of business on 6 May 20...

3. Write up D. Lobley's bank cash book from the following particulars:

(a) His balance at the bank at the close of business on 27 May 20.., according to his cash book, was $893.

(b) The counterfoils of his paying-in book give the following details:

28 May	Total paid in $596, consisting of cash from sales $448.50, cheque from A. Plum for $50 and cheque from B. Berry for $97.50. Berry's cheque was accepted in full settlement of $100 owed by him.
29 May	Total paid in $448, consisting entirely of cash from sales.
30 May	Total paid in $575, consisting of cash from sales $540 and a cheque from C. Flower for $35.

(c) The counterfoils of his cheque-book show:

28 May	Orchard and Co. Ltd $327.
29 May	Hedges and Co. $195.
30 May	Petty cash $129 and self $120—one cheque for $249.
31 May	Wood's Garage $118.

The cheque to Hedges and Co. was accepted in full settlement of $200 owing to them. The cheque to Wood's Garage was for petrol, oil and servicing for the previous month and no previous record of this had gone through the books.

The particulars columns of the cash book should show clearly the name of the ledger account which is to be debited or credited in respect of each entry.

Rule off and balance the cash book at the close of business on 30 May 20...

20.4 Revise and Test 20. The Bank Cash Book

Answers	*Questions*
—	**1.** What is the idea behind a Bank Cash Book?
1. It is a way of controlling a business being run by a manager.	**2.** How does it work?
2. It separates the money being received from any money being paid out. The takings each day (the money in the till) must be paid in down to the last penny, every day. If the business is open late, the takings are paid in to the night safe at the local bank. If the manager needs cash for items, it is paid out of petty cash, on the imprest system.	**3.** What effect does this have on the Cash Book?
3. The middle column on each side—the Cash Column—is not required because no Cash Account exists. Instead this column is just used as an adding-up column, to show the takings in cash, or by cheque, paid into the bank each day and the payments out by cheque (including any cheque to restore the imprest in the Petty Cash Book).	**4.** Supposing branches pay in by the night safe service; what happens next day?
4. The accountant will call at the bank, open the leather case and pay the money in. Alternatively the Bank may be authorized to open the bag in secure conditions (i.e. two persons present) and make the lodgement.	**5.** What is the effect of all this on the Petty Cash Book?
5. It will play a larger part in the arrangements, because more payments for day-to-day expenses will be paid out of the Petty Cash Book.	**6.** Go over the page again until you are quite clear about it.

UNIT 21

Stock Valuation

21.1 The Valuation of Stock

At the end of any financial period the value of the stock in hand is handed on by the current period to the next period, at a figure which has to be determined. The purchase of stock during the year is a revenue expense, because it is the purchase of goods for resale, but at the end of the year the balance in hand has, for a few hours, to be capitalized, and handed on to the next year as an asset of the business. As soon as the business commences on the first day of the new period, the customers start once again to purchase the goods and the revenue activities of selling goods and replacing them with new stock begin again, for a further trading period.

The process of valuing stock is one of the *adjustments* which have to be taken into account at the end of the financial year. These are dealt with more fully in Unit 22, but it is convenient to treat stock as a special case.

To value stock the following activities must be carried out.

(a) *The counting of the stock—physically checking it to discover how many units remain on the shelves.* Ideally, this activity should be performed by special 'stock-takers'. A manager who has been misappropriating cash or stock can cover his/her dishonest activities by exaggerating the stock in hand. Stock-taking by specialist staff frequently uncovers such *defalcations*.

(b) *The valuation of units.* This is a most important point. How shall we value an item of stock? If we value it at the price at which it is marked on the shelves, i.e. the selling price, we shall in effect be valuing it with the profit 'mark-up' on it, and shall be overstating its value. It is generally better to value it at cost price, but sometimes the item has depreciated in value and is worth less now than we paid for it, so that even the cost price overstates its value. The rule is:

stock is valued at cost price or net realizable value, whichever is lower.

This rule is laid down in *Statement of Standard Accounting Practice No. 9*, published by the accounting bodies. The effect of Statement No. 9 is to make firms value stock at cost price, unless the goods have actually deteriorated below cost price so that they can only be disposed of at a lower figure. You are advised to learn the above rule by heart and also the name of the Accounting Standard in which it is laid down.

(c) *The multiplication of the unit value by the number of units in hand, and the addition of all these items into a grand 'closing stock' figure.* Thus, for example, where we have 136 tins of baked beans at 22c per tin (valued at cost price) the value of this item of stock is 136 × 22c = $29.92. When added to the other stock, a grand total of several thousand dollars may well result.

21.2 Stock-taking Sales

The labour of counting and valuing stock and calculating the total closing stock figure can be very great. It may be reduced if a stock-taking sale is held just before the stock-taking period, and large sections of the stock are disposed of. This is an excellent opportunity to review the stock, and consider those items that appear to be slow-moving. Who purchased these items? The buyer concerned may be consistently buying lines that do not sell, perhaps because of bad judgement, perhaps because of a strong personal interest in a particular subject. Thus a photography enthusiast may overbuy cameras, or a racing-car enthusiast may overbuy gadgets for fast cars. The buyer may actually be accepting bribes from a particular supplier, or may be under 'undue influence' or duress in some respect. Corrective action to restrain the buyer will have a salutary effect.

The Effect of Stock-taking Sales on Profit Margins

If sales are held, the reduction of prices involved necessarily results in a fall in profit margins. The slow-moving items disposed of at cut prices will reduce the total profit earned from the expected profit margin to something rather lower. We shall see (in Unit 28.3) how these margins—called *gross profit percentages*—can be used to control business activities. A fall in gross profit percentage is always investigated by an astute management. Clearly the necessity to sell goods at cut prices indicates bad buying, and will cause a fall in gross profit percentage achieved during the trading period.

21.3 Importance of Correct Stock-taking

Where stock is incorrectly valued there are two principal effects.

(a) *The gross profit is affected.* An overvalued stock exaggerates the profit made, and an undervalued stock understates the profit made.
(b) As stock is also a Balance Sheet item, the *Balance Sheet will not give a true and fair view of the affairs of the business*, stock being either overstated or understated in the current assets.

For these reasons it is very important to have accurate stock-taking figures, so that an honest profit figure and an honest Balance Sheet are produced.

Stock-taking in Inflationary Times

In periods of rapidly changing prices the method used to value stock can have a very important effect on the accounts. For example, suppose I have a stock of ten motor car components, five of which cost me $25 each, while the other five were purchased later at $30 each. If I use four of them to repair a customer's car, what is the value of the six which I have left in stock?

I might use the 'first in, first out' principle, and say:

stock value = 1 @ $25 and 5 @ $30 = $175

Or, instead, I might use 'last in, first out' and say:

stock value = 4 @ $25 and 1 @ $30 = $155.

Alternatively, I might work on the basis of the average cost of the components. This problem is fully discussed in Unit 34.

21.4 Stock Valuation: an Example

A firm has the following information about its stock of ladies' cardigans:

		Cost price	*Quantity*
		$	
Opening balance 1 January 20..		4.50	1400
Purchases	January	4.60	4000
	February	4.95	3500
	March	5.55	2800
		Selling price	*Quantity*
Sales	January	8.20	3000
	February	9.50	3800
	March	11.90	3900
Closing stock		?	?

Current selling price of the articles is now $12.50. All goods are sold in strict rotation, first in first out.

Calculate:

a) the value of the closing stock, and
b) the gross profit for the three months shown.

a) Total stock purchases = 1 400 + 4 000 + 3 500 + 2 800 = 11 700
Total sales = 3 000 + 3 800 + 3 900 = 10 700

Therefore stock left in hand = 1 000

This stock was clearly all part of the purchases made in March.
These cost \$5.55 each, and are now being sold for \$12.50.
Therefore closing stock is worth 1 000 × \$5.55 = \$5 550

b) To calculate the gross profit we shall need to draw up a Trading Account. The necessary figures are as follows:

Opening stock = \$4.50 × 1 400 = \$6 300
Purchases = (4 000 × \$4.60) + (3 500 × \$4.95) + (2 800 × \$5.55)
= \$18 400 + \$17 325 + \$15 540
= \$51 265
Sales = (3 000 × \$8.20) + (3 800 × \$9.50) + (3 900 × \$11.90)
= \$24 600 + \$36 100 + \$46 410
= \$107 110
Closing stock = \$5 550 (calculated in (a) above)

The Trading Account would therefore be drawn up as follows:

Trading Account
for three-month period ending 31 March 20.. L169

	\$		\$
Opening stock	6 300	Sales	107 110
Purchases	51 265		
Total stock available	57 565		
Less Closing stock	5 550		
Cost of sales	52 015		
Gross profit (to P & L A/c)	55 095		
	\$107 110		\$107 110

The gross profit figure, which is taken to the Profit and Loss Account, is thus \$55 095.

Now try this sort of calculation for yourself, using the exercises that follow.

21.5 Exercises Set 31. The Valuation of Closing Stock

1. At stock-taking, a firm found that it had 420 of a certain article in stock. Of these, 200 had been purchased at $1.50 each, 100 at $1.70 each and the remainder at $2.00 each. The current price of these articles is $2.25 each. Some 20 of the items purchased at $1.50 have become discoloured due to bad storage, and are valued as only likely to sell at $1.00 each by the manager. The firm usually sells at 50 per cent above cost. Calculate the stock-taking valuation placed upon this item on the stock sheets.

2. Badbuyers Ltd find that on taking stock at 31 December they have 84 units of a certain article in stock. Four of these originally cost $32 each, but are now damaged and offered for sale at only $20 each, 16 of the rest cost $39.50 each, and the remainder were bought at $45.50 each. The current price of such goods from their usual supplier is now only $41.50, but a competitor is offering them at $40. The firm usually adds 50 per cent to cost price to find its selling prices. Value these articles in accordance with sound accounting practice.

3. a) On what basis is stock valued at the end of the financial year?

b) Ann Lawson had, on 1 January 20.., a stock of 4000 pairs of shoes valued at cost price ($15 each). In January she sold 1800 pairs and bought 2500 pairs at $16.50 each. In February she bought a further 2500 at $17.25 each and sold 3000 pairs. At the end of February she still has 100 pairs of the 1 January stock unsold and the shoes bought in February have not yet been offered to her customers. Calculate the value of her stock on 28 February, if the current selling price of these shoes is $25.95 per pair.

4. a) What is the basis for stock valuation at the end of the financial year?

b) John Richards, a sugar merchant, prepared his Trading Account at 31 December 20... His stock consisted of 200 tonnes:

40 tonnes @ $189.00 per tonne
60 tonnes @ $191.50 per tonne
100 tonnes @ $197.50 per tonne

On 31 December the price of sugar on the market was $204 per tonne. Richards always sells sugar at 25 per cent above current market price. Draw up a statement showing the value of Richards' stock of sugar for Trading Account purposes at 31 December 20...

5. A. Trader had in stock on 1 March 20.. 8000 articles at $1.15 each. During March he purchased a further 16000 costing $1.17 each, but was given an allowance of 25c each on 2000 of these, as they arrived in a damp condition. His sales during the month were 14000 articles at $1.60 each and 1400 of the damaged articles at $1.18 each. Goods are disposed of under the 'first in, first out' rule. The current selling price of similar articles was $1.65 on 31 March. In view of this he intends to sell in future at $1.65 each, but will dispose of the rest of the damaged items at only $1.00 since these are the more seriously damaged of the batch. Show the Trading Account of the trader for the month ended 31 March.

21.6 Practical Difficulties in Stock-taking

The owner of a small business often finds it difficult to take stock for the purposes of the Final Accounts, since the end of a financial year often falls on a weekday when there are customers to serve and staff to supervise. A sole trader may therefore decide to do the stock-taking on the Sunday, or on the half-day closing, even if this does not fall on the last day of the financial year. The true closing stock figure is then calculated by taking into account the changes in the stock position that have occurred in the two or three days between the stock-taking date and the end of the financial year.

Example

Tom Smith's financial year ends on 31 March. He decides to postpone his stock-taking figure until Sunday 5 April. He values the stock at that date at a figure of $6700. In the first five days of April the following occurred:

> Takings at the tills totalled $2455.
> Goods were also sold on credit $460.
> Goods were delivered by suppliers $1280.
> A customer returned goods originally sold to him for $30.

Tom has always added 25 per cent to his cost prices to give his selling prices. What was his true closing stock figure on 31 March?

We must think very clearly about these figures. In logical sequence these points must be taken into account:

(i) Stock valuation at 5 April = $6700
(ii) Sales during the first five days of April = $2455 + $460
= $2915

Since these items were not sold on 31 March they would still have been in stock at that date and must be added back, *but this adding back must be at cost price, not selling price.*

To find out what the cost price was we must deduct one-fifth from $2915 (if you don't understand why this is so, read the arithmetical note after the calculation):

$2915 − $583 = $2332

Valued at cost price these items were worth $2332.
Therefore stock in hand must be increased by $2332 to give the true 31 March figure.

(iii) Goods delivered by the suppliers in the first five days of April were not in stock on 31 March and must be deducted from the stock figure.

(iv) Goods returned by the customer in early April ($30 at selling price) must be deducted from the stock figure since they were not in stock at 31 March. This deduction must be made at cost price, i.e. $30 − $\frac{1}{5}$ of $30 = $24.

			$
Therefore closing stock on 5 April		=	6 700
Add Sales made in early April, but at cost price		=	2 332
			9 032
Deduct:	$		
Goods taken into stock in early April	1 280		
Returns in the same period at cost price	24		
			1 304
Closing stock at 31 March			$7 728

Notice that if Tom Smith had valued his stock on Sunday 29 March, the adjustments would have been made the opposite way. Sales made in the last two days of March would have been deducted from the 29 March figure (since they were lost to stock before the end of the year). Stock received and returns by customers would have been added in to give the true end-of-the-year position.

Arithmetical note: You must grasp, first, that if the mark-up is 25 per cent (one-quarter) added to our cost price, then it is also 20 per cent (one-fifth) of the selling price. For example, if the cost price is $100 the mark-up is $25 and the selling price is $100 + $25 = $125; the mark-up in this case is $25 ÷ $125 = one-fifth of the selling price—and this relationship will hold whatever the cost price figure.

In our example, we know (from (ii) above) that the sales in early April were $2 915. This includes a mark-up of one-fifth of $2 915 = $583, and the cost price of the goods was therefore $2 915 − $583 = $2 332.

You can work out similar relationships for other rates of mark-up. You will find:

mark-up of $\frac{1}{2}$ on cost price = $\frac{1}{3}$ off selling price
mark-up of $\frac{1}{3}$ on cost price = $\frac{1}{4}$ off selling price
mark-up of $\frac{1}{4}$ on cost price = $\frac{1}{5}$ off selling price

Suppose, however, that the mark-up is not a simple fraction—40 per cent, say. We can write:

selling price = cost price + 40% = 140% of cost price

Thus, whatever the selling price, we can write

$$\text{cost price} = \frac{100}{140} \times \text{selling price}$$

For example, goods sold at $280 after a 40 per cent mark-up must have cost

$$\$280 \times \frac{100}{140} = \$200$$

Burglaries and Fires

Occasionally situations arise where we may have to do a stock-taking exercise because of some unfortunate event, such as a burglary or a fire. Most businesses are covered by insurance against such events, and in order to make a claim for the loss we need to discover how much stock has been lost. We start by valuing the stock that we still have—that which was not stolen or destroyed in the fire, as the case may be. Our records can be expected to show the stock we had at the last stock-taking, and how much stock we have purchased in the period since. They will also show how much we have sold in that period (although we may need to bring this down to cost price, since it will be recorded at selling price). We can now calculate the stock stolen (or destroyed) as follows:

opening stock + purchases = total stock available in the period
total stock available − sales (at cost price) = balance of stock that should be available
balance of stock − actual stock in hand = stock lost by burglary or fire

Let us look at an example.

Example

A. Manufacturer suffers a fire in January in which his entire stock is destroyed except for \$500 of timber kept in an outside shed. His records show that total stock on 1 January was \$18275. Since then purchases of \$38529 have been taken into stock, and sales of \$28500 have been made. He always adds 50 per cent to cost prices to get his selling prices. How much should A. Manufacturer claim from his insurance company for the loss?

First let us reduce the sales of \$28500 to cost price.

Mark-up on cost price = 50%
Therefore selling price = cost price + 50%
= 150% of cost price

Cost price $= \frac{100}{150}$ of selling price

$= \frac{2}{3}$ of selling price
Therefore sales at cost price $= \frac{2}{3} \times \$28500$

$= \frac{\$57000}{3} = \$19000$

Now we can calculate the loss:

Opening stock + purchases	=	\$18275 + \$38529
	=	\$56804
Deduct sales at cost price	=	\$19000
		37804
Deduct timber (undamaged)		500
Amount of claim	=	\$37304

21.7 Stock Cards

It is essential to keep some record of stock, not only to ensure that we never run out of items that are essential to keep production lines going but also to keep control of pilfering and other forms of theft. It is common to keep a *stock card* or *bin card* for every item of stock; alternatively records are kept by computer, and can be called up on a visual display unit for checking and amendment as stock is ordered or requisitioned by departments.

A typical stock card is shown in Fig. 21.1.

STATIONERY STOCK CARD

Description	A4 White bond	Maximum stock	50 reams
Cupboard no.	23	Re-order period	14 days
Code no.	B1475	Minimum stock	10 reams
Unit of issue	Ream	Re-order level	15 reams
Other details		Re-order quantity	25 reams

Received			Issued			Balance
Date 20..	Order no.	Quantity	Date 20..	Requisition no.	Quantity	Quantity
1 Aug	Balance in hand					32
			4 Aug	1725	10	22
			11 Aug	1851	10	12
22 Aug	10945	25				37

Fig. 21.1 A stock card

Notes on Fig. 21.1:

(i) *Maximum stock* is specified to save waste of capital tied up in stocks.
(ii) The *re-order period* is the time the supplier takes on average to fulfil an order.
(iii) *Minimum stock* is the stock required to run the factory during the re-order period, while new stock is being ordered in.
(iv) *Re-order level* is just above minimum stock level, allowing the requisition time to be processed.
(v) The *re-order quantity* is the agreed order to make an economic order, taking account of bulk discounts.

21.8 Exercises Set 32. Stock-taking Problems

1. R. and T. Traders are retailers whose financial year ended on Thursday 31 December. They took stock on the following Saturday after closing their premises for the day, and then presented the accountant with the following figures:

	$
Stock at cost on Saturday 2 January	8180
Cost price of goods taken into stock from suppliers delivering on 1 and 2 January	1340
Sales on 1 and 2 January (cash takings)	1488
Credit sales on these days	408
Credit note to customer for goods returned on 1 January	32

R. and T. Traders add $33\frac{1}{3}$ per cent to cost prices to fix their selling prices. Calculate the correct stock figure for 31 December 20...

2. A Trader began stock-taking for the year ended 30 June 20.. on that date. He did not complete the stock-taking until the close of business on 4 July 20.., when he ascertained the value of stock at cost price as $7250. The following information is available for the period 1–4 July 20..:

Purchases included in stock figure	$1460
Sales of goods not included in stock figure	$2725

The stock figure included goods invoiced to a customer on 30 June 20.. at $120 but held in the factory pending instructions as to delivery.
Percentage of gross profit on *sales* is 25 per cent.

Draw up a statement to show the correct value of stock at cost price on 30 June 20...

3. R. Marshall did her stock-taking on Sunday 27 December, although her financial year did not end until 31 December. She valued her stock on 27 December at $12725. Records for the end of December were as follows:

28–31 December:	$
Sales in cash	1895
Stock received from suppliers at cost	1055
Sales on credit	585
Returns by customers (at selling price)	60
Returns to suppliers (at cost price)	48
A 200-litre drum of paraffin oil leaked in a shed where dried goods were also stored. This stock had to be thrown away. Value (at cost)	128
The proprietor took home stock (cost price)	12

Ms Marshall adds 50 per cent to cost prices to find her selling prices. Calculate the stock figure as at 31 December (to the nearest $1).

4. In a burglary at the warehouse of P. Grimes and Son on the night of 30 September 20.., part of the stock was stolen.

From the following particulars show in account form the estimated value of the loss of stock. Show any calculations below the account to make your method clear.

	$
Stock at cost 1 July 20..	7840
Purchases from 1 July to 30 September 20..	15600
Sales from 1 July to 30 September 20..	18400
Stock remaining after the burglary was valued at	2420

P. Grimes and Son's usual gross profit is 25 per cent of selling price.

5. During the year 20.., M. Lomax bought goods value $8400 and his sales, on which he made a gross profit of 25 per cent, were $11600. The value of his stock at the beginning of the year was $1600. What was the value of his stock at the end of the year? Show details of your calculations.

6. From the following information calculate the value of R. Butler's stock on 30 September 20..:

	$
1 September 20.. stock (at cost)	4300
Purchases during month	15000
Sales during month	20000
Sales returns during month	800
Goods taken by Butler (selling price)	400

Gross profit is 20 per cent on turnover.

7. Carol Draper began to take stock at 5 p.m. on Saturday 28 December 20... She used cost price as the most suitable valuation. By the time the shop reopened on Monday 30 December she knew that the value of the stock in hand was $7280.

On that day and the next day new stock arrived (cost price = $1240), and a customer also returned goods sold to her in early December (invoice value = $300). Cash sales for the two days were $700 and $580 respectively, and credit sales were $240 and $220 respectively.

Miss Draper always adds 20 per cent to cost price to fix her selling prices.

Adjust the stock-taking figure of $7280 to allow for the movements of stock on the last two days of the year, and thus arrive at the closing stock figure for 31 December 20...

All working is to be shown clearly.

8. Rule up a stationery stock card similar to the one shown in Fig. 21.1 and record on it the following orders and requisitions for A4 bond paper:

20..		
1 Jan.	Opening balance	28 reams
3 Jan.	Requisition no. 2184	12 reams
5 Jan.	Order no. 1685	25 reams
17 Jan.	Requisition no. 2279	20 reams
19 Jan.	Requisition no. 2312	5 reams
29 Jan.	Order no. 1712	25 reams

9. Rule up a bin card similar to the stationery stock card shown in Fig. 21.1 and record on it the following orders and requisitions for volume control knobs. The bin number is 273, the item code is V/141/5, and the unit of issue is 1 000 items.

20..		
1 October	Opening balance	12 000
3 October	Requisition no. 1784	4 000
11 October	Order no. 29	15 000
12 October	Requisition no. 1798	11 000
19 October	Requisition no. 1894	3 000
26 October	Order no. 38	15 000

The maximum stock is 30 000, the re-order period 1 week, the minimum stock 5 000, the re-order level 10 000 and the re-order quantity is 15 000.

21.9 Revise and Test 21. Stock Records and Stock Valuation

Answers	*Questions*
—	**1.** What is stock?
1. Stock is goods or materials purchased for re-sale, or manufactured for re-sale. Like other assets stock must be protected from theft, deterioration of various sorts, fire, etc.	**2.** How do we control stock?
2. With stock records, often on cards such as bin cards, rack cards, stock ledger cards, or electronic records.	**3.** What is stock-taking?
3. It is an activity carried out from time to time to check that the actual stock in hand is the same as the stock shown on the stock record card. Any shortage should be investigated.	**4.** What is an advice note?
4. It is a copy of an invoice delivered with goods to tell the buyer what goods are being supplied and taken into stock. Any shortage calls for an investigation, and may lead to an insurance claim.	**5.** What is the usual requirement about complaints?
5. Notice in writing must be given within 3 days.	**6.** What should a bin card tell us about an item of stock?
6. It should show a running balance of the stock available of the item concerned, together with details that help keep control of the stock, such as maximum stock, re-order level, re-order quantity, etc.	**7.** How does a department requiring an item obtain it?

7. By putting in a requisition for the part required, number wanted, etc., to the Stores Department.	**8.** When it has been supplied and recorded on the bin card etc., what happens to the requisition?
8. It goes to the Costing Department to be charged out to the job that the item was used on.	**9.** Why do we do a stock-taking at the end of every financial year?
9. Because we cannot work out our profits until we know what stock we have left on our books. The value of the stock has to be handed on from the old year to the new year.	**10.** How do we value stock?
10. Stock is valued at cost price or net realizable value, whichever is the lower.	**11.** Explain this rule.
11. If an item is in stock in good condition we value it at cost price. If it is not in good condition for any reason, we value it at the price we could get for it (the realizable value) less any costs of disposal (transport charges, auctioneer's fees, etc.). This gives us the net realizable value. If the net realizable value is less than the cost price then we value the item at this lower figure.	**12.** How is the value of closing stock at the end of the year used in working out the profits?
12. It comes in the Trading Account to work out the cost of goods sold.	**13.** Go over the page again until you are sure of all the answers.

	$
Opening stock	2000.00
Add Purchases	27000.00
	29000.00
Less Closing Stock	4500.00
Cost of goods sold	$24500.00

UNIT 22

Adjustments in Final Accounts

22.1 Recapitulation

You have now reached a point in your studies where you are about to leave behind the more routine aspects of accounting and move on to a slightly higher level of activity—interpreting and controlling the business's situation. At this point we have considered the following aspects:

(a) the basic idea of double-entry accounting;
(b) the recording of original documents in the books of original entry, i.e. the day books, the cash book and the petty cash book;
(c) the posting of these original entries into the ledger, which is the main book of account;
(d) the extraction of a Trial Balance from the ledger;
(e) the preparation from this Trial Balance of Trading Accounts, Profit and Loss Accounts and Balance Sheets.

We must now move on to consider the finer points of accounting, and we begin with the examination of what are called *adjustments*.

22.2 Adjustments in Final Accounts

There are two guiding principles in the preparation of Final Accounts:

(a) Every Trading Account and every Profit and Loss Account must be prepared accurately, so that the correct profit for the period is obtained. This can only be achieved if the accounts carry every penny of the losses for the year, and include every penny of the profits earned.
(b) Every Balance Sheet must give a 'true and fair view' of the affairs of the business, showing the assets and the liabilities at their 'true' values.

In order to achieve these two aims, we need to take into account many matters which require adjustment. For example, the Wages Account may include some wages given in advance for next year to an employee who has requested an advance of salary to help him meet some domestic difficulty. This amount must be removed from the wages bill to be charged to the Trading Account; if it is not removed, the Trading Account for this year will be carrying next year's losses. Similarly, a commission earned for selling a piece of property for a client may not have been paid yet although it is definitely due from the customer. If it is omitted from the Profit and Loss Account this year's profits will be understated and next year's profits will be exaggerated. A full list of adjustments includes:

(a) payments in advance by the firm;
(b) payments in advance to the firm;
(c) payments accrued due by the firm;
(d) payments accrued due to the firm;
(e) bad debts and provisions for bad debts;
(f) provisions for discounts;
(g) closing-stock adjustments;
(h) depreciation of assets;
(i) appreciation of assets;
(j) amortization of leases;
(k) depreciation of goodwill.

These are considered in turn in Units 22.3 to 22.11.

22.3 Payments in Advance by the Firm

Certain payments are always made in advance. The best example is insurance payments, for no insurance company will offer cover until the first premium is paid. Whenever we make out the Final Accounts of the business there is usually some balance of insurance cover due, which has been paid for but the protection afforded will carry over into the next year. Consider the following:

Insurance Account L175

20..		$
1 Jan.	Motor Vehicle A (Bank A/c)	175.50
1 April	Motor Vehicle B (Bank A/c)	66.00
30 June	Motor Vehicle C (Bank A/c)	156.00
30 Sept.	Fire insurance (Bank A/c)	25.00

Clearly the premium paid on 1 January has given cover for a whole year by 31 December and its protection has been fully enjoyed. The whole of this $175.50 is a loss chargeable to this year's Profit and Loss Account. The other items are not fully used: one-quarter of the 1 April payment has still to be enjoyed and it will give protection until 31 March next year. Half of the June payment and three-quarters of the September payment similarly represent unexpired benefits. So the charge to the Profit and Loss Account for this year is:

		$
The whole of the January payment	=	175.50
Three-quarters of the April payment	=	49.50
Half the June payment	=	78.00
One-quarter of the September payment	=	6.25
Charge to Profit and Loss Account	=	$309.25

The Journal entry for the transfer of this charge to Profit and Loss Account and the balance on the account are shown below.

				J27
			$	$
20..				
31 Dec.	Profit and Loss Account Dr.	L206	309.25	
	Insurance Account	L175		309.25
	Being transfer of correct portion of insurance paid to Profit and Loss Account			

Insurance Account L175

20..		$	20..			$
1 Jan.	Motor Vehicle A (Bank A/c)	175.50	31 Dec.	Transfer to Profit and Loss A/c	J27	309.25
1 April	Motor Vehicle B (Bank A/c)	66.00	31 Dec.	Balance	c/d	113.25
30 June	Motor Vehicle C (Bank A/c)	156.00				
30 Sept.	Fire insurance (Bank A/c)	25.00				
		$422.50				$422.50
31 Dec.	Balance B/d	113.25				

The balance is a debit balance, an asset, and will appear in the Balance Sheet as an asset—payment in advance:

Balance Sheet as at 31 December 20..

	$
Current asset:	
Premiums in advance	113.25

Payments in advance are also commonly made for rates, for advertising and occasionally for wages when an employee, for some domestic reason, seeks an advance of salary. Very often, too, there is a balance of postage stamps, advertising brochures and stationery in stock. All these should be carried forward to the next year.

22.4 Payments in Advance to the Firm

If payments are made in advance by firms, then clearly some other firms are receiving them in advance. The insurance premiums referred to in the last section will be part of a mass of premium revenue received by the insurance companies, much of which will represent a liability for cover in the new year. Where an insurance company still owes clients protection in the early months of the year ahead, it will not be able to treat these sums as revenue income for the year that has passed. It will instead carry them forward as a liability for the coming year. Some typical entries are shown below.

Premiums Received Account L121

20..			$	20..			$
31 Dec.	Profit and Loss A/c		850 000	Jan.–Dec.	Sundry cash items		1 375 254
31 Dec.	Balance	C/d	525 254				
			$1 375 254				$1 375 254
				20..			$
				1 Jan.	Balance	B/d	525 254

Balance Sheet as at 31 December 20..

	$
Current liability:	
Premiums in advance	525 254

The accounts of insurance companies present special difficulties, however, and are not within the range of discussion of this book.

22.5 Payments Accrued Due by the Firm

At the end of a financial year there are invariably some payments due which will not be paid until the next financial period. These are often called *accruals*, that is, debts which have collected and are due for payment.

A common example of accrued expenses is that part of the wages for the year which is left unpaid because the financial year-end has not coincided with a pay-day. Clearly only once every five or six years will 31 December be a Friday; in other years the last Friday of the year falls on some other day. If Friday is pay-day, and wages are only paid on that day, then clearly in most years a few remaining days' wages will have 'accrued due' by the last day of the year. This amount of wages should be added to the wages paid to give a complete picture of the expense for the year. Entries would appear as follows:

Wages Account L162

		$				$
20..			20..			
1 Jan.–27 Dec.	Cash payments	17 246	31 Dec.	Transfer to Trading A/c		
31 Dec.	Wages due c/d	122				17 368
		$17 368				$17 368
			1 Jan.	Balance	B/d	122

Trading Account L177

		$
20..		
31 Dec.	Opening stock, etc.	–
31 Dec.	Wages	17 368

Balance Sheet as at 31 December 20..

	$
Current liabilities:	
Wages due	122

Other common accrued expenses are such items as rent due, light and heat bills due, advertising expenses due, and so on.

What is the Effect of the Credit Balance?

As shown above, any expense due appears as a credit balance on the account. What is the effect of this credit balance? In our example, consider the first wages payment of the new year, made, let us say, on 5 January. Clearly this payment will be credited on the cash book and debited in the Wages Account as a revenue expense for the new year, thus:

Wages Account L162

			$				$
20..				20..			
5 Jan.	Cash A/c	CB19	368.50	1 Jan.	Balance	B/d	122.00

Not all this payment of $368.50 is a revenue expense for the new year. That part of it ($122) which was taken into account as a loss of the previous year will not also be a loss for the new year. The effect of the balance on the credit side of the Wages Account is therefore to reduce the revenue expense for the new year to the proper figure of $246.50.

22.6 Payments Accrued Due to the Firm

Just as debts can collect which are due for payment by the firm, it is also possible for items to collect due to the firm. Sometimes a sub-tenant may be behind with his rent, or a firm may delay paying commission to which we are entitled. In such circumstances the profit earned from these transactions is taken into account even if it has not been paid. What is needed is to arrive at a true profit figure for the year, even though some of this profit has not yet been collected from those who owe it to us. The treatment is shown below.

Rent Received Account L134

			$				$
20..				20..			
31 Dec.	Transfer to Profit and Loss A/c	L178	600	31 Mar.	Cash	CB5	150
				29 June	Cash	CB11	150
				27 Sept.	Cash	CB19	150
				31 Dec.	Balance	c/d	150
			$600				$600
20..							
1 Jan.	Balance	B/d	150				

Profit and Loss Account L178

		$
20..		
31 Dec.	Rent Received	600

Balance Sheet as at 31 December 20..

	$
Current assets:	
Rent due from sub-tenant	150

Now try some of the following exercises on payments in advance and accrued expenses.

22.7 Exercises Set 33. Payments in Advance and Accrued Expenses

1. The Trial Balance extracted from the books of J. Thomas at 31 December 20. . includes the following debit balances:

	$
Rent paid	750
Rates	500
Wages	36 000
Interest on loan	100
Insurance	120

The following adjustments have to be made before the preparation of the Final Accounts:

	$
Rent outstanding	250
Rates paid in advance	125
Wages accrued due	500
Interest on loan unpaid	100
Insurance paid in advance	30

Show the ledger accounts from which the Trial Balance was prepared, give the closing entries and bring down all balances.

2. Antiques Ltd commenced trading on 1 January 20. ., on which date it took over a showroom suite at an annual rent of $2 700.

On 1 August 20. . a section of the premises was sub-let at an annual rental of $1 200.

During the year ended 31 December 20. ., at which date Antiques Ltd ends its financial year, the following payments had been made in respect of rent:

25 March, $675; 24 June, $675; 29 September, $675

and the following amounts had been received from the sub-tenant:

2 August, $300; 1 November, $300

Write up separate accounts for rent payable and rent receivable and balance them at the financial year-end, showing the appropriate transfers to Profit and Loss Account.

3. From the following particulars write up R. Taylor's Electricity Account for the year ending 31 December 20... Show the amount transferred to the Profit and Loss Account.

		$
1 January	Electricity used since last reading and already charged to Profit and Loss Account	20
8 February	Paid Electricity Board cash	138
13 May	Paid Electricity Board cash	136
11 August	Paid Electricity Board cash	127
12 November	Paid Electricity Board cash	131

On 31 December, R. Taylor read her meter and found she had used 1 680 units since the meter was last read for the account in November. She is charged 7c per unit, and wishes to bring this charge into account for the year just ended.

4. At 1 January 20.. A. Metcalfe, a grocer, owed $250 for rent, and his rates were paid in advance to the extent of $72. During the year he made the following payments:

Rent: 27 March, $500; 29 September, $520
Rates: 4 April, $144; 8 October, $180

You are required to write up Metcalfe's combined Rent and Rates Account for the year, taking into consideration the following matters outstanding at 31 December:

Rent accrued, $260; Rates prepaid, $90

and showing the transfer to Profit and Loss Account for the year ended 31 December 20...

5. A. Jenkins sub-lets the flat over his shop at an annual rental of $1 300 payable quarterly in arrears. During 20.. the tenant paid the rent due from her on 25 March, 30 June and 29 September, but at 31 December she had not yet paid the quarter's rent due. Show the rent account in the retailer's ledger, as it would appear after the preparation of his Profit and Loss Account for the year.

6. The Readywear Wholesaling Co. Ltd pays its wages on the system of keeping a week in hand. On 1 January 20.. the company held $7 000 in hand. During the year they paid $360 000 in wages and held $6 500 on 31 December 20...

Of the wages paid, it was calculated that $12 000 should be charged to warehouse maintenance.

Write up the Wages Account for the year ended 31 December 20.., and show the amount transferred to the Trading Account.

7. Here is the Trial Balance of Helen Hollow as at 31 March 20... Prepare her Trading Account, Profit and Loss Account and Balance Sheet.

	Dr.	*Cr.*
	$	$
Capital (H. Hollow)		40200.00
Cash	125.00	
Bank	6975.00	
Premises	34000.00	
Motor Vehicles	5850.00	
Plant and Machinery	4270.00	
Office Furniture	1866.50	
Office Salaries	12735.25	
Factory Wages	11624.00	
Office Light and Heat	538.00	
Commission Received		3594.00
Loan from M. Long		4406.00
Office Expenses	228.25	
Advertising	464.00	
Discount Allowed and Discount Received	127.00	236.75
Purchases and Sales	25246.00	68294.75
Sales Returns and Purchases Returns	1124.00	1196.75
Drawings (H. Hollow)	9600.00	
Stock at 1 March 20..	4320.00	
Debtors and Creditors	2686.50	4339.75
Carriage In	160.00	
Carriage Out	328.50	
	$122268.00	$122268.00

Stock at the end of March was valued at $4800.00. $48.50 is owing for factory wages and is to be included in the above accounts. Commission amounting to $26.00 has not yet been received, but is to be included as part of the year's profits.

8. On 1 January 20.. R. Regent, a computer salesman, owed $15 for stationery and had in his office, stationery valued at $118. During the three months ended 31 March he made the following payments to his stationery suppliers (for whom personal accounts are not kept):

28 January, $43; 26 February, $47; 29 March, $57

At 31 March Regent had unpaid bills for stationery amounting to $81 and he estimated the value of his stationery stock at $82.

Write up Regent's Stationery Account, balancing it at 31 March 20.., at which date he prepares his quarterly Profit and Loss Account.

9. On 1 January 20.. V. Dance, who owns her premises, lets the flat over her shop for an annual rent of $1 440, payable in cash monthly in advance. During the first six months of his tenancy the tenant paid the rent due on 1 January, 3 February, 2 March, 9 April and 14 May, but the rent due for June had not been paid when the Profit and Loss Account for the six months was prepared on 30 June. Show the Rent Account as it would appear in her ledger as at that date.

10. From the following Trial Balance prepare a Trading Account and Profit and Loss Account for the year ended 31 December 20.., and a Balance Sheet as at that date. The adjustments given below the Trial Balance are to be taken into account.

F. Grosvenor's Books
Trial Balance as at 31 December 20..

	Dr.	*Cr.*
	$	$
Postage	385	
Printing and Stationery	525	
Capital (F. Grosvenor)		11 535
Cash in hand	125	
Cash at bank	4 560	
Opening stock	11 250	
Purchases and Sales	124 750	246 650
Returns In and Returns Out	3 150	4 650
Carriage In	250	
Carriage Out	490	
Wages (Trading Account)	12 500	
Office Salaries	13 100	
Rent Received from Sub-tenant		1 355
Bad Debt Recovered		25
Rent and Rates	3 800	
Premises	45 500	
Plant and Machinery	23 250	
Drawings (F. Grosvenor)	10 000	
Insurance	1 250	
Discount Allowed and Discount Received	150	520
Debtors and Creditors	4 150	15 750
Advertising	3 300	
Distribution Expenses	6 700	
Loan from P. Carr		4 000
Furniture and Fittings	3 800	
Motor Vehicles	11 500	
	$284 485	$284 485

Closing stock on 31 December 20.. = $10 000.
Rates paid in advance = $200.
Wages due = $500.

22.8 Adjustments for Bad Debts and Provision for Bad Debts

At the end of a financial year the accountant should appraise the list of debtors, to consider whether there are any bad debtors among them. If there are any they should be written off at once, the loss being charged to Profit and Loss Account for the year (see Unit 12.3).

Even when such bad debtors have been eliminated the accounts do not represent a 'true and fair view' of the debtors, since every accountant knows that a certain percentage of debts will be bad. This percentage varies with the type of trade, the locality, and so on. How shall the accountant provide for these bad debts? They cannot be written off at once, because we have no idea which debtor will eventually fail to pay. The answer lies in setting aside an agreed percentage of the total debtors figure in a special account called the Provision for Bad Debts Account. This account represents some of the owner's profits, tucked away here instead of being made available to the proprietor as profit for the year. The Journal entry and accounts are shown below.

					J1
20..				$	$
31 Dec.	Profit and Loss Account	Dr.	L178	240	
	Provision for Bad Debts Account		L163		240
	Being profits set aside equal to 5 per cent of the debtors figure at this date				

Profit and Loss Account L178

		$
20..		
31 Dec.	Provision for Bad Debts J1	240

Provision for Bad Debts Account L163

			$
20..			
31 Dec.	Profit and Loss A/c	J1	240

(a) Displaying the Debtors on the Balance Sheet

The Provision for Bad Debts Account is an account with a credit balance—a liability of the business. To whom is it owed? The answer is that it is owed to the proprietor; it is some of this year's profit tucked away in a special account, since we have an uneasy feeling that it might not really be profit at all, but could be lost as some of the debts become bad debts. How shall we show it on the Balance Sheet? Clearly it should be on the liabilities side, but it is much better to show it as *a deduction from the assets* side in order to bring out the estimated true value of the debtors, thus:

Balance Sheet as at 31 December 20..

	$	$
Current assts:		
Debtors	4800	
Less Provision for Bad Debts	240	
		4560

(b) The Provision for Bad Debts Account in Subsequent Years

In the next year, three possible situations could arise:

(i) The bad debts could prove to be *exactly the same* as the provision made for them—$240 in our example. This is so extremely unlikely that we will disregard it.
(ii) The bad debts could be *less* than the sum set aside. There will then be a balance left on the Provision Account which will reduce the charge for bad debts in the coming year.
(iii) The bad debts could *exceed* the sum set aside. This is the most likely case, for not only would bad debts be expected on the debts outstanding on 1 January, but also on new debts incurred during the year as it proceeded.

The best thing to do in both (ii) and (iii) is to charge the Provision for Bad Debts Account, not the Profit and Loss Account, and adjust any outstanding balance when the provision for the new year is made. In a good year (ii), the account might look like this:

Provision for Bad Debts Account L163

20..			$	20..			$
31 Dec.	Bad Debts for year	J1	139	1 Jan.	Balance	B/d	240
31 Dec.	Balance	c/d	200	31 Dec.	Profit and Loss A/c	J5	99
			$339				$339
				20..			
				1 Jan.	Balance	B/d	200
				(*Note:* Being 5% of debtors at end of year)			

The result of a bad year (iii) might be as follows:

Provision for Bad Debts Account L163

20..			$	20..			$
31 Dec.	Bad Debts for year	J11	396	1 Jan.	Balance	B/d	200
31 Dec.	Balance	c/d	250	31 Dec.	Profit and Loss A/c	J11	446
			$646				$646
				20..			
				1 Jan.	Balance	B/d	250
				(*Note:* Being 5% of debtors at end of year)			

22.9 Provision for Discounts

(a) Discount to be Allowed

If it is correct to reduce the debtors figure by the amount of the expected bad debts, it could equally be argued that it is also desirable to reduce it by the amount of discount that the debtors will claim as they pay their accounts. In the Balance Sheet in Unit 22.8(a) the debtors of $4800 have been reduced by $240 for expected bad debts. The remainder of the debtors are expected to pay, but will they pay the figure of $4560 shown on the Balance Sheet? Almost certainly not, for they will probably claim discount. We ought therefore to prepare a Provision for Discount Account very similar to the Provision for Bad Debts Account. The necessary Journal entry is shown below; note that the Provision for Discount is only calculated on the *remaining* debtors figure.

					J15
20..				$	$
31 Dec.	Profit and Loss Account	Dr	L154	228	
	Provision for Discounts Account		L155		228
	Being discount at 5 per cent on the balance of debtors deemed to be good				

The entries in the accounts will result in a reduction of the profits for the year by the amount provided $228, and this would be balanced on the Balance Sheet by the following entries:

Balance Sheet as at 31 December 20..

	$	$
Current assets:		
Debtors	4800	
Less Provision for Bad Debts	240	
	4560	
Less Provision for Discounts	228	
		4332

(b) Discounts to be Received

If it is fair to provide for possible losses, such as bad debts or discounts to be allowed, is it also fair to take account of the discount to be received? Clearly the creditors we must pay will not be as great as appears on the Trial Balance if discount is to be earned by early payment. This is one of those debatable points which some accountants would be prepared to consider, while others would reject the idea. Since it offends against that important rule that we should always accept a loss when it is likely to occur, but should never take a profit until we actually make it, it is better not to anticipate a profit in this way.

Now you should try some exercises on the treatment of provision for bad debts.

22.10 Exercises Set 34. Bad Debts and Provision for Bad Debts

1. At 31 December 20.. a company's debtors totalled \$2670 and its Provision for Bad Debts Account from 1 January 20.. amounted to \$140. It was decided to write off as irrecoverable debts of \$130 and to carry forward a provision of 5 per cent of the debtors.

Prepare the Provision for Bad and Doubtful Debts Account, the entries in the Profit and Loss Account, and the entry for debtors on the Balance Sheet at 31 December 20...

2. At 1 January 20.. a firm's debtors amounted to \$24240 and at 31 December 20.. \$26360. It is the firm's practice to have a bad debt provision of 5 per cent of the debtors at the end of each year.

During the year, a debt amounting to \$132 was written off, and a debt of \$24, previously written off, was paid in full.

Draw up a statement showing the amount of the charge to Profit and Loss Account for the year 20.. in respect of bad debts (including adjustment of the bad debt provision).

3. At 1 April 20.. a firm's debtors amounted to \$18750, and at 31 March a year later to \$11500. It is the firm's practice to have a bad debt provision of 5 per cent of the debtors at the end of each year.

During the year, a debt amounting to \$380 was written off, and a debt of \$46 previously written off, was paid in full.

Draw up a statement showing the amount of the charge to Profit and Loss Account if any for the financial year in respect of bad debts (including adjustment of the bad debt provision).

4. N. Thorn maintains a bad and doubtful debts provision equal in amount to 5 per cent of the debts outstanding at the end of each financial year.

From the following information prepare the Provision for Bad and Doubtful Debts Account for the year 20..:

		$
Total debtors on 1 January 20..		4500
Total debtors on 31 December 20..		5360
Debts written off as irrecoverable:		
On 31 May 20..	T. Tomkins	26
On 31 May 20..	S. Carter	145
On 31 July 20..	P. Lane	40
On 30 November 20..	N. Lucas	57

On 1 October a first and final dividend of 15c in the dollar was received in respect of the debt from P. Lane written off on 31 July. On 17 November 20.. \$30 was received in respect of a debt due from K. Jones which had been written off in a previous year.

Balance the account as on 31 December 20.., and show the amount charged to the Profit and Loss Account for the year.

5. The Balance Sheet of J. Wilson, dated 1 January 20.., gave his total debtors as $5 500 and there was a provision of 8 per cent against bad debts. During the following year the bad debts written off amounted to $350, but a debt of $72 written off in the previous year was paid in full.

At 31 December 20.. Wilson's debtors were $6 500 and he decided to increase his provision to 10 per cent of that amount.

You are to prepare the Bad Debts and Provision Accounts for the year 20.. and to show the relevant entries in the Profit and Loss Account for 20.. and in the Balance Sheet dated 31 December 20...

6. On 1 January 20.. the Sales Ledger of Roberts and Brown Ltd showed the following debtors:

	$
Hall	480
Smith	260
Stevens	320
Peterson	150
Johannsen	56

The firm had a bad debt provision equal to 10 per cent of the total debts outstanding. Trading continued during the year 20.. with these and other customers, except that there were no sales to Peterson or Johannsen and that the former made no payment in respect of the amount due from him, while Johannsen paid only $30 during the year. On 31 December 20..:

(a) it was found that the Sales Ledger debit balances, including those due from Peterson and Johannsen, totalled $876;

(b) it was decided to write off as bad debts the amounts then due from Peterson and Johannsen, and

(c) it was decided to adjust the bad debts provision to 20 per cent of the remaining debts.

You are asked to show the entries recording the above in the appropriate impersonal ledger accounts for the financial year ended 31 December 20.., including the entries in the firm's Profit and Loss Account for the year.

7. The Balance Sheet of P. Sheldrake, dated 1 January 20.., gave his total debtors as $8 500 and there was a provision of 5 per cent against bad debts. During the following year the bad debts written off amounted to $500, but a debt of $150 written off in a previous year was paid in full.

At 31 December a year later, Sheldrake's debtors were $9 000 and he decided to increase his provision to 10 per cent of that amount.

You are to prepare the Bad Debts and Bad Debts Provision Accounts for the year 20.. and to show the relevant entries in the Profit and Loss Account and in the Balance Sheet dated 31 December 20...

8. M. Rooselar's Trial Balance was as follows on 31 December 20... Prepare his Trading Account, Profit and Loss Account and Balance Sheet. The following adjustments are to be taken into account:

Stock at 31 December 20.. was $8 000.
Debts worth $250 are considered bad and are to be written off. A Provision for Bad Debts of 5 per cent of the outstanding debtors is to be created (correct to the nearest $1).

Trial Balance as at 31 December 20..

	Dr.	*Cr.*
	$	$
Opening stock	11 950	
Capital		20 883
Carriage Out	526	
Sundry Expenses	3 300	
Purchases and Sales	125 000	234 000
Returns In and Returns Out	586	236
Salaries	22 350	
Cash	425	
Land and Buildings	43 500	
Plant and Machinery	11 500	
Office Furniture	4 850	
Discount Allowed and Discount Received	326	425
Debtors and Creditors	4 534	3 670
Light and Heat	490	
Commission Paid to Travellers	3 760	
Cash at bank	12 875	
Rent and Rates	1 242	
Drawings	12 000	
	$259 214	$259 214

9. The Trial Balance of Gerard Eliasson on 31 December 20.. is given below. You are asked to prepare his Trading Account and Profit and Loss Account for the year and his Balance Sheet as at this date, bearing in mind the adjustments given below the Trial Balance.

Trial Balance as at 31 December 20..

	Dr.	*Cr.*
	$	$
Cash in hand	327	
Cash at bank	2465	
Purchases and Sales	58248	113612
Returns In and Returns Out	612	448
Stock (at 1 January 20..)	9780	
Wages (Trading Account)	7450	
Salaries	13580	
Light and Heat	1420	
Commission Received		3650
Rent Received		2100
Telephone Expenses	420	
Insurance	250	
Motor Vehicles	7250	
Land and Buildings	44000	
Plant and Machinery	21400	
Loan from Southern Bank		12000
Interest Paid	750	
Capital		46112
Debtors and Creditors	3250	4280
Drawings	11000	
	$182202	$182202

Notes:

1. At 31 December 20.. stock was valued at $11250.
2. Debtors include one debt of $450 which is regarded as definitely bad.
3. It is decided to provide for future bad debts at 10 per cent of the *remaining* debtors, and then to provide for discount at 5 per cent on the outstanding balance.

22.11 Other Adjustments

To return to our list of adjustments to Final Accounts (Unit 22.2), we will now look at the last five items on the list.

(a) Closing Stock

Closing stock has been fully discussed in Unit 21, and in the Unit on the Trading Account (Unit 5.4).

(b) Depreciation of Assets

This has been fully discussed in Unit 13.

(c) The Appreciation of Assets

We have said already that one of the important principles of accounting is that one should never anticipate a profit; it should be left to be enjoyed in the period when it is actually realized. There is one exception to this rule. It is the appreciation (increase in value) of land, which is the result of the pressure of population and higher living standards on available housing and property. It is a matter of some concern to limited companies, whose shares may be purchased on the Stock Exchange. These firms may find that unrealized appreciations in the values of the sites they occupy may lead to take-over bids by speculators anxious to take over the company—not to continue it as a going concern, but to close it down and realize the very considerable sums of money to be obtained by selling the site for redevelopment.

If it is decided to recognize the increase in site values and raise the value of land and buildings above its original cost, the resulting profit is of a capital nature, and should be credited to Capital Account or a Capital Reserve Account. It should not be treated as a revenue profit, since it would then be taxable. The increase in value would be caught for taxation purposes only at a later date, if at all. The recognition of the true site value in this way will be reflected in the price of shares on the market and will reduce the profitability of a take-over bid. It is the presence of a 'secret reserve' of which other investors are not aware that gives the speculator his/her opportunity. The Journal entry and relevant entries in the Balance Sheet would be as shown below.

				J27
20..			$	$
31 Dec.	Land and Buildings Dr.	L1	3000	
	Capital Account (or Revaluation of Premises Account)	L2		3000
	Being revaluation of premises to take account of changing site values			

Balance Sheet as at 31 December 20..

	$	$		$
Fixed assets:			Capital:	
Land and Buildings	20 000		At start	17 500
Revaluation	3 000		*Add* Capital appreciation	3 000
		23 000		20 500
				etc.

(d) Amortization of Leases

This subject has been discussed in the Unit on depreciation (Unit 13.9).

(e) Goodwill—an Unusual Asset

When a business is purchased as a going concern, there is nearly always an additional sum to pay for the *goodwill* of the business. This is a payment to compensate the previous owner for his/her hard work in the past, since that hard work will continue to earn profits for the new owner in the future. One judge defined goodwill as 'a payment for the probability that the old customers will return to the old place'. It is often referred to as an *intangible asset*, in that the payment purchases an asset which, though it has a real value, exists only in people's minds. It cannot be physically touched like other assets taken over.

(i) The paradox of goodwill Accountants sometimes talk of the 'paradox of goodwill'. A paradox is something which is self-contradictory. The paradox of goodwill arises because of the practice of depreciating goodwill. Let us consider a simple example.

Mr A buys a grocery retail business paying $35 000 for the premises, stock and so forth, and $3 000 extra for goodwill. He does not know anyone in the district and no one knows him. On the commencement of business, say 1 January 20.., no one bears him any goodwill at all, despite the balance on his Goodwill Account which reads '$3 000'. Clearly this goodwill is not borne to him, but to the previous owner. It is not truly worth the stated value to Mr A, and should be written off. He decides to write the goodwill off over three years at $1 000 per annum. As he does so, the Goodwill Account first diminishes on the Balance Sheet, and finally vanishes from it. Yet at the same time the goodwill actually borne to Mr A is increasing. He is now the life and soul of the local Chamber of Trade, perhaps, and is a popular and respected trader in the district. The paradox of goodwill is that *when valued on the books at a high figure it is really worth nothing, and when valued on the books at nothing it is really worth a high figure.*

(ii) Writing off goodwill—an appropriation of profit The important point about writing off goodwill is that it is not a revenue expense, nor a charge against the profits, but an appropriation of profit towards the reduction of capital assets.

The difference between a *charge against the profits* and an *appropriation of profit* is an important one. A charge against the profits is a revenue expense, which reduces the profit for the year. It is admissable by the Inland Revenue authorities as a legitimate cost incurred in earning the income received, and reduces tax payable. An appropriation of profit is quite different. It is a voluntary decision by the owner of a business to appropriate the profit earned, after tax has been paid, in a particular way which results in the writing off of an intangible or a fictitious asset. (A *fictitious asset* is one for which there is nothing real to show at all. The best example is the Preliminary Expenses Account of a limited company, where legal and other expenses have been paid just to get the company organized and under way.) Appropriations of profit only take place after the profit has been assessed for the year—they do not determine the profit made.

It follows that the Journal entry for the depreciation of goodwill charges the reduction to Capital Account (not Profit and Loss Account), as shown below.

					J27
20..				$	$
31 Dec.	Capital Account	Dr.	L2	1000	
	Goodwill Account		L3		1000
	Being appropriation of profit to reduce goodwill at this date				

Balance Sheet as at 31 December 20..

	$	$		$	$
Fixed assets:			Capital:		
Goodwill	3000		At start		38000
Less Appropriation	1000		*Less* Goodwill reduction		(1000)
		2000	*Add* Net profit	12850	
etc.			*Less* Drawings	2850	
					10000
					47000

You should now attempt the Final Accounts exercises shown overleaf. They are designed to give you practice in all the adjustments we have discussed.

22.12 Exercises Set 35. More Final Accounts Exercises

1. The following Trial Balance was extracted from the books of D. Archer, a wholesale merchant, on 31 December 20..:

	$	$
Capital		15 100
Drawings	8 000	
Leasehold Premises (lease to run 5 years from 1 January of this year)	15 000	
Advertising	1 138	
Motor Vans	9 938	
Purchases and Sales	168 496	273 572
Stock at 1 January 20..	22 036	
Debtors and Creditors	24 898	9 570
Insurance	1 203	
Bad Debts	637	
Returns Inwards	1 567	
Returns Outwards		1 403
Furniture and Fittings	4 110	
Telephone Expenses	1 245	
Rates and Water	1 112	
Wages (Trading Account)	12 848	
Lighting and Heating	1 102	
Postage	2 149	
Cash in hand	363	
Goodwill	5 000	
Balance at bank	18 803	
	$299 645	$299 645

Prepare the Trading and Profit and Loss Accounts for the year ended 31 December 20.., and the Balance Sheet at that date. In preparing the accounts, the following matters should be taken into consideration:

(a) The stock at 31 December 20.. was valued at $19 645.
(b) An appropriate rate of amortization should be written off the leasehold premises.
(c) 20 per cent per annum on cost ($12 500) should be written off motor vans.
(d) 10 per cent per annum should be written off the value of furniture and fittings at the start of the year.
(e) Wages accrued amounted to $346.
(f) A Provision for Bad Debts of $1 230 is to be created.
(g) In view of the excellent profits made, it is decided to write off the intangible asset goodwill against Capital Account.

2. The following balances were extracted from the books of K. Richards at 31 December 20..:

	$
Capital—Richards	72 459
Stock in trade, 1 January 20..	12 720
Petty cash	64
Bank Overdraft	2 522
Sundry Debtors	7 000
Sundry Creditors	6 735
Motor Vans (cost $8 000)	6 000
Drawings	10 459
Fixtures and Fittings (cost $4 000)	3 800
Purchases	83 436
Provision for Bad Debts	662
Sales	130 261
Purchase Returns	1 120
Carriage Inwards	1 546
Rent and Rates	2 626
Salaries and Wages (Profit and Loss Account)	15 226
General Expenses	3 920
Interest on Bank Overdraft and Bank Charges	356
Carriage Outwards	3 720
Discounts Allowed	965
Discounts Received	859
Returns Inwards	1 240
Freehold Buildings	60 300
Bad Debts	1 240

You are given the following information:

(a) The stock in trade at 31 December 20.. was valued at $14 270.
(b) Wages and salaries outstanding at 31 December 20.. were $426.
(c) Rates paid in advance at 31 December 20.. amounted to $100.
(d) The Provision for Bad Debts is to be increased to $700, and a Provision for Discounts of 5 per cent of the net debtors is to be created.
(e) Depreciation is to be charged as follows:
motor vans, 25 per cent per annum on cost;
fixtures and fittings, 5 per cent per annum on cost.
(f) Richards is advised by a valuer that his premises are now worth $100 000 and that it would be advisable to revalue them to that figure. He decides to do so and to take the increase as an increase in capital.

Now prepare a Trading and Profit and Loss Account for the year 20.. and a Balance Sheet as at 31 December 20...

3. The Trial Balance extracted from the books of Wilkinson, a trader, as at 31 December 20.. was as follows:

	$	$
Capital		7699
Furniture and Equipment (cost $2100)	1640	
Motor Vans (cost $8000)	5600	
Purchases	36291	
Rent and Rates	2800	
Salaries	13969	
Bad Debts	281	
General Expenses	2062	
Bank Balance	4308	
Sales		75622
Provision for Doubtful Debts as at 1 January 20..		269
Stock in trade as at 1 January 20..	8726	
Debtors	4289	
Creditors		3164
Drawings	6788	
	$86754	$86754

You are given the following additional information:

(a) Stock in trade 31 December 20.. $9428.
(b) Rates paid in advance at 31 December 20.. $60.
(c) General expenses unpaid at 31 December 20.. $466.
(d) Provision for Doubtful Debts is to be adjusted to $430.
(e) A motor van purchased on 1 January of this year at a cost of $2800 was traded in for $2000 on 31 December 20.. and a new van purchased at a cost of $4000 on the same day. The amount due on the new van was payable within one month. No entries had been made in the books in respect of this transaction when the Trial Balance at 31 December 20.. was extracted.
(f) Depreciation is to be charged on furniture and equipment at the rate of 5 per cent per annum on cost and on the vans at the rate of 25 per cent per annum on cost.

You are asked to prepare Wilkinson's Trading and Profit and Loss Account for 20.. and his Balance Sheet as at 31 December 20...

22.13 Revise and Test 22. Adjustments in Final Accounts

Answers	*Questions*
—	**1.** What are adjustments?
1. They are changes in the amount of any expenses of the business or receipts of the business to establish the true amount paid or received in the financial year.	**2.** What is the principle behind them?
2. There are two principles really: a) that each year should carry every penny of expense properly incurred in that year, but no more. It should also take account of every bit of income earned in that year, but no more; b) that the Balance Sheet should present a 'true and fair view' of the affairs of the business at the end of the financial year.	**3.** Who imposed these requirements upon accounts?
3. They are traditional, since accountancy first began, but for companies they are actually enacted into law in the Companies Act 1985. However, the principles apply to all businesses.	**4.** What do these principles ensure?

---

4. That the final accounts
a) result in an accurate figure for profits for the year, so that the trader knows what his/her true income is (and so does the tax inspector);
b) that the Balance Sheet is honest and accurate (so far as it can be). Businesses are bought and sold on the basis of Balance Sheet valuations; so an accurate Balance Sheet enables business transfers to take place honestly and to the mutual benefit of both parties.

5. What are the commonest adjustments?

---

5. a) Payments in advance;
b) accrued expenses;
c) receipts in advance;
d) accrued receipts.

6. Give an example of a payment in advance.

---

6. Insurance is almost always paid in advance (you don't get cover until you pay the premium). Suppose I insure a car on 1 July and pay an annual premium of $300. On 31 December what amount should be treated as an expense of the year just ending. Clearly only half ($150). The rest is paid in advance for next year and must be carried over as an expense of the next year. It counts as an asset on the Balance Sheet.

7. Give an example of an accrued expense.

7. An accrued expense is one that has built-up and is due for payment. At the end of the year an expense that has not been paid, and will now be paid in the first few weeks of the new financial year must be included as an expense of the present year on the Profit and Loss Account. The amount due appears as a liability on the Balance Sheet.	**8.** What about receipts in advance?
8. If someone pays us for goods to be supplied at a later date the income is not counted as income of the present year. It is not included as a profit on the Profit and Loss Account, but is carried over to the next year. It is therefore a liability on the Balance Sheet.	**9.** What about accrued receipts?
9. If money has accrued due to us, for example where members of a club or society do not pay their membership dues, the income we should have received is counted as income of the present year and the debt is carried forward as a current asset on the Balance Sheet.	**10.** What other adjustments might be met with?
10. a) We might need to take depreciation into account on motor vehicles, plant and machinery and furniture; b) we might need to write off bad debts or make a provision for doubtful debts; c) we might need to amortize a lease; d) we might need to appreciate (increase the value of) premises.	**11.** Go over the list again until you are sure of all the answers.

UNIT 23

Partnership Accounts

23.1 Partnerships

In many situations in business life, a partnership seems to be the best type of business unit. For example, in family businesses it is sometimes helpful to recognize the merits of various interested parties by designating them as partners in the business. Names such as Harrison Bros, Sorrell and Son, and Scammell and Nephew are common. In professional businesses the partnership is often the only satisfactory form of business unit, for many professional bodies do not permit their members to practise through limited companies, and a single person rarely has all the time and expertise required for a sophisticated professional service in medicine, dentistry, the law or management consultancy.

The chief reasons for forming partnerships may be listed as follows:

(a) In order to increase the capital of an enterprise, so that improved machinery, equipment and buildings may be obtained.

(b) In order to broaden the knowledge and experience available, and thus to offer a more comprehensive service to the public. Thus a group of lawyers specializing respectively in divorce, motor accident, criminal and conveyancing law may form a partnership to pool their knowledge and experience in these fields.

(c) In order to unite wisdom and experience with youth and vitality. A doctor of mature years who is finding all the calls he is required to make too great a strain upon his health may seek a young and lively partner who will take on the more active part of the practice in exchange for consultations with his senior colleague on tricky cases where a second opinion is desirable.

(d) In order to reduce the onerous responsibilities of a one-man concern, where it is impossible to take time off, and where sickness can endanger the very existence of the business. Partners are able to take annual vacations and days and week-ends off, and in times of sickness they can cover the absence of the partner who is not well.

23.2 Agreements Between Partners

Two people can hardly work together at all unless they are in agreement about most things, though such agreements are often not reduced to written form. A mere handshake is sufficient to inaugurate a partnership, and early partnerships were often called 'common ventures' or 'joint ventures'—phrases which include the idea that all business is to some extent an adventure in the way of trade.

Partnerships may be held to have existed by the courts if either partner can prove:

(a) an oral agreement (proved by witnesses), or
(b) a systematic course of dealing together by way of trade or professional services, or
(c) a written agreement, either formal (drawn up by a solicitor in deed form) or informal (a simple undertaking in writing to be associated with one another). Clearly the formal *partnership deed* is most desirable, since an experienced lawyer will bring to the partners' attention many points that have caused controversy between partners in the past. Even where people agree to work together at the start of a partnership it does not follow that disagreement will not arise at a later date.

Matters to be Included in a Partnership Deed

The following major points should be included in any partnership agreement.

(a) The amount of capital to be contributed by each partner.
(b) Whether this capital is to earn interest for the partner, and if so at what percentage rate. Usually it is desirable to give interest on capital if the amounts contributed are unequal. This prevents the partner contributing the greater sum from developing a sense of grievance.
(c) Whether any partner is to receive a salary, and if so how much. It often happens that a young person contributes very little to a partnership in terms of capital (and so is entitled to only a very small share of the profits) but a great deal in terms of health, strength and energy. While the older partner sits and thinks, the younger one is actively engaged on the routine but diverse requirements of the firm's day-to-day activities. The older partner should recognize this contribution as entitling the younger one to a reward in the form of a basic salary.
(d) The ratio for sharing the remaining profits and losses. Simple fractions are usually adopted, such as half and half, three-fifths and two-fifths, two-thirds and one-third, and so on. Note that salaries, interest on capital and so forth are part of the profits and are appropriated first. Only the residue of profit left after these appropriations can be shared in the agreed manner.

(e) The date the partnership shall commence, and the duration of the partnership. If the duration is to be 'at will', i.e. indefinitely so long as they are in agreement, then it is also wise to specify what arrangements are to be made in the event of the death of a partner. Consider, for instance, the death of a partner whose share in the business is $40 000. The heirs, as well as the Inland Revenue authorities, will be interested in obtaining their share of the estate. This could result in the collapse of the whole enterprise if assets have to be sold to realize the funds required. It is a wise policy to insure every partner's life, so that if he or she dies the partnership will receive a sum of money which may be used to pay the heirs their shares of the inheritance.
(f) How much each partner is permitted to draw as 'drawings' each month, or week, and whether it is intended to charge interest on these drawings.
(g) In the event of disputes, how the dispute shall be resolved. Some partners specify a particular person to act as arbitrator. Others suggest a formula for choosing an arbitrator, such as a bank manager for financial matters and a solicitor for legal points.

23.3 The Partnership Act 1890

Partnership law was codified in 1890, that is to say, the legal cases on which the law had formerly depended were enacted as a formal set of rules by Parliament, and modified in line with the thinking of the times. It was an age when legislators still believed that controls in business affairs were largely undesirable. The Act therefore established rules to which reference could be made as a last resort, when partners failed to agree on how certain specific points were to be settled; an original agreement, however informal, to behave differently from the way suggested in the Act is always upheld by the courts. These rules are residual only, that is to say they are used in cases (nowadays very few) in which partners entered into no clear arrangements with one another on the point at issue, and are as follows:

(a) Partners must share equally in the profits and contribute equally to the losses, regardless of whether their capitals are different.
(b) No partner may have a salary.
(c) No partner may have interest on capital.
(d) A partner lending money to the firm, over and above his/her capital contribution, is entitled to interest at 5 per cent per annum. This interest is a charge against the profits, i.e. it will appear in the Profit and Loss Account as one of the expenses of the business. (We shall see below that it is credited to the partner in his/her Current Account.)
(e) Any partner may see and copy the books of the firm, which must be kept at the ordinary place of business.
(f) No new partner may be introduced without the general consent of all the partners.

23.4 The Partners' Accounts

It is usual to keep the original capital contributions of the partners recorded unchanged in their Capital Accounts. That is to say, the Capital Accounts are not varied from year to year as profit is ploughed into the business or drawings are made from time to time, but each remains at the original figure for the duration of the partnership (unless a change in arrangements is agreed between the partners).

Since it is essential to have some account to which profits may be credited and from which drawings may be deducted (in this case debited), each partner has a Current Account (i.e. a running account) where these adjustments may be made. Each partner in fact has three accounts:

- a Capital Account, credited with the original capital contributed by the partner, and possibly remaining unchanged during the life of the partnership;
- a Current Account, credited with all profits earned and debited at the end of the year with all drawings, whether in cash or in kind;
- a Drawings Account, into which cash drawings are accumulated as the months go by. This account is cleared at the end of the financial year into the Current Account of the partner.

Typical accounts for a partner are illustrated below. For privacy they are often recorded in a separate ledger, called the Private Ledger, and kept by the partners separate from the ordinary books of account.

Capital Account (A. Partner) L1

				20..			$
				1 Jan.	Bank A/c	J1	25 000

Current Account (A. Partner) L2

20..			$	20..			$
30 June	Computers A/c	J4	25	31 Dec.	Salary	J8	4 200
31 Dec.	Drawings A/c	J8	4 550	31 Dec.	Interest on capital	J8	2 000
31 Dec.	Balance	c/d	4 475	31 Dec.	Share of residue of profit	J8	2 850
			$9 050				$9 050
				20..			$
				1 Jan.	Balance	B/d	4 475

Drawings Account (A. Partner) L3

20..			$	20..			$
31 Mar.	Bank	CB5	1 400	31 Dec.	Current A/c	J8	4 550
30 June	Bank	CB12	1 400				
30 Sept.	Bank	CB19	1 400				
31 Dec.	Bank	CB27	350				
			$4 550				$4 550

23.5 The Appropriation Account

The accounts of partnerships are identical with the accounts of sole traders as to routine books of original entry, the ledger and the Final Accounts, the Trading and Profit and Loss Accounts. Where they differ from the accounts of sole traders is in the allocation of the profits between the partners. This requires a special account, called the Appropriation Account, though some accountants regard it merely as a section of the Profit and Loss Account and call it the Appropriation Section of the Profit and Loss Account.

In the Appropriation Account the net profit achieved, instead of being credited to the Capital Account as with a sole trader, is appropriated between the partners in accordance with the partnership agreement. The chief matters are as follows, and they are entered in the order shown below.

(a) There may be goodwill to be written off.
(b) A partner, or partners, may be entitled to a partnership salary.
(c) A partner, or partners, may be entitled to interest on capital.
(d) The residue of the profit will then be shared in the agreed manner.

Example

Hills and Hobbs are in partnership with capitals of $25 000 and $15 000 respectively. The partnership agreement provides that profits shall be shared $\frac{5}{8}$ and $\frac{3}{8}$ after giving Hobbs a salary of $7800 and giving both partners interest on capital at 8 per cent per annum.

Write up the Appropriation Account for the year. The net profit for the year was $42 900. $500 is to be written off the Goodwill Account.

Appropriation Account for year ending 31 December 20.. L184

20.		$	$	20..		$
31 Dec.	Goodwill		500	31 Dec.	Net profit	42 900
31 Dec.	Salary (Hobbs)		7 800			
31 Dec.	Interest on capital:					
	Hills	2 000				
	Hobbs	1 200				
			3 200			
31 Dec.	Share of residue:					
	Hills	19 625				
	Hobbs	11 775				
			31 400			
			$42 900			$42 900

Notes:

(i) Goodwill is treated as discussed in Unit 22.11(e).
(ii) Hobbs' salary is credited to his Current Account.
(iii) The interest for each partner is credited to his Current Account.
(iv) The residue of the profit is then shared in the proper proportions.

23.6 Appropriating a Loss

Sometimes there is a net loss on the year's activities. This might appear to give some difficulty, but in fact it presents no accounting problems. The various items—salary, interest on capital and so on—are still given to the partners entitled to them. Of course this increases the loss, but the final sharing of the residue appropriates this loss in a proper manner. For example:

Appropriation Account for year ending 31 December 20.. L184

20..		$	$	20..		$
31 Dec.	Net loss		4560	31 Dec.	Share of loss:	
31 Dec.	Salary (Hobbs)		7800		Hills	9725
31 Dec.	Interest on capital:				Hobbs	5835
	Hills	2000				
	Hobbs	1200				
			3200			
			$15560			$15560

23.7 Interest on Drawings

Where a partner is receiving interest on capital, it is sometimes felt desirable to charge him/her interest if any drawings are made. The simplest way to do this is to add an extra column to the Drawings Account. Interest is calculated on the period outstanding until the end of the year. It is credited in the Appropriation Account, and thus is eventually shared between the partners as a further portion of profit. An example, with interest calculated at 8 per cent per annum, is shown below:

Drawings Account (Hills) L185

20..		*Interest* $	$	20..		$
30 June	Bank	90	2250	31 Dec.	Transfer to Current A/c	4590
31 Dec.	Bank	–	2250			
31 Dec.	Appropriation A/c		90			
			$4590			$4590

Drawings Account (Hobbs) L186

20..		*Interest* $	$	20..		$
31 Mar.	Bank	66	1100	31 Dec.	Transfer to Current A/c	4532
30 June	Bank	44	1100			
30 Sept.	Bank	22	1100			
31 Dec.	Bank	–	1100			
31 Dec.	Appropriation A/c		132			
			$4532			$4532

23.8 Exercises Set 36. Partnership Appropriation Accounts

1. Sybrandt and Cornelis are in partnership. They have a written agreement which says:

(a) partnership capitals shall carry interest at 10 per cent;
(b) Cornelis shall have a salary of $4 500 per annum;
(c) goodwill shall be reduced each year by 20 per cent;
(d) profits over and above those required for the first three clauses shall be shared two-thirds to Sybrandt and one-third to Cornelis.

Capitals are Sybrandt $40 000, Cornelis $24 000. Goodwill is valued at $2 000. Show the Appropriation Account (i.e. the Appropriation Section of the Profit and Loss Account) for the year if the profits for the year to 31 December 20.. were $20 000.

2. Wheel and Barrow are in partnership under an agreement which provides that profits and losses shall be shared three-fifths and two-fifths respectively and that, before this division is made, Barrow shall be entitled to a salary of $7 800 per annum and partners shall be credited with 8 per cent per annum interest on their capitals which are as follows: Wheel $40 000, Barrow $30 000.

The profit for the year ended 31 December 20.., before making any of these adjustments, amounted to $42 000.

Write up the Profit and Loss Appropriation Account for the year.

3. The Partnership Agreement of Able, Baker and Charles contains the following provisions:

(a) the partners' fixed capital shall be: Able $40 000, Baker $28 000, Charles $16 000;
(b) Able and Baker are each to receive a salary of $7 800 per year;
(c) interest on capital is to be calculated at 8 per cent per annum;
(d) Able, Baker and Charles are to share profits and losses in the ratios 3:2:1.

The Profit and Loss Account for the year showed a profit of $59 520 before charging interest on capital or partners' salaries.

Show the Profit and Loss Appropriation Account for the year ended 31 December 20...

4. At 1 January 20.. R. Hawtrey owned a business in which he had $28 000 capital. As from 1 July 20.. W. Grigg came in as a partner on the following terms:

(a) The capital to be brought in by Grigg would be $12 000. Hawtrey's capital would remain at $28 000.
(b) Grigg should have a salary of $4 500 per annum.
(c) Interest at 8 per cent per annum was to be allowed on both partners' capitals from the start of the partnership.
(d) After charging both salary and interest on capital any further profit should be shared $\frac{3}{4}:\frac{1}{4}$, Hawtrey taking the larger share.

You are asked to show the Appropriation Section of the Profit and Loss Account at 31 December 20.. for the half-year ended on that date. The net profit available for division between the partners was $48 850.

5. Melville and Ahab entered into partnership on 1 April 20.. with capitals of $15 000 and $5 000 respectively. The Partnership Agreement provided as follows:

(a) Ahab to draw a salary of $10 400 per annum;
(b) interest on capitals to be given at 9 per cent per annum;
(c) residue of profit to be shared two-thirds to Melville and one-third to Ahab.

On 31 December 20.. they prepared Final Accounts for the nine-month period, showing that the profits were $47 220.

You are to show the Appropriation Account which shares these profits between the partners.

23.9 The Current Accounts of the Partners

We have seen that every partner has three private accounts: a Capital Account to record the original contribution of capital, a Drawings Account to record cash drawings, and a Current Account to record the fluctuating part of the partner's relationship with the business. Here are shown the profits accumulated and the drawings made in cash (transferred from the Drawings Account) and in kind (transferred by means of Journal entries—see below).

The result of any year's activities is either a credit or a debit balance on the Current Account of a partner. Imaginary Current Accounts for two partners, B. Careful and A. Spendthrift, are shown below.

Current Account (B. Careful) L195

20..			$	20..			$
30 June	Motor Vehicle		660	1 Jan.	Balance	B/d	415
31 Dec.	Drawings		11200	31 Dec.	Travelling Expenses A/c		42
31 Dec.	Balance	c/d	2137	31 Dec.	Interest on capital		1300
				31 Dec.	Share of residue		12240
			$13997				$13997
				20..			$
				1 Jan.	Balance	B/d	2137

Current Account (A. Spendthrift) L196

20..			$	20..			$
31 Jan.	Sales		125	1 Jan.	Balance	B/d	201
31 Dec.	Motor Vehicle Expenses		330	31 Dec.	Salary		4200
31 Dec.	Drawings		12500	31 Dec.	Interest on capital		1100
				31 Dec.	Share of residue		6120
				31 Dec.	Balance	c/d	1334
			$12955				$12955
20..			$				
1 Jan.	Balance	B/d	1334				

These accounts could also be shown as columnar accounts, thus:

Current Accounts (B. Careful and A. Spendthrift) L197

			Careful	*Spend-thrift*				*Careful*	*Spend-thrift*
20..			$	$	20..			$	$
31 Jan.	Sales			125	1 Jan.	Balance	B/d	415	201
30 June	Motor Vehicle		660		31 Dec.	Travelling Expenses		42	
31 Dec.	Motor Expenses			330	31 Dec.	Salary		–	4200
31 Dec.	Drawings		11200	12500	31 Dec.	Interest on capital		1300	1100
31 Dec.	Balance	c/d	2137		31 Dec.	Share of residue		12240	6120
					31 Dec.	Balance	c/d		1334
			$13997	$12955				$13997	$12955
20..			$	$	20..			$	$
1 Jan.	Balance	B/d		1334	1 Jan.	Balance	B/d	2137	

Notes on these Current Accounts

(i) The opening balances Usually a Current Account will have an opening balance. In both cases these accounts open with a credit balance, showing that the business owes the balance to the partner—it is a liability for profit made by the partner and not withdrawn.

(ii) The profits earned The profits appropriated to the partners in the Appropriation Account have been credited in the partners' Current Accounts. These items are (i) Spendthrift's salary, (ii) interest on capital to both partners, (iii) both partners' shares of the residue of the profit—in this case shared up two-thirds to Careful and one-third to Spendthrift.

(iii) Drawings in kind These are drawings made in the form of goods taken from the business by the partner. The most usual item here is the removal for personal use of goods purchased for resale. Following the ruling in Sharkey *v.* Wernher 1953 these must be regarded as sold to the partner at selling price. To comply with the law on this point we must debit the partner's Current Account (he has received goods) and credit Sales Account (which has given value). This requires a Journal entry as shown below.

				J19
20..			$	$
31 Jan.	Current Account (Spendthrift) Dr.	L196	125	
	Sales Account	L36		125
	Being goods taken home for partner's private use			

Another example of the same sort of charge to Current Account is where a partner takes a vehicle, or other asset of the business, at an agreed valuation, because it is surplus to the requirements of the business. Another is the payment of some portion of motor vehicle expenses, in return for the use of firm's vehicles for private purposes. All such matters lead to a debit entry in the Current Account, and a credit entry in the asset account or expense account.

Conversely, where a partner is to be recompensed for some out-of-pocket payment made on behalf of the business, his or her Current Account is credited and the loss or asset account debited. Typical Journal entries are shown overleaf.

					J19
20..				$	$
30 June	Current Account (Careful)	Dr.	L195	660	
	Depreciation Account	Dr.	L37	40	
	Motor Vehicles Account		L52		700
	Being sale of motor vehicle valued at $700 on book for $660 to a partner (Careful)				
31 Dec.	Current Account (Spendthrift)	Dr.	L196	330	
	Motor Vehicles Expenses Account		L55		330
	Being portion of motor vehicle expenses agreed to be chargeable to Spendthrift for private use of the firm's motor vehicle				
31 Dec.	Travelling Expenses Account	Dr.	L56	42	
	Current Account (Careful)		L195		42
	Being refund of fares to Exeter paid by Careful out of his own pocket for business purposes				

(iv) The balance at the close of the year The balances of Careful's and Spendthrift's accounts above illustrate that the final result of any Current Account may be either a credit or a debit. The credit balance represents a liability of the business to the partner; it is the part of his profit for the year which the partner has not withdrawn, but has left in the business. A debit balance represents an excess of drawings over profits earned, and leaves the partner a debtor for the sum. It is a current asset of the business, but it is unlikely that the partner will pay the balance in. It is more likely to remain as a debit balance to be set against next year's profits.

The end of the year might be a suitable moment for the partners to consider their long-term capital positions. For example, where a year has been profitable they might agree to transfer some of the balances on their Current Accounts to their Capital Accounts as long-term capital to be used for the development of the business.

You should now attempt some of the exercises given below.

23.10 Exercises Set 37. Current Accounts of Partners

1. Potton and Dover are in partnership with capitals of $15000 and $10000 respectively. The partnership deed provides that:

   (a) Dover is entitled to a salary of $8750 per annum;
   (b) each gets 8 per cent interest on capital per annum;
   (c) the remaining profits are shared three-quarters to Potton, one-quarter to Dover.

   Each partner has a Current Account to which all items of personal income arising from the firm are posted, and against which any drawings, either of cash or goods, are charged.

   Show Dover's Current Account for the year 20... On 1 January 20.., he had a credit balance of $180. During the year he drew $10500 in cash and took home goods valued at $378. Profits for the year were $31542.

2. Johnson is a partner in a business and is entitled to one-third of the net profit of the firm. From the following particulars write up the Capital and Current Accounts of Johnson for the year to 31 December 20.. as they would appear in the ledger of the partnership:

20..		$
1 January	Balance on Johnson's Capital Account (credit)	23000
1 January	Balance on Johnson's Current Account (credit)	450
1 May	Additional capital brought in by Johnson	3600
31 December	Johnson's drawings for the year	11600
31 December	Interest allowed on Johnson's capital	2070
31 December	Johnson's salary	4800
31 December	Net profit for the year (after adjustment of partner's salaries and interest) divisible between the partners	26310
31 December	Amount transferred from Johnson's Current Account to his Capital Account	1400

3. Messrs Hayling and Wight are in partnership, sharing profits and losses in the ratio Hayling three-fifths, Wight two-fifths. Their fixed capitals are: Hayling $8000, Wight $5000. The partnership agreement provides that interest of 9 per cent per annum shall be paid on fixed capital and that Wight is to receive a salary of $14400 per annum and 2 per cent commission on the trading profit.

   The balances of the Current Accounts at 1 January 20.. are: Hayling credit $420, Wight credit $350.

   Drawings during the year: Hayling $16000, Wight $14000.

   The trading profit for the year ended 31 December 20.. was $45800.

   Prepare the Current Account of each partner for the year ended 31 December 20...

4. a) What are the reasons for keeping a Current Account as well as a Capital Account for each partner?
   b) A Capital Account can show only a credit balance. Do you agree with this statement?
   c) In what circumstances would a Current Account show a debit balance?

5. Smith and Edwards are in partnership sharing profits and losses in the ratio 2:1. Their accounts are made up for the year ending 31 December 20... From the following information write up the Profit and Loss Appropriation Account of the partnership, and the Current Accounts of Smith and Edwards as they would appear in their private ledger.

1 January 20..	Current Account balance:	
	Smith	$400 *Cr.*
	Edwards	$350 *Dr.*
31 December 20..	Drawings during year:	
	Smith	$17 000
	Edwards	$15 600
	Interest on capital:	
	Smith	10 per cent of $13 000
	Edwards	10 per cent of $7 000

Salary: Edwards $5 400
Net profit to be divided, *after* charging interest on capital and paying Edwards's salary, was $47 490.

23.11 The Balance Sheet of a Partnership Enterprise

The Final Accounts of a partnership consist of a Trading Account, a Profit and Loss Account, an Appropriation Account, two or more Current Accounts and a final Balance Sheet. This Balance Sheet is different from the sole trader's Balance Sheet only in that it has two or more entries for the Capital Account, which are merely added together. The Current Account balances appear in appropriate places either as liabilities to the partners or, if they have debit balances, as current assets of the business, as shown below.

Balance Sheet of Brighton and Hove as at 31 December 20..

	$	$		$	$
Fixed assets:			Capital:		
Land and Buildings		25 000	At start Brighton		26 000
Plant and Machinery		14 000	Hove		24 000
Furniture and Fittings		1 000			50 000
Motor Vehicles		11 750	Current Account:		
		51 750	Brighton		55
Current assets:			Long-term liability:		
Current A/c Hove	160		Mortgage		3 500
Stock	11 800		Current liabilities:		
Debtors	1 520		Creditors	12 350	
Cash at bank	900		Wages due	350	
Cash in hand	125				12 700
		14 505			
		$66 255			$66 255

23.12 Exercises Set 38. Final Accounts of Partnerships

1. From the following list of balances you are required to prepare the Profit and Loss Appropriation Account and the Current Accounts of the partnership of Holden and Didsbury for the year ended 31 December 20.. and their Balance Sheet as at that date.

	$
Profit and Loss Account (net profit)	24 612
Cash in hand	236
Cash at bank	3 630
Trade Debtors	1 930
Trade Creditors	2 416
Provision for Bad Debts	193
Insurance prepaid	125
Rent owing	340
Furniture and Equipment (at cost)	24 000
Provision for Depreciation on Furniture etc.	1 800
Stock	12 840
Loan (from Holden)	4 000
Capital Accounts (1 January):	
Holden	18 000
Didsbury	6 000
Drawings Accounts:	
Holden	5 210
Didsbury	5 920
Current Accounts (*Cr.*) (1 January):	
Holden	208
Didsbury	122
Motor van (at cost)	4 600
Provision for Depreciation on Van	800

Notes:

(i) The loan—for the purchase of the van—is for five years and bears interest at 12 per cent per annum; this has not been provided for. (Since the Profit and Loss Account has been done, make it the first Appropriation Account item.)

(ii) Didsbury is entitled to be credited with a partnership salary of $4 000.

(iii) The partners share profits and losses in the proportions: Holden three-quarters, Didsbury one-quarter.

2. A. Bull has been having a quarrel with his partner T. Cow over the distribution of the profits made last year ($25 800). Bull and Cow are agreed on one thing, that it never entered the heads of either to discuss the question of how profits should be shared when they started business on 1 January, as they were more concerned with avoiding losses. Bull is now claiming 10 per cent interest on capital (Bull $10 000, Cow $500) and a salary for his work (he does 60 per cent of the work to Cow's 40 per cent). Advise the partners.

3. Able and Kinder are in partnership sharing profits and losses equally. Interest on capital is allowed at 8 per cent per annum. From the following Trial Balance (extracted after the Trading and Profit and Loss Accounts had been completed) prepare the partners' Profit and Loss Appropriation Account, Current Accounts in columnar form for the year ended 31 December 20.., and a Balance Sheet on that date.

	$	$
Capital Accounts (1 January 20..)		
Able		28000
Kinder		20000
Current Accounts (1 January 20..)		
Able		375
Kinder	125	
Net profit (year ended 31 December 20..)		23600
Drawings during year ended 31 December 20..		
Able	6300	
Kinder	11800	
Creditors		2450
Rates due		250
Premises	28000	
Vans	12000	
Shop Fittings	1900	
Stock	11700	
Debtors	30	
Bank balance	2400	
Cash in hand	360	
Insurance in advance	60	
	$74675	$74675

During the year ended 31 December 20.. the following depreciation had been written off: motor vans $3000, shop fittings $100.

4. At 30 June 20.. R. Short owned a business in which he had $20000 capital. As from 1 July 20.. P. Lovelace came in as a partner on the following terms:

(a) Short's capital was to remain unchanged and Lovelace was to bring in $10500 of which $500 was to be credited to his Current Account.
(b) Interest at 8 per cent was to be allowed on both capitals from the start of the partnership.
(c) Lovelace was to be credited with a salary of $8500 per annum.
(d) Profits, after charging interest and salary, were to be divided Short two-thirds and Lovelace one-third.

Lovelace withdrew $1000 on the last day of each month, commencing with 31 July. At 31 December 20.. the net profit available for division before charging the partnership interest and salary was $48485.

You are required to prepare the partnership's Appropriation Account and the Current Account of P. Lovelace.

5. Ross and Glass were in partnership sharing profits equally. The following Trial Balance was extracted from their books as at 31 December 20.., after various adjustments such as depreciation had been made:

Trial Balance as at 31 December 20..

	$	$
Capital: Ross (as at 1 January 20..)		24000
Glass (as at 1 January 20..)		22500
Drawings: Ross	6580	
Glass	6025	
Current Account: Ross (as at 1 January 20..)		1324
Glass (as at 1 January 20..)	125	
Motor vans at cost *less* depreciation	6450	
Stock in trade, 1 January 20..	5875	
Debtors	4320	
Creditors		5840
Purchases	37850	
Sales		96251
Rates and insurances	785	
Wages (Profit and Loss Account)	10057	
Bad Debts	184	
Provision for Bad Debts		260
Premises	45000	
Plant at cost *less* depreciation	17250	
Bank balance	2475	
General Expenses	2814	
Van Running Expenses	3185	
Depreciation	1200	
	$150175	$150175

Stock in trade at 31 December 20.. amounted to $11765.
The Provision for Bad Debts is to be changed to $432.

You are required to prepare a Trading Account, Profit and Loss Account, Appropriation Account and Current Accounts in columnar form for the year ending 31 December 20.., and a Balance Sheet as at that date.

6. Brown and Marshall are in partnership sharing profits and losses in the ratio of 2 to 1. They have agreed to keep their drawings in that ratio. At the end of their financial year they have attempted to draw up a Balance Sheet, and have produced the following:

Balance Sheet as at 31 December 20..

	$		$	$
Premises	40 000	Capital invested:		
Machinery	16 000	Brown	50 000	
Motor Vehicles	14 000	Marshall	20 000	
Fixtures and Fittings	5 000			70 000
Stock	23 000	Profit for the first year		48 000
Debtors	21 500	Creditors		17 000
Bank	8 200	Depreciation:		
Cash	500	Motor vehicles	3 500	
Drawings	15 000	Fixtures	1 200	
				4 700
		Provision for Bad Debts		3 500
	$143 200			$143 200

Set out the Balance Sheet in acceptable form, with fixed Capital Accounts and Current Accounts for each partner.

7. Troy and Sparta were partners sharing profits and losses in the proportion Troy two-thirds and Sparta one-third. The following Trial Balance was extracted from their books as at 31 December 20..:

Trial Balance as at 31 December 20..

	$	$
Capital: Troy		30 000
Sparta		15 000
Drawings: Troy	7 250	
Sparta	6 120	
Current Accounts: Troy		1 850
Sparta	850	
Repairs to Buildings	1 482	
Stock in trade, 1 January 20..	7 245	
General Expenses	3 815	
Motor Cars	8 250	
Car Expenses	794	
Trade Debtors	12 140	
Trade Creditors		3 250
Freehold Land and Buildings	28 000	
Furniture and Fittings	5 200	
Wages and Salaries	17 850	
Purchases	59 600	
Sales		123 250
Rates and insurances	1 254	
Bad Debts	186	
Provision for Bad Debts, 1 January 20..		450
Balance at bank	13 764	
	$173 800	$173 800

The following matters are to be taken into account:

(a) Stock in trade 31 December 20.. amounted to $9 658.
(b) Wages and salaries outstanding at 31 December 20.. were $150.
(c) The Provision for Bad Debts to be increased to 5 per cent of the outstanding debtors.
(d) The item 'repairs to buildings $1 482' includes $700 in respect of alterations and improvements to the buildings.
(e) Rates and insurances paid in advance at 31 December 20.. were $154.
(f) During the year Troy withdrew goods valued at $120 (sale price) for his own use and Sparta paid car expenses for the firm's car out of his own pocket amounting to $87. No entries had been made in the books for either of these matters.

You are required to prepare a Trading and Profit and Loss Account, etc., for the year to 31 December 20.. and a Balance Sheet as at that date.

Note: Ignore depreciation of fixed assets.

8. Richard and Stanley Bridges formed a partnership on 1 January 20.., in which they invested $10 000 and $5 000 respectively. At the same time they obtained a five-year lease on a property, for which they paid $4 000.

They agreed that interest should be allowed on their capitals at 10 per cent per annum and that profits and losses should be divided as follows: Richard three-fifths and Stanley two-fifths.

Prepare the Journal entries at the year ending 31 December 20.. to deal with the two following items:

(i) the charge against revenue in respect of the lease at the end of the year;
(ii) the discovery after the preparation of the Balance Sheet dated 31 December 20.. that the entries for interest on capital had been omitted from the Profit and Loss Appropriation Account.

9. The following Trial Balance was extracted from the books of Messrs Bristol and Avon, wholesale merchants, who share profits and losses three-quarters and one-quarter respectively, correct to the nearest dollar. From it you are required to prepare their Trading and Profit and Loss Account, etc., for the year ended 31 December 20.. and Balance Sheet as at that date.

Trial Balance as at 31 December 20..

	$	$
Capital Accounts (1 January 20..):		
Bristol		54000
Avon		18000
Drawings: Bristol	6000	
Avon	4800	
Current Accounts (1 January 20..):		
Bristol		851
Avon		1200
Trade Debtors and Creditors	3600	4519
Purchase and Sales	57200	85320
Warehouse Wages	7240	
Office Salaries	8250	
Returns	320	1200
Stock (1 January 20..)	5850	
Cash in hand	420	
Balance at bank	6639	
Freehold Premises	45000	
Furniture and Equipment	5000	
Motor Vehicles	8250	
Bad Debts	180	
Stationery	400	
Advertising	1250	
Lighting and Heating	860	
Rates	740	
Postage and Telephone	465	
Insurance	480	
Discounts	326	850
Motor Vehicles Expenses	2450	
Sundry Expenses	380	
Provision for Bad Debts		160
	$166100	$166100

Attention must be paid to the following matters which have not yet been put into effect in the books:

(a) The stock at 31 December 20.. was valued at $12720.
(b) Three-quarters of the expenses for rates and lighting and heating are to be charged to the warehouse and the remainder to the office.
(c) The furniture and equipment are to be depreciated by 10 per cent and the motor vehicles by 20 per cent.
(d) Insurance unexpired amounts to $120.
(e) The Provision for Bad Debts at 31 December 20.. is to stand at 4 per cent of the trade debtors at that date.

10. Ross and Cromarty carry on business in partnership and the following are the balances on the books of the firm as at 31 March 20..:

	$	$
Ross Capital Account		30 000
Cromarty Capital Account		15 000
Ross Drawings Account	5 258	
Cromarty Drawings Account	4 758	
Ross Current Account (1 April last)	122	
Cromarty Current Account (1 April last)		1 425
Purchases and Sales	97 128	167 545
Sales Returns and Purchases Returns	545	1 128
Stock at 1 April previous year	14 756	
Salaries	9 425	
Rent and Rates	1 850	
Insurance	630	
Carriage Inwards	720	
General Expenses	2 956	
Debtors and Creditors	4 700	5 862
Discounts Allowed and Received	78	560
Office Furniture and Fittings (cost)	3 800	
Provision for Depreciation of Office Furniture and Fittings at start of year		1 152
Balance at bank	19 664	
Provision for Bad Debts at start of year		460
Bad Debts written off	186	
Motor vehicles (cost)	20 000	
Provision for Depreciation of Motor Vehicles		1 744
Computers and peripherals (cost)	32 500	
Patents owned	5 800	
	$224 876	$224 876

Prepare the Trading and Profit and Loss Account, etc., for the year ending 31 March 20.. and the Balance Sheet at that date, making such adjustments as are required by the following:

(a) The partners' Capital Accounts are to remain constant and to carry interest at the rate of 8 per cent per annum.

(b) Profits and losses are to be divided in the proportions of two-thirds to Ross and one-third to Cromarty (correct to the nearest $1).

(c) The stock on hand at 31 March 20.. was valued at $11 476.

(d) Rent owing at 31 March 20.. was $500.

(e) Insurance paid in advance at 31 March 20.. was $130.

(f) Depreciation of office furniture to be charged at the rate of 10 per cent per annum on the cost.

(g) The Provision for Bad Debts is to be made up to $470.

(h) Motor vehicles are to be depreciated on cost by 20 per cent, and computers and peripherals by 25 per cent. Computers were new on 1 April last.

23.13 Revise and Test 23. Partnerships

Answers	*Questions*
—	**1.** What is a partnership?
1. It is a type of relationship which subsists between persons carrying on a business together with a view to earning profits.	**2.** What is the legal basis of the relationship?
2. Agreement between the parties. There may be a formal deed of partnership.	**3.** What matters should be included in a partnership deed?
3. a) The name of the business; b) its address; c) the nature of the business; d) details of any contributions of capital, the sharing of profits and arrangements about drawings; e) the powers of the parties; f) details about the book-keeping and accounting arrangements.	**4.** What are the advantages of partnerships?
4. a) Increased capital; b) wider experience—partners may have different skills and expertise; c) recreation and sickness can be covered by the partner who is not on holiday, or ill; d) affairs are still private.	**5.** What are the disadvantages of partnerships?
5. a) Liability is still unlimited—the partners are liable to the limit of their personal wealth for all debts; b) profit must be shared; c) consultation is necessary and delay in decisions may consequently occur; d) death or retirement may bring a firm to an end.	**6.** Who controls the firm?
6. Every partner is entitled to manage the firm.	**7.** What Act controls partnerships in the United Kingdom?

7. The Partnership Act of 1890	**8.** How is it effective?
8. It is an Act that takes effect residually—it is only used to decide matters on which the partners have not reached agreement.	**9.** How can you prove an agreement?
9. a) By a formal deed drawn up by a solicitor; b) by a written agreement (not formal—but still in writing); c) by witnesses to an oral agreement; d) by a course of dealing over a period of time.	**10.** What is special about the accounts of a partnership?
10. It is usual to regard the Capital Accounts as fixed, except for the changes made at very long intervals when some rearrangement of the partnership occurs. This means that profits are not added to Capital Account, and drawings are not deducted from Capital Account. Instead each partner has a Current Account, which is allowed to fluctuate from year to year.	**11.** How many accounts does each partner have?
11. Three—a fixed Capital Account; a Current Account and a Drawings Account in which Drawings are collected as the year goes by.	**12.** What happens to the Drawings Account at the end of the year?
12. It is cleared off (i.e. debited) into the Current Account of the partner.	**13.** What other account is important in partnership accounts?
13. The Appropriation Account (sometimes called the Appropriation Section of the Profit and Loss Account).	**14.** What happens in this account?

14. It is used to split up the profit in the agreed way so that each partner receives an appropriate amount. We appropriate the profit to the individuals entitled to receive it.	**15.** What sort of appropriations are made?
15. There are three chief types: a) some partners may have a salary—a basic wage to meet their needs. This is often done to help a younger partner; b) sometimes interest on capital is allowed—a basic recognition of the importance of capital to the firm. This benefits the partner who has contributed more funds than the others; c) the profit left after these appropriations is called the residue, and is shared in the agreed manner.	**16.** What are the special features of Partnership Balance Sheets?
16. a) The partners' Capital Accounts will not vary from year to year and appear on the Balance Sheet at their original values; b) the partners' Current Accounts will also appear. They may have a credit balance (in which case they appear on the liabilities side because the business owes the partners this extra amount—profit ploughed back). They may have a debit balance, in which case the partner owes the business money and this would appear as an asset—a special kind of debtor.	**17.** Go over the test again until you are sure of all the answers.

UNIT 24

Non-profit-making Organizations

24.1 Non-profit-making Institutions

Most enterprises are run for private profit. There are, however, many institutions in society whose aims are not to make profits but to provide useful services to other people, or to promote activities which interest or amuse them. Such institutions are called *non-profit-making* bodies, or more commonly 'clubs'. They exist wherever interested people come together to form a body of members, elect a committee, subscribe funds, and proceed to conduct affairs. Local hockey clubs and cricket clubs, football supporters' clubs and even world-famous clubs like the United Nations Association or the International Red Cross, are examples. Many of these bodies are very small; others, such as many professional organizations, are enormous. In this Unit we shall study the accounting principles behind all such activities.

From the legal point of view, the important feature of clubs is that they have no separate legal status. In the eyes of the law a club is nothing but a mere collection of individuals. These individuals are totally responsible for all the things done in the club, and their officers (chairperson, secretary, treasurer) are personally liable for the actions they take, the contracts they make, etc.

The *treasurer* is the committee member responsible for the collection of funds, and is often also responsible for paying bills, rent of premises and so on. It is often considered desirable that more than one person shall be concerned with these payments, to prevent the treasurer misappropriating funds, so it is frequently laid down in the club rules that the chairperson and the treasurer must both sign cheques. Any misappropriation of funds in such circumstances must involve a criminal conspiracy, or forgery, both of which are more severely punished than theft.

The chief functions of the treasurer are the collecting of subscriptions and other funds and the paying of any bills that arise. He or she must also prepare and submit to the committee at the Annual General Meeting (AGM) of the club suitable Final Accounts for the year that has just passed. These accounts may be very simple, in which case they are called *Receipts and Payments Accounts*. For large clubs, especially those with substantial assets, they take the form of an *Income and Expenditure Account*, followed by a Balance Sheet as at the last day of the year (or season, if the club's activities are seasonal). Both these types of 'Final Accounts' are prepared from the club's cash book.

24.2 Keeping the Cash Record of a Club

The chief concerns of the treasurer—collecting subscriptions and paying bills—are mainly cash activities (though most clubs also have bank accounts, where club funds can be deposited, or at least safeguarded in a current account). A simple cash record can be kept in a cheap cash notebook. The treasurer goes to club meetings, prepared to accept any subscriptions that are offered. There may also be donations to be accepted and recorded, raffles and other fund-raising activities to be organized and perhaps pay-boxes for billiard-tables and pin-ball machines to be emptied. Often the balance of the proceeds of the sale of refreshments—after the responsible person has deducted the expenses paid out for the purchase of sandwich materials, tea, milk, sugar and so on—is also paid over to the treasurer after each meeting.

The treasurer's cash record, a simple Cash Account, might be as follows:

The Merry Players' Drama Society
Cash Account

20..		$	20..		$
7 Sept.	Balance in hand	49.50	7 Sept.	Hire of hall	8.00
7 Sept.	Subs—Mrs Dillon	5.00	7 Sept.	Refreshment expenses	12.50
7 Sept.	Subs—Mr Metcalfe	5.00	7 Sept.	Raffle prize	4.80
7 Sept.	Refreshments	27.50	14 Sept.	Hire of hall	8.00
7 Sept.	Raffle proceeds	12.25	14 Sept.	Raffle prize	5.50
14 Sept.	Subs—Miss Latymer	5.00	14 Sept.	Leaflet printing	17.00
14 Sept.	Subs—Mr Lidyard	5.00	14 Sept.	Refreshment expenses	13.50
14 Sept.	Subs—Rev. P. Stacey	5.00			
14 Sept.	Refreshments	31.00			
14 Sept.	Raffle proceeds	11.50			

Analysing Receipts and Payments

One of the chief disadvantages of such a club cash book is that the transactions recorded day by day are not analysed under various headings, but simply appear in date order. To analyse these items, it is necessary to go through the figures collecting together similar items. For example, using the figures above:

Receipts	$	*Payments*	$
Subscriptions		Hire of hall $8.00 + $8.00	= 16.00
$5 + $5 + $5 + $5 + $5	= 25.00	Refreshment expenses	
Refreshments $27.50 + $31.00	= 58.50	$12.50 + $13.50	= 26.00
Raffle proceeds $12.25 + $11.50	= 23.75	Raffle prizes $4.80 + $5.50	= 10.30
		Printing $17.00	= 17.00
	$107.25		$69.30

This type of analysis work is laborious, especially if a busy treasurer has a whole year's takings to analyse. A better system is to keep an analysed cash book, for example, the *Simplex School Fund and Club Accounts Book*, obtainable from George Vyner Ltd, Holmfirth, Huddersfield, designed by Geoffrey Whitehead. The entries would then be as shown in Fig. 24.1.

The Merry Players' Drama Society

Date	*Details*	*Sub-scrip-tions*	*Com-peti-tions*	*Ref-resh-ments*	*Sun-dry R'pts*	*Total*	*Date*	*Details*	*Equip-ment*	*Com-peti-tions*	*Ref-resh-ments*	*Gen. Exp-enses*	*Total*
20..		$	$	$	$	$	20..		$	$	$	$	$
1 May	Balance in hand				49.50	49.50	7 Sept.	Hire of hall				8.00	8.00
7 Sept.	Sub—Mrs Dillon	5.00				5.00	7 Sept.	Refresh. expenses			12.50		12.50
7 Sept.	Sub—Mr Metcalfe	5.00				5.00	7 Sept.	Raffle prize		4.80			4.80
7 Sept.	Refreshments			27.50		27.50	14 Sept.	Hire of hall				8.00	8.00
7 Sept.	Raffle		12.25			12.25	14 Sept.	Raffle prize		5.50			5.50
14 Sept.	Sub—Miss Latymer	5.00				5.00	14 Sept.	Leaflet printing				17.00	17.00
14 Sept.	Sub—Mr Lidyard	5.00				5.00	14 Sept.	Refresh. expenses			13.50		13.50
14 Sept.	Sub—Rev. P. Stacey	5.00				5.00	21 Sept.	Hire of hall				8.00	8.00
14 Sept.	Refreshments			31.00		31.00	21 Sept.	Cups	14.00				14.00
14 Sept.	Raffle		11.50			11.50	21 Sept.	Postage				2.50	2.50
14 Sept.	Sub—Mr Darby	5.00				5.00	21 Sept.	Raffle		5.00			5.00
	and so on throughout the season until							and so on throughout the season until					
29 Apr.	Sub—Mr Way	5.00				5.00	29 Apr.	Hall charge				8.00	8.00
29 Apr.	Raffle		14.50			14.50	29 Apr.	Refreshments			10.25		10.25
29 Apr.	Refreshments			25.00		25.00	30 Apr.	Hall charge				8.00	8.00
30 Apr.	Donation				50.00	50.00	30 Apr.	Refreshments			17.30		17.30
30 Apr.	Refreshments			28.00		28.00	30 Apr.	Balance in hand				164.55	164.55
		185.00	387.50	426.50	129.50	1128.50			162.50	228.50	325.80	411.70	1128.50
1 May	Balance in hand				164.55	164.55							

Fig. 24.1 The analysed cash book of a club

24.3 The Receipts and Payments Account

At the Annual General Meeting (AGM) of a club, the treasurer will present to the members a statement of the club's financial position. The simplest type of statement that can be presented is a Receipts and Payments Account, prepared from the analysis figures revealed either by a physical analysis of the club's cash book as shown above, or from the analysis columns of the type of cash book shown in Fig. 24.1. The Receipts and Payments Account may be defined as *the analysed cash book of a club listing the receipts and payments for the year and revealing any cash balance in hand.*

When the members arrive for the meeting, copies of the Receipts and Payments Account will be distributed to all members present. They listen to the secretary's and treasurer's accounts of the year's proceedings, and are then free to comment on the conduct of the club and its affairs.

Using the same figures as before, the Receipts and Payments Account would look like this:

The Merry Players' Drama Society
Receipts and Payments Account for Winter Season 20..–20..

20..		$	20..		$
1 May	Balance from last season	49.50	Sept. to Apr.	Purchase of equipment	162.50
Sept. to Apr.	Subscriptions	185.00		Competitions and raffle expenses	228.50
	Competitions and raffles	387.50		Refreshment expenses	325.80
	Refreshment sales	426.50		General expenses	247.15
	Sundry receipts	80.00	30 Apr.	Balance in hand	164.55
		$1 128.50			$1 128.50
20..		$			
1 May	Balance in hand	164.55			

As you see, the figures are not exactly the same as those in the analysis columns of the cash book. The figure for sundry receipts, for instance, does not correspond, since in fact it also includes the opening cash figure: you might say that on the receipts side of the cash book the opening cash balance is received by this season from last season. Similarly, on the payments side the 'general expenses' item is reduced by the amount of the closing balance of cash in hand, which is not really an expense of the season but is handed on to the next season by the present season.

You should now prepare several Receipts and Payments Accounts from the information given in Exercises Set 39 below.

24.4 Exercises Set 39. Simple Receipts and Payments Accounts

1. Prepare a Receipts and Payments Account from the cash book of the treasurer of Newtown Football Club, at the end of the season, 31 May 20..:

   Cash in hand at start $48.00; earnings from gate $2778.00; payments for goal posts $45.00, for players' kits $123.50, for a deposit on the Club House $500.00; earnings from refreshments $2026.54; payments for refreshment materials $827.78 and for annual dinner $286.25; donation from Supporters' Club $726.62; payments for postage $47.62; wages of secretarial help $1256.50; balance of cash in hand $42.51; balance at bank $2450.00. (*Note:* The bank account was opened during the present year.)

2. Prepare the Receipts and Payments Account of the Jolly Wanderers Rambling Club for the year ended 31 December 20..:

   Balance in hand at start of year, cash $57.50, bank $120; sales at bar $6485; subscriptions received $955; dividends on club investment received $105; purchases of bar stocks $3600; wages $1713; purchases of new furniture $125; rent and rates $290; repairs to premises $420; general expenses paid $401; cash in hand at end of year $55; cash at bank $1118.50.

3. Prepare the Receipts and Payments Account of the Roman Camp Archaeological Society, for the season ended 31 October 20..:

   Balance in hand at 1 January 20.. $127.50; subscriptions collected $1276.00; cost of new digging equipment $345.40; weather-protection material $116.00; sale of surplus finds from digs $432.75; earnings from conducted tours of digs $1585.50; cost of printing brochures and reports $347.20; contribution to local museum fund $400.00; expenses of labourers $1285.00; transport $284.50.

4. Prepare the Robert Burns Society's Receipts and Payments Account for the year ended 31 December 20.. given that:

   a) balance in hand at start was $175.50;
   b) expenses by cheque were as follows: transport to outings $225.50; refreshments $131.50; hire of musicians $231.00;
   c) expenses in cash were: secretary's honorarium $150.00; stationery $37.50; postage $112.25; repairs to dresses and outfits $117.55;
   d) subscriptions of $10.50 each were paid by 147 members;
   e) entrance fees paid to festivals totalled $247.50.

5. On 1 January 20.. the Kingswood Community Association had a balance of cash in hand of $133.81. Its receipts and payments for the year were:

   subscriptions received $675.35; donation from past president $100.00. Payments: for use of hall $240.00; for refreshments $228.30; for Christmas party $237.35; for summer outing $128.25. The treasurer and secretary were given $50.00 each as an honorarium and the Christmas bazaar raised $373.35 for club funds.

   a) Prepare the Receipts and Payments Account of the club for the year, bringing out the balance of cash in hand.
   b) This balance is kept at the treasurer's home. What change in this arrangement would you suggest?

24.5 Defects of the Receipts and Payments Account

The Receipts and Payments Account is an unsatisfactory record of the club's activities, for several reasons:

(a) The record shows no assets of the club other than the cash balance and assets purchased during the year. This is very unsatisfactory where a club owns substantial assets (such as motor vehicles or a club house) worth, perhaps, many thousands of dollars.
(b) There is no record of liabilities, so that members cannot tell whether the club is in debt or not. They may of course ask the treasurer to clarify this point, but it may not occur to them to ask.
(c) Members do not know whether the club's activities for the year resulted in a profit or loss for the year. This information, if available, would tell them whether the subscription was too high, or too low.

Where a club has valuable assets which should be accounted for, therefore, it is usual to present a more sophisticated set of Final Accounts: an Income and Expenditure Account, and a Balance Sheet. Before discussing these records one or two special points must first be made.

24.6 Profits and Non-profit-making Organizations

All clubs make profits on such activities as bazaars and raffles, which are designed to raise funds for various club purposes. Such profits will appear in the accounts, but it is not usual to regard the final profit on the year's activities as 'profit' in the normal meaning of that word. A non-profit-making organization does not make 'profits'. If there is any extra money it must represent a surplus contribution by the members over and above what it was really necessary for them to contribute in view of the activities they enjoyed. The better term therefore is *surplus for the year*. If the result of the year's activities is a loss, this is described as a *deficit for the year*, the members' contributions being insufficient for the functions they held.

24.7 Capital and Non-profit-making Organizations

When a club starts its activities it usually begins by collecting the first year's subscriptions from the members, which are payable in advance. Sometimes a fee is charged on joining, besides the annual subscription. These sums are not quite the same as the capital of a business enterprise, but clearly a club which eventually owns valuable assets must have some sort of capital to record on the balance sheet. *Capital* is not a particularly good word to describe the liability the club owes to its members who have contributed or raised funds for its activities. It is usual to call this liability an *Accumulated Fund*, since this name aptly describes the way the fund is built up. Any surplus in the first year which is carried over to the second year may be said to have been 'accumulated'. Therefore the Balance Sheet of a club records on one side the club's assets, and on the other side its liabilities, including the Accumulated Fund.

At the start of any given year the club will have an opening balance on this Accumulated Fund. It is calculated by using the formula:

Accumulated Fund = assets owned at the date named − liabilities

Consider the following example. The Marco Polo Society has the following assets and liabilities at 1 January 20. .:

Assets:	$
Furniture	240
Projector and other visual aids	120
Various Chinese artefacts	150
Library of reference books	200
	$710
Liabilities:	$
Printing bill due	25
Members' subs in advance	20
	$45

Using the formula given above we have:

Accumulated Fund = $710 − $45
= $665

24.8 Trading by Non-profit-making Organizations

Where a club carries out a considerable amount of trading it is sometimes deemed desirable to prepare one or more Trading Accounts. Thus, where a club operates a bar for members it is usual for the sub-committee concerned to prepare a Bar Trading Account. Other sub-committees might act similarly so that, for example, a Dances and Social Committee Trading Account or a Publications Committee Trading Account might be prepared. These would be no different from the normal Trading Accounts of a sole trader or partnership, and any closing bar stocks or unsold books and pamphlets would be brought on to the Balance Sheet as assets of the club.

In the United Kingdom clubs and non-profit-making organizations may need to register for VAT if they engage in substantial trading activities—for example, if they run a bar. At the time of writing, where sales exceed £13 000 (say, $19 500) a quarter, or £53 000 (say, $78 000) in a full year, they must register as non-profit-making organizations and account for VAT in the usual way. For simplicity's sake, however, VAT has *not* been taken into account in the exercises in this Unit.

24.9 Final Accounts of a Non-profit-making Organization

Sole traders prepare Profit and Loss Accounts. The comparable account for a club is an *Income and Expenditure Account*. The income is entered on the credit side, like the profits of a sole trader. The expenditure is entered on the debit side, like the losses of a sole trader. The surplus (if any) is transferred to the Accumulated Fund, to increase the fund, in the same way that the net profit increases the sole trader's capital when he/she ploughs it back into the firm. The deficit (if any) is transferred to the Accumulated Fund and reduces the fund, indicating that members have been 'consuming capital' during the year by enjoying more facilities than they paid for.

The two starting points for the preparation of an Income and Expenditure Account and the Balance Sheet of a club are the Accumulated Fund calculation and the Receipts and Payments Account. It is now time to prepare one of these more sophisticated sets of Final Accounts for a club, and the example which follows illustrates all the points mentioned.

Example

The Harrison's Rocks Mountaineering Club was formed some years ago and on 1 January 20.. had assets and liabilities as follows:

Club premises and gymnasium $12 000; equipment $1 500; motor van $1 450; cash at bank $1 360 (on deposit); cash in hand $32.50. $30 is owed to the Snowdonia Instruction Club for the services of visiting lecturers and $25 for a printer's bill.

During the year it was resolved to obtain and sell to members at a reasonable profit any climbing gear or camping equipment they might need, and a special sub-committee called the Climbing Gear Committee was appointed to supervise this activity.

At 31 December 20.. a Receipts and Payments Account was prepared as follows:

Receipts and Payments Account for the year ending 31 December 20..

Receipts:	$	Payments:	$
Balance of cash in hand B/d	32.50	Snowdonia Instruction Club	130.00
Subscriptions	424.00	Refreshment materials	122.50
Sale of gear to members	458.00	Printing, etc.	42.25
Sale of refreshments	236.50	Club gear for club house	148.50
Donation from Anne Enthusiast	125.00	Purchase of gear for resale	200.00
Insurance claim paid	20.00	Ambulance expenses	15.50
		Medical expenses (injured member)	125.00
		Insurance premium	40.00
		Motor van expenses	285.00
		Balance of cash in hand c/d	187.25
	$1 296.00		$1 296.00
Balance of cash in hand B/d	187.25		

You are required to:

(a) calculate the Accumulated Fund at the start of the year,
(b) draw up a Trading Account for the Climbing Gear Committee,
(c) prepare an Income and Expenditure Account for the year ending 31 December 20.. and
(d) prepare a Balance Sheet as at 31 December 20...

Notes: On 31 December stocks of gear for resale were valued at $52, and $4 of the subscriptions listed as receipts were payments in advance for the coming year. The motor van is to be depreciated by 20 per cent and equipment in hand at 31 December 20.. by 10 per cent.

(a) Calculation of Accumulated Fund at start of year

Assets:	$	Liabilities:	$
Premises	12 000.00	Snowdonia Club	30.00
Equipment	1 500.00	Printer	25.00
Motor van	1 450.00		
Cash at bank	1 360.00		
Cash in hand	32.50		
	$16 342.50		$55.00

Accumulated Fund = $16 342.50 – $55.00
= $16 287.50

Notes:

(i) When the Accumulated Fund has been calculated in this way it is carried straight to the Balance Sheet, where it occupies the position usually taken by the Capital Account in a sole trader's accounts (see page 263).
(ii) When this figure is entered on the liabilities side of the Balance Sheet it must clearly be balanced by an equal and opposite figure. This means that *every figure that gave rise to it, i.e. the assets and liabilities above, must also be carried to the Balance Sheet, either unchanged or in a modified form.* If the assets or liabilities will still be in existence at the end of the season (that is, the premises, equipment, motor van and bank deposit in our example) they are entered unchanged on the Balance Sheet. Those that would not be still in existence at the end of the season are entered in the Cash Account, or are taken into account in the preparation of the Income and Expenditure Account. They therefore play their part in deciding what modified cash figure, or surplus or deficiency figure, eventually appears on the Balance Sheet.

(b) Preparation of Trading Account

Climbing Gear Committee Trading Account for the year ending 31 December 20..

20..		$	20..		$
31 Dec.	Purchases	200	31 Dec.	Sales	458
	Less Closing stock	52			
	Cost of sales	148			
	Profit on sales of gear	310			
		$458			$458

Notes:

(i) As this club activity began only in the current year, there was no opening stock.

(ii) The profit on trading is taken to the Income and Expenditure Account, just as the gross profit of a sole trader is transferred to Profit and Loss Account.

(c) Preparation of Income and Expenditure Account

Income and Expenditure Account for the year ending 31 December 20..

20..		$	$	20..		$	$
31 Dec.	Snowdonia Club	130.00		31 Dec.	Subscriptions	424.00	
	Less Last year's amount overdue	30.00			*Less* Subs paid in advance	4.00	
			100.00				420.00
	Refreshment materials		122.50		Refreshment sales		236.50
	Printing (for year)		17.25		Donation		125.00
	Ambulance expenses		15.50		Insurance claim		20.00
	Medical expenses		125.00		Profit on sales of gear		310.00
	Insurance premium		40.00				
	Motor van expenses		285.00				1111.50
	Depreciation:						
	Equipment	164.85			Deficiency for year (transferred to Accumulated Fund)		48.60
	Motor vans	290.00					
			454.85				
			$1160.10				$1160.10

Notes:

(i) You may have noticed that items appearing on the Receipts and Payments Account have crossed over sides as they enter the Income and Expenditure Account. For example, 'refreshment sales' appears on the debit side of Receipts and Payments Account, and on the credit side of the Income and Expenditure Account above. The explanation is that the

Receipts and Payments Account is a cash book, not a Trial Balance. It has never been posted to any account, for most clubs do not have any accounts. It follows that the profit items are on the debit side of the cash book (receipts) and the losses are on the credit side (payments).

(ii) The subscriptions figure has been adjusted to take account of the subscriptions paid in advance, which therefore appear on the Balance Sheet as a liability—we owe the members concerned a year's entertainment.

(iii) The outstanding payments to Snowdonia Instruction Club at the start of the year and for printing due do not appear in this year's accounts, since they refer to last year's expenses.

(iv) The club gear purchased was a capital item and therefore does not appear on the Income and Expenditure Account, but goes straight to the Balance Sheet.

(v) The deficiency for the year is carried to the Balance Sheet and deducted from the accumulated fund.

(d) Balance Sheet

Balance Sheet as at 31 December 20..

	$	$		$	$
Fixed assets:			Accumulated Fund:		
Premises		12 000.00	At start	16 287.50	
Equipment	1 500.00		*Less* Deficiency	48.60	
+ Additions	148.50				
	1 648.50				16 238.90
Less Depreciation	164.85				
		1 483.65			
Motor van	1 450.00				
Less Depreciation	290.00				
		1 160.00			
		14 643.65			
Current assets:			Current liabilities:		
Stock of gear for re-sale	52.00		Subs in advance		4.00
Cash at bank (deposit)	1 360.00				
Cash in hand	187.25				
		1 599.25			
		$16 242.90			$16 242.90

Notes: The presentation is similar to that of a sole trader's Balance Sheet, and may be presented either in the order of liquidity or in the order of permanence as shown above.

You should now try some of the exercises given in Unit 24.10.

24.10 Exercises Set 40. Final Accounts of Non-profit-making Organizations

1. Choose from the items shown below those necessary to prepare the Income and Expenditure Account of the Snowdonia Young Climbers' Club for the summer season ended 31 October 20... A Balance Sheet is not required.

	$
Subscriptions for current year	1 240.00
Subscriptions for previous year	5.50
Refreshment profits	125.00
Accumulated Fund of club at start	1 225.00
Purchases of magazines for club house	40.25
Purchase of climbing ropes and other gear (expected to last only two years)	260.50
Payments to farmer for camping fees	125.00
Printing and stationery	45.00
Charges to visiting parents	165.50
Train fares—accident victim	32.50
Ambulance charges	23.15
Donation by club to Mountain Rescue Service	100.00
Purchase and erection of mountain hut	400.00

2. The following figures were supplied to you by the treasurer of the Blewbury Tennis Club. They refer to the year ended 31 December 20...

		$
1 January 20..	Balance in bank and in hand	1 300
	Rates due and unpaid	40
	Subscriptions owing to the club	5

Receipts and payments for the year ended 31 December 20.. were as follows:

	$
Subscriptions (including $5 arrears)	2 350
Tournament (entrance fees received)	370
Tournament (cost of prizes)	140
Postage and stationery	40
Light and heat (club house)	130
Rates (including arrears for previous year $40)	460
Cost of new roller, bought for cash	140
Repairs to netting	40
Club house decorations (expected to last 5 years)	350
Wages of part-time groundsman	1 250

On 31 December 20.. subscriptions of $45 due for the year had not been paid, but were certain to be received.
The rates paid included $70 for the first quarter of the next year.
The club's furniture and fittings are depreciated by $120 every year.

You are asked to prepare the Blewbury Tennis Club's Receipts and Payments Account and Income and Expenditure Account for the year ended 31 December 20... A Balance Sheet is not required.

3. From the following information prepare a Cash Account and an Income and Expenditure Account for the year ended 31 March 20.. of the Seashore Pierrots Society:

20..	
1 April	The treasurer held $229 in the Cash Account.
23 April	The council paid a grant of $250.
3 October	The council paid a further grant of $250.

Paid engagements during the year were as follows:

		$
28 May	Chalkwell Seashore	30
3 June	Chalkwell Park	35
10 June	Pier Head	15
24 June	Chalkwell Seashore	30
1 July	Leigh Clifftop Pavillion	30
8 July	The Football Stadium	30
29 July	Nursery Funday	30
1 September	Pier Head	15
15 September	Leigh Theatre	35

All cash was received on the day of the engagement.
Payments made during the year were as follows:

		$
28 May	Two guest instrumentalists @ $15 each	30
30 June	Payment for performing rights	28
8 July	One guest instrumentalist	20
23 October	Music	12
20 February	Music	32

During the year the group entered for one contest. This was held on 11 March 20.. at Scarborough. In connection with this event the following payments were made:

		$
17 February	Entrance fee	25
21 February	Hire of rehearsal room	15
11 March	Hire of coach	145

A charge for friends on the coach brought in $65. The group won the second prize, which included $25 in cash.
On 31 March 20.. the following accounts were due and unpaid:

	$
Piano transport	27
Two new outfits (treated as a revenue expense)	86

4. The treasurer of the Coldfall Estate Sports Club provided the following analysis of his receipts and payments during the year ended 31 December 20... From it and the notes given below, draw up the club's Income and Expenditure Account as it should have been presented to the members on 31 December.

	$
Receipts:	
Subscriptions:	
Current year	2272
Previous year	112
Profit on refreshments	435
Competition fees	118
Payments:	
New games equipment	824
Printing, postage and stationery	113
Periodicals	118
Competition prizes	112
Sundry expenses	620
Wages	1278
Rent	420
Rates	249

Notes:

(i) Subscriptions due but unpaid for current year amount to $188.

(ii) The club furniture and games equipment at the beginning of the year was valued at $480. It is to be written down—ignoring additions during the year—by 20 per cent.

(iii) At 1 January, rates paid in advance amounted to $42, and of the rates payment made during the year $73 was in respect of the following year.

5. On 1 January 20.. the financial position of the Dog Schooling Society was:

Assets:	$	Liabilities:	$
Equipment	425	Accumulated Fund	1220
Subscriptions due	135	Trainer's fees accrued	110
Cash at bank	770		
	$1330		$1330

During the year ended 31 December 20.. receipts and payments were as follows:

Receipts:	$	Payments:	$
Balance at bank (1 January 20..)	770	Printing	80
Subscriptions for previous year	120	Stationery and postage	123
Subscriptions for current year	640	New equipment	118
Subscriptions in advance for following year	25	Hire of training ground	150
Field Trials entrance fees	144	Trainer's fees (including $110 for previous year)	340
Receipts from advertisements in Society year book	55	General expenses	215
		Field Trials:	
		Judges' fees	100
		Expenses	21
		Balance at bank (31 December 20..)	607
	$1754		$1754

The following items must also be taken into account:

(i) $48 is owing for subscriptions for current year.
(ii) The balance of subscriptions for previous year still outstanding is to be written off as a bad debt.
(iii) The balance of equipment at 1 January 20.. is to be depreciated by 20 per cent.
(iv) There is an amount of $12 owing for printing expenses.

You are required to prepare the Income and Expenditure Account for the year ended 31 December 20.. and a Balance Sheet as at that date. All calculations are to be shown in detail.

6. In preparing the Income and Expenditure Account of a gardening club you find:

(i) Rent owing at beginning of the year $18, paid during the year $380, owing at the end of the year $128.
(ii) Members' subscriptions overdue at the beginning of the year $10; received during year $340; payments in advance included in receipts $6.
(iii) Rates prepaid at the beginning of the year $84; paid during the year $349 which sum includes $53 in respect of the following year.

You are required to calculate (showing details of your workings) the amounts which would be shown in the Income and Expenditure Account for the year in respect of

a) rent,
b) subscriptions,
c) rates.

Note: You are not required to present the accounts.

7. The accounts of a social club are made up annually as at 31 December. At 31 December, year 1, subscriptions in arrears amounted to $69 and subscriptions received in advance for year 2 amounted to $43. During year 2 $837 was received in respect of subscriptions; this included the $69 arrears for year 1 and $29 in advance for year 3. At 31 December, year 2, subscriptions in arrears amounted to $76.

The annual Income and Expenditure Account is credited with all subscriptions in respect of the year to which the account relates, on the basis that all arrears will afterwards be collected.

Show the Subscriptions Account for year 2.

Note: There are no separate accounts for subscriptions in arrears or for subscriptions in advance.

8. a) The Daleshire Social Club was founded on 1 January 20.. with one hundred members, the annual subscription per member being $10. By the end of that year two members had not paid their subscriptions but nine had paid for a year in advance.

Prepare the Club's Subscription Account as it would appear after the closing of the Income and Expenditure Account at 31 December 20...

b) A trader uses the term 'net profit'. What is the comparable term used by the treasurer of a non-profit-making club?

9. The following information was extracted from the books and records of the Fenland Angling Club:

Bank Account for 20..

	$		$
Balance 1 January 20..	762	Bar supplies	17146
Subscriptions for 20..	1864	Cost of social events	722
Subscriptions in advance for next year	21	Wages	2468
		General expenses	1962
Bar takings	22184	Repairs and decorations to premises	1400
Receipts from social events	794		
Balance 31 December 20..	573	New furniture purchased 1 July 20..	2500
	$26198		$26198
		Bank overdraft B/d	573

Notes:

(i) All bar takings and other receipts are banked intact.

(ii) The buildings belonging to the club were valued on 1 January at $15000. The written-down value of the furniture at that date was $1600. Subscriptions in advance amounting to $26 were received in the previous year.

(iii) Depreciation on furniture is to be provided at the rate of 10 per cent per annum on the written-down value of the old furniture and on the cost of the new purchases.

(iv) The following additional details are given:

	1 January 20..	31 December 20..
	$	$
Bar stock	861	928
Creditors for bar supplies	1241	1266

You are asked to give the club's Bar Trading Account and Income and Expenditure Account for 20.., together with the Balance Sheet as at 31 December 20...

10. a) How does a Receipts and Payments Account differ from an Income and Expenditure Account?

b) On 1 April 20.., the start of the financial year, the Deanery Recreation Club's records showed cash in hand and at savings bank $210; furnishings and equipment $370; subscriptions outstanding for the previous year $8.

From the following information relating to the year ended 31 March one year later, prepare the Receipts and Payments Account, the Income and Expenditure Account of the club for the year and the Balance Sheet of the club as at that date.

	$
Payments:	
Rent and rates	160
Light and heat	142
New darts boards	17
Repairs to billiard table	39
Sundry expenses	112
Receipts:	
Subscriptions (including those outstanding at 1 April 20..)	496
Darts and billiards	172
Savings bank interest	11

Bring the following matters into account:

(i) Subscriptions $36 were outstanding for the year ended 31 March.

(ii) Equipment is to be depreciated by $37.

(iii) An account for $44 is outstanding for light and heat.

(iv) One month's rent $10 is paid in advance.

24.11 Household Accounts

The accounts of a household present book-keeping considerations very similar to those relating to the accounts of a club. Both are non-profit-making organizations, and household accounts can be kept using the layout similar to that of a club's analysed cash book shown in Fig. 24.1. As many analysis columns as are required may be ruled up. Many stationery shops sell analytical paper of this sort, ruled with as many as 24 columns to each side (i.e. 24 analysis columns on the debit side and 24 analysis columns on the credit side). To give some idea of this in a textbook is not easy because the pages are not wide enough, but Fig. 24.2 shows a simplified layout. The analysis columns, when totalled, show how expenditure was divided up under the various headings chosen, and who provided the housekeeping money. At the end of the month a Receipts and Payments Account similar to the one in Unit 24.3 could be prepared if required.

Receipts (debit side)

Date 20..	Details	PCV	1 Father $	c	2 Mother $	c	3 John $	c	4 Peter $	c	5 Susan $	c	6 $	c	Balance 7 in hand $	c	Total $	c
			Analysis columns - you may head the spare columns to suit your own needs															
1 July	Balance in hand														17	52	17	52
5 July	Housekeeping allowance		30	00													30	00
6 July	Other allowances						8	00	6	00	5	00					19	00
		$	30	00			8	00	6	00	5	00			17	52	66	52
6 July	Balance in hand	B/d													35	15	35	15

Pay

Da

See below

Payments (credit side)

Date 20..	Details	PCV	1 Food $	c	2 Rent $	c	3 Light & heat $	c	4 Telephone $	c	5 Cleaning $	c	6 $	c	Balance 7 in hand $	c	Total $	c
			Analysis columns - you may head the spare columns to suit your own needs															
1 July	Groceries		3	85													3	85
1 July	1 Pair socks										1	20					1	20
2 July	Meat		6	32													6	32
6 July	Rent				20	00											20	00
6 July	Balance in hand	c/d													35	15	35	15
	$		10	17	20	00					1	20			35	15	66	52

Fig. 24.2 An analysed cash record of household expenses

24.12 Exercises Set 41. Household Accounts

1. A family has three members contributing to the family budget and also receives some income from the sale of eggs from the domestic hens. The expenses of the household are analysed into food, rent and rates, light and heat, sundry expenses and balance in hand. Enter the following items in an analysed cash book (rule up suitable paper and invent headings on both sides to suit your own purposes):

4 April	Received cash from father \$40.00. Purchased food \$9.22, newspapers \$0.64. Paid rent \$16.50.
5 April	Sale of eggs \$2.34. Purchased food \$4.23, cups and saucers \$5.12.
6 April	Son Tom paid \$22.00 into housekeeping. Purchased food \$3.80. Paid electricity bill \$47.25.
7 April	Daughter Jean paid \$15.00 into housekeeping. Purchased food \$8.25, electric light bulbs \$1.30, plants for front garden \$1.75.
9 April	Purchased food \$3.25.
10 April	Received cash from father \$40.00. Paid for food \$8.80, cleaning materials \$3.25.

Balance off the cash book, total all columns and find the balance of cash in hand.

2. A family has two members contributing to the family budget and also receives some income from the sale of fruit and flowers. The expenses of the household are analysed into food, rent and rates, light and heat, sundry expenses and balance in hand. Enter the following items in an analysed cash book (rule up suitable paper and invent suitable column headings as required):

14 April	Cash in hand \$25.00. Received from father \$40.00. Purchased food \$5.32, cleaning materials \$1.55. Paid rent \$20.50.
15 April	Sale of flowers \$3.36. Purchased food \$4.85, household items \$5.42.
16 April	Son Peter paid \$20.00 into housekeeping. Purchased food \$5.80. Paid gas bill \$53.50.
17 April	Purchased food \$4.25, electric light plug \$1.50, cleaning materials \$1.85.
18 April	Purchased food \$5.25.
20 April	Received cash from father \$40.00. Paid for food \$5.75, kitchen utensils \$3.25.

Balance off the cash book, total all columns and find the balance of cash in hand.

3. Three members of a family contribute to the family budget, and some income is received from the sale of vegetables from the garden. The expenses of the household are analysed into food, rent and rates, light and heat, sundry expenses and balance in hand. Enter the following items in an analysed cash book (rule up suitable paper and invent suitable column headings):

24 October	Received cash from father \$50.00. Purchased food \$8.24, magazines \$1.64. Paid rent \$18.50.
25 October	Sale of brussels sprouts and turnips \$3.50. Purchased food \$4.28, crockery \$4.80.
26 October	Mother paid \$20.00 into housekeeping. Purchased food \$2.52; paid milk bill \$6.50.
27 October	Daughter Anne paid \$18.00 into housekeeping. Purchased food \$7.55, washing powder \$2.30, spring bulbs for window box \$1.85.
28 October	Purchased food \$3.25.
29 October	Received cash from father \$50.00. Paid for food \$6.95, cleaning materials \$4.25.

Balance off the cash book, total all columns and find the balance of cash in hand.

24.13 Revise and Test 24. Non-profit-making Organizations

Answers	*Questions*
—	**1.** What sort of organizations are 'non-profit-making'?
1. Voluntary associations such as clubs and societies of every type. There are hundreds and thousands of such organizations and some (like the Royal Automobile Club) have thousands of members.	**2.** What type of accounts is used to report back to the membership?
2. A special type of 'final accounts' called 'club accounts'.	**3.** What are the distinguishing features of club accounts?
3. a) The club exists to provide services to the members—for example, a tennis club provides courts and recreational facilities, runs tournaments, etc.; b) it does not make 'profits' in the normal way—any profits made are called 'surpluses', since they are funds which the members contributed over and above what was really necessary to cover the costs of the enterprise; c) the organization does not have 'capital' in the way capital is supplied by the owners of a business. The capital which does accumulate over the year is called the 'Accumulated Fund'. It behaves like a Capital Account in every way, but it is not called a Capital Account.	**4.** Who is in charge of club accounts?
4. A member of the committee called the treasurer.	**5.** What does the treasurer do?

5. a) Keeps the accounting records, which are chiefly based on receipts and payments over the course of the year;
b) reports back to the members at the AGM.

6. What is the simplest form of reporting to members at the AGM?

---

6. A Receipts and Payments Account. This is a summary of the receipts and payments over the year, and shows the balance of cash in hand, and at the bank at the end of the year.

7. Why is a Receipts and Payments Account not suitable as a report to the AGM of a large organization?

---

7. a) It doesn't tell us everything that we need to know—for example, we know what assets were purchased this year but not what the total value of assets is (or where they are);
b) it doesn't tell us anything about the capital that has been accumulated in the Accumulated Fund.

8. What do we need to report fully on a club's activities?

---

8. We need:
a) an Income and Expenditure Account, which is like a Profit and Loss Account. It tells us the surplus (or deficit) actually created (or suffered) in the year;
b) a Balance Sheet, showing the assets and liabilities at the end of the financial year.

9. Does a club ever have a Trading Account?

---

9. Yes, or several trading accounts, if it suits the club to do so. Thus a Working Men's Club would probably produce a Trading Account for the bar, and we could have trading accounts for refreshments or fund-raising activities of various sorts.

10. So what is the starting point for a full set of Club Accounts?

10. We need to know (or be given enough information to be able to work out) the Balance Sheet at the start of the year. We need to have the Receipts and Payments Account for the year (sometimes we get two separate ones, one for Cash and one for Bank entries). Finally we need to know any end-of-year adjustments.

11. So list the activities in drawing up Final Accounts for a really big club.

---

11. a) We start with the Opening Balance Sheet at the start of the year, because that gives us the 'Capital' of the Club (the Accumulated Fund);

b) then we draw up any Trading Accounts (for example on the Bar, or on the Socials and Entertainments). Each of these gives us either a 'surplus' or a 'deficit'. These surpluses or deficits will be carried to the Income and Expenditure Account (which is the Profit and Loss Account of the club);

c) then we use the Receipts and Payments Account of the club to draw up the Income and Expenditure Account of the club. This gives us the overall surplus or deficiency for the year. This is added to (or taken from) the Accumulated Fund;

d) we then draw up a closing Balance Sheet;

e) the final result can be submitted to the members at the AGM.

12. Go over the page until you are sure of all the answers.

UNIT 25

Manufacturing Accounts

25.1 Manufacturing and Manufacturing Accounts

Manufacturing is the process of taking raw materials provided by nature, or some primary industry like agriculture, and turning them into more sophisticated and useful products. Thus the steel industry converts iron to steel, and the oil industry converts crude oil to petrol and other materials. The cotton industry takes raw cotton, an agricultural product, and converts it into cloth and clothing. These activities are at the root of much of our national wealth, and the accounting activities connected with them are of great importance. Many of these accounting activities are in the specialized field of *cost accounting*, which is chiefly concerned with controlling costs to eliminate wasteful activities and keep our goods competitive in price on world markets. Cost accounting is mentioned below, but a detailed study of this difficult branch of accountancy is not appropriate in this text.

A *Manufacturing Account* is part of the Final Accounts of a manufacturing concern; it precedes the Trading Account (before the firm can trade in the product it has to manufacture it). The Manufacturing Account is used to collect together the costs of manufacture, so that the goods may be passed on to the Sales Department for trading purposes either at cost, or at some agreed 'notional value' which will include an element of manufacturing profit.

25.2 Types of Cost in a Manufacturing Account

In the preparation of Manufacturing Accounts it is necessary to discover the total cost of manufacturing goods. The costs met with fall into two main groups, each of which has several alternative names.

(a) Prime Costs

These costs are those that are embodied in the product ('prime' meaning 'first'). Raw materials are typical costs in this first group, as are wages of workers employed in the actual manufacturing process. They are also often called *direct costs*, since they are embodied directly in the product, or *variable costs*, since they vary fairly directly with output—for example, if we double the output of cars on a production line we shall double the quantity of sheet steel used.

(b) Overheads

These costs are not directly embodied in the product, but are necessary to the production process just the same. For example, the rent of a factory cannot be said to be embodied in the goods manufactured, but it must still be borne by the product when we price it to recover total costs, over and above the prime costs—hence the names *overhead*, *secondary* or *supplementary costs*. If 10000 suits are made per week in a clothing factory, we must add on one-ten-thousandth part of the week's rent to each suit, and hence the word *oncosts* is sometimes used to describe this type of cost. Other names are *indirect costs* (since they do not vary with output—a manager's salary will not be doubled just because output is doubled; he/she will be expected to supervise the factory activities whatever the output may be). All these names are commonly used, and are interchangeable. The commonest costs of this type are items such as factory rent and rates, light and heating, insurance, salaries of supervisory staff, repairs to machinery, oil and lubricants, and so forth.

In order to separate these two groups of costs the Manufacturing Account is built up in two sections: the *Prime Cost Section*, in which are listed raw materials, wages of operatives and all other variable costs, and the *Cost of Manufactured Goods Section*, in which the total of the prime costs is brought down and the overheads, or fixed costs, are added.

25.3 Stocks in Manufacturing

Manufacturing stocks can present an accounting problem. Not only will there be *stocks of raw materials* at the start of the process, and *stocks of finished goods* at the end, but there will also be *stocks of work in progress* or partly finished goods going through the production lines as well.

Imagine a furniture manufacturer who is about to prepare his Final Accounts for the year, and arranges for stock to be taken at the close of business on 31 December. The stock-taking will involve the counting and valuation not only of all the finished furniture that is in stock, but also of all the raw materials and components in stock too. Besides this, between the start of the production line and the finish there will be many partly finished units of output, ranging from sawn planks which have barely started the production process to nearly finished articles needing merely labelling and packaging. Clearly it will require some calculation to decide the value of this work in progress. The accountant must decide what value to place upon it and whether to include overhead charges as well as prime costs in the calculations. It is probably most common to value the work in progress at 'factory cost', that is to say at prime cost (raw materials, labour and other variable costs) plus overheads (a proportion of total overhead costs being added). If this procedure is adopted, the work in progress will appear in the second part of the Manufacturing Account (the Cost of Manufactured Goods Section).

25.4 The Final Accounts of a Manufacturer

A manufacturer's Final Accounts include the following sections of work:

(a) a Manufacturing Account in two parts, a Prime Cost Section and a Cost of Manufactured Goods Section;
(b) a Trading Account;
(c) a Profit and Loss Account;
(d) for a partnership or a limited company, an Appropriation Account;
(e) a Balance Sheet.

This is a fairly lengthy series of activities and for textbook and examination purposes it is usual to produce only the Manufacturing Account and Trading Account. You have, in any case, mastered the preparation of the other accounts. In the example below a manufacturer's accounts are prepared in this way. Work through them carefully and make sure that you understand the preparation of each part.

Example

R. Wilkinson is a manufacturer. Prepare his Manufacturing Account and Trading Account for the year ending 31 December 20.. and carry the gross profit to the Profit and Loss Account.

	$
Stocks at 1 January 20..:	
Raw materials	1900
Work in progress	3300
Finished goods	16850
Purchase of raw materials	27550
Sales	166345
Returns in	305
Factory:	
Wages (variable)	27910
Power (fixed)	710
Salaries (fixed)	12949
Rent and rates (fixed)	1350
Stocks at 31 December:	
Raw materials	3000
Work in progress	5550
Finished goods	22376
Factory:	
Lighting (fixed)	400
Repairs (fixed)	1600
Depreciation (fixed)	2275
Warehouse:	
Wages	24450

Manufacturing Account for year ending 31 December 20..

Prime Cost Section

	$			$
Raw materials:		Prime cost	c/d	54 360
Opening stock at 1 January	1 900			
Purchases	27 550			
	29 450			
Less Closing stock	3 000			
Cost of raw materials used	26 450			
Wages	27 910			
	$54 360			$54 360

Cost of Manufactured Goods Section

	$	$		$
Prime cost	B/d	54 360	Cost of finished goods (transferred to Trading Account)	71 394
Overheads:				
Factory power	710			
Factory salaries	12 949			
Factory rent and rates	1 350			
Factory lighting	400			
Factory repairs	1 600			
Factory depreciation	2 275			
		19 284		
		73 644		
Work in progress:				
Stock at 1 January	3 300			
Less Stock at 31 Dec.	5 550			
		(2 250)[1]		
		$71 394		$71 394

[1] It is customary in published accounts to show a minus quantity (which has to be deducted) in brackets.

Trading Account for year ending 31 December 20..

	$		$
Finished goods:			
Opening stock at 1 January	16850	Sales	166345
Cost of finished goods	71394	*Less* Returns	305
	88244	Net turnover	166040
Less Closing stock	22376		
Cost of goods sold	65868		
Warehouse wages	24450		
Cost of sales	90318		
Gross profit	75722		
	$166040		$166040

Profit and Loss Account for year ending 31 December 20.

	$
Gross profit	75722

Notes:

(a) In the Prime Cost Section of the Manufacturing Account, it is for the accountant to decide which costs will be regarded as prime costs. Raw materials and wages are of course always embodied in the finished product. Some accountants would regard power for machines as a prime cost.

(b) As you see, the total cost of the manufactured goods is given by

prime costs + overheads + (or −) net work in progress

If the opening stock of work in progress is bigger than the closing stock the effect will be an increase in the cost of manufactured goods. If the closing stock of work in progress is greater than the opening stock there will be a decrease in the total cost of finished goods. It really means that more work in progress has been held back—to be passed on to next year's accounts—than was handed on to this year by the previous year, on 1 January.

(c) In the Trading Account, the manufacturer does not have 'purchases' in the usual way. The raw materials that are purchased appear in the Manufacturing Account. Instead the 'finished goods' manufactured are transferred to the warehouse, in this case at their manufactured cost. This manufactured cost therefore becomes part of the calculations to determine the cost of sales, and this is used to determine the gross profit in the usual way.

25.5 Finding a 'Manufacturing Profit'

As described in (c) above, where the manufacturer transfers the finished goods to the warehouse at 'factory cost price' the gross profit is found by deducting this cost price, or rather the cost of sales based upon it, from the selling price. Unfortunately this is not entirely satisfactory, because it does not give any indication of the profitability of the factory. The gross profit achieved is the result of two processes: the manufacturing process and the trading process. If the results of these two activities can be separated to show their respective results we improve our control of the business. Suppose the factory is very efficient, but the sales manager is lax, and negotiates sales at too low a price? The profit made from the factory will be lost by this weakness. In contrast a very efficient sales manager, striking good bargains with customers, will bring us no benefit if the factory is inefficient and running at an unnecessarily high cost.

Where it is possible to bring out a manufacturing profit it is desirable that we do so. This can be achieved by comparing the 'factory cost' with the current market price at which goods like the ones we manufacture can be purchased on the open market. Where such a figure can be obtained, a revised Manufacturing Account can be prepared with the Cost of Manufactured Goods Section showing a manufacturing profit. The effect of this on the profit figures calculated in Unit 25.4 is illustrated below. The market value of the goods manufactured, i.e. the total we would have to pay to buy them from an outside firm, is taken as $90 000.

Cost of Manufactured Goods Section

	$	$		$
Prime cost	B/d	54 360	Market value of finished goods (transferred to Trading A/c)	90 000
Overheads:				
Factory power	710			
Factory salaries	12 949			
Factory rent and rates	1 350			
Factory lighting	400			
Factory repairs	1 600			
Factory depreciation	2 275			
		19 284		
		73 644		
Work in progress:				
Stock at 1 January	3 300			
Less Stock at 31 Dec.	5 550			
		(2 250)		
		71 394		
Manufacturing profit		18 606		
		$90 000		$90 000

Trading Account for year ending 31 December 20..

	$		$
		Sales	166345
		Less Returns	305
			166040
Finished goods:			
Opening stock	16850		
Market value of goods manufactured	90000		
	106850		
Less Closing stock	22376		
Cost of goods sold	84474		
Warehouse wages	24450		
Cost of sales	108924		
Gross profit	57116		
	$166040		$166040

Profit and Loss Account for year ending 31 December 20..

	$
Manufacturing profit	18606
Gross profit	57116
	75722

Notes:

(i) The total profit is unchanged, but now the proportion attributable to the factory can be seen. It leads us to conclude that the factory is earning profits and is therefore worthwhile.

(ii) Imagine that the market value of the finished goods had been only $60000. This would have meant that a manufacturing loss of $11394 would have been suffered. This would have been completely hidden, because the Trading Account, which was making a $27116 profit, would have obscured it. The factory should be shut down, in these circumstances, and the goods purchased from our (obviously more efficient) competitors.

25.6 Break-even Analysis

Every manufacturer who is planning production needs to know at what point he/she will *break even* and start to earn profits. The points we need to understand here are as follows:

(i) We break even when we have covered our total costs, and from that point on everything extra we receive is profit.

(ii) Total costs are made up of fixed costs and variable costs (see Unit 25.2). Variable costs are the costs directly incurred in making our product, and they are called 'variable' because they vary with output. So if I make pizzas with pizza pastry costing 20 cents and other items costing 20 cents for each pizza, and if the labour cost is 10 cents, the variable costs of my pizzas are 50 cents each. So long as I sell them for more than 50 cents I shall make a gross profit on any particular pizza. Let us say I sell them for $1 each. Then I have covered my variable costs, and have 50 cents left over. This 50 cents is called the *contribution.*

(iii) To what does the contribution contribute? The answer is it is a contribution towards covering my fixed costs (overheads), and once they are covered the business can start to make profits. The fixed costs have to be borne whatever the output of the business. Thus I need a factory whether I make 1 000 pizzas or 100 000 pizzas. I need a managing director, a lorry for distribution purposes and so forth. These are all part of the fixed costs, which do not vary directly with output—though I might need a bigger lorry if output grows. Suppose my total fixed costs are $10 000 and I sell one pizza. I have a contribution of 50 cents towards my fixed costs and no profit. I shall need to sell 20 000 pizzas to cover my fixed costs, so 20 000 pizzas is my *break-even point.* After that I shall begin to make a profit.

This can best be followed by looking at the break-even chart in Fig. 25.1.

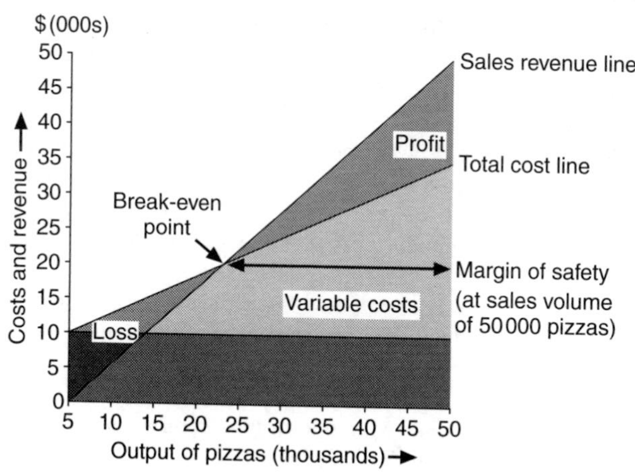

Fig. 25.1 A break-even chart for pizza production: pizzas are sold at $1 each

Notes to Fig. 25.1:

(i) As the output of pizzas rises from zero to 50 000 the variable costs increase by 50 cents per pizza. As these are incurred over and above the fixed costs we see the total cost line sloping up towards the $35 000 point ($10 000 fixed and $25 000 variable).

(ii) At the same time revenue from the sale of pizzas is rising—$10 000 from 10 000 pizzas, $20 000 from 20 000 pizzas, and so on.

(iii) Break-even point is at 20 000 pizzas, the sale of which brings in $20 000. This exactly covers $10 000 fixed costs and $10 000 variable costs.

(iv) After that point we have profits being made and at 50 000 pizzas we get profits of $15 000, since revenues are $50 000 and costs $35 000.

(v) The *margin of safety* is that range of the graph above break-even point where we are making profits. If costs rise the break-even point will move to the right (reducing the margin of safety), but we could resist that by raising the selling price to restore the *status quo*. If competition causes us to cut prices, this will reduce the contribution from each pizza, again reducing the margin of safety. We could meet that by lowering our costs, perhaps by negotiating cheaper costs with our suppliers and our workers, lower rents from our landlords, and so on.

The Limitations of Break-even Charts

Cost behaviour is the response of cost to a variety of influences. Therefore when working out a cost–contribution–sales analysis, we must take into account any factors which may affect the results, and realize that the break-even graph is only a pictorial expression which relates costs and profit to activity. The graph tends to oversimplify the real situation as there are other effects besides volume.

(a) Costs and revenues are shown in Fig. 25.1 as straight lines, but selling prices are not necessarily fixed, and the revenue may change depending on the quantities of goods sold direct, sold through agents, and sold at a discount. The slope of the graph will not be constant but will vary according to the circumstances.

(b) Variable costs may not be proportional to volume, perhaps because of overtime working, reductions in the price of materials when bulk discounts are negotiated, or an increase in the price of materials when demand outstrips supply. If sales are made over a wider area, distribution costs tend to rise considerably.

(c) Fixed costs do not always remain constant during the period of activity.

(d) The efficiency of production or a change in production methods may have an affect on variable costs.

You should now prepare some Manufacturing Accounts and work out some questions on break-even analysis, using the exercises given below.

25.7 Exercises Set 42. Manufacturing Accounts

1. R. Rayner is a manufacturer. From the following details prepare

a) a Manufacturing Account in the usual two sections, a Prime Cost Section and a Cost of Manufactured Goods Section, and

b) a Trading Account for the year ended 31 December 20...

	$
Stocks at 1 January 20.. (valued at cost):	
Raw materials	7250
Finished goods	29275
Stocks at 31 December 20.. (valued at cost):	
Raw materials	8500
Finished goods	26375
Purchases of raw materials	38250
Carriage on raw materials	550
Sales of finished goods	99500
Factory wages (prime cost)	27300
Factory expenses	14700
Work in progress (valued at factory cost):	
1 January 20..	2755
31 December 20..	3900

2. M. Lockhart Ltd is a manufacturing company and the following details for the year 20.. are extracted from their books:

	$
Stock of raw materials, 1 January 20..	15275
Stock of raw materials, 31 December 20..	14385
Stock of manufactured goods, 1 January 20..	27350
Stock of manufactured goods, 31 December 20..	26000
Work in progress, 1 January 20.. (valued at factory cost)	3800
Work in progress, 31 December 20.. (valued at factory cost)	3250
Purchases of raw materials	43850
Manufacturing wages	22725
Sales	168000
Factory expenses	12500
Rent, rates of factory	4500
Rent, rates of office	1500
General administration expenses	13250
Salesmen's salaries	11750
Motor expenses (for delivery to customers)	2550
Other selling expenses	1340
Depreciation: plant and machinery (Manufacturing Account)	1500
motor vans	1400

Prepare the firm's Manufacturing Account, Trading Account and Profit and Loss Account for the year ending 31 December 20...

3. Robespierre Ltd is a manufacturing company and the following details for the year 20.. are extracted from their books:

	$
Stock of raw materials, 1 January 20..	13585
Stock of raw materials, 31 December 20..	13400
Stock of manufactured goods, 1 January 20..	22725
Stock of manufactured goods, 31 December 20..	21855
Work in progress (valued at factory cost), 1 January 20..	12725
Work in progress (valued at factory cost), 31 December 20..	13000
Purchases of raw materials	35850
Manufacturing wages	37000
Sales	227000
Factory expenses	14000
Rent, rates of factory	3620
Rent, rates of office	3280
General administration expenses	12200
Motor expenses (for delivery to customers)	2480
Salesmen's salaries	21550
Other selling expenses	14350
Depreciation: plant and machinery (Manufacturing Account)	2800
motor vans	2400

Robespierre Ltd valued the goods manufactured at $120000, and 'sold' them to the Trading Account at this price so as to reveal the profitability (or otherwise) of the factory. Draw up the Manufacturing Account, Trading Account and Profit and Loss Account of Robespierre Ltd for the year ending 31 December 20...

4. Rymer and Ross Ltd is a manufacturing company and the following details for the year 20.. are extracted from their books:

	$
Stock of raw materials, 1 January 20..	23854
Stock of raw materials, 31 December 20..	23600
Stock of manufactured goods, 1 January 20..	22724
Stock of manufactured goods, 31 December 20..	20500
Work in progress, 1 January 20..	4816
Work in progress, 31 December 20..	4450
Purchase of raw materials	47275
Manufacturing wages	28425
Sales	149258
Factory expenses	4100
Rent, rates of factory	2750
Salary of factory manager	12850
Repairs to factory	4650
Repairs to warehouse	2880
Depreciation: plant and machinery (Manufacturing Account)	3600
warehouse fittings	1580

It is decided to value the factory output at a market value of $110000. Prepare (a) a Manufacturing Account which brings out clearly (i) the prime cost, (ii) the cost of goods manufactured, and (iii) the manufacturing profit, and (b) a Trading Account bringing out the gross profit. Transfer both these profits to the Profit and Loss Account.

5. Suffolk Ltd is a manufacturing company and the following details for the year 20. . were extracted from its books:

	$
Stock of raw materials, 1 January 20. .	32 330
Stock of raw materials, 31 December 20. .	36 480
Stock of manufactured goods, 1 January 20. .	38 550
Stock of manufactured goods, 31 December 20. .	34 000
Work in progress, 1 January 20. .	25 500
Work in progress, 31 December 20. .	26 750
Purchases of raw materials	279 800
Manufacturing wages	166 900
Sales	735 500
Factory expenses	42 550
Rent, rates of factory	20 000
Rent, rates of office	9 050
General administration expenses	45 250
Salesmen's salaries	14 924
Motor expenses (for delivery to customers)	8 725
Other selling expenses	15 717
Depreciation of plant (Manufacturing Account)	16 850
Depreciation of motor vans	3 400

a) You are asked to prepare Suffolk's Manufacturing Account and a Trading and Profit and Loss Account for the year 20. . . The goods are valued at a notional figure of $480 000 for the purpose of determining the profitability of the factory.

b) During the year 500 000 units were manufactured. Another manufacturer who has excess capacity in his workshops offers to supply these at a cost of $1 per unit. What arguments would you put forward for accepting this offer? What arguments are there against acceptance?

6. Potter & Co. manufacture milk jugs which sell for $5 each in their chain of seaside souvenir shops. The fixed costs of production are $14 000 per annum and the variable costs are $1.50 per jug. Draw a graph to show the break-even point on jug manufacture, and likely profits up to their maximum output of 10 000 jugs per year. State on your graph the profits at an output of 8 000 jugs.

7. Marshall Ltd make security locks which retail at $20 each. The overheads of their factory total $45 000 per annum and the variable costs of production are $5 per lock. Draw a break-even chart to represent output up to a total of 10 000 locks. Where is the break-even point, and what profit will be made at outputs of 5 000 locks, 7 500 locks and 10 000 locks?

25.8 Revise and Test 25. Manufacturing Accounts

Answers	*Questions*
—	**1.** What is manufacturing?
1. It is the process of taking the raw materials provided by nature, or the produce of some primary activity like agriculture and turning them into some more useful, convenient or sophisticated product.	**2.** What is our chief interest in accounting for manufacturing activities?
2. We are chiefly interested in costs. The costs we incur form the basis of the prices we must charge if we are to operate profitably. We must recover our costs and a profit on top.	**3.** What are prime costs, direct costs and variable costs?
3. They are different names for the same thing; the basic costs in manufacturing. Prime costs means 'First costs'; the cost of basic raw materials. As these costs are embodied directly in the product they are often called direct costs. As they also vary with output (double the quantity of garments calls for double the amount of cloth), they are often called variable costs.	**4.** What are the chief prime costs?
4. Raw materials, labour, components included in manufacture, power for machines.	**5.** Where do these items appear on a Manufacturing Account?
5. In the first part of the account—the Prime Cost Section.	**6.** What is the other part of the Manufacturing Account called?
6. The Cost of Manufactured Goods Section.	**7.** What costs appear in this Section?

7. a) The Prime Costs, brought down from the Prime Cost Section;
b) the overhead costs;
c) Work in Progress.

8. Explain about overhead costs, oncosts, indirect costs and fixed costs.

---

8. These are all different names for the same thing. Overhead costs are costs like light and heating, repairs, rent and rates, which are not embodied in the actual product. Oncosts are the same (their cost has to be added on to Prime Costs). Because they are not embodied directly in the finished goods we say they are indirect costs and because they do not vary with output we say they are fixed costs. (Double the output does not mean we need two factory managers).

9. What is the Work in Progress (WIP) adjustment?

---

9. At the end of the financial year it is usual to have a lot of work going through the factory. Some of it is nearly finished, some of it has hardly started. The old year hands on all this work in progress to the new year. Commonly we value it all at half price—an average valuation.

10. What happens to the total 'Cost of Manufactured Goods'?

---

10. It is carried to the Trading Account in the place usually occupied by Purchases. (We haven't purchased our goods to sell again—we manufactured them ourselves.)

11. Finally how can we tell if our manufacturing effort made a profit?

---

11. We 'sell' the finished goods to the Trading Account at a fair price. This gives a profit on manufacture but reduces the Gross Profit on Trading. Some of the profit was made by the factory, not by the Marketing Department.

12. Go over the page again until you are sure of all the answers.

UNIT 26

Incomplete Records

26.1 The Accounts of a Small Trader

There are many business which are very small-scale enterprises. Their proprietors are untrained in accounting and yet succeed in making profits year after year. Such small traders often deal exclusively in cash, buying at wholesale produce markets and selling from local market stalls, or from specially adapted vans calling at customers' homes. Such a trader has really no need for written records; the entire business is conducted from the trader's wallet or handbag. In former times the only 'accounts' for such a business would have been a Balance Sheet drawn up at the death of the trader so that his/her heirs could share up their inheritance.

Today things are not quite so simple. In most countries the government requires its share of the profits of every enterprise and has a government agency, the Inland Revenue, to collect the money. In the United Kingdom every business, however small, is required to keep basic book-keeping records and to keep all documents, invoices, credit notes, cheque-book stubs, etc., for six years so the Inland Revenue have time to check the profits declared by the proprietor. In cases of difficulty where records are not available a system known as 'the increased net-worth method' of finding profits is used. Sometimes the few records that are kept are called 'single-entry' records.

26.2 'Single-entry' Records

The term *single entry* is given to any type of book-keeping record which is not double entry. There are many such records kept, which often help the accountant in preparing a full set of Final Accounts from *incomplete records*. For example, a trader who uses a cash register often has a till roll showing the total cash sales for the period. A small retailer often keeps a book in which are recorded the names of debtors and the amounts owed. When the debtor calls in to pay the debt the trader crosses it out on the book, the debtors gradually being deleted until a few 'slow payers' only are left. All such records are known as *single-entry records*, as distinct from proper accounting records which are always double entries.

26.3 The Increased-net-worth Method of Finding Profits

The method used to find what profits a small trader has made is the increased-net-worth method. The *net worth* of a business to its owner is the same thing as the capital he or she has invested in it at a particular time. This usually means not only the capital that was put in originally but also any profits that have been ploughed in over the years. The method requires the preparation of two *statements of affairs*. A statement of affairs corresponds to a Balance Sheet drawn up at a particular moment of time, showing the assets and liabilities of a small trader. 'Statement of affairs' is a better name than 'Balance Sheet', since the latter implies that there are accounts with balances on them. Since this type of trader keeps no accounts, but only at best single-entry records, the title Balance Sheet is inappropriate.

Consider the following statement of affairs.

A. Stallholder
Statement of Affairs as at 1 January 20..

Fixed assets:	$		$
Motor van	180	Capital (net worth)	380
Current assets:			
Cash in hand	200		
	$380		$380

Notes:

(i) At the commencement of the year, the trader has only a sum of money in cash and an old motor van.
(ii) The capital of the business is $380.

At the end of the year a second statement of affairs is drawn up. Here it is:

A. Stallholder
Statement of Affairs as at 1 January 20..

Fixed assets:	$	$		$
Motor vehicles		2850	Capital (net worth)	3329
Scales and cash registers		165		
		3015		
Current assets:			Current liability:	
Stock	58		A. Supplier	350
Bank balance	480			
Cash in hand	126			
		664		
		$3679		$3679

Notes:

(i) There has been a considerable increase in the value of the assets. Clearly Stallholder has bought a new van, or vans, and also other equipment. He has saved money and has a certain amount of stock.

(ii) The total value of the business—its 'worth'—is $3679. However some of this value is owned by the external creditor A. Supplier, who has supplied goods but not been paid. The balance is the 'net worth' of the business to the owner of the business. The word 'net' here, as usual, means 'clean' or 'clear'—we are talking about the worth of the business clear of any debts to outsiders.

Note that capital is not just money but includes as well the value of other assets contributed by the proprietor.

The profit in this case is calculated in the following way:

1. Calculate the increase in capital. Clearly the extra wealth must have come from somewhere, and it can only be from the success of Stallholder's trading activities.
2. Adjust this figure to take account of drawings. Let us suppose that Stallholder admits taking $80 per week to give to his wife for housekeeping money, while he himself takes $25 per week for personal use.
3. Take into account any extra capital supplied during the year. Suppose Stallholder declares that $500, won on the football pools, was paid into the business during the year. Clearly this is responsible for some of the increase in value of the assets.

The calculations will be as follows:

	$
Final capital	3329
Less Original capital	380
Increase in capital	2949
Add Drawings (since if they had not been extracted from the business the increase in net worth would have been greater) $105 × 52 weeks	= 5460
	8409
Deduct New capital paid in (since without it the increase in net worth would have been smaller)	500
	$7909

Clearly this is the sum Stallholder has earned as a result of his business and on this figure he would pay an appropriate level of taxation.

It might be thought that this method of assessing profits is wide open to abuse by the small trader, who might not truthfully reveal the value of the business assets when drawing up his statement of affairs. While it is conceivable that some people might attempt minor tax evasions, these are made less easy by the statistics available to most tax authorities, who have been accumulating tax records for well over a century. They are able to compare Stallholder's profits with those of many similar enterprises all over the country. If Stallholder proves to be the least profitable small trader in his area they will probably re-examine the assessment, and increase it.

You should now attempt some questions from the set of exercises given below. In most of these the simplest approach is to draw up two statements of affairs, thus revealing the capital (net worth) at the beginning and the end of the period. It will then be easy to calculate the increased net worth.

26.4 Exercises Set 43. Simple Incomplete Records

1. Joyce Brown's Statement of Affairs at 31 December 20.. showed the value of her assets as $21 000, and amounts owing to creditors $9000.

At 1 January 20.. assets had been $15 000 and amounts owing to creditors $8000.

During the year she had introduced $2000 as additional capital, and had drawn $80 per week for personal use.

Calculate the amount of Ms Brown's profit for the year.

2. R. Shires owns a store. His records are incomplete and you have been called in to prepare his accounts. You ascertain the following:

At 1 January 20..	Stock	$2100	Debtors	$1300
	Creditors	$960	Rates in advance	$80
	Motor Vehicles	$1200	Cash at bank	$900
At 31 December 20..	Stock	$2240	Debtors	$1040
	Creditors	$1000	Rates in advance	$96
	Motor vehicles	$1000	Cash at bank	$2344

Drawings during the year were $4200 and a legacy of $1400 received on 1 March 20.. had been paid into the bank. You are required:

a) to draw up two statements showing
   (i) net worth at 1 January 20..,
   (ii) net worth at 31 December 20.., and
b) to compile a statement showing the profit for the year ended 31 December 20...

3. The following are summaries of the assets and liabilities of Paul Schofield, a retail trader, at the dates stated:

	1 January 20..	*31 December 20..*
	$	$
Debtors	4186	5319
Creditors	2918	2184
Stock	13750	24100
Loan from J. Green (repayable at the end of 5 years)	3000	3000
Cash in hand	475	2425
Bank balance	2273	
Bank overdraft		628
Plant and machinery	18500	15000
Land and buildings	35000	35000
Fixtures and fittings	1800	1700

During the year, Schofield had drawn $500 per month on account of profits.

Required:

a) a statement showing Schofield's capital at 1 January 20..,
b) a statement showing the profit/loss for the year, and
c) a statement of affairs at 31 December 20.. showing the Capital Account in detail.

4. From the following figures calculate M. Shah's profit or loss for the year ended 30 June 20..:

	At start	*At close*
	$	$
Fixed assets	3250	8000
Stock	1860	2140
Debtors	620	950
Creditors	490	350
Balance at bank	1100	4730

Shah's drawings totalled $4800, and he had also taken home goods valued at $425.

5. On 1 October 20.. M. Padley started a business. His assets then were: bank balance $2350; debtors $120; a van worth $2600 and stock valued at $2300. His only liability was $75 for van repairs. Three months later he owed $1009 to his creditors. His assets were: bank balance $1264; debtors $488; stock $3628 and the van now estimated to be worth $2500. There were pre-payments amounting to $110 for the van licence and insurance.

During the quarter Padley brought in no fresh capital, but he had with-drawn $1104 for personal expenses.

Calculate the profit or loss made by Padley during the period, showing clearly the method you adopt to obtain your result.

6. A. Page started business on 1 January 20.. with a balance at the bank of $4000, of which he had borrowed $1000 from A. Franchisee. Page did not keep a complete set of records but at 31 December 20.. a valuation showed the following assets and liabilities:

	$
Furniture and fittings	3200
Motor van	2900
Stock in hand	4700
Trade debtors	540
Cash at bank	4300
Trade creditors	4240

The loan from A. Franchisee was still outstanding and interest at 10 per cent per annum was due to him on this loan. During the year, Page had drawn $80 per week in anticipation of profits.

From the above information draw up a statement showing the profit and loss for the year ended 31 December 20.. and a Balance Sheet at that date.

26.5 Final Accounts from Incomplete Records

Sometimes it is necessary to build up a complete picture of the profits of a business from incomplete records. Usually it is possible to start from the statement of affairs at the beginning of the year, and to know the cash and cheque payments during the year. The outstanding debts can be found by adding up the entries in the debtors' records book, and the creditors can be found by adding up the invoices unpaid. With this kind of detail an attempt can be made to draw up the Trading, Profit and Loss Account and Balance Sheet. The following plan of attack on the problem will help:

1. Draw up the opening statement of affairs (if it is not available already) and hence calculate the capital (net worth) of the business.
2. Draw up a Receipts and Payments Cash Account, if the trader deals in cash during the year. Hence discover the balance of cash in hand.
3. Draw up a Receipts and Payments Bank Account of receipts and payments by cheque, and hence discover the bank balance.
4. Draw up a Total Debtors Account and hence find the sales for the year.
5. Draw up a Total Creditors Account and hence find the purchases for the year.
6. From the figures now available draw up a Trading Account, Profit and Loss Account and Balance Sheet.

Now read carefully through the following worked example. Make sure you understand each stage before going on to the next.

Example

The Balance Sheet of Trevor Ford, a trader, on 1 January 20.. was as follows:

Balance Sheet as at 1 January 20..

	$		$
Furniture	4790	Capital	28992
Stock in trade	12836	Trade creditors	8126
Trade debtors	5464	Creditors for expenses	54
Balance at bank	14082		
	$37172		$37172

Trevor pays all his takings into his bank account and draws cheques for all business payments.

The following figures relating to the year 20.. have been taken from his books:

	$
Receipts from customers	142120
Payments to suppliers	63646
General expenses paid	11832
Drawn from bank for private purposes	14600
Discounts allowed	3553
Discounts received	3180
Salaries and wages paid	24300

At 31 December 20.. trade debtors amounted to $12 712 and trade creditors amounted to $12 204. General expenses paid in advance were $806 and the stock in trade was valued at $13 246.

During 20.. Trevor incurred travelling expenses for business purposes amounting to $184 which he paid in cash from his own pocket.

There were no transactions other than those which can be ascertained from the information given above.

Depreciation on furniture is to be charged at the rate of 10 per cent per annum on the value at 1 January in each year.

You are required to prepare:

a) a summary of Trevor's Bank Account for 20..,
b) total accounts for debtors and for creditors for 20..,
c) a Trading and Profit and Loss Account for 20.. and
d) a Balance Sheet at 31 December 20...

The plan outlined above is applied.

1. The opening Balance Sheet is given so that it need not be prepared.
2. Trevor does not deal in cash, paying in all his takings as received into the Bank Account. A Cash Account is therefore not required.
3. The Bank Account is prepared as shown below.

Receipts and Payments Bank Account

20..			$	20..			$
1 Jan.	Balance	B/d	14 082	31 Dec.	Creditors		63 646
31 Dec.	Debtors		142 120	31 Dec.	General expenses		11 832
				31 Dec.	Drawings		14 600
				31 Dec.	Salaries and wages		24 300
				31 Dec.	Balance	c/d	41 824
			$156 202				$156 202
20..			$				
1 Jan.	Balance	B/d	41 824				

4. The Total Debtors Account is then drawn up from the figures given as follows. The item needing care is the closing balance of Debtors. Since it must be a debit balance *after* being brought down it must be a credit entry *before* being carried down. From this it is possible to calculate the Sales figure.

Total Debtors Account

20..			$	20..			$
1 Jan.	Balance	B/d	5464	31 Dec.	Bank		142 120
31 Dec.	Sales		152 921	31 Dec.	Discount		3553
				31 Dec.	Balance	c/d	12 712
			$158 385				$158 385
31 Dec.	Balance	B/d	12 712				

5. Similarly the Total Creditors Account enables us to calculate the Purchases figure for the year.

Total Creditors Account

20..			$	20..			$
31 Dec.	Bank		63646	1 Jan.	Balance	B/d	8126
31 Dec.	Discount		3180	31 Dec.	Purchases		70904
31 Dec.	Balance	c/d	12204				
			$79030				$79030
				31 Dec.	Balance	B/d	12204

6. Finally, the Trading Account, Profit and Loss Account and Balance Sheet of the trader appear thus:

Trading Account for year ending 31 December 20..

20..	$	20..	$
Opening stock	12836	Sales	152921
Purchases	70904		
	83740		
Less Closing stock	13246		
Cost of stock sold	70494		
Gross profit	82427		
	$152921		$152921

Profit and Loss Account for year ending 31 December 20..

20..	$	$	20..	$
General expenses	11832		Gross profit	82427
Less Amount for previous year	54		Discount received	3180
	11778			85607
Less Amount for next year	806			
		10972		
Discount allowed		3553		
Salaries and wages		24300		
Travelling expenses		184		
Depreciation		479		
		39488		
Net profit		46119		
		$85607		$85607

Balance Sheet as at 31 December 20..

	$	$		$	$	$
Fixed assets:			Capital:			
Furniture	4790		At start			28992
Less Depreciation	479		*Add* Net profit		46119	
		4311	*Less* Drawings	14 600		
Current assets:			– Travelling expenses	184		
Stock	13246					
Debtors	12712					
Bank	41824					
Expenses in advance	806				14416	
		68588				31703
						60695
			Current liabilities:			
			Creditors			12204
		$72899				$72899

Now you should try some exercises of this kind yourself.

26.6 Exercises Set 44. Final Accounts from Incomplete Records

1. A. Wholesaler does not keep proper books of account. The following information was obtained from his records on 31 December 20..:

	$
1 January 20..	
Stock	17400
Trade debtors	6000
Trade creditors	2100
1 January to 31 December 20..	
Receipts from trade debtors	85530
Payments to trade creditors	46320
Warehouse wages	12000
Carriage on purchases	1570
31 December 20..	
Stock	18200
Trade debtors	5750
Trade creditors	2740

From the above information you are required to:

(a) calculate Wholesaler's Purchases and Sales, showing your workings, and

(b) draw up his Trading Account for the year ended 31 December 20...

2. Kate Farley started business on 1 January 20.. by renting a shop at $3000 per annum and opening a business bank account into which she paid $2400.

She sells all goods for cash.

She uses some of this cash for running expenses and for her private expenses, paying the remainder into the bank.

She does not keep proper books of account but the following information is available at 31 December 20..:

(a) Business Bank Account:

		$
Receipts:	Cash sales paid in	34200
Payments:	Rates	1360
	Shop fittings	2300
	Rent	3250
	Delivery van	3800
	Trade creditors	14740
	Insurance	240

(b) Kate paid bills for light and heat $405 out of cash takings and estimates that she also paid sundry expenses $650 out of these takings.

(c) She retained $4500 of cash takings for her private use.

(d) On 31 December 20..:
   (i) Rates $1 240 for the half-year 1 October 20.. to 31 March following had not been paid.
   (ii) There was an outstanding bill for electricity $235.
   (iii) Trade creditors amounted to $1 210.
   (iv) Stock in trade was valued at $6 150.
   (v) One month's rent was paid in advance.
   (vi) Shop fittings were depreciated by 5 per cent and the delivery van by 20 per cent.
   (vii) Kate had cash takings in hand $430.

Prepare her Trading and Profit and Loss Accounts for the year ending 31 December 20.. and a Balance Sheet as at that date.

3. Thomas Jones did not keep proper books of account. The following information relates to his business for the year ended 31 December 20...

(a) His assets and liabilities at 1 January 20.. were as follows: cash in hand and balance at bank $8 541; sundry trade debtors $8 194; stock $5 989; furniture and fittings $2 250; motor van $3 600; sundry trade creditors $11 240.

(b) His cash book summary for the year ended 31 December 20.. was as follows:

Receipts:	$	Payments:	$
Cash sales	76 943	Payments to trade creditors	25 988
Receipts from trade debtors	11 236	Drawings	8 700
		Rent, rates and insurance	1 540
		Light and heat	442
		Motor van expenses	1 226
		Repairs and renewals	517
		New shop fittings	1 050
		Refunds to customers	73
		Wages and salaries	20 000
		General expenses	1 984

Prepare Jones's Trading and Profit and Loss Account for the year ended 31 December 20.. and a Balance Sheet as at that date taking into account that on 31 December 20..:

(i) Stock was valued at cost $6 910; sundry trade debtors were $4 136 and sundry trade creditors $7 570.
(ii) Light and heat outstanding was $211.
(iii) Rates and insurance prepaid were $330.
(iv) Depreciation at 10 per cent is to be written off the balance of furniture and fittings at 31 December 20.. and 20 per cent off the value of the motor van at 1 January 20...

Note: All calculations must be clearly shown immediately before or after the accounts.

4. On 1 January 20.. M. Coster started business as a building decorator and repairer with $3 000 in the bank. He kept no books but banked all receipts and paid all accounts by cheque. His bank statement disclosed the following information for the year ended 31 December 20..:

	$
Receipts for work done	24 000
Cost of second-hand motor van	2 000
Cost of materials purchased	4 750
Motor van expenses	1 270
Insurance	420
Cost of new equipment	3 300
Drawings for private expenses	5 000
Payments to building society for private house	2 400
Rent of yard	1 400

On 31 December 20.. stock was valued at $1 250, and debtors amounted to $1 150. Coster decided to write 20 per cent depreciation off his motor van, and 10 per cent off his equipment.

Prepare Coster's Trading and Profit and Loss Account for the year ended 31 December and a Balance Sheet on that date.

Note: You will find it useful to calculate his balance at bank on 31 December 20.. before attempting the Balance Sheet.

5. W. Davis is the proprietor of a small café. His sales are strictly cash, and he banks all takings every night. All purchases are paid for by cheque on delivery. He lives on the premises with his family.

A statement of affairs on 1 January 20.. showed his position to be as follows:

	$		$
Premises	33 000	Capital	44 870
Furniture	4 000		
Stock	4 150		
Bank	3 500		
Cash	220		
	$44 870		$44 870

A study of his cash book provides the following information relating to the year ended 31 December 20..:

	$
Takings	50 000
Purchases	17 400
Personal expenses	11 500
Light and heat	1 200
Cleaning	330
Wages	4 500
New furniture bought during year	2 200
Cash in hand 31 December 20..	630
Bank balance 31 December 20..	?

You are asked to prepare a statement showing W. Davis's profit or loss for the year ended 31 December 20.. and a Balance Sheet on that date. The following are to be taken into consideration:

(a) valuation of stock on 31 December 20.. $3 180.
(b) $400 of the light and heat expenditure was allocated to his private accommodation.

6. M. Glover started business on 1 January 20.. by renting a shop at $1 800 per annum and opening a business bank account into which he paid $3 500.

He sells all goods for cash.

He uses some of this cash for running expenses and for his private expenses, paying the remainder into the bank.

He does not keep proper books of account but the following information is available at 31 December 20..:

(a) Business Bank Account:

		$
Receipts:	Cash sales paid in	45 700
Payments:	Rates	1 420
	Shop fittings	2 400
	Rent	1 950
	Delivery van	3 700
	Trade creditors	22 340
	Insurance	450

(b) Glover paid bills for light and heat $424 out of cash takings and estimates that he also paid sundry expenses $372 out of these takings.
(c) He retained $4 600 of cash takings for his private use.
(d) On 31 December 20..:
   (i) Rates $840 for the half-year 1 October 20.. to 31 March next had not been paid.
   (ii) There was an outstanding bill for electricity of $242.
   (iii) Trade creditors amounted to $4 670
   (iv) Stock in trade was valued at $4 280.
   (v) One month's rent, $150, was paid in advance.
   (vi) Shop fittings were depreciated by 5 per cent and the delivery van by 20 per cent.
   (vii) Glover had cash takings in hand $465.

Prepare Glover's Trading and Profit and Loss Accounts for the year ended 31 December 20.. and a Balance Sheet as at that date.

26.7 Revise and Test 26. Incomplete Records

Answers	*Questions*
—	**1.** What is the danger of 'incomplete records'?
1. With 'incomplete records' there is no easy way of finding out what profit has been made in the year (or what loss has been suffered).	**2.** What does UK law say about incomplete records?
2. That it is an offence not to keep proper books of accounts, and all records must be kept for six years.	**3.** If records are incomplete how can we find the profit for the year?
3. By the 'increased-net-worth' method.	**4.** How does it work?
4. The 'net worth' of a business to the owner of a business is the same thing as saying the capital of the proprietor. The method uses two Statements of Affairs, which are exactly like Balance Sheets but drawn up by questioning the proprietor about his/her assets and liabilities. (We can't draw up a real Balance Sheet because that shows the balance on accounts, and we have no proper accounts.) We work out two Statements of Affairs, one, at the start of the year, the other at the end of the year. If the net worth has increased during the year it must have been because the trader made profits. If the net worth has declined during the past year it must be because he/she made losses.	**5.** Here are two Statements of Affairs of a trader at 1 January and the 31 December. What is the increase in net worth?

(i) Statement of Affairs of A. Trader
as at 1 January 20.

	$		$
Assets		*Liabilities*	
Cash at bank	3000	Capital (Net Worth) at start	3000

(ii) Statement of Affairs of A. Trader
as at 31 December 20..

	$	$		$
Fixed assets			*Capital (Net worth)*	
Furniture		680	At close	6500
Motor vehicles		3200		
		3880		
Current assets			*Long term liability*	
Stock	2250		Bank loan	2000
Debtors	460			
Cash at bank	2350		*Current liabilities*	
Cash in hand	150		Creditors	590
		5210		
		$9090		$9090

Two Statements of Affairs of A. Trader

---

5. The increase in net worth = $6500 – $3000 = $3500

6. Is that the profit figure for the year?

---

6. No. There are usually other things to adjust for, especially Drawings. Very few people can live for a whole year without drawing money from the business. This has to be added to the increased net worth to get the profit figure. Had this money not been withdrawn the increased net worth figure would have been greater. Suppose drawings were $100 per week ($5200 per year). The profit would have been $8700. Increased net worth = $3500 + Drawings $5200 = $8700.

7. Is there anything else that affects the calculation of profits by the increased net worth method?

7. Yes—if extra capital has been contributed during the year it would explain some of the increase in net worth. So, where a trader can show that he/she has invested extra capital (a legacy perhaps) during the year this has to be deducted from the increased net worth.

8. Suppose in 5 above the trader had received a premium bond prize of $3000 during the year and had invested it in the business, what would the profit figure have been?

---

8. Instead of $8700 it would only have been $5700 ($8700 – $3000).

9. Supposing a firm has kept some records, like cash records, bank records, debtors and creditors, how can you prepare a set of accounts from them?

---

9. It is a long story, but, briefly: We would:

a) Draw up an opening Statement of Affairs (if it was not available from last year's work) by questioning the proprietor, and hence find the capital at the start of the year;
b) draw up a Receipts and Payments Cash Account if the trader dealt in cash over the year—from such records as bank paying in slips, etc.;
c) draw up a Receipts and Payments Book Account from such records as cheque books, paying-in slips, Bank Statements, etc.;
d) draw up a Total Debtors Account and hence find the sales for the year;
e) draw up a Total Creditors Account and hence find the purchases for the year;
f) draw up a set of final accounts and a final Statement of Affairs.

10. Go over the page until you are sure of all the answers.

UNIT 27

The Accounts of Companies

27.1 The Limited Liability Company

In this Unit we have used the currency symbol for the euro (€) to familiarize students with this new symbol.

Limited companies are the commonest business units today. There are over half a million *private limited companies* and about eight thousand *public limited companies* in the United Kingdom alone. Between them limited companies carry out the vast majority of business activities in the United Kingdom, and in almost all the free-enterprise countries of the world. The popularity of companies is explained by the *limited liability* of the owners (the shareholders). Whereas sole traders or partners are liable to the full extent of their personal wealth for all the obligations of the business, the liability of shareholders is limited to the value of their shareholdings. They cannot be held personally liable for the debts of the business in excess of the nominal value of the shares they have purchased, or agreed to purchase. This concession to shareholders was originally made by Parliament in order to reduce the hardships suffered by early shareholders, whose liability was unlimited. As a result, when their company collapsed, they were held fully liable for the debts of the company, even though they were not directors of the company and had no chance of influencing personally the conduct of its affairs.

When the shareholders were thus freed from liability, a new group, the *creditors*, was placed in difficulties. If the shareholders could not be held liable for the debts of the business, who could be? The answer is 'no one'. The creditors must look to the contributed capital as the sole source of repayment. This places them in a difficult position. To warn them of this possibility Parliament has enacted that company names must include the word *Limited* (Ltd) or the words *Public Limited Company* (PLC) to warn suppliers to check on the financial soundness of a company before doing business with it. You may think that a limited company is a sound and reliable organization. Of course many are, but many have only €150 or less as the capital to which creditors may look should the company get into difficulties. Such important organizations must be regulated to some extent, and in the United Kingdom control is achieved through two Acts of Parliament, *The Companies Acts of 1985 and 1989*. All companies must be registered with the Registrar of Companies.

27.2 The Accounts of Limited Companies

There are many unusual features of company accounts, and a complete explanation would be far too long and complex for this elementary book. There are many texts on the market which go into greater detail. In the UK, the accounts of large companies, at the time of writing those with a turnover of more than £90 000 (say, €135 000), must be audited each year by professionally qualified accountants, who are required to certify that the accounts do give a 'true and fair view' of the affairs of the business.

(a) The Capital of Companies

The capital of companies is subscribed not by an individual or even a few individuals but by many people, known as *shareholders*. There are many different types of shares but the two major classes of shareholders are *ordinary shareholders* and *preference shareholders*. Holders of ordinary shares, often called *equity shares*, take an equal share of any profit that is available, but give way to preference shareholders who, as their name implies, have preferential rights to dividends. It might be thought that a preferential right to a dividend is so desirable that everyone would buy preference shares, but in fact preference shares only take an agreed percentage of dividend, often perhaps 5 per cent or 7 per cent. This would not be attractive to a wealthy investor who hoped to earn perhaps a 20 per cent or 25 per cent dividend, even if there was a risk that in a bad year he might receive no dividend at all. Small investors, seeking security and a regular dividend, may buy preference shares, which besides their fixed dividend often have a prior right to repayment when a company is dissolved.

When applying to form a company the founders must state what they consider to be the desirable sum for capital, and if this is approved by the Department of Trade and Industry it becomes the *authorized capital*. This sum must be shown on the Balance Sheet.

(b) The Profits of Companies

After all charges against the profit have been met, the net profit is available to be appropriated among the various classes of shareholders. This does not mean that it will necessarily be shared up to the last penny. It is for the directors to recommend a dividend. They usually do recommend that the preference share dividend shall be paid in full, but even this is not obligatory, and they may pass it over, arguing that it is better for the company to do so. Indeed a special class of *cumulative preference shares* has been specially created to take account of this possibility. Such shares are allowed to claim, in a subsequent year when good profits are made, any dividends passed over in earlier bad years; the dividends due accumulate. *Non-cumulative preference shares* do not have any right to claim back-dividends, which are lost for all time. Naturally, shareholders who do not receive a dividend may be disgruntled about the conduct of the company's affairs, but the only redress for their grievances is to remove the board of directors at the Annual General Meeting. It does not follow that they will be able to do so, since voting is arranged 'one vote for each share'. If the chairman of the board, or the directors between them, own 51 per cent of the voting shares it will be impossible to remove the board. Under the Companies Act 1985 it is possible for the minority shareholders to complain to the Department of Trade and Industry about unfair treatment. In practice, such complaints have not been numerous and although the Department of Trade and Industry is alive to the problem, actual investigations of companies from this point of view are rather rare events.

Generally speaking, the directors will pay the agreed preference dividend, and will also pay a reasonable ordinary dividend, depending upon the position of the company and their plans for its future development. What is a *reasonable* dividend is discussed later (see Units 28.9 and 28.10). For the purpose of this Unit it is sufficient to enumerate the reasons why it is often undesirable to pay out the full profit earned. These are:

(i) When dividends are paid, actual cash has to be available to pay them. It may be that there are not sufficient liquid funds to pay out, and the directors will be forced to pass the dividend.

(ii) Profits are not usually steady over the years, and it is wise to *equalize the dividend* by building up a *general reserve* of profits. Consider a shareholder who receives a 75 per cent dividend one year and a 1 per cent dividend the next. 'Marvellous company, mine,' will be the comment the first year. 'What have the stupid fools been up to?' will be said twelve months later. The average shareholder would be happier to receive, say, a 30 per cent dividend each year. They are actually worse off yet they feel contented. For this reason directors appropriate profits to general reserves in good years, so that money can be transferred back from reserves in bad years to equalize the dividend. Remember that this does not automatically mean that cash will be available to pay the dividend, and the directors must ensure that cash is available.

(iii) It is often necessary to build up reserves of profits to meet eventualities such as plant replacement, lease renewal and so on. In inflationary times a machine may double in price over ten years. It is necessary to avoid paying out dividends at too high a rate so that funds will be available to meet these charges when renewal becomes inevitable. In industries where the pace of technology is advancing rapidly, such as the computer industry, the possibility of obsolescence requiring premature replacement of assets must also be borne in mind.

(c) Debentures

Sometimes companies raise funds for the expansion of the enterprise in the form of loans secured on the assets of the company. This type of money is sometimes loosely referred to as loan capital, but this is a bad term since it is not in any way capital of the business. The security issued is called a *debenture*, or *debenture bond*. A bond is a *written promise*, and a debenture bond is a promise to repay. Debenture-holders are not shareholders in the company, but are its *secured creditors*. This means that they are able to seize the assets that form their security and sell them in order to regain the funds they have loaned to the company. They are able to exert this right in preference to the unsecured creditors of the company, so that a company which has many debentures on issue is a less satisfactory firm to deal with for ordinary suppliers of goods and services. Debentures must be recorded on a separate schedule of charges registered with the Company Registrar at Companies House.

There are three kinds of debenture.

(i) Fixed debentures are secured on the fixed assets.

(ii) Floating debentures are secured on the floating assets, i.e. the stock. The difference between these two lies in the nature of the assets forming the security. A fixed debenture, secured on plant and machinery, prevents the company from selling the assets concerned without the debenture-holders' permission. A floating debenture, secured on the stock, does not prevent the company selling the stock—that would be ridiculous—but at the least sign of financial difficulty it *crystallizes* over the stock in hand, preventing its sale except for the benefit of the debenture-holders.

(iii) Naked debentures, unusually, are not secured on any assets—hence their name (the holder is rather exposed). They do constitute a formal acknowledgement of the debt and can sometimes be issued by very reputable companies.

Debentures are very safe, and are therefore desirable investments to timid small-scale investors whose chief concern is to avoid losing their capital. To exert the rights of the debenture-holders a *debenture trustee* is appointed, usually a bank or a firm of accountants. Debentures, like most secure investments, do not receive a high return, say 7–9 per cent. This is a *payment of interest to creditors*, not a dividend (which is a payment to shareholders).

(d) Classes of Assets and their Depreciation

The Companies Act 1985 requires assets to be displayed in two main classes—fixed assets and current assets. Fixed assets are then sub-divided into three groups—intangible assets, tangible assets and trade investments.

(i) Intangible assets are assets which have no physical existence, but exist as legal rights which may be enjoyed. Thus an inventor's rights to payment for the use of patents, an author's rights to royalties on his books and a proprietor's right to goodwill (see Unit 22.11(e)) are intangible assets.

(ii) Tangible assets you are already familiar with. They are assets which have a physical existence and can actually be touched (which is what 'tangible' means). Examples are land and buildings, plant and machinery, office equipment and motor vehicles.

(iii) Trade investments require some explanation. It often happens that a company wishes to gain effective control of other companies. In such cases the parent company is known as a *holding company*, the company that is controlled is a *subsidiary*, and the whole enterprise is called a *group*. The parent company keeps control of its subsidiaries by securing 51 per cent of the voting shares. These shares are known as *trade investments*, that is to say they are investments in other companies in the same trade as the parent company. A holding company does not hold trade investments in order to sell them again, but in order to retain control of the subsidiary. It therefore will not sell them, and they are fixed assets. The requirement to show trade investments as a separate item is useful to investors thinking of investing in a company, since it helps them to judge the financial position of the company. Trade investments are displayed on the Balance Sheet as the third class of fixed assets. The Companies Act calls them 'shares in group companies' or 'shares in related companies'.

Other investments, which are often held by companies as a method of earning temporary profits on funds not yet required for the company's affairs, are shown as current assets because they can be turned into cash very easily when required.

The Companies Act 1985 requires that fixed assets be shown 'at cost, less the total depreciation to date'. This is a very useful requirement to those investing in companies, since it enables them to judge how modern the firm's assets are. It has led to the method of recording depreciation in separate provisions for depreciation (see Unit 13.10).

(e) Reserves of Companies

(i) Revenue reserves Where a company sets aside sums out of profits for particular purposes, such as to equalize dividends over the years or to replace plant when it wears out, these are known as *revenue reserves*. All such reserves are required to be shown on the Balance Sheet at the end of the year, with an indication of any increases in the reserves made during the last trading period. Three points are of interest with regard to these revenue reserves.

1. Revenue reserves, since they have been set aside out of profits, are the property of the ordinary shareholders only, and not of the preference shareholders. This is because the preference shareholders always take the full dividend to which they are entitled, and never plough any profits back into the business. Many companies, in their Balance Sheets, muddle up the ordinary share capital with the preference share capital, following this mixture with the reserve figures. This is highly undesirable, because it obscures from view exactly 'who' owns 'what'. The best way, as illustrated in Fig. 27.1, is to separate the ordinary shareholders' interest in the company from the preference shareholders' interest in the company.
2. Revenue reserves may always be recouped as profits for distribution purposes, whether they have been set aside for more permanent use, say as *plant replacement reserves*, or for general use—as *general reserves*. *Capital reserves* (see below) may *never* be distributed as dividends (though they may be given away as bonus shares).
3. The last revenue reserve that is shown on every Balance Sheet is the final balance left on the Appropriation Section of the Profit and Loss Account. Unlike partnerships, where the residue of the profit can usually be shared up to the very last cent, a company can rarely share up its profits exactly. For example, if a company has 100 000 shares and makes a profit of €35 751 it can only pay out €0.35 per share (making a total distribution of €35 000). There will be €751 on the Appropriation Section of the Profit and Loss Account that is undistributed. This is inevitable. It is more likely that the directors will pay out a simple round figure—say €0.20 per share, and leave €15 751 as a balance on the account.

(ii) Capital reserves These are a quite different type of reserve. They have not been set aside out of profits like the revenue reserves just described, but instead have been earned in unusual ways, which are of a capital nature. They need not concern us here, but you will meet them in more advanced studies.

27.3 Appropriating the Profits of a Limited Company

Just as the profits of a partnership must be shared between the partners, the profits of a limited company must be appropriated among the various classes of shareholders. A typical Appropriation Section of a Profit and Loss Account, with notes, is given below.

Profit and Loss Account for the year ending 31 December 20.. L170

Appropriation Section

20..			€	20..			€
31 Dec.	Reserve for corporation tax		8200	1 Jan.	Balance	B/d	1475
	Plant Replacement Reserve		2000	31 Dec.	Net profit		27284
	General Reserve		5000				
	Preference dividend		1400				
	Ordinary dividend		6000				
	Balance	c/d	6159				
			€28759				€28759
				20..			€
				1 Jan.	Balance	B/d	6159

Notes:

(i) The opening balance on the Appropriation Section is that part of the profit that was not distributed or placed to a reserve account in the previous year.

(ii) The net profit was transferred in from the first section of the Profit and Loss Account.

(iii) Corporation tax, roughly calculated at about 30 per cent but still awaiting proper assessment, was placed to a Corporation Tax Reserve Account.

(iv) €2000 has been set aside in Plant Replacement Reserve, and €5000 in General Reserve, to provide for plant replacement and the equalization of dividend in future years respectively.

(v) Preference dividends and ordinary dividends have been appropriated for the year, and will in due course be paid.

(vi) The balance on the Appropriation Section of the Profit and Loss Account, which is to be retained as a further reserve, is carried down to the credit side of the account.

The double entries for these items are as follows:

Corporation Tax Reserve Account L171

			€
20..			
31 Dec.	Appropriation A/c	L170	8200

Plant Replacement Reserve Account L172

			€
20..			
1 Jan.	Balance	B/d	6921
31 Dec.	Appropriation A/c	L170	2000

General Reserve Account L173

			€
20..			
1 Jan.	Balance	B/d	6500
31 Dec.	Appropriation A/c	L170	5000

Preference Dividend Account L174

			€
20..			
31 Dec.	Appropriation A/c	L170	1400

Ordinary Dividend Account L175

			€
20..			
31 Dec.	Appropriation A/c	L170	6000

The Difference Between Provisions and Reserves

As you see, the first three accounts above are designated 'reserve' accounts. Remember that *reserves are appropriations of profit made after the profits have been calculated*. Provisions, like provisions for bad debts and provisions for discounts, *are charges against the profits* and appear in the Profit and Loss Account where they assist in the calculation of a correct profit.

27.4 The Balance Sheet of a Limited Company

The Companies Act 1985, which incorporates the requirements of the European Economic Community's Fourth Directive on the harmonization of company law, gives two alternative formats for the Balance Sheet. Company Balance Sheets must follow one or other of these formats. One format shows the Balance Sheet in traditional double-sided style, with the assets displayed on the left-hand side, and the liabilities on the right-hand side (Fig. 27.1, pages 408–9). The other format shows the Balance Sheet in vertical style (Fig. 27.2, pages 410–11). The following points are important in considering these Balance Sheets.

(a) In this example one requirement of the Companies Act cannot be complied with because of the size of the pages in this book. This is the requirement to show the previous year's figures alongside the current year's figures for purposes of comparison. However, in examinations at this stage it is not usual for these figures to be given anyway.

(b) The ordinary shareholders' interest in the company has been kept separate from the preference shareholders' interest in the company so that a clear indication is given of the value of their holding. This enables prospective investors to judge how much they should pay for a share. This interest is called the *ordinary shareholders' equity*.

(c) The assets have been separated into fixed assets and current assets, and the fixed assets have been further sub-divided into intangible assets, tangible assets and trade investments.

(d) The current liabilities have been taken over to the assets side, and deducted from the current assets. This brings out the net working capital (also called the net current assets) position. This presentation also shows the 'total assets less current liabilities', sometimes called the 'net assets' position. In the final total of the Balance Sheet the net worth of the business to the owners can clearly be seen.

The order in which current assets and current liabilities are listed is now laid down by the Companies Act 1985. They are given in order of permanence, with the most permanent items shown first and the most liquid item last.

(e) The Companies Act requires that the book value of investments shown on a Balance Sheet must also be accompanied by the current market value (i.e. the value on the Stock Exchange of the company's holding at the end of the financial year). If the shares are in a private company the directors must give their considered opinion of the value of the investment if it should be sold privately.

After studying Figs 27.1 and 27.2, you should attempt the preparation of some sets of limited company Final Accounts. You should be able to prepare a Trading and Profit and Loss Account, an Appropriation Section of the Profit and Loss Account and a Balance Sheet, in both vertical and horizontal styles.

Clearview Ltd Balance Sheet as at 31 December 20. .

	€ *At cost*	€ *Depreciation to date*	€ *Present value*
Fixed assets:			
Intangible assets:			
Patent rights owned	3000	1000	2000
Tangible assets:			
Land and buildings	28000	–	28000
Plant and machinery	33000	25000	8000
Furniture and fittings	7000	1500	5500
Motor vehicles	8500	2500	6000
	79500	30000	49500
Trade investments:			
Shareholdings in subsidiaries at cost (valued by directors at €33500)			27500

Ordinary shareholders' interest in the company:		€ *Authorized*	€ *Issued*
€1 ordinary shares (fully paid)		100000	50000
Reserves:			
Plant Replacement Reserve	6921		
+ Additions	2000		
		8921	
General Reserve	6500		
+ Additions	5000		
		11500	
Profit and Loss A/c (balance)		6159	
			26580
Ordinary shareholders' equity			76580

(continues below)

Fig. 27.1 The Balance Sheet of a limited company in horizontal style (see page 407 for text references to this Balance Sheet)

	€	€	€
Current assets:			€
Other investments			
(market value €18 500)		15 000	
Stock		18 000	
Debtors		2 250	
Cash at bank		9 250	
Cash in hand		1 050	
		45 550	
Less Creditors: amounts falling due within one year			
(current liabilities):	€		
Ordinary dividend	6 000		
Preference dividend	1 400		
Trade creditors	8 215		
Wages due	155		
		15 770	
Net current assets			29 780
Total assets *less* current liabilities			€106 780

	Authorized	
Preference shareholders' interest in the company:		
7% preference shares of €1	20 000	20 000
Creditors: amounts falling due after one year:		
6% debentures of €100		2 000
Reserve for corporation tax		8 200
		€106 780

Fig. 27.1 (continued)

Clearview Ltd
Balance Sheet as at 31 December 20..

	€	€	€
Fixed assets:	*At cost*	*Depreciation to date*	*Present value*
Intangible assets:			
Patent rights owned	3000	1000	2000
Tangible assets:			
Land and buildings	28000	–	28000
Plant and machinery	33000	25000	8000
Furniture and fittings	7000	1500	5500
Motor vehicles	8500	2500	6000
	79500	30000	49500

Trade investments:			
Shareholdings in subsidiaries at cost (valued by directors at €33500)			27500
Current assets:			
Other investments (market value €18500)	15000		
Stock	18000		
Debtors	2250		
Cash at bank	9250		
Cash in hand	1050		
		45550	
Less Creditors: amounts falling due within one year (current liabilities):			
Ordinary dividend	6000		
Preference dividend	1400		
Trade creditors	8215		
Wages due	155		
		15770	
Net current assets			29780
Total assets *less* current liabilities			€106780

Financed by:
Ordinary shareholders' interest in the company:

	Authorized	Issued
€1 Ordinary shares fully paid	100000	50000

(continues opposite)

Fig. 27.2 A Balance Sheet in vertical style

	€	€	€
		(carried forward)	50 000
Reserves:			
Plant Replacement Reserve	6 921		
+ Additions	2 000		
		8 921	
General Reserve	6 500		
+ Additions	5 000		
		11 500	
Profit and Loss A/c (balance)		6 159	
			26 580
			76 580
Preference shareholders' interest in the company:		Authorized	
7% preference shares of €1		20 000	20 000
Creditors: amounts falling due after one year:			
6% debentures of €100			2 000
Reserve for corporation tax			8 200
			€106 780

Fig. 27.2 (continued)

27.5 Exercises Set 45. Company Final Accounts

1. The following Trial Balance was extracted from the books of Pizzatops Ltd at 31 December 20.., after the Profit and Loss Account had been prepared.

	€	€
Authorized and issued capital 80 000 shares of €1 each		80 000
General Reserve		10 000
6 per cent Debentures		20 000
Freehold property (at cost)	70 000	
Furniture and fittings (at cost)	4 000	
Stock-in-trade at end of year	28 950	
Wages and salaries due		350
Provision for Bad Debts, 1 January 20..		400
Provision for Depreciation of Furniture and Fittings		1 200
Trade Debtors	15 000	
Trade Creditors		9 280
Balance at bank	27 200	
Debenture interest due		600
Rates in advance	50	
Profit and Loss Account balance, 1 January 20..		3 300
Net profit for year		20 070
	€145 200	€145 200

You are given the following information:

(a) The directors propose to transfer €12 000 to General Reserve.
(b) They propose a dividend of 10 per cent on the issued capital.

You are required to prepare an Appropriation Section of the Profit and Loss Account for the year 20.. and a Balance Sheet as at 31 December 20... Ignore taxation.

2. The following Trial Balance was extracted from the books of Jacklin Ltd, as on 31 December 20..:

	€	€
Share capital (authorized and issued)		
80 000 ordinary shares of €1 fully paid		80 000
20 000 7 per cent preference shares of €1 fully paid		20 000
Motor vans at cost	24 460	
Freehold property at cost	95 200	
General Reserve		10 000
Machinery Replacement Reserve		2 000
Provision for Depreciation of Motor Vans		10 142
Stock in trade at 31 December 20..	17 754	
Provision for Bad Debts at 31 December 20..		3 400
Profit and Loss Account Balance at 1 January 20..		10 680
Balance at bank	24 170	
Trade Debtors and Creditors	28 325	24 150
Rates and insurance in advance	272	
Wages due		944
Net profit for year		28 865
	€190 181	€190 181

You are told that the directors propose

(a) to place a further €5 000 to General Reserve Account,
(b) to pay 7 per cent preference dividend, and
(c) to pay a 20 per cent dividend on the ordinary shares.

Draw up an Appropriation Section of the Profit and Loss Account, and a Balance Sheet as at 31 December 20...

3. The following Trial Balance was extracted from the books of E. C. Quarries Ltd on 31 December 20..:

Trial Balance

	€	€
Share capital, authorized and issued:		
200 000 ordinary shares of €1 each		200 000
6 per cent Debentures		40 000
Freehold properties at cost	272 000	
Furniture and fittings at cost	12 000	
Trade Debtors	18 950	
Trade Creditors		12 930
Renewal of Properties Reserve		5 000
Stock in trade, 1 January 20..	18 930	
Provision for Bad Debts, 1 January 20..		900
Debenture interest to 30 June 20..	1 200	
Provision for Depreciation of Furniture and Fittings		6 000
Bank overdraft		2 490
Wages and Salaries	23 360	
Rent and Rates	4 650	
General Expenses	5 120	
Bad Debts	1 510	
Profit and Loss Account: balance on 1 January 20..		14 740
Purchases	164 740	
Sales		240 400
	€522 460	€522 460

You are given the following information:

(a) Stock in trade at 31 December 20.. amounted to €20 470.
(b) The Provision for Bad Debts is to be increased to €1 000.
(c) Depreciation at 5 per cent per annum on cost is to be charged on furniture and fittings.
(d) Rates paid in advance at 31 December 20.. were €75.
(e) Wages outstanding on 31 December 20.. amounted to €240.
(f) A sum of €400 is to be appropriated to the Renewal of Properties Reserve.
(g) The outstanding debenture interest is to be paid (to 31 December).
(h) The directors have decided to recommend a dividend of 10 per cent on the share capital.

You are required to prepare a Trading and Profit and Loss Account for the year 20.. and a Balance Sheet as at 31 December 20... Ignore taxation.

4. The following Trial Balance was extracted from the books of Apex Ltd at 31 December 20..:

Trial Balance

	€	€
Share capital—authorized and issued 60 000 shares of €1 each		60 000
Stock in trade 1 January 20..	23 428	
8 per cent Debentures		20 000
General Reserve		10 000
Freehold property (at cost)	59 600	
Furniture and fittings (at cost)	13 000	
Bad Debts	601	
Wages and Salaries	29 820	
Purchases	90 620	
Sales		181 498
Provision for Bad Debts, 1 January 20..		850
Provision for Depreciation of Furniture and Fittings 1 January 20..		750
Insurance	693	
Office Expenses	4 142	
Balance at bank	14 294	
Debenture interest paid to 1 July 20..	800	
Rates	1 210	
Profit and Loss Account balance at 1 January 20..		3 900
Trade Debtors	16 923	
Trade Creditors		12 989
Rent Received		2 390
Directors' Salaries	26 000	
General Expenses	11 246	
	€292 377	€292 377

You are given the following information:

(a) Stock in trade 31 December 20.. €26 426.
(b) The Provision for Bad Debts is to be increased to €1 300.
(c) €3 400 has been included in the Wages and Salaries Account which represents the wages cost of extending the company's freehold property.
(d) Rent receivable due at 31 December 20.. €130.
(e) Insurance paid in advance at 31 December 20.. amounted to €86.
(f) Depreciation of furniture and fittings is to be provided for at the rate of 5 per cent per annum on cost.
(g) The outstanding debenture interest is to be paid.
(h) €7 000 is to be transferred to General Reserve and provision is to be made for a dividend of 20 per cent on the issued capital.

You are required to prepare a Trading and Profit and Loss Account for the year 20.. and a Balance Sheet in vertical style as at 31 December 20... Ignore taxation.

5. Hale and Harty Ltd has an authorized share capital of €200 000, divided into shares of €1 each and of which 100 000 shares have been issued.

After the preparation of the Profit and Loss Account for the year ending 31 March 20.. the following balances remained on the books:

Share Capital Account €100 000; Freehold land and buildings at cost €40 000; Machinery Replacement Reserve €10 000; Machinery at cost €60 000; Stock as valued €37 040; Sundry creditors €19 743; Sundry debtors €43 221; Provision for Bad Debts €524; Balance at bank €22 028; General Reserve Account €25 000; Investments at cost €25 000; Loan secured on land and buildings €20 000; Dividend payable €10 000; Provision for Depreciation of Machinery €32 000; Fixtures and Fittings at cost €22 506; Provision for Depreciation of Fixtures and Fittings €10 006; and Profit and Loss Account, undistributed profit €22 522.

a) List the above balances in the form of a Trial Balance.
b) Prepare the Balance Sheet of the company. (Investments have a market value of €28 050.)

6. The balances appearing below were those remaining on the books of Sky Ltd after the Profit and Loss Account for the year ended 31 December 20.. had been prepared:

	€
Share capital: authorized, 80 000 shares of €1 each; issued, 60 000 shares of €1 each	60 000
6 per cent Debentures	9 000
Premises at cost	42 000
Machinery at cost, *less* depreciation to date of €5 000	24 000
Creditors	7 430
Debtors	16 150
Stock in trade	22 920
Machinery Replacement Reserve	4 000
Profit and Loss Account balance at 1 January 20..	3 420
General Reserve	8 000
Fixtures at cost, *less* depreciation to date of €1 000	2 200
Provision for Bad Debts	1 250
Balance at bank	15 030
Profit for year to 31 December 20..	29 200

It was resolved that:

(a) the General Reserve be increased by €10 000;
(b) a dividend of 20 per cent on the issued capital be declared.

Prepare a Trial Balance, the company's Appropriation Account for the year ended 31 December 20.. and the Balance Sheet at that date. Ignore taxation.

7. The following Trial Balance was extracted from the books of Express Ltd as at 31 December 20.. whose authorized capital is €80 000.

Trial Balance

	€	€
Share capital 80 000 ordinary shares of €1 each		80 000
6 per cent Debentures (issued 1 January 20..)		20 000
Plant Renewal Reserve		25 000
Freehold buildings at cost	100 000	
Plant at cost	40 000	
Motor vehicles at cost	14 000	
Provision for Depreciation on Plant as at 1 January 20..		18 000
Provision for Depreciation on Motor Vehicles as at 1 January 20..		1 500
Sales		184 720
Purchases	97 468	
Returns In	621	
Returns Out		417
Debtors	13 099	
Creditors		8 698
Bad Debts	427	
Provision for Doubtful Debts 1 January 20..		621
Motor Expenses	4 127	
Rent and Rates	4 850	
Insurances	2 160	
Salaries	21 206	
General administration expenses	10 426	
Stock in trade at 1 January 20..	23 846	
Bank balance	10 641	
Directors' fees	15 000	
Profit and Loss Account as at 1 January 20..		19 469
Discount Received		907
Discount Allowed	1 461	
	€359 332	€359 332

You are given the following additional information:

(a) Stock in trade at 31 December 20.. €32 779.
(b) Rent owing at 31 December 20.. €550.
(c) Insurance in advance at 31 December 20.. €40.
(d) Provision for Doubtful Debts is to be increased to €685.
(e) Debenture interest is payable annually on 1 January and the amount due is to be provided for.
(f) Depreciation on plant is to be provided for at 10 per cent of cost and on motor vehicles at 25 per cent of cost.
(g) €25 000 is to be transferred to a new General Reserve.
(h) A dividend at the rate of 20 per cent on the ordinary share capital is to be provided for.

You are asked to prepare a Trading and Profit and Loss Account for 20.. and a Balance Sheet in vertical style as at 31 December 20... Ignore taxation.

8. The following Trial Balance was extracted from the books of Dark Shadows Ltd as at 31 December 20..:

Trial Balance

	€	€
Share capital, authorized and issued 80 000 shares of €1 each		80 000
General Reserve		10 000
6 per cent Debentures		20 000
Sales		182 620
Purchases	116 940	
Returns In	1 227	
Returns Out		1 359
Bad Debts	348	
Provision for Doubtful Debts		1 260
Rent and Rates	4 050	
Lighting and Heating	4 420	
Salaries	26 240	
General Expenses	12 661	
Debtors and Creditors	16 260	9 180
Freehold buildings at cost	80 000	
Furniture and equipment at cost	20 000	
Provision for Depreciation of Furniture as at 1 January 20..		7 400
Stock in trade, 1 January 20..	28 260	
Balance at bank	12 955	
Debenture interest	600	
Profit and Loss Account as at 1 January 20..		12 142
	€323 961	€323 961

You are given the following additional information:

(a) Debenture interest is paid on 1 January and 1 July each year.
(b) Provision for Doubtful Debts is to be reduced by €240.
(c) Rates paid in advance at 31 December 20.. amount to €350.
(d) €10 000 is to be appropriated to General Reserve Account.
(e) Lighting and heating due at 31 December 20.. amounts to €71.
(f) Depreciation is to be charged on furniture and equipment at the rate of 10 per cent per annum on cost.
(g) Stock in trade at 31 December 20.. was valued at €29 621.
(h) A dividend of $12\frac{1}{2}$ per cent is proposed for 20...

You are asked to prepare a Trading and Profit and Loss Account for the year 20.. and a Balance Sheet in vertical style at 31 December 20... Ignore taxation.

27.6 Revise and Test 27. The Accounts of Companies

Answers	*Questions*
—	**1.** What is the unique feature of limited companies?
1. The owners of the company have limited liability. Other people, partners and sole traders, have unlimited liability and are consequently very vulnerable should they get into financial difficulties. They are liable for every loss that occurs, to the limit of their personal wealth.	**2.** If the shareholders of companies have limited liability and are not placed in a vulnerable position as far as the debts of the business are concerned, who does suffer when a company collapses?
2. The creditors, who have supplied goods to the company. For this reason the government requires certain warnings to creditors that they are dealing with a limited liability company (the name must end with the word 'limited', or the words 'public limited company' or their Welsh equivalent). It also requires special attention to be given to the accounts of companies.	**3.** What are these special requirements?
3. The chief one is that both the Profit and Loss Account and the Balance Sheet shall give a 'true and fair view' of the profitability in the accounting period to which they refer, and the state of the company's affairs at the end of the accounting period.	**4.** What are the simple features of the accounts of limited companies?

---

4. a) The Trading Account and Profit and Loss Account are no different from the accounts of sole traders or partnerships;
b) the Appropriation Account is special in that it is used to appropriate the profits to those entitled to them;
c) the Balance Sheet is often presented in vertical style.

5. What entries would you expect to find on the Appropriation Account of a company?

---

5. a) On the credit side we would have the balance of profits left from last year and this year's profit coming from the Profit and Loss Account;
b) on the debit side we would have a Provision for Corporation Tax, and any amounts put into reserves, special reserves or a General Reserve. Then we would have the Preference Dividend (if any) and the Ordinary Dividend. Finally the balance carried down to next year.

6. Why do companies accumulate large reserves?

---

6. a) To meet specific needs such as plant replacement;
b) to equalize the dividend over the years. Shareholders get restless if dividends fluctuate;
c) to finance growth—self-financing is better than borrowing. Many shareholders prefer it too, in that a capital gain is better than a dividend when taxation is high.

7. What would you expect to find on the assets side of a company Balance Sheet?

---

7. a) The Fixed Assets, at cost, less the depreciation to date;
b) the Trade Investments (assets neither fixed nor current);
c) the Current Assets (less the Current Liabilities) to give the Net Current Assets;
d) the final total is then called the Net Assets.

8. And what would you expect to find on the liabilities side of the Balance Sheet?

---

8. a) The Preference Shareholders' interest in the Company;
b) the Ordinary Shareholders' interest in the Company (which includes all the reserves);
c) the debentures (long-term loans);
d) the provision for Corporation Tax.

9. If presented in vertical style how would it be listed?

---

9. a) Assets side first;
b) Then the words 'Financed by:';
c) Then the liabilities below.

10. Go over the page until you are sure of all the answers.

UNIT 28

Interpreting Final Accounts

28.1 How Businesses are Controlled

When a business has been running for some time, it becomes possible to compare the current trading period with earlier periods. Such comparisons are almost always interesting, especially if attention is paid to *relative changes* and not *absolute changes*. For example, a manager who tells his/her employer that sales have increased by $1 000 per week is quoting the actual figures—the absolute change that has taken place. It sounds very impressive, but before giving the manager a bonus, the employer should inquire what relative change the increase represents, i.e. what percentage change. If sales were previously running at $100 000 per week anyway it is only a 1 per cent increase and no one will think it miraculous. The success of an advertising campaign, for example, is always best judged in percentage terms.

Even if the business has only been running for a short time it is possible to compare it with similar businesses, if statistics are available from trade associations and similar bodies which analyse the activities of enterprises in their particular field. It is also possible, if a certain amount of planning is undertaken, to draw up in advance estimates of future performance in selling, expenditure, cash, turnover and so forth. These budgets may then be compared with actual performance as the weeks go by. This is the system known as *budgetary control*.

For the purpose of this Unit it is proposed to consider the most useful control figures which can be derived from the Final Accounts and, incidentally, while dealing with these matters you will learn many useful pieces of accounting vocabulary.

Before preparing any such figures it is essential to have a set of Final Accounts in good style, prepared in the way suggested throughout this book. When attempting to analyse the affairs of a business whose accounts have been prepared poorly the first step is to rearrange them in good style. Most of the control figures may then be prepared immediately.

28.2 A Trading Account for Analysis

Consider the following Trading Account.

Sunshine Boutique (E. Rawlinson)
Trading Account for year ending 31 December 20..

20..		$	$	20..		$
31 Dec.	Opening stock		12820	31 Dec.	Sales	211200
	Purchases	148625			*Less* Returns	1200
	Add Carriage in	675			Net turnover	210000
		149300				
	Less Returns	2120				
			147180			
	Total stock available		160000			
	Less Closing stock		32500			
	Cost of stock sold		127500			
	Wages		27500			
	Cost of sales		155000			
	Gross profit		55000			
			$210000			$210000

Last year the gross profit was $47500 on sales of $160000, so that both turnover and profit have increased.

The points to consider in analysing the results shown by a Trading Account are the *gross profit percentage* and the *rate of stock turnover*.

28.3 The Gross Profit Percentage on Turnover

This is given by the formula

$$\textit{gross profit percentage on turnover} = \frac{\textit{gross profit}}{\textit{turnover}} \times 100$$

Turnover is the net sales of the business, i.e. the sales *less* the returns inwards. In this case the percentage is

$$\frac{55000}{210000} \times 100$$
$$= \frac{550}{21}$$
$$= 26.2\%$$

It is interesting that, if business conditions are steady, the *gross profit percentage will be constant*, i.e. the same from year to year. For example, supposing business were to double in the coming year? Sales would be twice as great, purchases would be twice as great, we should probably need to take on more workers so that wages would rise, and profits ought to double as well. The gross profit percentage would be

$$\frac{\textit{gross profit}}{\textit{turnover}} \times 100 = \frac{110000}{420000} \times 100$$
$$= 26.2\%$$

The gross profit percentage remains the same even though everything has doubled. Its usefulness is that it shows the *relative profitability* of the business, this year compared with the previous year.

Returning to the Trading Account above, it is possible to compare this figure of 26.2 per cent with last year's, when the figures were $47 500 gross profit and $160 000 sales.

$$\textit{gross profit percentage} = \frac{47500}{160000} \times 100$$
$$= 29.7\%$$

Clearly the gross profit percentage has fallen off from 29.7 per cent to 26.2 per cent. This is a significant fall. There may have been perfectly good reasons for it, but it certainly detracts to some extent from the performance of the business.

Let us examine the possible causes of a decline in gross profit percentage.

(a) Causes of a Decline in Gross Profit Percentage

(i) Cash losses If the manager takes money out of the till before cashing up the daily takings, the sales figure will be reduced and hence the gross profit, and the gross profit percentage. It is unwise to accuse a manager of theft, but if his or her life style seems unexpectedly extravagant, it may be wise to take some corrective action. If the manager is not at fault, someone else may be the culprit. Where there are several cash registers it is possible for staff to steal money by incorrect ringing up of receipts. If a till has been deliberately placed so that the customer cannot see the amount being rung up an owner should be suspicious. Modern tills do much to overcome this type of theft by preventing any money being rung up unless the drawer is shut. Every amount rung up is totalled into daily totals which cannot be reset without an automatic record being made. If customers are always given till receipts this also reduces the chances of sharp practice. Staff training to emphasize the ease with which theft of takings can be detected is helpful in reducing cash losses.

(ii) Stock losses If the takings are being properly recorded, the fall in gross profit percentage may be caused by the theft of stock. Regular theft of small quantities of stock by staff will reduce the stock in hand at the end of the trading period. Where the trader takes home goods for his own use the effect will be similar (see Unit 4.3). Both will increase the 'cost of stock sold' and reduce the gross profit and hence the gross profit percentage. A general term for all stock losses is *shrinkage*.

Passing out, the deliberate handing over of stock without payment to friends or accomplices, is a common form of theft. *Shoplifting* is a common practice, believed to cost at least £20 million each year to shops in the United Kingdom. The provision of store detectives, two-way mirrors and other measures helps to deter and detect this activity.

Other forms of stock losses include *breakages* in departments where fragile goods are sold. Some assistants are naturally fumble-fisted and should be transferred from departments where this is a disadvantage. Skylarking and tomfoolery should be discouraged and action taken against offenders. Stock losses due to *the spoiling of perishable commodities* may indicate bad buying. Too many tomatoes, fresh fruit, etc. may result in stocks going bad, while bad storage may lead to stock losses due to evaporation, blowing away of powdery stocks like meal and flour, and the contamination of foods by other substances or by insects or other vermin.

(iii) Mark-downs Sometimes stock has to be disposed of at reduced prices because it is shop-soiled, or slow-moving. This indicates bad buying. Some buyers may be out of touch with what is fashionable and readily saleable. Products which for some reason do not achieve anticipated sales figures may have to be marked down, thus reducing the gross profit and the gross profit percentage. An appraisal of such 'clearance items' may reveal that a particular buyer is responsible for a high proportion of them. Clearly some action may be needed to end this situation.

(iv) Increased purchase prices Sometimes world prices of raw materials change, and result in higher purchase prices for goods. This increased price should be passed on to the consumer as increased selling prices. Sometimes this is not possible because of competition, and the result is falling profit margins and a lower gross profit percentage. At least managers who are aware of these falling profit margins can be ready, when circumstances are less competitive, to recoup past losses. They may also vary their mixture of goods to include more items where competition is less fierce, reducing those where rivals are particularly efficient and are able to undercut them.

(v) Expenses Even in the Trading Account there are certain expense items. An increase in these may explain a falling gross profit percentage. This type of change is discussed more fully below (see Unit 28.7).

(vi) Incorrect stock valuation A fall in gross profit percentage may be the result of incorrect stock valuation. An overvalued stock overstates the profit and gives an artificially high percentage of gross profit. As this stock then becomes the 'opening stock' of the next period, it will artificially inflate the 'cost of stock sold' and lower the percentage of gross profit in the following year. This will give a difference between the two successive years which is not the fault of the manager. It is simply caused by the bad stock-taking.

(b) Causes of a Rise in Gross Profit Percentage

Many of the reasons for a fall in gross profit percentage indicate dishonesty or incompetence somewhere in the business. A *rise* in gross profit percentage is almost certainly due to increased efficiency in the conduct of the business. More careful supervision, more systematic working or some other improvement has produced the beneficial change.

Clearly, every effort should be made by a business to improve the gross profit percentage wherever possible—for example, by seeking to buy at lower cost from suppliers, and by raising prices to consumers when the chance arises. Thus at festival times we might raise the prices of items required for the festival, lowering them again when the festival is over and they are less strongly demanded. Where a manager has been successful in raising the gross profit percentage through greater honesty and greater efficiency, he or she should be rewarded with a bonus for good work.

You should now try the simple calculations given below to practise dealing with gross profit percentages.

28.4 Exercises Set 46. Gross Profit Percentage

1. Mr A had the following results in successive years:

	Year 1	*Year 2*
Sales	$27 000	$35 000
Gross profit	$5 000	$6 000

Compare the two years by finding, and commenting upon, the gross profit percentage.

2. R. Dawson makes two products, a Junior model and a Senior model of an electrical appliance. His records show the following results at the end of the year.

	Junior	*Senior*
Sales	$29 000	$128 000
Sales returns	$9 000	$8 000
Cost of sales	$19 000	$82 500

He has no room to expand, and at present allocates half his available space to each model. Calculate the gross profit on each model, the gross profit percentage on each model, and offer Dawson some advice. You may assume that an unlimited market exists for each product.

3. R. Marshall, a retailer, finds that his gross profit percentage has fallen from 38 per cent last year to 23 per cent this year. Is he justified in considering the following as perhaps responsible for the fall in gross profit percentage?

a) The takings have been deliberately reduced by embezzlement.
b) One of the assistants has been conspiring with friends to charge less than the full price for goods each time they come in to purchase supplies.
c) The accountant has had a large increase in salary.
d) A supermarket four doors away has caused him to offer cut prices on many articles.
e) Marshall's wife has not been well and he has taken home regularly goods for domestic use which have not been recorded in any way.
f) An assistant buyer has placed several large orders with suppliers for goods which proved to be unpopular and were sold off in an end-of-year sale.

4. a) What is the meaning of 'gross profit'?
b) What is the meaning of 'gross profit percentage'?
c) Using the figures given below, prepare the Trading Account of Keith Newing, to find the gross profit and the gross profit percentage earned during the year.

	$
Stock, 1 January 20..	22500
Cash Purchases	5000
Credit Purchases	62500
Carriage Inwards	2500
Returns Outwards (Purchases Returns)	5000
Cash Sales	115000
Credit Sales	40000
Returns Inwards (Sales Returns)	5000
Stock, 31 December 20..	27500

5. a) At 31 December 20.. the Trial Balance of E. Randall contained the following items:

	$
Stock, 1 January 20..	27850
Purchases	69080
Sales	76420
Returns Outward	1950
Returns Inward	2620
Wages (Trading Account)	7000
Wages owing	200
Import Charges	1260

Randall's stock at 31 December 20.. was valued at $44400. Prepare the Trading Account for the year ending 31 December 20...
b) What was Randall's percentage gross profit or loss on his turnover?

28.5 The Rate of Stock Turnover

The rate of stockturn, or rate of stock turnover, shows how many times the stock turns over in a year. Rate of stock turnover is important because every time the stock turns over it yields a profit, so that rapid turnover will increase the total profit earned in the year. Turnover must be rapid with some merchandise; perishable foods and daily papers, for example, must turn over every day if possible. At least one supermarket chain throws away all cut-meat products unsold at the end of the day. Overstocking in such circumstances can be very expensive.

The formula for finding this control figure is:

$$\textit{rate of stock turnover} = \frac{\textit{cost of stock sold}}{\textit{average stock at cost price}}$$

The average stock is given by any of the following:

$$\frac{\textit{opening stock} + \textit{closing stock}}{2}$$

or
$$\frac{\textit{sum of the four quarterly stock figures}}{4}$$

or
$$\frac{\textit{sum of the twelve monthly stock figures}}{12}$$

It depends upon the frequency with which stock is taken as to which method is used.

In the case of the Trading Account in Unit 28.2,

$$\textit{rate of stock turnover} = \frac{\$127\,500}{(\$12\,820 + \$32\,500) \div 2}$$

$$= \frac{\$127\,500}{\$22\,660}$$

$$= 5.6 \text{ times per annum}$$

Is this a satisfactory rate of turnover? The answer is that we must know what the product is before we can say. It would be satisfactory for grand pianos but quite inadequate for groceries. It would perhaps do well enough for antiques, but not well enough for sweets or tobacco.

How long is the average item in stock? The rate of stockturn tells us how many times the stock turns over in a year. If we divide the 52 weeks of the year by the rate of stockturn we find how long the average item is in stock. In our example it is clearly $52 \div 5.6 = 9.3$ weeks.

28.6 Exercises Set 47. The Rate of Stock Turnover

1. L. Perry carries an average stock (at cost price) of $5250. Her annual sales are $78750 (selling price) of which 20 per cent is profit. What is the rate of stockturn in her business?

2. A. Reddington sells cars valued at $159375 (selling price) of which 20 per cent is profit. His average stock (at cost price) is $8500. What is his rate of stock turnover?

3. Using the figures available in the Trading Account below, find:
   a) the average stock held,
   b) the rate of stock turnover for the year, and
   c) the average length of time an article of stock was in the possession of A. Trader.

Trading Account of A. Trader
for year ended 31 December 20..

	$	$		$
Opening stock		25200	Sales	90000
Purchases	60480		*Less* Returns	240
Less Returns	1080		Net turnover	89760
		59400		
		84600		
Less Closing stock		18720		
Cost of stock sold		65880		
Gross profit		23880		
		$89760		$89760

4. Using the figures available in the Trading Account of M. Datta, find:
   a) the average stock held,
   b) the rate of stock turnover for the year,
   c) the average length of time an article of stock was in the possession of M. Datta, to the nearest day.

Trading Account of M. Datta
for the year ended 31 December 20..

	$	$		$
Opening stock		2400	Sales	69540
Purchases	51550		*Less* Returns	420
Less Returns	190		Net turnover	69120
		51360		
		53760		
Less Closing stock		1920		
Cost of stock sold		51840		
Gross profit		17280		
		$69120		$69120

5. Using the figures available in the Trading Account of D. Hancock, find:
a) the average stock held,
b) the rate of stock turnover for the year, and
c) the average length of time an article of stock was in the possession of D. Hancock (to the nearest day).

Trading Account of D. Hancock
for year ended 31 December 20..

	$	$		$
Opening stock		50000	Sales	488000
Purchases	414000		*Less* Returns	2240
Less Returns	8000		Net turnover	485760
		406000		
		456000		
Less Closing stock		51200		
Cost of stock sold		404800		
Gross profit		80960		
		$485760		$485760

6. The proprietor of Downtown Do-It-Yourself Stores prepares his Final Accounts annually and the following figures relate to the year ended 30 September 20..:

	$
Purchases	129090
Sales	160650
Stock at start	21340
Stock at close	20860
Returns inwards	8730
Returns outwards	2970

You are required to:
a) prepare a Trading Account for the year ended 30 September 20..;
b) state the cost of the goods sold during the year;
c) calculate the gross profit/sales percentage;
d) calculate, in months, the average time for which goods were held in stock.

7. J. Cole manufactures bicycles. He holds an average stock of 70 bicycles. The manufacturing cost of each bicycle is $72 and the selling price $100. During 20. . he sold 910 bicycles.

a) Calculate
   (i) Cole's rate of turnover of stock for the year 20. ., and
   (ii) Cole's gross profit for the year 20. . .

b) For the next year Cole reduced the selling price by 10 per cent and holding the same average stock, his rate of turnover of stock was 15. His gross profit was $27 300. Calculate
   (i) the value of Cole's turnover for the year, and
   (ii) the cost of manufacture of each bicycle in this second year.

8. M. Regent manufactures vacuum cleaners. He holds an average stock of 80 cleaners. The manufacturing cost of each cleaner is $25 and the selling price $40. During 20. . he sold 1 200 cleaners.

a) Calculate
   (i) Regent's rate of turnover of stock for the year 20. ., and
   (ii) Regent's gross profit for the year 20. . .

b) For the next year Regent reduced the selling price by 10 per cent and holding the same average stock, his rate of turnover of stock was 20. His gross profit was $19 200. Calculate
   (i) the value of Regent's turnover for the year, and
   (ii) the cost of manufacture of each vacuum cleaner.

28.7 The Net Profit Percentage on Turnover

The gross profit is carried forward to the Profit and Loss Account where other profits are added to it and losses are deducted. The resulting net profit can be used to find the *net profit percentage*, using the formula

$$net\ profit\ percentage = \frac{net\ profit}{turnover} \times 100$$

Again, this should be reasonably constant from year to year, and if it is not the causes of the change should be sought.

In the case of the Trading Account shown in Unit 28.2 the gross profit to be carried forward was $55 000. The Profit and Loss Account may be as follows:

Sunshine Boutique (E. Rawlinson)
Profit and Loss Account for year ending 31 December 20..

20..		$	20..		$
31 Dec.	Salaries	7 500	31 Dec.	Gross profit	55 000
	Administration Expenses	2 100		Discount Received	3 750
	Light and Heat	3 400		Commissions Earned	7 750
	Rent and Rates	8 250			66 500
	Insurance	2 250			
	Advertising	6 200			
	Carriage Out	500			
		30 200			
	Net profit	36 300			
		$66 500			$66 500

From the above we have

$$net\ profit\ percentage = \frac{net\ profit}{turnover} \times 100$$

$$= \frac{36\,300}{210\,000} \times 100 = 17.3\%$$

(a) Analysing the Net Profit Percentage

The figure of net profit percentage achieved here seems a fairly adequate one. Most firms would be very satisfied to achieve this net profit margin, and in many of the more competitive industries smaller profit margins than this are common. The chief advantage of the net profit percentage is that it enables us to compare one year with another, or one trading period with the previous trading period if we take out Final Accounts more frequently. Suppose that last year the net profit percentage was 20 per cent. This means that in the last year the net profit percentage has fallen by 2.7 per cent. What can have caused this decline? Let us assume that the gross profit percentage has remained constant, so that clearly there is nothing wrong with the trading activities of the firm. There can only be two explanations:

(a) The expenses may have increased for some reason.
(b) The 'other profits' may have declined for some reason.

Here it is useful to prepare *expense ratios*, which enable us to compare every expense with the same expense the previous year and to detect whether they have risen abnormally. The formula is

$$\textit{expense ratio} = \frac{\textit{expense item}}{\textit{turnover}} \times 100$$

In the case of salaries, for instance, the ratio in our example is

$$\textit{salaries ratio to turnover} = \frac{7500}{210000} \times 100$$

$$= 3.57\%$$

Suppose that last year the salaries were $5000 and turnover $160000. Then

$$\textit{salaries ratio (previous year)} = \frac{5000}{160000} \times 100$$

$$= 3.12\%$$

There has been quite a large increase in the salaries figure relative to the volume of trade done, and this seems to indicate some inefficiency somewhere. Some managers build 'empires' of staff under their control, and this may have happened here to some extent.

(b) Falling 'Other Receipts'

If the decline in net profit percentage does not seem to have been caused by an increase in expenses, it may have been caused by a decrease in 'other receipts', such as commission received, or rent received. If such items have yielded less profit than in previous years, we should try to discover the reasons. Perhaps a sub-tenant has been given notice to quit because his share of the building was required for expansion; in such a case there is nothing we can do about the lost rent. Or we might discover that commission previously earned has not been forthcoming for some reason; extra attention to this matter might ensure that this type of earnings was pursued more vigorously in the following year.

Regular comparison of the gross profit percentages and net profit percentages in successive trading periods is extremely useful, and reveals changes of a favourable or unfavourable nature that are taking place in the business. Many firms prepare interim Final Accounts at three-monthly, or even monthly, intervals so that they can check the profitability of their enterprises.

28.8 Exercises Set 48. Net Profit Percentage

1. F. Azouqua has the following results for two successive years. Present the two sets of figures in such a way as to make a comparison between them, and state any conclusions you are able to draw.

	Year 1	*Year 2*
Turnover	$72 000	$80 000
Gross profit	$14 400	$16 200
Net profit	$8 000	$9 000

2. K. Penn takes out Final Accounts at six-monthly intervals. He finds the following results. Compare the two sets of figures and comment upon them.

	January–June	*July–December*
Gross profit	$18 400	$22 400
Net profit	$5 520	$7 520
Turnover	$46 000	$80 000

3. How would the following transactions affect
a) the gross profit and
b) the net profit of B. Cook's manufacturing business?
(i) Sold goods on credit (cost price $100) for $120.
(ii) Paid commission to salesmen $650.
(iii) Paid bonus to works manager $250.
(iv) Paid office wages $210.
(v) Purchased new machinery on credit $2 000.
(vi) Paid customs duty on raw material $60.
(vii) Depreciated machinery by $300.

Your answers are to be given under the two headings:

Effect on gross profit *Effect on net profit*

You are required to show, under the appropriate heading, the amount of increase or decrease. Indicate an increase by the sign + (plus) and the amount and a decrease by the sign − (minus) and the amount. If there is no effect write the words 'no effect'.

4. a) What is meant by the term *expense ratio*?
b) Calculate the expense ratios for the expenses of R. James's business listed below. His turnover is $150 000.

Expense item	*Amount*
Discount allowed	$3 750
Office light and heat	$6 000
Office salaries	$16 000

5. At 1 January 20.. M. Truman valued his stock in trade at $16 700. For the ensuing year he made the following estimates: sales $60 000; returns inwards $1 500; carriage inwards $1 100; manufacturing wages $9 800; purchases $22 000. The ratio of gross profit on net turnover was $17\frac{1}{2}$ per cent.

   You are required to prepare:

   a) Truman's Estimated Trading Account showing the estimated value of his stock in trade at 31 December 20.. and
   b) his Profit and Loss Account, assuming a net profit percentage of 10 per cent.

   All Truman's expenses are assembled in a single General Expenses Account.

6. a) The following balances were extracted from the accounts of R. Harper at 31 December 20... Prepare Harper's Trading and Profit and Loss Accounts for the year ended 31 December 20...

	Dr.	*Cr.*
	$	$
Purchases	83 600	
Sales		109 425
Sales Returns	675	
Stock (at cost) 1 January 20..	14 400	
Delivery of Goods Sold	1 210	
Rent and Rates	7 125	
Bad Debts	515	
Light and Heat	710	
Insurance	225	
Discount Received		1 020
Discount Allowed	1 480	
Wages of Shop Assistant	3 640	
Bank Charges and Interest	205	

   The following matters are to be brought into account:

   On 31 December 20.. stock was valued at cost, $13 700.
   Rates $1 150 for the half-year to 31 March next were paid and are included in the balance of Rent and Rates Account.
   Harper's annual rent was $4 800. Rent for December 20.. had not been paid.
   A Provision for Bad Debts of $200 is to be created.

   b) What is the amount of Harper's turnover for the year 20..?
   c) Calculate his rate of turnover of stock for the year.
   d) During the year Harper purchased a delivery van for $4 800. To what extent (if any) do you think this would affect Harper's profit for the year?
   e) Calculate Harper's net profit percentage.

7. From the following information from M. Tyler's accounts ascertain:

a) turnover for the month;
b) cost price of goods sold during the trading period;
c) percentage of gross profit to turnover;
d) percentage of net profit to turnover;
e) the general expenses ratio to turnover.

	$
Capital	8000
Stock, 1 December	6000
General Expenses	180
Purchases	3080
Stock, 31 December	5080
Returns Inwards	600
Returns Outwards	80
Sales	5500

8. a) During the year 20.. E. Block held an average stock at cost price of $16920. She marked up her purchases by 25 per cent to obtain her selling prices. Her turnover for the year was $253800. Her selling and administrative expenses were 11 per cent of turnover.

Calculate:

(i) her gross profit for the year;
(ii) her rate of turnover of stock for the year;
(iii) her net profit for the year.

b) For the following year she plans to reduce her mark-up on cost price to 20 per cent and to spend $3000 on advertising. What must be her minimum rate of turnover of stock if she is to earn, at least, a net profit of $22800?

Assume that the average stock remains the same in amount and cost as in 20.. and that selling and administrative expenses, other than the additional advertising, are estimated at $28334.

9. a) During the year 20.. T. Wabash held an average stock at cost price of $18000. He marked up his purchases by 50 per cent to obtain his selling prices. His turnover for the year was $324000. His selling and administrative expenses were 12 per cent of turnover.

Calculate:

(i) his gross profit for the year;
(ii) his rate of turnover of stock for the year;
(iii) his net profit for the year.

b) For the following year, Wabash plans to reduce his mark-up on cost price to 40 per cent and to spend $12000 on advertising. What must be his minimum rate of turnover of stock if he is to earn, at least, a net profit of $60000? (Answer correct to one decimal place.)

Assume that the average stock remains the same in amount and cost as in 20.. and that selling and administrative expenses, other than the additional advertising, are estimated at $40000.

28.9 Interpreting a Balance Sheet

By now you are very familiar with the Balance Sheet of a business as a 'snapshot' of the affairs of the business at a moment of time. Here is the Balance Sheet of Sunshine Boutique, as a basis for discussion.

Sunshine Boutique (E. Rawlinson)
Balance Sheet as at 31 December 20..

	$	$	$		$	$
Fixed assets:				Capital:		
Goodwill			4000	At start		56000
Land and buildings			48000	*Add* Net profit	36300	
Fixtures and fittings			3600	*Less* Drawings	13600	
Motor vehicles			11000			22700
			66600			78700
Current assets:						
Stock		32500		Long-term liabilities:		
Debtors	2560			Mortgage		15000
Less Provision	320			Current liabilities:		
		2240		Creditors	12350	
Cash at bank		4800		Wages due	150	
Cash in hand		60				12500
			39600			
			$106200			$106200

The Vocabulary of Balance Sheet Appraisal

You are now familiar with well-presented Balance Sheets, sub-divided into fixed and current assets, and into capital, long-term liabilities and current liabilities. Now you are going to meet a further range of concepts, some of which simply offer alternative ways of handling those you already know while others will be new to you and will increase your ability to appraise a Balance Sheet.

In making such an appraisal it is most useful to know the total value of the business, and who 'owns' it. The simple answer would be that it all belongs to the proprietor(s), i.e. the sole trader, the partners or the shareholders as the case may be. This would be too simple a view, however, as we shall see.

(i) Capital employed This is a concept that must be handled carefully. Look first at our example. In the Balance Sheet of Sunshine Boutique, the owner's capital at start is given as $56000, yet the business is worth $106200, as the total of the Balance Sheet shows. It follows that the capital employed in this business is greater than $56000, and some of it must have been provided in some other way than by the original contribution of the proprietor, E. Rawlinson. It is easy to see where these extra funds came from. A mortgage provided $15000, creditors supplied goods without payment $12350, employees are waiting for their wages and to this small extent are providing funds for the business, while $22700 was ploughed back out of profits over the year. The capital employed in this business has therefore been provided in five different ways.

The definition of capital employed is different in different situations. We can answer the question 'What is the capital employed in this business?' in several different ways:

1. *capital employed* = *total value of the funds used in the business*
   = *total value of the business liabilities*
   = *total value of the business assets*
   = *total of the Balance Sheet* = $106 200

2. *capital employed* = *total of the* long-term *funds used by the business*

Here 'long-term funds' means the funds provided by the long-term investors in the company. This means that we count into the capital employed the following items:

capital invested at start	= $56 000
+ *profits retained in the business*	= $22 700
+ *long-term liabilities (the mortgage)*	= $15 000
	$93 700

The fact that there are two definitions in common use may seem a little tricky when examination questions have to be answered, but there will usually be some hint of which is the correct one to use in the context of the question. If in doubt give both, and explain why you have used them.

(ii) Fixed and circulating capital The 'capital employed' above is being used to provide two classes of assets, fixed (or capital) assets and current assets. The components of capital used in this way are called *fixed capital* and *circulating capital* respectively; the latter is sometimes also called *floating capital*. Defining these terms we may say:

Fixed capital is capital tied up in fixed assets, which are in permanent use in the business forming the framework for running its affairs.

Circulating capital or *floating capital* is capital tied up in current assets (see Unit 7.6(a)), which are in the process of turning over, or circulating, in the way shown in Fig. 7.1 on page 89 (i.e. stock, sold to debtors, which becomes cash again, which is used to buy stock, and so on).

For Sunshine Boutique, the figures are:

fixed capital = *total of fixed assets* = $66 600

circulating capital (floating capital) = *total of current assets* = $39 600

(iii) Liquid capital is capital tied up in liquid assets, which may be defined as cash and 'near cash' items. Liquid assets are cash in hand, cash at the bank, debtors (who have a legal obligation to pay) and any other near-liquid assets such as investments which are readily marketable. The best way to define liquid capital is:

liquid capital = current assets − stock

In the case of Sunshine Boutique the figure for liquid capital is:

liquid capital = \$39 600 − \$32 500
= \$7100

(iv) Working capital This is the most important guiding figure when appraising a Balance Sheet. It is that portion of the capital employed which is not tied up in fixed assets (fixed capital) but is available to 'work' the business, in other words to meet its revenue expenditure. The figure is found by the formula:

working capital = current assets − current liabilities

In the case of Sunshine Boutique it is:

working capital = \$39 600 − \$12 500
= \$27 100

(v) Working capital ratio and liquid capital ratio. These two important figures can be shown as numbers, or ratios.

working capital ratio = *current assets : current liabilities*
liquid capital ratio = *liquid assets : current liabilities*

The first tells us the *ratio between the circulating part of a firm's assets and its current liabilities*, and is also known as the *current ratio*. For Sunshine Boutique the ratio is:

working capital ratio = \$39 600 : \$12 500
= 3.2 : 1

It is generally recognized that 2 : 1 is an adequate working capital ratio, so that this appears to be very satisfactory. A more crucial test is the liquid capital ratio, however. The liquid capital ratio tells us the *ratio between a firm's readily available cash or near-cash assets and its current liabilities (due for payment in one month)*. For Sunshine Boutique the ratio is:

liquid capital ratio = (*current assets − stock*) : *current liabilities*
= (\$39 600 − \$32 500) : \$12 500
= \$7100 : \$12 500
= 0.57 : 1

This shows that Sunshine Boutique is short of liquid capital: it could not meet its short-term liabilities easily, and would need to borrow to pay them. The liquid capital ratio should never be less than 1:1, except where the management has anticipated it as a temporary situation for which they have provided—by arranging an overdraft, for example. To the investor, considering whether he should invest in a firm or not, the liquid capital ratio is a particularly valuable guide to the financial position of the firm and it is therefore often called the *acid-test ratio*.

Ratios like these two should always be expressed as shown—for example, as 3.2:1, rather than 16:5. The latter is arithmetically valid, but is less useful for the purposes of comparing one company, or one trading period, with another.

(vi) Capital owned and capital invested You have already met the idea of 'net worth' (see Unit 26.3). The net worth of any business is the difference between the total value of the business and the external liabilities, both current and long-term. An alternative name for net worth is *capital owned*, and it is calculated thus:

capital owned (net worth total) = value of the business − external liabilities

The Balance Sheet of Sunshine Boutique shows that:

capital owned	=	$106 200 − $27 500
	=	$78 700

This amounts, of course, to the *capital invested* at the start of the year plus the profits ploughed back during the year.

(vii) Return on capital employed Here a little care is needed. Whichever of the definitions of capital employed we use (see (i) above), we need to include in the profits earned any interest paid on external loans (such as the mortgage), because that interest has been deducted from the profits that have been earned in the year, and we must add it back before we make our calculation. We can normally find this figure in the Profit and Loss Account: suppose it is $1 500. Then:

profits earned	=	*net profit*	+ *interest on mortgage*
	=	$36 300	+ $1 500
	=	$37 800	

Let us use the second formula for calculating the capital employed:

capital employed	=	*capital at start*	+ *retained profits*	+ *mortgage*
	=	$56 000	+ $22 700	+ $15 000
	=	$93 700		

Now we have the information for calculating the return on capital employed (ROCE):

$$ROCE = \frac{\$37\,800}{\$93\,700} \times 100$$

$$= 40.3 \text{ per cent}$$

(viii) Return on capital invested This ratio enables us to see how the proprietor of the business has profited as a result of the investment he or she made at the start of the year. The figure is more narrowly based than ROCE, because it leaves out of the calculation both the interest on the mortgage and the mortgage itself. The formula is as follows:

$$\textit{return on capital invested} = \frac{\textit{net profit}}{\textit{capital invested at start}} \times 100$$

For Sunshine Boutique,

$$\textit{return on capital invested} = \frac{\$36\,300}{\$56\,000} \times 100$$

$$= \frac{\$3\,630}{\$56} = 64.8\%$$

Now we will use the figures discussed in the last few pages to appraise the affairs of Sunshine Boutique.

28.10 A Balance Sheet Appraised

In considering the Balance Sheet of any business, we are anxious to decide whether the enterprise appears to be soundly based. In order that it may be regarded as 'sound' we should expect to find the following:

(a) The *fixed assets* should be appropriate for the type of business concerned, and offer prospects of future profitability when they are used to conduct the enterprise. Having too many fixed assets is called *overcapitalization.*

(b) The *working capital* should be adequate, that is to say the current assets should be great enough to pay the current liabilities, preferably about twice over, i.e. a 2:1 ratio. If not, the firm is *overtrading*, that is to say it is buying too much and selling too little, piling up debts which will mean trouble. Should it continue overtrading, it will be forced to recognize that it cannot pay its debts and continue operations. Such a firm is said to be *insolvent.* It must realize its fixed assets (that is, sell them for what they will fetch) and use the funds so obtained to pay its creditors. (Insolvency is not the same as bankruptcy, which is only imposed on a person who cannot pay his/her creditors and who has to be prevented from getting into debt again by legal restrictions on his/her business activities in the future.)

   On the other hand, if the working capital ratio is much higher than 2:1 the firm is *undertrading*. It has funds that are lying idle, and is therefore less profitable than it could be.

(c) The *liquid capital* should be adequate, that is, sufficient to pay the current liabilities of the firm. This is the 'acid-test' of a sound firm.

(d) The *return on capital employed* should be good enough to justify the investors' decision to allow the business to use their capital in this way—more than could be earned, for example, in a safe investment without trading risks.

(e) Finally the *return on capital invested* should be adequate, representing a reasonable reward to the proprietor for the effort he/she has put in.

Appraising the figures for Sunshine Boutique, we find the following:

(a) *Fixed assets.* These are valued at $66 600. They seem to be a fairly reasonable mixture. $4 000 of the total represents the goodwill of the business. This is an *intangible asset*: it exists only in the minds of customers, and is not a very satisfactory sort of asset—however, it is not a high proportion of the total fixed assets. The amount of fixed assets that are actually used in the business, $3 600 of fittings and $11 000 of motor vehicles, seems about right for the enterprise. We should need to inspect them to ascertain whether they were adequate.

   On the whole we can feel fairly satisfied, at least *prima facie*, with the fixed assets of Sunshine Boutique.

(b) The *working capital ratio* is 3.2:1. This appears to be sound enough, but it is rather illiquid, as is shown by (c) below.

(c) The *liquid capital ratio* is 0.57:1; this is inadequate, since it should be about 1:1. We may therefore advise the proprietor to improve his position by reducing purchases of stock until his present stocks are cleared, and to do everything possible to improve liquidity by selling off his slow-moving items, preferably for cash.
(d) The *return on capital employed* is 40.3 per cent. This is very good.
(e) The *return on capital invested* seems excellent. If invested in other ways, for example in a building society, the gross return would probably be about 9 per cent, so a profit of 64.8 per cent seems very good indeed. It is usual, however, to take another factor into account as well—the *opportunity cost*, as economists call it. By working in this business Rawlinson has lost other opportunities of employment, and so perhaps has his wife. If the money they could have earned in other employment—say $9000 apiece—is deducted from the $36300, we have a clear profit of $18300, or 32.7 per cent. This is still a very good return on capital invested.

'Flow of Funds' Statements

It sometimes happens that business people who are not too knowledgeable about book-keeping and accounting complain to their accountants that they cannot understand why they are so short of cash when the business has made excellent profits. To them it seems that a business that is making good profits must have plenty of funds available. This is not necessarily so. If the expenses are carefully watched, so that the working expenses are kept as low as possible and the capital expenditure is kept down to safe levels, there is usually enough cash available to meet the needs of the business. If these precautions are not taken, however, financial difficulties will soon become evident.

Or consider the position of a businessman who sells on credit to unreliable customers. Suppose goods costing $1000 are sold for $2000 to A. Slowpayer. The profit is $1000, but when Mr Slowpayer fails to pay at the end of the month the cash position of the business will be adversely affected. The trader must pay the suppliers the $1000 for the goods now in Slowpayer's possession, even though the $2000 that was to yield such a handsome profit is unpaid. The profits are excellent on paper, but a bank overdraft may be needed to keep the business solvent.

In order to demonstrate the source and application of funds it is usual to draw up a *flow of funds statement*. Let us look at an example.

Example

R. Smith, a businessman, points out to you that in the past year he has made excellent profits, yet his bank overdraft has increased. His drawings have been very moderate for such a prosperous business. Where has all the profit gone? Here are his Balance Sheets which record the situation:

Balance Sheets (R. Smith) as at 31 December each year

		Last year		*This year*			*Last year*		*This year*
	$	$	$	$		$	$	$	$
Fixed assets:					Capital		25 000		44 500
Land and buildings		35 000		57 500	Net profit	23 000		28 500	
Fixtures		2 000		3 250	*Less* Drawings	3 500		4 500	
Motor vehicles		1 300		6 000			19 500		24 000
		38 300		66 750			44 500		68 500
Current assets:					Current liabilities:				
Stock	20 000		22 500		Creditors	24 000		21 000	
Debtors	11 000		12 500		Bank				
Cash	200		250		overdraft	1 000		12 500	
		31 200		35 250			25 000		33 500
		$69 500		$102 000			$69 500		$102 000

Flow of Funds Statement

Sources of funds in the current year:	$
Net profit	28 500
Increase in bank overdraft	11 500
	$40 000

Application of these funds:	$
Purchase of extra land and buildings	22 500
Purchase of extra fixtures	1 250
Purchase of extra motor vehicles	4 700
Purchase of extra stock	2 500
Extension of credit to extra debtors	1 500
Extra cash in hand	50
Prompter settlement of creditors	3 000
Drawings	4 500
	$40 000

An alternative way of displaying the same facts to bring out the need for the increased overdraft would be as follows:

Flow of Funds Statement

Activities carried out in current year which required funds:	$
Purchase of extra land and buildings	22 500
Purchase of extra fixtures	1 250
Purchase of extra motor vehicles	4 700
Purchase of extra stock	2 500
Extension of credit to extra debtors	1 500
Extra cash in hand	50
Prompter settlement of creditors	3 000
Drawings	4 500
	40 000
Financed by net profit	28 500
Financed by increased overdraft	$11 500

We have to point out to Smith that although he made $28 500 profit and only drew out $4 500 as drawings to live on, he purchased a lot of extra assets (about $30 000 worth) as well as increasing his debtors and reducing his creditors. Obviously he was overtrading, and he is threatened by financial difficulties as a result.

You should now attempt some of the exercises on the interpretation of Balance Sheets given below.

28.11 Exercises Set 49. Appraising Balance Sheets

1. State from the following Balance Sheet of A. Brewis, showing calculations if necessary:

a) the capital owned by the proprietor on 31 December 20..;
b) the long-term capital employed in the business;
c) the fixed capital of the business;
d) the working capital of the business.

Balance Sheet as at 31 December 20..

	$	$		$	$	$
Fixed assets:			Capital:			
Land and buildings	23000		At start		35000	
Furniture and fittings	4500		*Add* Profit	8550		
Motor vehicles	11000		*Less*			
		38500	Drawings	6000		
					2550	
Current assets:						37550
Stock	12250					
Debtors	3000		Long-term liabilities:			
Balance at bank	4050		Mortgage			18000
Cash in hand	450		Current liabilities:			
		19750	Creditors		2580	
			Wages due		120	
						2700
		$58250				$58250

2. From the following Balance Sheet of R. Hemingway state, showing calculations if necessary:

a) the capital owned by the proprietor on 31 December 20..;
b) the capital employed (long-term) in the business;
c) the fixed capital of the business;
d) the working capital of the business.

Balance Sheet as at 31 December 20..

	$	$		$	$	$
Fixed assets:			Capital:			
Land and buildings	33000		At start		75000	
Furniture and fittings	4500		*Add* Profit	12550		
Motor vehicles	8000		*Less* Drawings	4000		
		45500			8550	
Current assets:						83550
Stock	44300		Long-term liabilities:			
Debtors	4800		Mortgage			15000
Balance at bank	9500		Current liabilities:			
Cash in hand	150		Creditors		5580	
			Rates due		120	
		58750				
						5700
		$104250				$104250

3. The following is the Balance Sheet of Sea Styles Ltd, a manufacturing company:

Balance Sheet as at 31 December 20..

	$		$
Freehold buildings	45000	Share capital	24000
Plant and machinery	10500	Net profit	7000
Stock	8500	7% Debentures	40000
Debtors	9000	Creditors	8000
Bank balance	6000		
	$79000		$79000

You are required to calculate:

a) capital employed (long-term),
b) current assets,
c) current liabilities, and
d) working capital.

4. The following balances remain on the books of Coolbawn Ltd on 31 March 20.. after the Profit and Loss Account to that date has been prepared:

	$
Share capital	100000
Profit and Loss Account	18922
6% Debentures	30000
General Reserve	25000
Freehold at cost	85000
Plant at cost	70600
Provision for Depreciation on Plant	25400
Stock in trade	32147
Debtors	21096
Bank balance in hand	15260
Creditors	24781

You are asked to:

a) prepare the Balance Sheet of Coolbawn Ltd at 31 March 20.. and
b) indicate from the figures in that Balance Sheet the amount of
   (i) the long-term capital employed and
   (ii) the working capital as at 31 March 20...

5. The following balances remain on the books of Holder Ltd on 31 March 20.. after the Profit and Loss Account to that date has been prepared:

	$
Share capital	180000
Profit and Loss Account	28500
7% Debentures	20000
General Reserve	26000
Freehold at cost	95000
Plant at cost	90000
Provision for Depreciation on Plant	20700
Stock in trade	44155
Debtors	26250
Bank balance in hand	30500
Creditors	10705

You are asked to:

a) prepare the Balance Sheet of Holder Ltd at 31 March 20.. and

b) indicate from the figures in that Balance Sheet the amount of

(i) the long-term capital employed and

(ii) the working capital as at 31 March 20...

6. A. Trader considers he could earn at least 8 per cent interest on his capital invested in his business without working for it. Assuming he had $45000 capital in his business on 1 January 20.. and invested a further $4000 on 1 July, what interest could he rightly claim out of profits at the end of the trading year 31 December 20..?

7. On 31 December 20.. the following balances appeared in R.T.'s ledger after preparation of the Trading and Profit and Loss Accounts:

	Dr. $	*Cr.* $
Capital (1 January 20..)		73000
Profit and Loss Account		18800
Drawings	8500	
Trade Debtors	4200	
Trade Creditors		2400
Expenses outstanding		2100
Freehold premises	40000	
Fixtures and fittings	6500	
Motor vans	12800	
Stock in trade	16200	
Cash in hand and balance at bank	8100	
	$96300	$96300

Prepare R.T.'s Balance Sheet to show *within the Balance Sheet*:

a) the total of fixed assets and the total of current assets,

b) the total of current liabilities,

c) the working capital, and

d) the net book value of the assets.

8. a) On 31 December 20.. the following balances appeared in M. Smith's ledger after preparation of the Trading and Profit and Loss Accounts:

	Dr.	*Cr.*
	$	$
Capital (1 January 20..)		71 780
Profit and Loss Account		25 705
Drawings	10 000	
Trade Debtors	3 668	
Trade Creditors		4 946
Expenses outstanding		572
Freehold Premises	45 000	
Fixtures and Fittings	4 150	
Motor Vans	12 340	
Stock in trade	15 610	
Cash in hand and balance at bank	12 235	
	$103 003	$103 003

Prepare Smith's Balance Sheet in such a way as to show within the Balance Sheet:

(i) the total of fixed assets,
(ii) the total of current assets,
(iii) the total of current liabilities,
(iv) the working capital, and
(v) the net book value of the assets.

b) How would the following transactions affect the amount of Smith's capital and the amount of his working capital?

(i) New fittings were purchased on credit for $120.
(ii) $342 was paid to trade creditors, by cheque.
(iii) Stock valued at $130 on 31 December 20.. was sold on credit for $170.
(iv) Trade debtors $76 were written off as bad debts.
(v) Smith withdrew $300 from the bank for private purposes.
(vi) Motor vans were depreciated by $470.

You are to present your answer in the following form:

Item	*Effect on capital*	*Effect on working capital*
(i)		
(ii)		
(iii)		

and so on.

Indicate an increase by the sign + and the amount, and a decrease by the sign − and the amount. If there is no effect write the words 'no effect'.

9. Malcolm Peters is puzzled because his business appears to be making good profits yet he is always short of cash to meet end-of-month requirements. With the help of the Balance Sheets presented below you are asked

a) to prepare for him a cash flow statement which explains his present position, and

b) to suggest to him how he can overcome the situation in the months ahead.

Balance Sheet as at 31 December each year

	$	*Previous year* $	$	*Current year* $
Fixed assets:				
Land		35 000		48 000
Fittings		3 600		4 000
Motor vans		5 650		6 550
		44 250		58 550
Current assets:				
Stock	8 250		8 350	
Debtors	1 550		5 750	
Bank	1 850		–	
Cash	150	11 800	50	14 150
		$56 050		$72 700

	$	*Previous year* $	$	*Current year* $
Capital:				
At start		50 000		55 500
Add Net profit	13 800		13 900	
Less Drawings	8 300	5 500	11 800	2 100
		55 500		57 600
Current liabilities:				
Creditors	550		2 850	
Overdraft	–	550	12 250	15 100
		$56 050		$72 700

10. John Wooding is puzzled because his business appears to be making good profits yet he is always short of cash to meet end-of-month requirements. The Balance Sheets presented below explain his situation. You are asked

a) to prepare for him a cash flow statement which explains the shortage of cash, and

b) to suggest to him how he can overcome the situation in the months ahead.

Balance Sheet as at 31 December each year

	$	*Previous year* $	$	*Current year* $
Fixed assets:				
Land and buildings		47 000		65 000
Fittings		4 500		12 500
Motor vans		11 000		13 800
		62 500		91 300
Current assets:				
Stock	11 000		7 950	
Debtors	1 500		4 800	
Cash	150	12 650	250	13 000
		$75 150		$104 300

	$	*Previous year* $	$	*Current year* $
Capital:				
At start		67 000		72 200
Add Net profit	14 000		16 500	
Less Drawings	8 800	5 200	15 500	1 000
		72 200		73 200
Long-term liability:				
Mortgage		–		18 000
Current liabilities:				
Creditors	2 500		3 300	
Overdraft	450	2 950	9 800	13 100
		$75 150		$104 300

28.12 Revise and Test 28A. Interpreting Final Accounts

Answers	*Questions*
—	**1.** What can we learn from the Final Accounts of a business?
1. If it is a profitable business; if it has any weak spots; how it compares with similar businesses.	**2.** As far as the Trading Account is concerned what are the chief figures revealed about the business?
2. a) The net turnover; b) the gross profit percentage; c) the rate of stock turnover.	**3.** What is the net turnover?
3. The Sales figure, less any sales returns. It is the total trading earnings, out of which all purchases, overhead expenses and profits have to be recovered.	**4.** What is the gross profit percentage?
4. A figure which shows how much of our turnover figure is profit. It is found by the formula: $\frac{\textit{Gross Profit}}{\textit{Turnover}} \times 100$	**5.** What is the chief point about the gross profit percentage?
5. It should be a constant (the same year after year) unless something is at work to change it. So if it is 45% one year and 39% the next year something has gone wrong. The question is what?	**6.** List some things that could have gone wrong.
6. a) The manager is stealing the takings; b) the staff are stealing stock; c) bad buying is leading to waste—groceries going bad, fruit rotting, garments not selling as well as hoped; d) price rises by our suppliers not being passed on to customers.	**7.** Why is the rate of stock turnover important?

7. Because every time stock turns over we make a profit. Sell one motorcycle, one lot of profit; sell 100 motorcycles 100 lots of profit.	**8.** What is the formula for finding the rate of stock turnover?
8. $\frac{\textit{Cost of Stock sold (sales at cost price)}}{\textit{Average stock at cost price}}$ Example: Cost of stock sold = \$90 000 Average stock at Cost Price = \$18 000 Rate of stock turn = $\frac{\$90\,000}{\$18\,000}$ = 5 times	**9.** If stock turns over 5 times in a year how long is an average item in stock? (Give the answer in weeks).
9. $\frac{52}{5}$ = 10.4 weeks (all right for furniture, no good for groceries, or newspapers or meat).	**10.** What is net profit percentage?
10. A figure that tells us how much of our turnover is net profit.	**11.** How do we find it?
11. $\frac{\textit{Net Profit}}{\textit{Turnover}} \times 100$	**12.** What is important about the net profit percentage?
12. It should be constant (the same from year to year), unless something is causing it to change.	**13.** What could cause it to fall. (You may assume the gross profit percentage is all right.)
13. Overheads have risen and not been passed on as increased prices. Profits earned last year have not been received this year (such as rent received).	**14.** How can we check on these things?
14. Take out expense ratios on this year's and last year's expenses: $\frac{\textit{expense}}{\textit{turnover}} \times 100$ If the expense ratio has risen in the year we must do what we can to reduce it in the year ahead, or pass on the increase to our customers in raised prices.	**15.** Go over the page again until you are sure of all the answers.

28.13 Revise and Test 28B. Interpreting Balance Sheets

Answers	*Questions*
—	**1.** What is a Balance Sheet?
1. It is a snapshot picture of the financial affairs of a business at a given moment in time (usually 23:59 hours on the last day of the financial year).	**2.** What can we tell from the Balance Sheet?
2. a) The working capital and the liquid capital available (which tells us if the company's current situation is sound); b) the return on capital employed and the return on capital invested.	**3.** Thinking about the assets side of a Balance Sheet, what does it usually show?
3. a) The fixed assets, shown at cost less depreciation to date, to give a net value; b) there may be some trade investments in subsidiary companies. These are assets which are neither fixed nor current; c) then we get the current assets and deduct from them the current liabilities (to show us the net working capital); d) finally the total figure is labelled 'net assets'.	**4.** What is working capital exactly?
4. It is the money left over, after buying the fixed assets and any trade investments. This is what we have left to work the business (i.e. engage in normal trading).	**5.** What can you tell us about the working capital ratio?

5. You find it by the formula:

$$\frac{\textit{Current assets}}{\textit{Current liabilities}}$$

This should work out to at least 2:1. This means the trader is able to pay the current liabilities twice over.

6. What is the liquid capital?

---

6. It is the total of the current assets which are in cash or near cash form (usually found by current assets—stock in hand). The ratio is (*Current assets – stock*) : *current liabilities*.

7. What is the point about the liquid capital ratio (often called the acid-test ratio)?

---

7. It should be at least 1:1 (i.e. the trader can pay debts in full).

8. What is capital employed?

---

8. Capital employed is the total capital used in the business. For a firm it is capital at start of year + profits retained in the business + long-term loans and mortgages.
For companies it is capital from ordinary shares + preference shares + reserves + debentures and other long-term loans.

9. What return should we hope for on capital employed? What is the formula to find the return?

---

9. We should hope for a better return than we could get from investment of the capital employed in another way, such as savings or a balanced portfolio of shares.
The formula is:

$$\text{ROCE} = \frac{\textit{Net profit} + \textit{Interest paid on loans \& mortgage}}{\textit{Capital employed}} \times 100$$

10. What is capital invested?

---

10. It is the actual capital invested by a proprietor—made up of the capital at the start of the year.

11. What is the formula for the return on capital invested (ROCI)?

11. $\frac{\textit{Net Profit}}{\textit{Capital at start of year}} \times 100$	**12.** But what must we remember?
12. The proprietor has worked in the business for one year and has had his/her capital tied up. We should therefore deduct these 'opportunity costs' to get the real return on the business. $\frac{\textit{Net Profit} - \textit{Opportunity Costs}}{\textit{Capital at start of year}} \times 100$	**13.** Go over the main text again if you are not sure of any of these answers.

UNIT 29

Departmental Accounts

29.1 A Business with Several Departments

There has been a tendency in recent years for businesses to grow in size, as large-scale enterprises have many advantages. Growth usually results in a departmental organization of some sort, and in many businesses, particularly wholesale and retail trade, different qualities and experience are required for each department. Thus a buyer of carpets will have very different experience from that of a buyer of groceries. It follows that the respective chief buyers will regard their own special fields as of paramount importance, and will have to be controlled if they exceed their authorities and destroy the 'balance' of the business.

Departments can be controlled by budgetary methods (see Unit 28.1). The system anticipates the expenditure, growth and so on of each department and prepares a budget of future performance which can be compared with actual performance to show whether the department concerned is reaching, exceeding or failing to achieve expectations. Budgetary control is one of the more advanced accounting techniques.

Departmental accounts are more routine—they endeavour to compare the performance of each department with those of others, in such matters as the gross profit percentage achieved, the net profit percentage achieved, and the expense ratios to turnover. It might, for example, be found that while the groceries department made a steady profit, the fruit and vegetable department frequently made a loss. This would indicate either that this department should be closed down, or that a drastic revision of its activities should be undertaken.

29.2 Figures for Departmental Accounts

If departmental Trading Accounts and Profit and Loss Accounts are to be prepared, the basic figures required must be obtained by a rearrangement of procedures. For example, analytical day books and cash books will be needed so that extra columns are available to collect figures for each department. Mechanized and computerized accounting systems use codes to distinguish the expenditure of one department from another. You can see this procedure for yourself the next time you visit a supermarket. Against every item on your till receipt you will find a code number telling the management whether the item is groceries, meat, fruit and vegetables or toiletries.

Analysis of the till records will reveal the total sales for each department, analysis of the invoices from suppliers will reveal the departmental purchases, while expenses will be similarly allocated to the department responsible. Some expenses (the indirect expenses or overhead expenses) cannot be directly allocated to any one department, and some logical basis must be found for their allocation between some or all of the departments of the business. For example, lighting expenses might be allocated on the basis of counter space occupied by the department, and general advertising expenses on the basis of departmental sales.

These rearrangements will make available the figures necessary for the preparation of departmental accounts of the type shown in Fig. 29.1. The layout with which you are already familiar is simply continued into the analysis columns, the cross-totting of which produces figures for the whole business. With computerized accounts it is extremely easy to take out departmental accounts. Purchases, sales, returns and overheads for each department can be collected by means of codes which alert the computer to the need to keep these figures separate for the departments concerned, and hence the achievements of each department can be studied.

29.3 A Comparison of Departments

From Fig. 29.1 it is possible to compare the departments, and the following statistics may be derived.

	Gross profit %	Net profit %
Department A	25.2	12.5
Department B	41.7	25.7
Whole firm	33.1	18.8

It is difficult to draw any real conclusions from these figures without actually knowing the business concerned. For example, it is clear that Department B is very much more profitable than Department A, and one might feel tempted to suggest that Department B should be expanded and Department A contracted. In real life this might be quite impossible. For example Department A might be selling essentials like groceries and might be attracting many customers into the shop. By contrast Department B, selling furniture and furnishings, might be saturating the demand of the neighbourhood and incapable of expansion.

Other figures seem to need investigation; for example Department B, with a smaller turnover, has higher advertising and 'general expenses'. It would be interesting to discover why, by analysing these expenditures.

You should now try one or two of these simple exercises in departmental accounts.

Departmental Trading and Profit and Loss Account for the year ending 31 December 20..

Date		*Dept. A.*		*Dept. B*		*Total*		Date		*Dept. A*	*Dept. B*	*Total*
20..		$	$	$	$	$	$	20..		$	$	$
31 Dec.	Opening stock		18400		12300		30700	31 Dec.	Sales	207250	188360	395610
	Purchases	128462		91784		220246			*Less* Returns in	1250	1360	2610
	Less Returns	1462		1784		3246						
			127000		90000		217000		Net turnover	206000	187000	393000
	Total stock available		145400		102300		247700					
	Less Closing stock		15840		11150		26990					
	Cost of stock sold		129560		91150		220710					
	Wages		24440		17850		42290					
	Cost of sales		154000		109000		263000					
	Gross profit		52000		78000		130000					
			$206000		$187000		$393000			$206000	$187000	$393000
20.			$		$		$	20..		$	$	$
31 Dec.	Salaries		23184		24750		47934	31 Dec.	Gross profit	52000	78000	130000
	Light and heat		1240		1160		2400		Rent received	1500	1300	2800
	General expenses		2026		3190		5216					
	Advertising		1300		2200		3500			53500	79300	132800
	Total		27750		31300		59050					
	Net profit		25750		48000		73750					
			$53500		$79300		$132800			$53500	$79300	$132800

Fig. 29.1 A departmental Trading and Profit and Loss Account

29.4 Exercises Set 50. Departmental Accounts

1. Prepare a departmental Trading Account from the following accounts in R. Rogers' books for the year ending 31 December 20... Calculate the gross profit on each department and on the business as a whole.

	Dept. A	*Dept. B*
Opening stocks	12 800	13 860
Purchases	45 290	127 420
Sales	80 234	241 040
Carriage In	1 144	1 142
Returns In	1 300	1 400
Returns Out	1 460	1 280
Closing stock	11 840	11 540
Wages	12 000	23 040

2. Prepare a departmental Trading and Profit and Loss Account from the following information from the books of V. Bartlett at 31 December 20..:

	Dept. A	*Dept. B*
Opening stocks	13 800	13 210
Purchases	127 000	115 000
Sales	255 000	207 000
Returns Out	2 450	1 230
Returns In	2 950	1 260
Closing stocks	12 500	12 650
Salaries	33 500	32 200
Warehouse Wages	14 850	12 700
Rent and Rates	2 320	2 180
Sundry Expenses	4 730	5 530

Calculate the gross profit and net profit percentages for each department, and for the business as a whole (correct to one decimal place).

3. Tinseltown Ltd is a large departmental store and the following figures appear in their books for the year ended 31 December 20..:

	$
Sales:	
Dept. A	521 400
Dept. B	533 600
Dept. C	424 800
Dept. D	418 600
Purchases:	
Dept. A	216 900
Dept. B	224 700
Dept. C	222 100
Dept. D	214 900
Stock, 1 January:	
Dept. A	32 940
Dept. B	33 760
Dept. C	44 100
Dept. D	31 670

Stock, 31 December:	
Dept. A	43 490
Dept. B	31 900
Dept. C	32 880
Dept. D	41 760

You find that purchases for Department D costing $4000 have been debited against Department C and that sales for $400 for Department A have been credited to Department B.

You are asked to prepare a departmental trading account in columnar form after making the adjustments for the wrongly analysed items. You should calculate the gross profit percentage for each department.

4. Style Furnishings Ltd is a large departmental store and the following figures appear in their books for the year ended 31 December 20..:

	$
Sales:	
Dept. A	778 000
Dept. B	666 000
Dept. C	758 000
Dept. D	512 000
Purchases:	
Dept. A	342 000
Dept. B	231 000
Dept. C	327 000
Dept. D	211 000
Stock, 1 January:	
Dept. A	35 950
Dept. B	37 280
Dept. C	28 640
Dept. D	42 150
Stock, 31 December:	
Dept. A	37 120
Dept. B	43 380
Dept. C	37 250
Dept. D	36 540

You find that purchases for Department C costing $850 have been debited against Department A and that sales for $800 for Department D have been credited to Department B.

You are asked to prepare a departmental Trading Account in columnar form after making the adjustments for the wrongly analysed items. You should calculate the gross profit percentage for each department correct to one decimal place.

29.5 Revise and Test 29. Departmental Accounts

Answers	*Questions*
—	**1.** What is the point of preparing Departmental Accounts?
1. It enables the accountant to compare the activity in the various departments and the profitability of various parts of the business.	**2.** How do we prepare these accounts?
2. We keep analysed records of purchases, sales, etc. so we can see which purchases, for example, are being issued to each department, and which takings are being earned by each department. We then draw up final accounts showing the profitability of each department.	**3.** How do we allocate expenses between departments where there is only one general bill for the whole firm?
3. In some fair way, depending on the facts. For example a) the floor space occupied; b) the number of employees in the department; or c) the number of machines (using the power, etc.).	**4.** What use can be made of this information?
4. We might adjust the business arrangements (e.g. give more floorspace etc. to the more successful products or services).	**5.** What about the weaker departments?
5. a) We might decide to close them down; b) we might increase their advertising budget or do special promotions about them; c) we might develop new products in these areas to increase turnover.	**6.** Go over the page again if necessary.

UNIT 30

Control Accounts

30.1 The Need for Control Accounts

Control accounts, as their name implies, seek to give management control over some aspect of a business. There are many types of control account, and in this book it is only possible to illustrate some of the simplest, in particular Debtors and Creditors Control Accounts.

In order to understand these, you must first understand why they are necessary. The reason is that the sub-division of the ledger, as business has grown more complex, has enabled management to delegate the posting of ledgers to less experienced employees. Control accounts are designed to check on the work of these employees and to ensure that errors are discovered.

Where accounts are maintained by computer, both a control account, and a printout of any disparity between the ledger itself and the control account, are prepared automatically. The principles are, however, exactly the same as those described below for use in manual accounting.

30.2 The Sub-division of the Ledger

When the work of keeping the ledger became too great for a single counting-house clerk, the ledger had to be sub-divided into sections each of which would provide employment for an individual clerk. First the *cash book* was introduced, with the cashier in charge of it. For security reasons the private accounts were removed into a *Private Ledger*, kept either by the proprietor personally or by the accountant. The very numerous debtors' accounts were removed into separate *Debtors Ledgers*. Later these were mechanized into a card system operated by junior typists. (Today they are frequently computerized, but many small firms still employ simultaneous systems using ledger cards.) The less numerous creditors' accounts were then removed into loose-leaf *Creditors Ledger* systems which again were kept by junior staff. This left the *General Ledger*, containing the nominal accounts (losses and profits of the business) and the real accounts (assets of the business). This ledger was usually kept by a chief accounts clerk, whose responsibilities included the preparation of the Trial Balance.

30.3 Getting the Trial Balance to Agree

Fig. 30.1 shows the sub-division of the ledger of a typical medium to large firm, and the staff in charge of each section. If we list the staff concerned and the accounts they keep, it is easy to see where mistakes might occur.

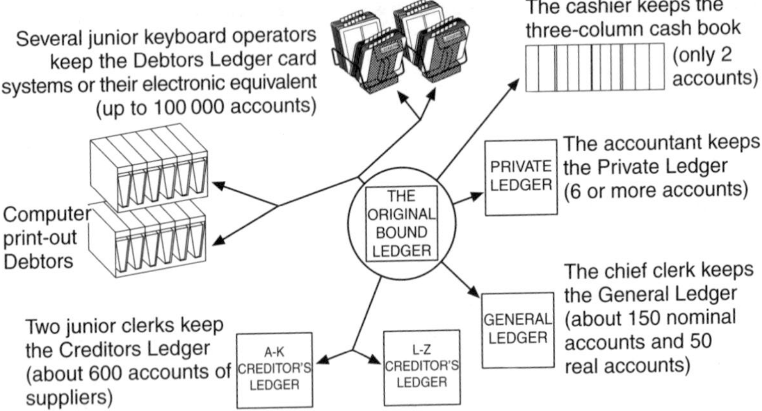
Several junior keyboard operators keep the Debtors Ledger card systems or their electronic equivalent (up to 100 000 accounts)
The cashier keeps the three-column cash book
(only 2 accounts)
PRIVATE LEDGER
The accountant keeps the Private Ledger (6 or more accounts)
Computer print-out Debtors
THE ORIGINAL BOUND LEDGER
The chief clerk keeps the General Ledger (about 150 nominal accounts and 50 real accounts)
GENERAL LEDGER
Two junior clerks keep the Creditors Ledger (about 600 accounts of suppliers)
A-K CREDITOR'S LEDGER
L-Z CREDITOR'S LEDGER

Fig. 30.1 The sub-division of the ledger

Staff	*Duties*	*Accounts kept*
Cashier	Three-column cash book	2 (Cash Account and Bank Account)
Accountant	Private Ledger	6 or more, depending on the number of partners (Capital Accounts, Current Accounts, Drawings Accounts)
Chief clerk	General Ledger	200 nominal accounts and real accounts
Junior clerks	Creditors Ledger	600–1 000 creditors' accounts
	Debtors Ledger	Up to 100 000 debtors' accounts

If the Trial Balance fails to agree it is likely that the mistake lies with the junior staff, especially as they have many accounts to keep. For this reason control accounts are used to check on the Debtors Ledgers and Creditors Ledgers—one for each sub-division if there are several. Thus an A–E Debtors Ledger would be controlled by an A–E Debtors Control Account.

Each control account will represent exactly the complete ledger section kept by a junior employee, whose work will thus be proved to be right before it is included in the Trial Balance. The accountant, or the chief clerk, will prepare the control accounts from figures obtained from the subsidiary books, and without direct reference to the sources used by the office junior. For example, the A–E Debtors Ledger is prepared from 'posting media', such as sales invoices, credit notes and statements. The A–E Debtors Control Account is prepared from *total figures* obtained from the subsidiary books, without reference to the posting media. Once the total of the book has been found to agree with the control account the junior in charge of the book can be praised for a creditable performance, and its figures can be included in the Trial Balance. This method is often called *sectional balancing*.

30.4 Preparing a Control Account

When drawing up a control account the clerk has to prepare, on a single page, an exact replica of the entire section of the ledger being kept by each junior accounts clerk or accounting machine operator. Consider, for instance, the types of entry made by the junior keeping the F–K Debtors Ledger. The first account in the ledger card system is A. Farr's Account; this account is shown below, with the F–K Control Account immediately following.

A. Farr Account DL171

20..		$	20..		$
1 July Balance	B/d	127.50	3 July Bank	CB17	121.12
9 July Sales	SDB5	68.60	3 July Discount Allowed	CB17	4.13
14 July Sales	SDB6	174.75	14 July Contra	J21	2.25
27 July Sales	SDB9	38.50	17 July Returns	SRB3	15.00
			31 July Balance	c/d	266.85
		$409.35			$409.35
1 Aug. Balance	B/d	266.85			

F–K Debtors Ledger Control Account CL29

20..		$	20..		$
1 July Balances	B/d	17254.50	1 July Balances	B/d	84.50
31 July Sales	SDB11	8572.65	31 July Bank	CB29	15175.65
31 July Carriage	J9	708.00	31 July Contras	J11	422.50
31 July Dishonoured cheques	J12	76.30	31 July Returns	SRB7	202.80
31 July Balances	c/d	28.50	31 July Bad Debts	J13	127.65
			31 July Motor Vehicles	J15	540.00
			31 July Balances	c/d	10086.85
		$26639.95			$26639.95
20..		$	20..		$
1 Aug. Balances	B/d	10086.85	1 Aug. Balances	B/d	28.50

Notes:

(i) In the Debtors Ledger we expect to have a large number of debit balances. In this example the total debit balances on the F–K section on 1 July were $17254.50.

(ii) We also find on control accounts that there is often a credit balance too. This means that somewhere in the ledger there is one account, or perhaps more, that bears a credit balance for some reason. This may be because the debtor, having paid for goods, then finds there is some reason for returning them. He/she becomes temporarily a creditor instead of a debtor. The existence of this credit is recognized on the control account.

(iii) On the debit side of the control account appear those items—in total—which appear as individual postings on the debit side of the customers' accounts. These figures will have been obtained from analysis columns in the books referred to in the folio column. For example, the sales figure will have come from the F–K analysis column of the Sales Day Book. An analytical day book of this sort is shown in Fig. 19.1. The 'carriage' and 'dishonoured cheques' figures will have come from the Journal Proper. Since there are very few such items it is usual to analyse them off by turning over the few pages of the Journal for the month, making a note of any items affecting the F–K ledger.

(iv) On the credit side of the control account appear those items which normally appear on the credit side of the customer's account. These figures will have been obtained from analysis columns in the cash book (see Fig. 19.2) and Sales Returns Book, or from direct analysis of the Journal, while in firms using mechanized or computerized accounting the figures will be collected in registers or data storage devices. The entry 'contras' is explained in Unit 30.5.

(v) The final balances represent the total F–K debtors' balances. The junior accounts clerk or typist keeping this part of the ledger should find that when the ledger cards are totalled they agree with the control account. If they do, the total debtors' figure is put into the Trial Balance.

(vi) Comparison of these two accounts thus shows that the control account imitates the ordinary ledger account of any debtor, but has entries in it to cover every possible type of entry made in the previous month, since these are sure to have occurred on at least one account in the ledger.

Examination Work on Control Accounts

Because the preparation of a control account is an excellent test of a student's ability, it is often required by examiners. The student is given information referring to either a Debtors Ledger or a Creditors Ledger, and is asked to draw up a control account. This information will have been derived from the appropriate records in analytical Sales Day Books, Purchases Day Books, cash books and so on. An example of this type of exercise is given below.

Example

Tom Jones keeps his Creditors Ledger controlled by drawing up monthly a Creditors Ledger Control Account in two parts A–K and L–Z. The following figures are available at 31 January 20.., when there is a difference on the Trial Balance of $1 000.

		A–K	*L–Z*
		$	$
1 Jan.	Balances on Creditors Ledger (credit side)	4 200	1 800
1 Jan.	Balances on Creditors Ledger (debit side)	25	42
1–31 Jan.	Purchases	7 256	3 686
1–31 Jan.	Returns	500	326
1–31 Jan.	Sundry charges by suppliers	100	22
1–31 Jan.	Cheques paid to suppliers	3 990	1 710
1–31 Jan.	Discount received from suppliers	210	90
31 Jan.	Balances carried down to debit side	25	16

The book-keeper in charge of the A–K ledger makes his accounts total $7856 while the clerk in charge of the L–Z ledger makes his ledger balances total $3356. Draw up the two control accounts and draw any conclusion you can from them.

Preparing the two accounts we find the following situation:

Creditors Ledger Control Account A–K

20..			$	20..			$
1 Jan.	Balances	B/d	25	1 Jan.	Balances	B/d	4 200
1–31 Jan.	Returns		500	1–31 Jan.	Purchases		7 256
1–31 Jan.	Bank		3 990	1–31 Jan.	Sundry charges		100
1–31 Jan.	Discount received		210	31 Jan.	Balances	c/d	25
31 Jan.	Balance	c/d	6 856				
			$11 581				$11 581
20..			$	20..			$
1 Feb.	Balance	B/d	25	1 Feb.	Balance	B/d	6 856

Creditors Ledger Control Account L–Z

20..			$	20..			$
1 Jan.	Balances	B/d	42	1 Jan.	Balances	B/d	1 800
1–31 Jan.	Returns		326	1–31 Jan.	Purchases		3 686
1–31 Jan.	Bank		1 710	1–31 Jan.	Sundry charges		22
1–31 Jan.	Discount received		90	31 Jan.	Balances	c/d	16
31 Jan.	Balances	c/d	3 356				
			$5 524				$5 524
20.			$	20.			$
1 Feb.	Balances	B/d	16	1 Feb.	Balances	B/d	3 356

The control accounts reveal that there is a difference of $1 000 between the control account for the A–K ledger and the totals discovered by the book-keeper in charge of that ledger. The L–Z ledger seems to be correct. The next thing to do is obviously to check the ledger entries in the A–K ledger very carefully. Almost certainly it is an adding-up mistake—it nearly always is when the error is $1, $10, $100 or $1 000.

30.5 Contra Accounts in the Ledger

When the ledger is sub-divided it often happens that a firm will appear in two sections of the ledger, as a debtor in the Debtors Ledger and as a Creditor in the Creditors Ledger. It means that we have dealings with this firm in both capacities—selling to it and buying from it. Keeping two accounts in this way is the most convenient method, since the two sets of ledgers may be in quite different parts of the building. At the end of the month, the smaller account will be set off against the larger account, and the words '*per contra*' or '*contra*' written to explain that an 'opposite' account is being cancelled out by this entry. This is a rather different kind of 'contra entry' from the type you are familiar with in the three-column cash book (see Unit 10.2).

30.6 Other Names for the Control Account

Control accounts are often called by other names. Sometimes they are called *total accounts* or *adjustment accounts*, and sometimes the system is called the *self-balancing ledger system*. Each of these names is simply a variation on control accounts, and you should treat any mention of them in an exercise as referring to the control account system described in this Unit.

A special kind of total or control account is used with hire purchase accounts. Here a single control account represents the hire purchase debtors in the General Ledger. The customers' individual accounts are kept separately and are called *memorandum accounts*. The system avoids a multiplicity of trivial accounts in the General Ledger.

30.7 The Control Account which is Wrong

The purpose of any control account is to discover mistakes in the work of junior members of staff. It is therefore very regrettable if the control account is itself incorrectly prepared, since it may mean that staff are kept behind because their ledgers do not balance when in fact the accountant is at fault. To save loss of face, the young accountant should be particularly careful in the preparation of control accounts, and should approach the discovery of errors in a set of ledgers in a friendly and conciliatory way. Until the books agree it is never absolutely safe to say where the error lies.

30.8 Exercises Set 51. Control Accounts

1. R. Martin maintains a system of self-checking ledgers. You are asked to prepare the Sales Ledger Control Account from the following figures:

	$
Debit balances, 1 January 20..	35 850
Credit balance, 1 January 20..	127
Sales	38 560
Cash received from customers	29 726
Discount allowed	743
Returns and allowances	1 026
Bad debts	154
Credit balance, 31 January 20..	36

2. Cyberview Ltd maintain a system of self-checking ledgers. You are asked to prepare the Sales Ledger Control Account from the following figures:

	$
Debit balances, 1 January 20..	34 296
Credit balance, 1 January 20..	26
Sales	51 264
Cash received from customers	28 629
Discount allowed	824
Returns and allowances	968
Bad debts	426
Credit balance, 31 January 20..	32

3. J. Peters keeps several Sales Ledgers and a Purchases Ledger. From the following details relating to his No. 1 Debtors and his Creditors, write up Peters' Sales Ledger No. 1 Control Account and the Purchases Ledger Control Account for the month of November 20..:

20..		$
1 November	Balance of Sales Ledger No 1 Control Account	2 670
	Balance of Purchases Ledger Control Account	4 140
30 November	Sales for month (No. 1 A/c)	12 890
	Purchases for month	8 960
	Receipts from debtors (No. 1 A/c)	6 405
	Payments to creditors	8 920
	Discounts allowed (No. 1 A/c)	625
	Discounts received	495
	Sales returns (No. 1 A/c)	265
	Purchases returns	145
	Transfer of a debit balance from the Purchases Ledger to Sales Ledger No. 1	120

4. L. Morris keeps several Sales Ledgers and a Purchases Ledger. From the following details relating to his No. 1 Debtors and his Creditors write up Morris's Sales Ledger No. 1 Control Account and the Purchases Ledger Control Account for the month of November 20..:

20..		$
1 November	Balance of Sales Ledger Account No. 1	3875
	Balance of Purchases Ledger Control Account	4182
30 November	Sales for month (No. 1 A/c)	8525
	Purchases for month	4395
	Receipts from debtors (No. 1 A/c)	3650
	Payments to creditors	3973
	Discounts allowed (No. 1 A/c)	91
	Discounts received	209
	Sales returns (No. 1 A/c)	127
	Purchases returns	382
	Transfer of a credit balance from the Purchases Ledger to Sales Ledger No. 1	36

5. a) S. Hardy keeps a Sales Ledger, a Purchases Ledger and a General Ledger. What kind of accounts would you expect to find in each of these ledgers?

b) In which ledger would the following accounts appear?
F. J. Doe, a supplier of Hardy's stock in trade
R. T. Ray, a customer
Sales Account
Stock Account

c) On 1 May 20.. Ray's Account had a debit balance of $329. On 10 May Hardy received payment of this amount by cheque and sold goods on credit to Ray $189. On 20 May Ray was allowed $17 on the goods sold to him on 10 May.

Prepare Ray's Account as it would appear on 31 May 20.. and balance it as at that date.

d) Hardy keeps a Sales Ledger Control Account and a Purchases Ledger Control Account. From the following details relating to the month of May 20.. draw up these accounts as they would appear on 31 May 20.. and balance them as at that date:

	$
Balances at 1 May 20..:	
Sales Ledger Control Account	3107
Purchases Ledger Control Account	4201
Sales on credit	13406
Receipts from trade debtors	2905
Sales returns and allowances	446
Purchases on credit	6803
Payments to trade creditors	3800
Discounts allowed	175
Discounts received	210
Bad debts	36

6. L. Martin keeps a Sales Ledger Control Account and a Purchases Ledger Control Account. From the following details relating to May 20.., draw up these accounts as they would appear on 31 May 20.. and balance them as at that date:

	$
Balances at 1 May 20..:	
Sales Ledger Control Account	4206
Purchases Ledger Control Account	5107
Sales on credit	13815
Receipts from trade debtors	4101
Sales returns and allowances	386
Purchases on credit	6258
Payments to trade creditors	4680
Discounts allowed	105
Discounts received	120
Bad debts	136

7. These figures are taken from the books of D. Badger for January 20..:

	$
Sales Ledger balances (*Dr.*), 1 January 20..	7249
Sales Ledger balances (*Cr.*), 1 January 20..	62
Sales	81296
Amounts received from customers and lodged at the bank (including the relodging of a cheque for $39 returned by the bank)	76424
Returns and allowances	1291
Discount allowed	3468
Bad debts written off	421
Sales Ledger balances (*Cr.*), 31 January 20..	149

You are asked to prepare a Sales Ledger Control Account for the month.

8. There is a difference in the balances on the books for Clover Ltd. In an attempt to locate the difference, total accounts for the Purchases and Sales Ledgers are prepared from the following figures:

20..		$
1 January	Balances on Purchases Ledger	40921
1 January	Balances on Sales Ledger	50420
31 January	Purchases during month	498216
31 January	Sales during month	628421
31 January	Discounts received	8289
31 January	Discounts allowed	10498
31 January	Purchases returns during month	825
31 January	Sales returns during month	1422
31 January	Bad debts written off	623
31 January	Cash paid to suppliers	456227
31 January	Cash received from customers	582989

Prepare the total accounts. The Purchases Ledger balances total $73976 and the Sales Ledger balances total $83309. What conclusions do you draw?

9. From the following particulars prepare
a) the Bought Ledger Control Account, and
b) the Sales Ledger Control Account for January, for Colvin and Hodge:

	$
Purchases	19000
Sales	40000
Total Creditors balance on 1 January	7000
Total Debtors balance on 1 January	6000
Discounts received	210
Discounts allowed	400
Returns outwards	20
Returns inwards	300
Cash paid	16000
Cash received	35000
Bad Debts written off	500

You are now told the following facts:

(i) The Trial Balance for Colvin and Hodge fails to agree by $820.50.
(ii) The book-keeper keeping the Sales Ledger on a card index system makes the debtors' account balances total $9800.
(iii) The book-keeper who keeps the Creditors Ledger lists the balances on the creditors' accounts and finds that altogether they total $9770.

What conclusion do you draw about the error on the Trial Balance?

30.9 Revise and Test 30. Control Accounts

Answers	*Questions*
—	**1.** What are Control Accounts?
1. Accounts which check on the accuracy of a section of the book-keeping, to see that the work has been done properly.	**2.** Which parts of the business accounts can be checked in this way?
2. The Debtors Ledger and the Creditors Ledger where a business has many accounts (more than can be managed by one employee).	**3.** What other names are given to the Control Account?
3. Sometimes they are called Total Accounts. Sometimes they are called Adjustment Accounts. The system is also called 'Self-balancing Ledgers'.	**4.** What do we actually do?
4. Each time we post a batch of invoices etc. to the ledger we enter the individual invoices in the accounts of the debtors (or creditors) but we also enter the total for the batch in a special Control Account, kept at the back of that section of the Ledger. It is these totals that give us the name Total Accounts.	**5.** Thinking of, say, the Debtors Ledger, what totals would get entered during any given month of the year?
5. a) The balances brought down from last month. There would be a big total of all the debtors still owing money, on the debit side of the account; b) in any section of the ledger we might have one or two debtors to whom we owed money. So there could be a small credit balance coming down from last month;	

c) the total of the Sales invoices sent to debtors in the month, coming from the Sales Day Book— a debit entry;
d) the total of the Credit Notes sent to debtors who had returned goods—a credit entry;
e) the total cash received from debtors who had paid their debts in the month—a credit entry (the debit entry would be in the Cash Book);
f) the total discount allowed to debtors—a credit entry (the debit entry would be in the Discount Allowed Account—one of the losses of the business);
g) there might even be the odd Journal Entry for a bad debt written off.

6. What would be the final effect of these entries at the end of the month?

---

6. The total of the Control Account (a large debit figure and a small credit balance, if any), would be the same as the total of the individual ledger accounts of all the debtors. If it is, we know the book-keeping is correct.

7. And if it isn't?

---

7. We have to look for the error.

8. Explain about Adjustment Accounts.

8. Sometimes the accountant puts the Control Account in his/her General Ledger and puts a mirror image of it (everything on the wrong side) in the back of the book-keeper's ledger. So now, if everything works out correctly:

a) the book-keeper will have a self-balancing ledger (because the last page has all the entries on the wrong side and makes the book balance) while

b) the accountant has an Adjustment Account in his/her general ledger which represents that section of the Debtors' Ledger all on one page, ready to go on the Trial Balance at the end of the month.

9. If you are at all doubtful about this go back and work through one or two of the exercises in Unit 30 again.

UNIT 31

Amalgamations

31.1 What is an Amalgamation?

An *amalgamation* is a joining together of two businesses. It usually results in more efficient operations, because *economies of large scale* can be achieved. There are many such economies—administrative, financial, marketing and so forth. For example, a sole trader who wishes to take a brief holiday may have to employ a qualified manager to take his/her place, and a reliable person may demand a sizeable salary for such a short assignment. If the sole trader amalgamates with another sole trader one will be able to take care of the joint enterprise while the other is away, in return for similar services later when he or she in turn needs a vacation. Advertising may be beneficial to both parties, and hence more economical, while the joint properties may provide better security for bank loans or overdrafts, making them easier to obtain.

In this Unit we shall look at the accounting problems of amalgamation.

31.2 Arrangements Between the Parties

Clearly both parties in a proposed amalgamation will have some existing assets and liabilities which could be set out in a Balance Sheet or Statement of Affairs at the date of amalgamation. This existing condition may, or may not, be mutually acceptable to the two people concerned. Usually some adjustments are made to one, or both, of the Balance Sheets to take account of objections raised by the other party. One may feel that the other's motor vehicles are overvalued. The other may feel that the debtors figure shown by the first is excessive, and includes certain debts that should be regarded as bad. Such objections will result in the adjustment of their respective Balance Sheets.

Another point that may be raised is the question of goodwill. In particular, this may arise where the new business is to make use of the business premises of one partner only, the other's premises being sold. The partner whose premises are to form the base of the new joint enterprise may insist upon some payment for goodwill, or its recognition as part of the asset values to be taken over.

31.3 An Example of Amalgamation

The following example illustrates the accounting procedures necessary when an amalgamation of businesses is arranged.

A. Brown and B. Green have businesses in the same district, with assets and liabilities as shown below:

A. Brown
Balance Sheet as at 31 December 20..

	$	$		$
Fixed assets:			Capital	38520
Premises		36000		
Furniture and equipment		12000	Long-term liabilities:	
Motor vehicles		2350	Mortgage	25000
		50350		
Current assets:			Current liabilities:	
Stock	14750		Creditors	5850
Debtors	1250			
Cash at bank	2880			
Cash in hand	140			
		19020		
		$69370		$69370

B. Green
Balance Sheet as at 31 December 20..

	$	$		$
Fixed assets:			Capital	42839
Premises		23000		
Furniture and fittings		4850		
Motor vehicles		12500		
		40350		
Current assets:			Current liabilities:	
Stock	4920		Creditors	4081
Debtors	1650			
		6570		
		$46920		$46920

They agree to amalgamate, using the premises and furniture of Brown, and the motor vehicles of Green. Brown will sell off his motor vehicles privately, Green will sell his premises and all the fixtures and fittings except weighing machines valued at $500. In place of these assets he will bring in $20 000 cash as extra working capital. Brown will open up a Provision for Bad Debts of $250 and Green will do the same for $150.

Brown will create a Goodwill Account of $4 000 and Green will create one of $2 000.

Modify the Balance Sheets to take account of these arrangements, and then amalgamate them to show the Balance Sheet of the new business as at 1 January 20...

The modified Balance Sheets are given below. Each has been adjusted to include only the assets actually brought into the new business, the capitals of each partner being altered to take account of the changes in the net worth he is contributing.

A. Brown
Adjusted Balance Sheet as at 31 December 20..

	$	$	$		$
Fixed assets:				Capital	39 920
Goodwill			4 000		
Premises			36 000	Long-term liabilities:	
Furniture, etc.			12 000	Mortgage	25 000
			52 000		
Current assets:				Current liabilities:	
Stock		14 750		Creditors	5 850
Debtors	1 250				
Less Provision	250				
		1 000			
Cash at bank		2 880			
Cash in hand		140			
			18 770		
			$70 770		$70 770

B. Green
Adjusted Balance Sheet as at 31 December 20..

	$	$	$		$
Fixed assets:				Capital	37 339
Goodwill			2 000		
Furniture and fittings			500		
Motor vehicles			12 500		
			15 000		
Current assets:				Current liabilities:	
Stock		4 920		Creditors	4 081
Debtors	1 650				
Less Provision	150				
		1 500			
Cash at bank		20 000			
			26 420		
			$41 420		$41 420

All that is now required is to merge these two adjusted Balance Sheets into an amalgamated Balance Sheet as shown below:

A. Brown and B. Green
Balance Sheet as at 1 January 20..

	$	$	$		$
Fixed assets:				Capital:	
Goodwill			6 000	A. Brown	39 920
Premises			36 000	B. Green	37 339
Furniture, etc.			12 500		
Motor vehicles			12 500		77 259
			67 000		
Current assets:				Long-term liabilities:	
Stock		19 670		Mortgage	25 000
Debtors	2 900				
Less Provision	400				
		2 500			
Cash at bank		22 880		Current liabilities:	
Cash in hand		140		Creditors	9 931
			45 190		
			$112 190		$112 190

31.4 Exercises Set 52. Amalgamations

1. A. Young and B. Old are to amalgamate their businesses. Young will contribute a motor lorry valued at $18 000 and capital in cash of the same amount $18 000. Old will bring in his premises $25 000, his fixtures and fittings $4 800, his stock $12 500 and debtors of $1 000. He has creditors to be paid of $2 200. Draw up the opening Balance Sheet, on 1 January 20...

2. Maker and Seller are to amalgamate their businesses. Their assets and liabilities are given below:

	Maker	*Seller*
	$	$
Premises	22 500	27 500
Furniture and fittings	4 000	4 800
Motor vehicles	12 000	11 800
Stock	7 450	15 250
Debtors	–	1 850
Creditors	3 650	1 650
Bank balance	2 850	800 (overdraft)
Cash in hand	130	50

All assets and liabilities will be brought into the new business except for the following:

(i) Seller will dispose of his vehicles privately and use the funds made available to pay up his overdraft. He will also bring in a bank balance of $5 000.

(ii) Seller's stock will be valued by the new business at $12 500, Maker's at $5 000.

(iii) Seller will create a Provision for Bad Debts of $250.

Draw up the Balance Sheet of the new business when it commences operations on 1 January 20...

3. W. Sandon and M. Sandon agree to amalgamate as from 1 January 20... On that day their records show the following situation:

	W. Sandon	*M. Sandon*
	$	$
Land and buildings	26 000	24 000
Machinery	12 500	11 500
Furniture and fittings	4 800	4 500
Stocks:		
Raw material	1 800	1 600
Work in progress	1 230	1 450
Finished goods	11 720	13 850
Cash	325	285
Bank	11 520	9 450
Creditors	2 850	1 450
Rents due	350	–
Debtors	3 650	4 850

W. Sandon will open a Provision for Bad Debts of $450. M. Sandon will sell her land and buildings and furniture and fittings. She will then pay off all her creditors and bring in $16000 extra in the Bank Account. W. Sandon will be allowed to open a Goodwill Account for $4000. Draw up the amalgamated Balance Sheet. (*Note:* The rents due are owing on a lock-up garage W. Sandon has rented to store materials prior to manufacturing.)

4. Tyler and Templeton have businesses in adjoining premises. They agree to combine and trade as partners from 1 January 20...

On that date they agreed the value of assets and liabilities of each business as follows:

	Tyler	*Templeton*
	$	$
Freehold premises	40000	38000
Furniture and fittings	3650	2440
Motor vans	11170	11840
Stocks	13250	12170
Trade debtors	1890	1640
Provision for Bad Debts	160	140
Trade creditors	2980	4965
Rates outstanding	470	–
Insurances prepaid	120	215
Bank overdraft	–	320
Cash at bank	3840	–

(i) Before combining the businesses Tyler paid off his outstanding rates from his business bank account and Templeton paid off his bank overdraft from his private bank account.

(ii) The goodwill of Tyler's business was agreed at $3490 and that of Templeton's business at $2000.

(iii) On amalgamation Tyler made a loan of $10000 to the partnership from private funds, at 7 per cent per annum. This was for additional working capital.

(iv) It was agreed that current accounts should be kept and that profits and losses should be shared equally.

a) Draft the opening Balance Sheet of the partnership at 1 January 20...

b) At the end of 20.. the partnership had made a net trading profit of $26770 before allowing for interest on Tyler's loan. It was agreed that $1490 should be written off goodwill.
During the year each partner had withdrawn $8000.
Prepare:
(i) the Appropriation Account of the partnership for the year ended 31 December 20.. and
(ii) the Current Accounts of the partners balanced as at 31 December 20...

31.5 Revise and Test 31. Amalgamations

Answers	*Questions*
—	**1.** What is an amalgamation?
1. It is a joining together of two businesses, usually similar businesses, to achieve economies and more effective working.	**2.** What are the chief economies that can be achieved?
2. Administrative economies, financial economies, marketing economies and economies in the use of personnel.	**3.** What is the first stage in an amalgamation?
3. To look at the assets and liabilities of both firms and make arrangements about their future use. We only bring into the new business the assets that are really necessary—other things being disposed of privately by the two parties.	**4.** What about the value placed upon the items being brought in?
4. They should be valued at today's prices so that each party feels he/she is being given a fair valuation for everything brought in.	**5.** Give some examples.
5. a) Premises: it may be necessary to get them valued by a professional valuer; b) motor vehicles—allow for depreciation; c) stocks—valued at cost price or net realizable value, whichever is less; d) debtors—provide for bad debts.	**6.** What else needs to be agreed?

6. There must be adequate capital. The parties must agree to bring in cash at the bank to cover the working of the business in the first few months. Drawing up a Cash Flow Forecast is desirable.

7. What is the final stage?

---

7. Sort out the legal side of the new arrangements—if it is a partnership draw up an agreement with a solicitor's help. If it is a new company register the details with Companies House (or other appropriate authority).

8. What is the final bit of book-keeping?

---

8. Amalgamate the two revised Balance Sheets to give the Opening Balance Sheet of the new business, and start trading.

9. Go over the page again until you are sure of all the answers.

UNIT 32

Purchase of a Business

32.1 Introduction

Businesses are bought and sold every day; some sensational take-overs capture the national headlines for days on end. There is little difference as far as accounting records are concerned between the purchase by one small trader of another's business, and the purchase of one huge public company by another. The basic elements in any purchase of a business may be listed as follows:

(a) The purchase price has to be agreed, between the vendor and the purchaser.
(b) The effective date of the transfer of ownership has to be decided upon and the necessary conveyances arranged if land and buildings are to change hands.
(c) The purchaser will review the assets being taken over to decide whether they are correctly valued. He/she will bring the new assets on to the books at the valuation placed on them, irrespective of what the vendor considered them to have been worth.
(d) The purchaser may also be taking over certain liabilities of the old business. Usually these cannot be varied from the vendor's figures, and they will have to be honoured in full, except that a settlement discount of some sort may be earned.
(e) The difference between the asset values and the liabilities taken over will be the net value of the business to the new owner. Yet nearly always the price paid will be in excess of this net value. The difference between what the assets are worth and what is paid for them must be the goodwill figure, i.e. the amount the purchaser considers it is worth paying the previous owner for the hard work done in years gone by.

The recording of these matters in the books of the new business is best considered by taking an example and working through all the necessary procedures in turn.

32.2 The Purchase of a Business: an Example

Consider the following set of circumstances.

J. Brown agrees to sell his business to M. Regan as from 1 July 20.., at a price of $60 000. The assets and liabilities on 30 June were as shown in J. Brown's Balance Sheet below. Regan will not take over the cash at bank or the cash in hand.

J. Brown
Balance Sheet as at 30 June 20..

	$	$		$
Fixed assets:			Capital	52 000
Premises		26 000		
Fixtures and fittings		5 500		
Motor vehicles		3 800		
		35 300		
Current assets:			Current liabilities:	
Stock	14 250		Sundry creditors	1 530
Debtors	2 650			
Cash at bank	1 300			
Cash in hand	30			
		18 230		
		$53 530		$53 530

Regan decides on the following changes in value:

Premises will be revalued to $35 000

Fixtures and fittings will be valued at $2 000, and motor vehicles at $2 500.

Stock will be valued at $13 500 and a Provision for Bad Debts of 10 per cent will be created.

Regan brings in capital of $45 000, arranges a mortgage of $18 000 on the premises, and pays Brown on 1 July in full by cheque.

(a) Calculation of the 'Goodwill' Figure

The goodwill is calculated as follows:

		$
Value of assets taken over:		
Premises		35000
Fixtures		2000
Motor vehicles		2500
Stock		13500
Debtors	2650	
Less Provision	265	
		2385
		55385
Less Current liabilities		1530
Net value of assets		$53855
Purchase price		= $60000
Less Net value of assets		= $53855
Goodwill		= $6145

Since Regan is prepared to pay $60000 for assets valued at a net figure of $53855, he must be prepared to consider the goodwill as worth $6145.

(b) The Opening of the Books of the New Business

This requires a series of simple Journal entries. The following stages are required to complete the opening entries.

(i) Take on the vendor as a creditor, and debit a Purchase of Business Account This is simply a convenience account, opened for a few minutes while the double entry is carried out.

				$	J1 $
20..					
1 July	Purchase of Business Account	Dr.	L1	60000	
	J. Brown Account		L2		60000
	Being agreed purchase price at this date				

Purchase of Business Account L1

			$
20.			
1 July	J. Brown	J1	60000

J. Brown Account L2

			$
20..			
1 July	Purchase of Business	J1	60000

(ii) Take on the assets, including goodwill, and credit the Purchase of Business Account. Of course each asset account will be debited.

					J1
20..				$	$
1 July	Goodwill Account	Dr.	L3	6145	
	Premises Account	Dr.	L4	35000	
	Fixtures and Fittings Account	Dr.	L5	2000	
	Motor Vehicles Account	Dr.	L6	2500	
	Stock	Dr.	L7	13500	
	Sundry Debtors Account	Dr.	L8	2650	
	Purchase of Business Account		L1		61795
	Being assets taken over at agreed valuations				

Goodwill Account L3

20.			$
1 July	Purchase of Business	J1	6145

Premises Account L4

20.			$
1 July	Purchase of Business	J1	35000

Fixtures and Fittings Account L5

20.			$
1 July	Purchase of Business	J1	2000

Motor Vehicles Account L6

20.			$
1 July	Purchase of Business	J1	2500

Stock Account L7

20.			$
1 July	Purchase of Business	J1	13500

Sundry Debtors Account[1] L8

20..			$
1 July	Purchase of Business	J1	2650

[1] In real life there would be many individual debtor accounts.

Purchase of Business Account L1

20..			$	20..			$
1 July	J. Brown	J1	60000	1 July	Sundry assets	J1	61795

(iii) The liabilities must now be taken on, including the Provision for Bad Debts

				J1
20..			$	$
1 July	Purchase of Business Account Dr.	L1	1795	
	Sundry Creditors Account	L9		1530
	Provision for Bad Debts	L10		265
	Being liabilities taken over at this date			

Purchase of Business Account L1

20..			$	20..		$
1 July J. Brown	J1		60000	1 July Sundry assets	J1	61795
1 July Sundry liabilities	J1		1795			
			$61795			$61795

Sundry Creditors Account[1] L9

			$
20..			
1 July	Purchase of Business	J1	1530

[1] In real life there would be many individual accounts.

Provision for Bad Debts Account L10

			$
20..			
1 July	Purchase of Business	J1	265

(iv) The capital is brought in, the mortgage arranged and the vendor is paid

20..			$	$
1 July	Bank Account Dr.	CB1	45000	
	Capital Account	L11		45000
	Being capital brought in at this date			
1 July	Bank Account Dr.	CB1	18000	
	Mortgage on Premises Account	L12		18000
	Being mortgage arranged at this date			
1 July	J. Brown Account Dr.	L2	60000	
	Bank Account	CB1		60000
	Being payment of vendor as agreed			

Bank Account CB1

20..		$	20..		$
1 July Capital	J1	45 000	1 July J. Brown	J1	60 000
1 July Mortgage	J1	18 000	1 July Balance	c/d	3 000
		$63 000			$63 000
2 July Balance	B/d	3 000			

Capital Account L11

			20..		$
			1 July Bank	J1	45 000

Mortgage Account L12

			20..		$
			1 July Bank	J1	18 000

J. Brown Account L2

20..		$	20..		$
1 July Bank	J1	60 000	1 July Purchase of Business	J1	60 000

(v) Finally, a Balance Sheet of the new business is drawn up

M. Regan
Balance Sheet as at 1 July 20..

	$	$	$		$
Fixed assets:				Capital:	
Goodwill			6 145	At start	45 000
Premises			35 000		
Furniture and Fittings			2 000	Long-term liabilities:	
Motor vehicles			2 500	Mortgage	18 000
			45 645		
Current assets:				Current liabilities:	
Stock		13 500		Creditors	1 530
Debtors	2 650				
Less Provision	265				
		2 385			
Bank balance		3 000			
			18 885		
			$64 530		$64 530

32.3 Exercises Set 53. Purchase of a Business

1. On 31 December 20.., A. Robertson purchased the business of R. Long. The assets were as follows:

	$
Freehold property	25 000
Furniture and fittings	2 200
Stock in trade	4 800
Debtors	550

The purchase consideration was $35 000, to be paid by cheque on 1 January. Robertson decided to revalue the premises at $27 500, and the stock at $2 500. He brings in cash at the bank $40 000 and pays Robertson as arranged.

Show the Journal entries opening the books of Robertson's new business and the Balance Sheet on 1 January 20...

2. The Balance Sheet of P. Fitzpatrick at 31 December 20.. was as follows:

Balance Sheet as at 31 December 20..

	$		$
Freehold property	32 000	Capital	59 500
Plant	18 500	Creditors	4 400
Motor vehicles	4 100	Bank overdraft	3 950
Stock in trade	13 250		
	$67 850		$67 850

He sold the assets only to R. Killinchy on 1 January 20.. for the agreed price of $55 000.

Killinchy valued the freehold at $28 000, plant at $12 800, motors at $3 600 and stock at $7 950.

You are asked to give the Journal entries necessary to record these matters in the books of R. Killinchy, who brings in capital of $60 000 cash at bank and pays Fitzpatrick by cheque on 1 January 20... Then draw up the opening Balance Sheet of the business.

3. The Balance Sheet of R. Morgan at 31 December 20.. was as follows:

Balance Sheet as at 31 December 20..

	$		$
Freehold property	45 000	Capital	86 300
Plant	28 000	Creditors	1 500
Motor vehicles	4 000	Bank overdraft	1 200
Stock in trade	12 000		
	$89 000		$89 000

He sold all the assets to M. Phillips on 1 January 20.. for the agreed price of $86 000, Phillips also agreeing to pay up the creditors.

M. Phillips valued the freehold at $40 000, plant at $25 000, motors at $4 800 and stock at $10 000.

You are asked to give the Journal entries necessary to record these matters in the books of M. Phillips, who brought in cash at bank of $75 000, and arranged a mortgage of $20 000 to provide further cash. The vendor was paid on 2 January. Then draw up an opening Balance Sheet.

4. On 30 September 20. . R. Lyons arranged to take over the business carried on by J. Kelleher. The assets were taken over at the following valuations: fixtures and fittings $4 850; stock $8 250; motor vehicles $1 850. Trade creditors amounted to $785 and it was also found that:

(a) telephone charges accrued on the date of transfer were $89.55;
(b) electricity due amounted to $87.45 against which could be set a deposit for the original connection of $55, which would be effectively transferred to the new owner;
(c) rent had been paid in advance of $150 for the month of October;
(d) rates $180 had been paid in advance for the quarter to 31 December.

The purchase price was agreed at $20 000, which Lyons paid on 1 October from funds he contributed on that date. These consisted of $24 000 in the bank account and $1 000 in cash.

Open the affairs of R. Lyons's business with appropriate Journal entries, and show the opening Balance Sheet. There is no need to post the Journal entries to the ledger accounts.

32.4 Revise and Test 32. Purchase of a Business

Answers	*Questions*
—	**1.** What are the problems when purchasing a business?
1. a) You have to agree a purchase price; b) you have to take over the assets of the old business but it doesn't mean that you will place the same valuation on them as the previous proprietor; c) if you take over any debtors make sure they know that they are to pay you the outstanding sums; d) if you take on any creditors make sure they are agreeable to deal with you on the same terms as with the old proprietor.	**2.** What is stage 1 of the book-keeping process?
2. Open a Vendor Account (a credit balance because you owe him/her the money) and debit a Purchase of Business Account.	**3.** What next?
3. Bring in all the assets (debit each asset account) and credit Purchase of Business Account. Don't forget Goodwill Account if you paid more for the business than the value of the assets you are actually recording on your books.	**4.** What next?
4. Bring on any liabilities taken over (credit each liability account, whatever they may be and debit Purchases of Business Account).	**5.** And finally.
5. Pay the vendor (debit Vendor Account and credit Bank Account).	**6.** Go over the page again if you are not sure of this set of answers.

UNIT 33

Accounting for Bills of Exchange

33.1 What is a Bill of Exchange?

The documents known as bills of exchange are used in many commercial transactions, and enable goods to be paid for under special arrangements that suit the parties concerned and that are legally binding upon them. Millions of dollars are handled in this way every day; a whole money market—the *discount market*—is based on them; all governments use bills of exchange (Treasury bills) to finance their short-term activities, and actually control the money market largely by changing the number of bills they issue each week.

A bill of exchange is defined in the Bills of Exchange Act 1882 as *an unconditional order in writing, addressed by one person to another, signed by the person giving it, requiring the person to whom it is addressed to pay on demand or at a fixed or determinable future time a sum certain in money to or to the order of a specified person, or to bearer.*

Now look at the bill of exchange shown in Fig. 33.1 and the notes following the figure, which explain how it fulfils the strict requirements of the definition given in the Act.

No. 1274 1 of 1

EXCHANGE FOR $ 5274.50 31 October 20

At 90 days after date pay this first Bill of Exchange to or to the Order of M. J. Spurling (Camside) Ltd, 1215 Camside, Cambridge CB4 1 PB

Five thousand two hundred and seventy four dollars 50 cents

Value Received which place to Account

To M. Lawrence & co
15784 High St
Newtown
Herts

Signed M. J. Spurling (Director)
for M. J. Spurling (Camside) Ltd

Fig. 33.1 An inland bill of exchange

Notes:

(i) The bill is an *unconditional* order in writing. It does not say 'provided the good ship *Peerless* reaches Bombay' or something like that. It says 'pay this bill of exchange 90 days after the date named on it', that is, without any conditions at all.
(ii) It is *addressed by one person*—M. T. Spurling (Camside) Ltd—*to another*—M. Lawrence & Co.
(iii) It is *signed by the person giving it* (one of the directors of the company).
(iv) It requires the person to whom it is addressed (M. Lawrence & Co.) to pay (not on demand) but *at a fixed and determinable future time*—90 days after 31 October. This is 29 January next.
(v) The sum of money is *certain*—it is $5274.50. It is not something uncertain, like the value of the television sets sold at auction when they reach Newtown. Everyone who handles this bill knows how much it is worth—$5274.50.
(vi) It says that it is payable *to, or to the order of, a specified person*—M.T. Spurling (Camside) Ltd.

The Act says if a document does not fulfil all the requirements of the definition it is not a bill of exchange. That is why it is a good idea to learn the definition off by heart. Do this now, and then go on to Unit 33.2.

33.2 How Bills of Exchange Work

There are three parties to a bill of exchange: the drawer, the acceptor and the payee. The *drawer* draws up the bill of exchange—that is, he or she writes it out. The drawer is the person who is owed money, usually as payment for goods or services that have been supplied. The person drawn upon is called the *drawee*; in the normal way the bill is sent straight to the drawee who is asked to *accept* the bill, that is, to accept the obligation to pay the bill on the due date. Paying the bill is called 'honouring' the bill, and the drawee accepts the obligation by writing 'accepted' across the face of the bill, and signing it. Even the signature alone will do, but it is better to write 'accepted' as well. The drawee has now become the *acceptor* of the bill and is liable to honour it on the due date. The *payee* is the person named on the bill as being entitled to receive payment on it; if the drawer has written *pay me* or *pay us* on the bill, then the payee and the drawer are the same person.

Notice three points about bills of exchange.

(a) A person who wants to buy goods but has no money may obtain them if he or she agrees to accept a bill of exchange for, say, 90 days' time. He or she hopes by the time the bill is due for payment to have sold the goods at a profit and consequently to have the funds to honour the bill on the due date.

(b) The person who has supplied the goods and drawn up the bill does not have to wait until the 90 days are up for the money. He or she can do so if they want to, but more likely they will *discount* the bill with a bank. This means they will get the bank to give its *present value*, that is, the value with interest deducted for the number of days it has to run. Since this is calculated on a day-to-day basis it is quite a small amount of interest. (If I have made, say, $5 000 profit on an order I don't mind paying $200 of it in interest—I have still made a nice profit.) The supplier therefore *endorses* the bill over to a bank (or to one of the specialist banks called *discount houses*) and they give them the money, less the discount charged. 'Endorsed' means 'written on the back' (Latin, *in dorsum*). They simply order the acceptor to pay the bank by writing 'Pay Helpful Discount House Ltd' on the back of the bill and signing it.

(c) The discount house now has the bill. They will keep it until *maturity*—that is, until the due date—when they will present it to the acceptor and demand payment. By then the acceptor can be expected to have sold the goods at a profit and should have the money needed to honour the bill of exchange and pay up cheerfully. The discount house will have earned the interest it is entitled to.

Fig. 33.2 shows what the situation would have been if bills of exchange had not been invented. Fig. 33.3, by contrast, shows how bills of exchange get business activity started, to the benefit of everyone.

Start here!

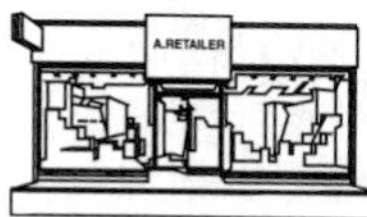

1 A. Retailer wishes to stock up his shop, but has no money.

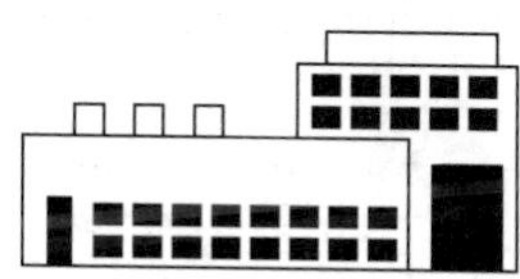

2 A. Manufacturer has electrical and electronic goods but no customers.

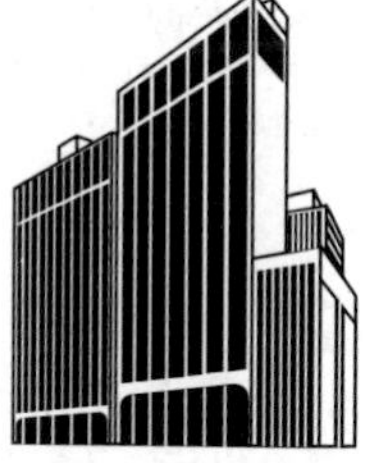

3 Merchant Bankers PLC have plenty of funds to lend out at interest, and charge 10% per annum. They would welcome borrowers.

4 The general public have money and wish to buy electrical and electronic appliances, but there are none on sale.

Fig. 33.2 Business inactivity without bills of exchange

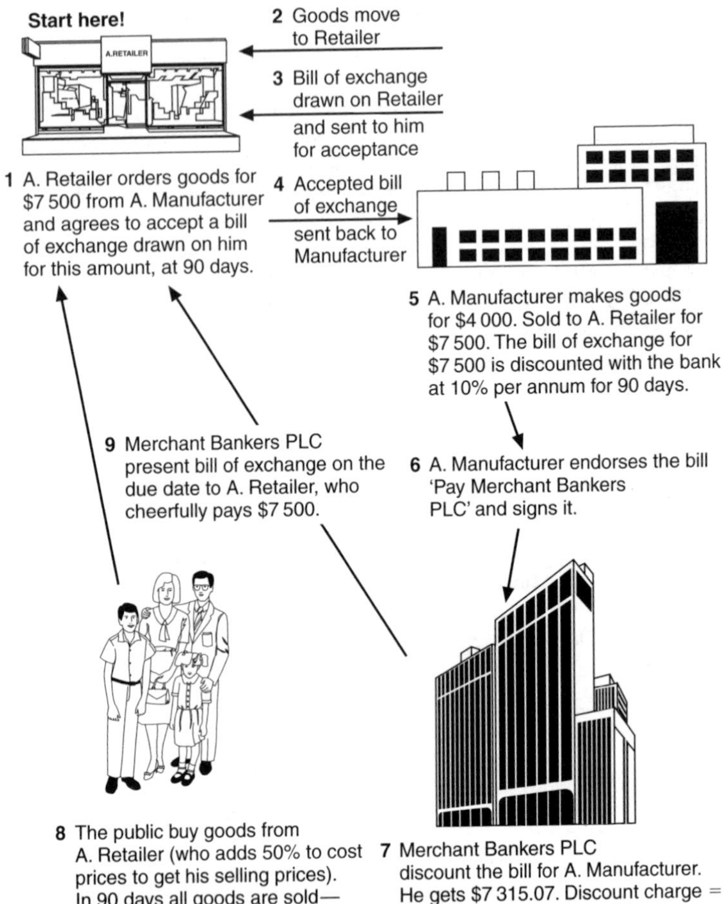

Fig. 33.3 Business activity when bills of exchange are used

Notes to Fig. 33.3:

(i) A. Retailer bought goods for $7500 and sold them for $11250. Profit $3750.

(ii) A. Manufacturer made goods for $4000 and sold them for $7500. Charges of $184.93 for discounting give a final profit of $3315.07.

(iii) Merchant Banker PLC buys bill for $7315.07. It is later honoured for $7500. Profit $184.93.

(iv) The general public have spent $11250 and are enjoying their purchases—watching television, playing with their home computers, using their calculators and, in general, participating in the pleasures of the consumer-oriented society.

33.3 Recording Bills of Exchange. 1. Bills Payable

If you accept a bill of exchange by writing 'accepted' across the face of it and signing your name, you become the primary person who is liable on the bill of exchange and must honour it on the due date. The bill is a *bill payable*. Look, for instance, at the bill of exchange illustrated in Fig. 33.1; as you can see, the acceptor of this bill (although he has not signed it yet) will be M. Lawrence & Co. Let us suppose that we work for M. Lawrence & Co.; as far as our firm is concerned this is a bill payable. The situation is as follows:

(a) We have a creditor, M. T. Spurling (Camside) Ltd, to whom we owe $5274.50, value received. This means they have supplied goods to that value. Their account looks like this:

M.T. Spurling (Camside) Ltd Account L73

20..		$
26 Oct. Purchases	PDB27	5274.50

(b) As soon as we accept the bill of exchange and return it to them we have cleared our debt—although we haven't paid anything, Spurling's can go off to a bank and discount the bill of exchange if they want to get their money. Of course, they will lose a bit of interest if they do, but that is up to them. We have cleared our debt completely, and no longer owe them money.

(c) To whom do we owe the money, then? The answer is that we have no idea—we owe it to the person who presents it to us on the due date (29 January) and says 'Pay me!' The bill may change hands a dozen times before then, but whoever has it on that date will present it for payment so we must have the money ready. In the meantime we open up a *Bills Payable Account* and put the bill on that as a credit item—we owe Bills Payable $5274.50 when the due date comes round.

The actual entries are made in a special kind of book of original entry, called the *Bills Payable Book*. This is then posted into the ledger to give the proper ledger entries. Fig. 33.4 shows an example; to make it look more realistic several bills have been entered in, but the bill for M. T. Spurling (Camside) Ltd is the last bill payable entered this month.

The total of the Bills Payable Book will be credited to Bills Payable Account at the end of the month, to give a total of bills payable. The credit entry in M. T. Spurling (Camside) Ltd's Account for the goods they supplied has been cleared from the books, but it has been replaced by this credit entry in the Bills Payable Account, although the $5274.50 is hidden in the grand total of $8179.75.

When 29 January comes round we shall pay the $5 274.50 to the person who holds the bill of exchange at that time and who presents it for payment. The money will be credited in the Bank Account and debited to Bills Payable Account, since M. T. Spurling (Camside) Ltd's Account has been cleared already. This will reduce the amount we owe on the Bills Payable Account. Look again at the Bills Payable Book shown in Fig. 33.4; you will see that this has happened with the bill for T. Miles (the first bill shown). T. Miles's bill has been presented by T. Freeman, who has been paid the money in cash, and the ledger entries are as follows:

T. Miles Account L73

		$			$
20..			20..		
4 Oct. Bill payable	BPB27	500.00	3 Oct. Purchases	PDB27	500.00

Bills Payable Account

		$			$
20..			20..		
31 Oct. Cash	CB28	500.00	31 Oct. Sundry bills payable	PDB27	8 179.75

Cash Book (cash column only) CB28

		$
20..		
31 Oct. Bills payable		500.00

Bills Payable Book

Page 27

No. of bill	*Date accepted*	*Date of bill*	*F*	*Amount* $ c	*Drawer*	*Acceptor*	*Payee*	*Where payable*	*Tenor*	*Due date*	*Presented by*	*Remarks (if any)*
1	20.. 4 Oct.	20.. 1 Oct.	L127	500 00	T. Miles	Self	T. Miles	15784 High St	30 days	31 Oct.	T. Freeman 2754 Lombard St	Paid in cash
2	11 Oct.	8 Oct.	L56	1720 25	R. Pocock	Self	M. Burton	15784 High St	91 days	10 Jan.		
3	15 Oct.	14 Oct.	L14	685 00	A. Ajakaiye	Self	R. Nakanda	15784 High St	60 days	13 Dec.		
4	31 Oct.	31 Oct.	L73	5274 50	M. T. Spurling (Camside) Ltd	Self	M. T. Spurling (Camside) Ltd	15784 High St	90 days	29 Jan.		
				$8179 75								
				L154								

Fig. 33.4 The Bills Payable Book

Bills Receivable Book

Page 33

No. of bill	*Date recd*	*From whom received*	*Date of bill*	*F*	*Amount* $ c	*Drawer*	*Acceptor*	*First Endorser (payee)*	*Other endorsers*	*Where payable*	*Tenor*	*Due date*	*Date of disposal*	*How disposed of*	*Discounting charges* $ c
78	4 Oct.	T. Giles	1 Oct.	L19	384 50	Self	T. Giles	Self	–	712 Lombard St EC3	180 days	30 Mar.	5 Oct.	Sold to Merchant Banker PLC	17 91
79	27 Oct.	Palgrave & Co.	14 Oct.	L28	3 500 00	R. T. Hart	P. Brough	R. T. Hart	Palgrove & Co.	2 Green Lane Edmonton	30 days	13 Nov.			
80	31 Oct.	Lawrence & Co.	31 Oct.	L169	5 274 50	Self	Lawrence & Co.	Self	–	Newtown Herts	90 days	29 Jan.	31 Oct.	Sold to Merchant Banker PLC	184 93
					$9 159 00										
					L42										

Fig. 33.5 The Bills Receivable Book

33.4 Recording Bills of Exchange. 2. Bills Receivable

As far as M. T. Spurling (Camside) Ltd are concerned this bill is not a bill payable but a *bill receivable*. If we now look at the bill from their point of view, we find that the situation is as follows:

(a) We have a debtor, Lawrence & Co., whose account shows a debit balance for $5 274.50 for goods sold to them on 26 October 20...

(b) As soon as Lawrence & Co. accept the bill of exchange it is entered in our Bills Receivable Book and posted to the ledger account of Lawrence & Co. to clear their debt. They no longer owe us any money for we have a bill of exchange in full settlement of the debt. Their account is therefore credited with $5 274.50.

(c) Although Lawrence & Co. are no longer in debt to us we have not yet received any money. Who owes us this money now? The answer is Bills Receivable Account, an imaginary debtor who will pay us as soon as we decide what to do with the bill. This account is debited with the total of the Bills Receivable Book for the month (Fig. 33.5), and the $5 274.50 is part of the total debit of $9 159.00. The ledger entries are as follows:

Lawrence & Co. L169

20..		$	20..		$
			31 Oct. Bills Receivable		
26 Oct. Sales	SDB29	5 274.50		BRB33	5 274.50

Bills Receivable L42

20..		$
31 Oct. Sundry bills receivable	BRB33	9 159.00

(d) We can now do one of three things:

(i) We could keep the bill until maturity on the due date, when it becomes payable. At one time we would then have gone round to Lawrence & Co., where we would present the bill for payment and collect the full value. Today it is usual to collect the bill through the banking system. In accepting the bill the debtor would write something like 'Accepted, payable at Mill Road branch, Barminster Bank, Cambridge'. The result will be a simple cash book entry. Debit Bank Account, and credit Bills Receivable Account, thus removing the bill from the Bills Receivable Account—it is no longer receivable.

(ii) We could discount the bill with a bank. If we do this at once the discount will be $184.93, as shown in the Bills Receivable Book in Fig. 33.5. What entry shall we need to make? Clearly the whole value of the bill must be removed from the Bills Receivable Account, but we shall only get $5 089.57 from the discount house. The balance is 'discount on bills', one of the losses of the business. The entries are therefore as follows:

					J21
				$	$
20..					
31 Oct.	Bank Account	Dr.	CB28	5089.57	
	Discount on Bills Account		L159	184.93	
	Bills Receivable Account		L42		5274.50
	Being discounting of bill from Lawrence & Co. at this date				

Cash Book (bank column only) CB28

20..		$
31 Oct.	Bills Receivable J21	5089.57

Discount on Bills Account L159

20..		$
31 Oct.	Bills Receivable J21	184.93

Bills Receivable Account L42

			$				$
20..				20..			
31 Oct.	Sundry bills receivable	BRB33	9159.00	31 Oct.	Bank and Discount on bills	J21	5274.50

(iii) We could use the bill to pay a debt to someone else to whom we owe money. Suppose we have a creditor to whom we owe $7000. We could say 'Will you accept the present value of this bill ($5089.57) in part payment?' If they agree we negotiate the bill to them, by endorsing it to the other party. We thus become the first endorser of the bill, and the value we get for it is the discounted value of the bill—its present value on the day of negotiation. The entries are exactly the same as before, but instead of a debit in the Bank Account we have a debit for $5089.57 in the creditor's account to reduce our debt to him. The Bills Receivable Account is still credited with the full value of the bill, and the balance is again 'interest payable'. 'Discount on bills' is really a form of 'interest payable'. Do you see why? We should have received $5274.50 in 90 days' time. Instead we decided to borrow $5089.57 today and repay it on the due date (or rather our debtor Lawrence & Co. will repay it). The $184.93 is the interest we paid for borrowing $5089.57 for 90 days.

33.5 Contingent Liabilities on Bills of Exchange Receivable

At the end of every financial year we are pretty certain to have some bills receivable outstanding. These will of course be assets, just as debtors are. There may also be some bills receivable which we have not kept, however. Perhaps we discounted them with a bank, or passed them on to someone else. Now on these bills we have had our money, but there is just a chance that the bills will be dishonoured on the due date. This brings us to a very important point about bills of exchange. Everyone who writes his name on a bill of exchange is liable on it, and must honour it in the sequence in which it is signed. Now the chief person liable is of course the acceptor, but if the acceptor dishonours the bill the drawer must honour it. Usually the drawer is also the first endorser (if he is not, the payee named on the bill will be the first endorser); the first endorser is also liable, so is the second endorser, and so on. The more signatures carried on a bill the safer it is, because the more likely it becomes that one of these signatories will honour it. So if the acceptor dishonours the bill we shall have to honour it. We therefore have a *contingent liability* on the bill—that is, in certain contingencies we might have to honour it. When we draw up a Balance Sheet at the end of the year we must add a note 'Contingent liabilities exist on bills of exchange for $\$x$ which have been discounted or passed on'. Otherwise the Balance Sheet will not give a 'true and fair view' of the affairs of the business.

33.6 Dishonour of a Bill

You have just seen that when a bill is dishonoured any party that has signed the bill is liable on it. Consider the following chain of signatures:

Acceptor
Drawer and first endorser
Second endorser, *M*
Third endorser, *N*
Fourth endorser, *O*, endorses it to *P*.

Now suppose that the acceptor dishonours the bill when *P* presents it to him. *P* has the bill *noted*, or *protested*, by a *notary public*. This is a legal process which entitles the bill to be presented in court as evidence of an insolvent's failure to honour the bill. *P* does not want to sue the acceptor, however; he simply wants his money. He can ask anyone who has signed the bill to pay him, but the only one he knows is *O*. He asks *O* to pay him. This is fair because *O* used the bill to pay *P* for goods and *P* has not been paid. *O* pays up and asks *N* to honour the bill. *N* pays up and asks *M*. The bill moves backwards towards the drawer. It is the drawer who then says to the acceptor, 'Now, what about this bill? Have I got to make you a bankrupt, or can you pay if I give you a little more time?' He may *renew the bill* for 30 days, if there is some prospect of payment.

What then will be the final piece of book-keeping as the drawer pays *M* the money for the bill that has been dishonoured? The answer is quite simple:

Credit the Bank Account, as money has been paid out.

Debit the acceptor, for the debt has to be restored to the debtor, just as with a dishonoured cheque.

The ledger entries are as follows:

				J36
20..			$	$
29 Jan.	Lawrence & Co. Dr.	L169	5274.50	
	Bank Account	CB49		5274.50
	Being restoration of a debt to a debtor Lawrence & Co., after a bill of exchange was dishonoured; payment made to *M* to honour the bill			

Lawrence & Co. L169

		$
20..		
29 Jan. Bank Account	J36	5274.50

Cash Book (bank columns only) CB49

		$
20..		
29 Jan. M Ltd	J36	5274.50

33.7 Exercises Set 54. Accounting for Bills of Exchange

(*Note:* In some of these exercises you will need to rule up paper similar to the Bills Payable Book and Bills Receivable Book shown in Figs 33.4 and 33.5.)

1. On 27 October M. Larkin agrees to purchase goods value $5600 from Microgames Ltd, and to accept a bill of exchange for 91 days drawn on them at this date and payable at 205 Fenchurch Street, London EC3 9XX. Show the ledger entries in M. Larkin's books to record the purchase of the goods, and the entries in the Bills Payable Book to record the acceptance of the bill, its posting to the ledger (pretend it was the only bill of exchange that month) and its settlement on the due date by payment in cash.

2. On 14 July A. Distributor agrees to purchase goods value $27500 from Chinaware Ltd, and to accept a bill of exchange at 60 days drawn on them at this date and payable at 2074 Hill Street, London WC1 1CW. Show the ledger entries only for the purchase of these goods, the entry in the Bills Payable Book for the bill (pretend it was the only bill payable that month) and the entries for settlement of the bill on the due date; it was paid by cheque.

3. On 25 May A. Retailer agrees to purchase goods value $4200 from A. Wholesaler and to accept a bill of exchange for that amount at 90 days, payable at 1795 Cornhill, London EC3 9XY. Show the ledger entries only for the original purchase, the entry in the Bills Payable Book (pretend it was the only entry that month) and the postings to the ledger. Show also the entries for the final settlement on the due date. It was paid in cash.

4. Using the data given in Question 1 above, show the records in the books of Microgames Ltd for the sale, the bill receivable and the final settlement if Microgames Ltd keep the bill to maturity. (For extra practice you could repeat this exercise using Questions 2 and 3 above.)

5. Using the data given in Question 1 above, show the records in the books of Microgames Ltd if they discount the bill receivable with the Helpful Bank Ltd the same day at 15 per cent per annum. What note will appear on the Balance Sheet at 31 December? (For extra practice you could repeat this exercise with Questions 2 and 3 above.)

6. Using the data given in Question 1 above, show the records in the books of Microgames Ltd, supposing that they pass the bill on seven days later to A. Creditor, to whom they owe $10000, with discount calculated at 16 per cent per annum. (For extra practice you could repeat this exercise with Questions 2 and 3 above.)

7. A. Brown accepted a bill of exchange for $580 for T Ltd, and his account is at present clear on T Ltd's books. On 12 July T Ltd are approached by S Ltd, to whom they negotiated the bill, who complain that the bill has been dishonoured.

a) Why is it fair that T Ltd should pay S Ltd?
b) What would be the book-keeping entries in T Ltd's books?

8. M Ltd accepted a bill of exchange for P Ltd, who discounted it with a bank, Q Ltd. On the due date they are approached by Z Ltd and told that the bill has been dishonoured by M Ltd. P Ltd are therefore liable as drawers.

a) Why is it fair for P Ltd to pay Z Ltd, a company they have never heard of before?
b) What would be the book-keeping entries for the payment of the money to Z Ltd?

33.8 Revise and Test 33. Bills of Exchange

Answers	*Questions*
—	**1.** What is a bill of exchange?
1. It is an unconditional order, in writing addressed .... (If you can't carry on turn back to page 493.) (Note: it is important to learn this definition by heart.)	**2.** Who are the parties to a bill of exchange?
2. a) The drawer; b) the drawee, who becomes the acceptor; c) the payee—usually the same person as the drawer, but it could be a third person; d) the holder in due course.	**3.** Who is the drawer?
3. The one who draws up the bill (i.e. writes it out). Usually he/she has supplied goods or services and wishes to be paid for them.	**4.** Who is the drawee?
4. The one who is drawn upon, because they have received goods or services from the drawer. If the drawee accepts the duty to pay he/she writes 'accepted' and signs the bill, and becomes the acceptor, fully liable on the bill.	**5.** What is the whole idea of a bill of exchange?
5. It is a way of keeping business going by making funds available through a secure system of credit.	**6.** How does it work?

---

6. a) A trader who wants goods to sell asks a supplier to make them available against his/her signature on a bill of exchange. He/she signs the bill (accepts the legal promise to pay it on the due date) and gets the goods;
b) the supplier asks his/her bank to discount the bill (give him/her the money less interest at an agreed rate for the tenor (time it has to run)). The bank is now a holder in due course;
c) by the due date the trader has sold the goods at a profit and has the money to pay;
d) the bank presents the bill and the trader pays it. All parties are happy.

7. Now explain the book-keeping in A. Trader's books.

---

7. a) The trader credits the supplier's account (because he/she has become a creditor);
b) the bill is recorded in the Bills Payable Book and posted from there to the Supplier's Account (Debit the supplier who has been paid with the bill);
c) but in fact he/she hasn't really been paid so we credit a Bills Payable Account. We now have a liability to the holder in due course (whoever that may be);
d) on the due date someone (the holder in due course) presents the bill. We pay him/her;
e) we now credit the Cash Account as we pay the money and debit Bills Payable Account to wipe out our liability to the holder in due course.

8. How would the entries in A. Supplier's book differ?

8. They would be the other way round i.e.

a) A. Trader would be a debtor, not a creditor;
b) the Bill Book would be the Bills Receivable Book not the Bills Payable Book;
c) the discounting of the bill would be a cash entry (cash being received) and there would be a small loss in the Discount on Bills Account;
d) Bills Receivable Account would be credited to close the account.

9. Go over the page again until you are sure of all the answers.

UNIT 34

The Basic Principles of Accounting

34.1 The Place of Accounting in the Economy

Now that you know a good deal about elementary accounting you are ready to stand back and take a look at the place of accounting in the modern economy, and the general principles, or concepts, of accounting that have developed in recent years. In the days when production was largely domestic in nature, there was little need to lay down principles of accounting to be adhered to by everybody. Today, wealth is created in complex ways, by people in vast organizations, and it can be moved quickly from place to place by means of sophisticated electronic systems. Governments want their share of the nation's wealth and have large taxation departments to collect it. Consequently we have to have systems of accountancy that everyone understands, and rules that all must keep. In this way, it is arranged that we pay our fair share of taxes, account to our shareholders, creditors and employees for the wealth our company has created, and discover fraud, embezzlement and theft as soon as they occur—we hope.

First let us remind ourselves of the purpose and functions of accounting.

The Purpose and Functions of Accounting

We have seen that accounting is primarily a method for *measuring profitability*, as well as a way of *keeping track of the uses of financial resources*, and we have concentrated on these aspects in this book, which is about elementary *financial accounting*. Another branch of accounting, management accounting, deals with the control of enterprises. It is more concerned with accounting for manufacturing activities, job costing, contract costing, process costing and so on. That branch of accounting too is concerned with keeping track of financial resources and budgeting manufacturing activities to ensure eventual profitability.

Much of accounting is about *keeping a record of past performance*, because a clear record of past performance is a useful guide for future decision-making. If we know what was done in the past, and the results that were achieved thereby, we may be able to avoid wrong decisions and improve on those results in the future.

A further purpose of accounting is embodied in the concept of *stewardship*. (A steward is a person in charge of an enterprise such as a landed estate, who is charged with operating it on behalf of the owner or owners.) We are all, in business, acting as stewards for other people. Today the owners are not the only people concerned, for the employees too are vitally interested in what happens to their firm, company or corporation. As we have seen, the Companies Act 1985 lays a duty on us, as accountants, to present accounts which give anyone interested a true and fair view of the business's affairs. (The concept of stewardship is discussed further in Unit 34.2.)

We can thus summarize the purposes and functions of accounting as follows:

(a) to measure profitability;
(b) to keep track of the use of financial resources;
(c) to supervise production and distribution activities from the financial point of view;
(d) to provide a record of past performance and hence provide guidelines for future decision-making;
(e) to report back to the owner or owners, the shareholders, the employees and—in the case of public corporations—to the government of the day about the conduct of the enterprise and the results achieved.

In preparing these reports to conform with the concept of stewardship we rely on certain basic principles, most of which you have studied earlier in this book. These principles or conventions have long been known as the *concepts of accounting*—ideas and rules which a good accountant will always bear in mind in preparing accounts. More recently, some of them have been embodied into the Companies Act 1985 as principles that must be followed, and they have therefore become positive legal requirements that must be adhered to in the preparation of accounts. The chief concepts are:

(a) the concept of business entity;
(b) the prudence concept;
(c) the going concern concept;
(d) the accruals concept;
(e) the substance and materiality concepts;
(f) the consistency concept;
(g) the objectivity concept;
(h) the stable money concept.

Having studied this book, you will already be familiar with many of the ideas involved in these concepts. We will look at them one by one.

34.2 The Concept of Business Entity

A business entity is a separate business unit, distinct from all other business units. A sole trader business is separate from all other sole traders, partnerships, limited companies, friendly societies or co-operative societies—indeed, from all other businesses. It is even distinct from the owner of the business, who may sometimes act for the business (as when he or she is buying goods for re-sale) and at other times act as an individual (as when he or she buys food for the family to take on a picnic).

The concept of business entity is recognized by law, and in some cases the business is given a special legal status—an *incorporation*. Thus a limited liability company is an incorporation—a body set up by process of law. This process is called the *registration* of the company. Some companies are set up by special Act of Parliament (statutory companies) and some are set up by royal decree (chartered companies).

Partnerships, sole traders and clubs are not incorporations and do not have separate legal status from the partners, proprietors or members of the club. However, the accountant still separates them off from one another; the business has its own accounts, and these are quite distinct from the partners' accounts, the sole trader's personal records and so on.

The concept of stewardship, discussed in Unit 34.1, is a development from the concept of business entity. Those who run a business must account to the owners of the business for all its financial affairs. A sole trader, of course, only has to account to himself (and to the Inland Revenue for the tax due). Partners must account to one another. The treasurer of a club must account to the members, and the directors of a company must account to the shareholders. It is necessary to keep honest books of account, produce receipts (or paid cheques) for all money spent, balance our books every month in a Trial Balance, and every year produce a set of Final Accounts and a Balance Sheet showing the affairs of the business at the end of the last day in the financial year. You have already learned how to do all these things.

34.3 The Prudence Concept

The prudence concept reflects the fact that a person in business is most likely to be successful if he or she is prudent (cautious) in everything he or she does, i.e. by trying to avoid such things as overspending and overtrading (see Unit 28.10). The Companies Act 1985 requires the accounts of a business to follow the same principle. You are already familiar with most of the basic ideas associated with the prudence concept. You have learned the rule 'stock is valued at cost or net realizable value, whichever is lower' (Unit 21.1). If stock has risen in value and we value it at this increased price, we are taking the profit on it before we have sold it. This is imprudent—we may never sell it and so may never actually achieve the profit. Similarly, if stock has fallen in value, it is prudent to take the loss into account at once and not leave it to be suffered at a later date. A prudent manager never takes a profit until it has actually been made, and always accepts a loss at once even if there is a chance it may be recovered later. If we hear that a debtor is in financial difficulties and a receiver has been appointed to deal with a debtor's affairs, the prudent trader treats the debt as bad at once, while doing what is possible to claim in the bankruptcy. Similarly, as we know from learning about provisions for bad debts (Unit 22.8) and provisions for discounts (Unit 22.9), the prudent trader anticipates some bad debts, even when he or she does not know which debtor is likely to default. By deducting something from our profits to provide for bad debts, we put away the profits for a future emergency. By providing for discounts we anticipate that customers will claim a discount and thus reduce the amount we can collect from them.

There is, however, another side to this prudent behaviour. If we reduce our profits more than is reasonable we shall also pay less taxes, for, as we know, the Government's revenues partly come from a share of business profits. Many legal cases result from disputes between the Inland Revenue and businesses about the amount of profit they are retaining for future hard times. We are allowed to be prudent—but not to defraud the revenue authorities.

34.4 The Going Concern Concept

This concept holds that an accountant is entitled to work out the Final Accounts of a business, and draw up a Balance Sheet, on the basis that the business will continue for the conceivable future—in other words that it is a 'going concern'. If there is some reason to believe that the business does not intend to continue, it would, of course, be fraudulent to prepare the accounts as if it did.

The reason for the importance of the going concern concept is that the value of things can change to a considerable extent according to their usefulness to the business as a going concern. If you visit a large engineering works or factory you will see expensive machinery producing the goods the company sells. As a going concern the machinery is valuable. If you visit the same factory six months after it has shut down, much of the machinery may be worth only what it would fetch as scrap metal. Therefore, if there is some prospect that the business, or some major part of it, may shut down or cease to operate, the accountant must reflect this in the accounts he or she prepares, and in particular in the Balance Sheet of the business.

The assumption is, in all businesses, that the accounts are prepared for a business that is a going concern, and that no intention or necessity to reduce activity or sell off parts of the business is envisaged.

34.5 The Accruals Concept

The accruals concept is the basis of preparing Final Accounts. It holds that the profits we earn and the costs we bear are recognized *at the time they take place*, and not at the time they are actually paid for (which may be several months later). For example, if we sell goods in January and they are paid for by our debtors in March, there is no problem of accrual for a business which keeps its accounts on a calendar year basis, for both the sale and the payment are made in the same year. By contrast, if we sell goods in November and they are paid for in February, there is a problem of accrual. When did the profit on these goods accrue—when we sold them or when we actually recovered the payment? The accruals concept lays down that the profit was earned when we sold the goods, and it must be counted as a profit for this year, when we do the Final Accounts in December. Similarly with expenses—an expense incurred in November counts as an expense of that financial year even though we don't actually pay the account until February of the following year. These are examples of 'adjustments' (see Unit 22).

There is one exception to this rule: the prudence concept (see Unit 34.3) can override the accruals concept in so far as is reasonable. We can carry forward a Provision for Bad Debts, if there is some prospect that some of the sales we are making in November may not actually be paid for when payment time comes round.

This exception apart, the basic idea of the accruals concept is a concept of 'matching' profits with the expenses of earning these profits. The basic rule which the Inland Revenue Department follows when deciding whether our accounts are satisfactory is as follows:

(a) on the credit side of the Trading and Profit and Loss Accounts appear *all the incomes we have earned this year, whether they have actually been received or not*; and
(b) on the debit side of the accounts appear *all the expenses incurred in earning these incomes, whether they have actually been paid or not.*

You have already met all these ideas when learning how to prepare Final Accounts.

34.6 The Substance and Materiality Concepts

These concepts deal with the problem of how much detail should be included in the accounts. The Final Accounts of a firm might be very complicated and take pages and pages of typescript to reproduce in full. We have to be allowed to group some things together to reduce the amount of detail. Thus things like flour, eggs and butter can be put together as stock. Should lorries and private cars be lumped together as 'motor vehicles'? The answer is provided by these two concepts.

First, the accounts must show the true *substance* of the firm's financial position. Suppose we have loaned one of the directors \$100 000 with which to buy a house. The director is in debt to the company for this amount. If we hide this debt from the shareholders by including it in the 'debtors', we shall not be revealing the true substance of the matter. Similarly, if a road haulage company owns a number of elderly lorries but has just purchased new cars for all the directors, it would not reveal the true state of affairs to put them together as 'motor vehicles'. Compare the following Balance Sheet entries:

Balance Sheet as at 31 December 20..

	At cost	*Less depreciation*	*Current value*
Fixed assets:			
Motor vehicles	$100 000	$50 000	$50 000

Balance Sheet as at 31 December 20..

	At cost	*Less depreciation*	*Current value*
Fixed assets:	$	$	$
Heavy lorries	60 000	45 000	15 000
Motor cars	40 000	5 000	35 000
	$100 000	$50 000	$50 000

Clearly, the first entry hides the true state of affairs, for it appears that all vehicles still have half of their useful life ahead of them. The second entry reveals the true substance of the firm's situation. Its heavy goods vehicles are almost at the end of their useful life and before long we can expect very substantial costs to replace them.

The substance concept thus requires the accounts to be prepared in such a way that they bring out the true state of affairs. The materiality concept has a very similar basis. If an item is *material*, i.e. sufficiently important to affect our judgement of the true position of the firm, it must appear as a separate item. If it does not affect our judgement, it can be merged with other items. Thus the item 'petty cash' does not appear on a Balance Sheet—it is merged with 'cash in hand', even though most of the cash is in the cashier's cash box and the petty cash is in the petty cashier's till.

34.7 The Consistency Concept

When we prepare the accounts of any organization we expect management to compare this year's records with the records of earlier years. For this reason we must be *consistent* from one year to the next. If we show the Balance Sheet headings in a different way from the headings used the year before, it will be difficult for management to detect 'trends', such as rises or falls in sales, stocks, wages costs and profit margins (see Unit 28).

If, for any reason, it is impossible to follow the same pattern as in previous years, we must give a full explanation in the form of a note to the accounts. This must explain why this year's accounts cannot be compared strictly with last year's. If, for example, the basis of valuing stock has changed from FIFO to LIFO we must explain why we have changed, and the effect it has had on the profits; if a revolution has affected our trading activities in an overseas country, we should similarly explain the situation and give a brief assessment of its likely effect on the firm.

34.8 The Objectivity Concept

The objectivity concept holds that the accounts should be prepared objectively, not subjectively. This means that they must be viewed not from the standpoint of someone inside the firm, but from that of an outside observer, looking at the firm and all other firms with the same attitude. If this doesn't happen, we may get into serious trouble. Many take-over bids succeed because of such mistakes. Suppose I purchased a piece of property in the city of Sydney twenty years ago for $10000, and that it is still valued on my books at cost price. An outside observer may know that this property is now worth $1 million. If he or she takes over my business and sells this asset for its full value, I shall not realize the profit, but he or she will. Had I valued my assets objectively I would have raised that value on my books in line with its change in value over the years, and when anyone tried to take over my business they would have had to pay the full value. Or, of course, they wouldn't have tried to take it over—and I should still be in business.

34.9 The Stable Money Concept

At one time money was stable in value. Between 1745 and 1939 the British Government always borrowed money at $2\frac{1}{2}$ per cent interest, and could always get as much as it wanted without any difficulty. Today money is liable to suffer from a disease called 'inflation'. With this disease prices of goods and services rise, so that the value of money falls, and rates of interest are variable and often very high. The basic idea in accounting is that money is stable in value; if I borrow $500, I expect to repay $500 in the future. Although this is how the records in our ledgers look, in inflationary times I don't repay $500, I repay $500 in *depreciated* currency. The notes I pay are worth much less than those I borrowed. That is why interest rates are sometimes so high: the interest payable makes the true value of what I repay about 'right' in an inflationary period.

(a) Inflation Accounting and Historical Cost Accounting

Some years ago it was formally recognized that final accounts prepared by traditional methods of accounting—known as *historical cost accounting*—could give a false view of the profits of a business, and since 1980 large businesses have been required to publish not only historical cost accounts but inflation accounts as well.

To illustrate how traditional accounts can be misleading, consider a Trading Account worked out on the basis of historical costs, i.e. what the goods sold actually cost at some past time when they were purchased:

Cost price in April	$30000
Sold in August	$50000
Gross profit	$20000

Now suppose we re-order the same goods to replace the ones sold, but by August the price has risen to \$35 000.

We may have appeared to make a profit of \$20 000, but to replenish our stocks we have had to spend an extra \$5 000. In inflationary times we are thus liable to overstate our profits. This is undesirable, because it has the following effects:

(a) We seem to be a very profitable enterprise. The shareholders may immediately feel that a big dividend should be paid—but if we pay it we shall not be able to replenish our stocks.
(b) Trade unions representing our employees may feel equally strongly that if the company is profitable their members should share in the good times. If we give wage increases all round we shall not have the funds we need to replace stocks.
(c) Excessive profitability may attract the interest of take-over bidders who may feel the company is worth taking over.

The rules for inflation accounting are complex and too difficult for this text. Here we will consider one example of the effects of inflation: the problem of stock valuation (see Unit 21.3).

(b) FIFO, LIFO and AVCO

Where stock consists of a collection of items purchased in inflationary times at a variety of prices it can be allocated for use in jobs or contracts in several different ways. Let us imagine motor vehicle tyres, all of the same type and quality, purchased at various times for \$18, \$20 and \$24. The stock card might look like this:

Tyres Type 2D radials	\$
16/cost \$18 each/value	288
12/cost \$20 each/value	240
20/cost \$24 each/value	480
	\$1 008

A customer now buys four tyres at \$36 each (current cost \$24 + 50 per cent mark-up).

The three most common methods of accounting for this transaction are as follows:

(i) FIFO—first in, first out The first tyres cost \$18 each. The stock would decrease by 4 × \$18 = \$72.

(ii) LIFO—last in, first out The last set of tyres to be delivered cost \$24 each. This time the stock would decrease by 4 × \$24 = \$96.

(iii) AVCO—average cost The tyres would be regarded as having all cost the same average price, i.e. $1 008 ÷ 48 = $21. The value of the stock would decline by 4 × $21 = $84.

Whichever method of valuation we adopt, it does involve keeping careful stock records. In the case of AVCO we have to recalculate the average price each time we take delivery of a new batch of stock.

Now consider the effect of these different valuation policies on the profits of a business. We will do a comparative Trading Account to see what the situation is, assuming this time that 30 tyres have been sold.

The sales value would be 30 × $36 = $1 080.

The tyres would be used as follows:

FIFO	(16 × $18) + (12 × $20) + (2 × $24)	= $576
LIFO	(20 × $24) + (10 × $20)	= $680
AVCO	(30 × $21)	= $630

The stock left would be as follows:

FIFO	(18 × $24)	= $432
LIFO	(16 × $18) + (2 × $20)	= $328
AVCO	(18 × $21)	= $378

The profit may be calculated as follows:

	FIFO	*LIFO*	*AVCO*
	$	$	$
Sales	1 080	1 080	1 080
Cost of sales	576	680	630
Profit	$504	$400	$450

We get the most profit with FIFO and the least profit with LIFO, while with AVCO we fall between these two extremes. Note that in this example the customer has been charged the same price, $36, in each case. Had we wished to do so, we could have maintained a more competitive stance in the market place by continuing to sell at old prices so long as we had 'old' items in stock. This would not have affected our stock valuation policy, but it would have altered our profits for the year, because the sales figure would have been reduced.

The stock values at the end of the year are in the same order. Under FIFO the stock left is valued at $432, whereas under LIFO it is valued at $328 and under AVCO at $378. As you will notice, when using AVCO it is not easy to comply with the rule about showing the value of stock at cost or net realizable value. We have the stock valued at an average price and do not really know the true original cost of any particular unit.

Note also that the order in which we value stock is an accounting problem and not necessarily connected with the order in which we use the stock. Just because we supply a customer at the latest price (plus our profit margin) does not mean we actually give him the latest item to come into stock. It is usual to use stock in the order in which it came into stock—oldest items first—irrespective of our accounting policy for valuation of stock.

(c) Unstable Money and the Revaluation of Assets

One difficulty that results from the changes of money values in inflationary times is the false valuation given on Balance Sheets to assets. Thus suppose a building was purchased in 1970 for $10 000 but in 2000 it is 'worth' $45 000. If the Balance Sheet value is not altered anyone who buys the business can sell the property and make a huge profit on the transaction. This change in values does not just affect premises—it can affect plant and machinery, equipment, stocks and so forth as well. If the purchaser of a business can take the business over without the present owner realizing how much the values have increased they can—provided they cease to trade—sell off the assets at a huge profit. This is called *asset-stripping*, and it is a very profitable business. It is also an unsavoury one, because the business is purchased not to keep it going, but to close it down, with all that means for employees in unemployment terms. The country also loses, in that the wealth creation that had been taking place has now ceased.

The solution to this problem is to revalue the assets every two or three years to give a true valuation. This revaluation must be professionally done by a qualified valuer. Take the example quoted in the last paragraph of a property that has risen in value from $10 000 to $45 000. Suppose the proprietor's Capital Account is at the figure of $23 000 (because of course he owns other property than the premises of $10 000). We decide to revalue the property to its current value. This will increase the assets side of the Balance Sheet by $35 000. This profit—which is in fact a *capital appreciation*—must be given to the proprietor, whose Capital Account will therefore rise to $58 000. Any person keen to take over the business for the sake of its assets will now have to pay the full price for the building and will, of course, be less likely to be interested. The entries will be:

					J1
20..				$	$
1 July	Premises Account	Dr.	L72	35 000	
	Capital Account		L7		35 000
	Being revaluation of premises in line with current values				

Premises Account L72

20..			$				
1 Jan.	Balance		10 000				
1 July	Capital	J1	35 000				

Capital Account L7

				20..			$
				1 Jan.	Balance		23 000
				1 July	Premises	J1	35 000

Where the accounts of a company are concerned it is not of course possible to vary the Capital Account in this way, because the capital is in the form of shares issued to shareholders. What we have to do is to place the capital profit in a *revaluation reserve account* (which is a capital reserve account), and we would usually call such an account Revaluation of Premises Account. (You will remember that we saw in Unit 27.2(e)(ii) that a capital reserve cannot be given away as profits to the shareholders because it is not a revenue gain, but a capital gain. It may, however, be given away at a future date in the form of bonus shares.) The Journal entry would be similar to the one shown above, but instead of crediting Capital Account we credit Revaluation of Premises Account. This will appear on the Balance Sheet as one of the capital reserves, and become part of the ordinary shareholders' interest in the company.

34.10 The Limitations of Accounting Statements

Finally, at the very end of a book about the presentation of accounting statements, which has argued all the way through that good accounting can tell us many things about a business, we have to admit that there are some things it cannot tell us.

We have already seen (in Unit 34.9) that historical cost accounting can mislead us because it does not tell us what is happening to the value of money over time.

The other things accounting cannot tell us are concerned with the quality of items like labour, supervisory staff and top management. Non-quantifiable items—such as the nature of the industrial relations in a company, its location, its access to a hinterland on the one hand and to ports and airports on the other—may be of very great importance to the business. These are not susceptible to explanation in financial terms, and must be studied and reported on as well if we are to evaluate an enterprise properly. Accounting then merges into the general pattern of management activities.

We have reached a new level in our studies—we understand accounting and the financial implications of what we are doing—but having struggled up to a higher position we only discover new horizons to be explored. That is, after all, what education is all about.

34.11 Exercises Set 55. The Concepts of Accounting

1. What is meant by an accounting concept? List the concepts with which you are familiar and explain any *one* of them in detail.

2. a) What is meant by 'prudence' in accounting?
b) Peter Jones has just completed a contract for Bigboy Ltd for the erection of plant at a factory. The profit amounts to $334000, but $134000 has to be kept in a special provision account in case the plant fails to work satisfactorily in the first six months. Peter Jones is a prudent accountant. How much should he declare as profit for the present financial year, which ends on Friday of this week?

3. a) What is meant by the going concern concept?
b) AB Ltd have decided to cease trading on the last day of the present financial year. What difference will this make to the accountant's thinking as he or she considers the preparation of the Final Accounts for the year?

4. Would you include the following items in your Final Accounts under a separate heading as being important items affecting the substance of your Final Accounts, or merge them with other items as being immaterial?

(a) $350000 paid to a firm of experts who extinguished a fire at No. 3 well which had caused a $15 million loss to the company.
(b) $30 paid to a member of staff who worked overtime to cure a plumbing leak.
(c) Timber worth $750 was used to rebuild a store damaged by vandals. Our annual turnover of timber is $3.5 million, and we frequently lose stock as valuable as this by theft, fire or road accident.
(d) The purchase of property valued at $85000. Our total property is valued at $650000.

Give your answer in the form of a list (a) to (d) with the words 'separate item' or 'immaterial item' written alongside. You do *not* need to give a written explanation.

5. a) What is meant by the consistency concept?
b) Up to now your firm has always valued stock on a FIFO basis, but you are in favour of adopting the LIFO system. Explain what this means in terms of the profit situation. How would you draw your shareholders' attention to this change of policy?

6. On 1 January 20.. a trader has the following items in stock. They are identical but were purchased at different times as prices rose during the previous year:

5 which cost $10 each;
8 which cost $14 each;
7 which cost $17 each;
10 which cost $20 each.

He always sells at a mark-up of 50 per cent on current cost price. What will be his profit, and what will be the value of closing stock on 31 January 20.., if he sells 18 items in the month and accounts for them on a FIFO basis?

7. Using the same figures as in Question 6, what will be the profit and what will be the value of the closing stock if he accounts for the 18 items on a LIFO basis instead?

8. On 1 January 20.. a trader has the following items in stock. They are identical but were purchased at different times as prices rose during the previous year:

3 which cost $50 each;
8 which cost $55 each;
4 which cost $60 each;
5 which cost $65 each.

He always sells at a mark-up of 60 per cent on current cost price. What will be his profit, and what will be the value of closing stock on 31 January 20.., if he sells 15 items in the month and accounts for them on a FIFO basis?

9. Using the same figures as in Question 8 above, what will be the profit and the value of the closing stock on 31 January 20.. if he accounts for the 15 items on a LIFO basis?

10. The books of Growing Fast Ltd on 31 December 20.. show premises valued at $15 000. This is the figure for which they were purchased 17 years ago. They have now been professionally revalued at $60 000.

a) Show the Journal entry to take account of the appreciation in value that has occurred and the ledger accounts affected by the revaluation.

b) To whom does this increased value belong?

34.12 Revise and Test 34. The Concepts of Accounting

Answers	*Questions*
—	**1.** What is a concept?
1. It is a fundamental idea which forms the basis of any philosophical or practical system.	**2.** What is the concept of 'business entity'?
2. It is a concept that holds that a business is a separate unit, different from all other businesses and even different from the owner or owners. The business is one thing, the owner and his/her relationship with the business is a separate thing altogether.	**3.** What is the 'prudence' concept?
3. A concept that holds that a wise trader is always prudent (cautious). The basic rule is 'Never take a profit until you've actually got the money in your hand, but always take a loss the moment you know about it.'	**4.** What is the 'going concern' concept?
4. A concept that holds that the business will go on trading from year to year, and that all the assets may be valued on that basis. The asset values of a business that is closing down (a 'gone' concern) are totally different. They are always worth much less.	**5.** What is the 'accruals' concept?
5. A concept that holds that the profits we earn and the losses we suffer must be accounted for at the time they happen, and not at some later date. In each year the profits made must be set against the costs incurred in earning the profits, to give the net profit for the year.	**6.** What is the 'substance' concept, and how does materiality affect the concept?

---

6. A concept that holds that the Final report to the owners of the business must bring out the real truth of the affairs of the enterprise; what has actually happened. Every material fact must be brought out in the report, but if an item is immaterial (too trivial to be worth a mention) it may be merged with other matters and not specifically referred to.

7. What does the 'consistency' concept hold?

---

7. That accounts should be prepared in the same way year after year, unless there is some very good reason for a change of policy. If that happens there should be a note about it in the accounts, and possibly an explanation of the effect on the business profits.

8. What is the concept of 'objectivity'?

---

8. A concept which holds that the affairs of the business should be reported on from the point of view of a disinterested outsider (an objective view) rather than from the subjective view of an insider with a personal interest in the matter.

9. What is the 'stable-money' concept?

---

9. A concept that holds that the value of money is steady from year to year, and that the accountant may assume this is true when preparing the accounts. This is called 'historical cost accounting'—as distinct from 'inflation accounting', when falls in the value of money are taken into account.

10. Go over the page again until you are sure of all these concepts.

Index